THIRD EDITION

PUBLIC SPEAKING FOR COLLEGE AND CAREER

Hamilton Gregory

Asheville-Buncombe Technical Community College

McGraw-Hill, Inc.

New York   St. Louis   San Francisco   Auckland   Bogotá   Caracas
Lisbon   London   Madrid   Mexico   Milan   Montreal   New Delhi
Paris   San Juan   Singapore   Sydney   Tokyo   Toronto

To my mother
Rachel Smith Gregory

**PUBLIC SPEAKING FOR COLLEGE
AND CAREER**

Photo credits appear on pages 424–425, and on this page by reference.

1 2 3 4 5 6 7 8 9 0   VNH   VNH   9 0 9 8 7 6 5 4 3

ISBN 0-07-024701-3

This book was set in Trump Medieval by Monotype Composition Company.
The editors were Hilary Jackson and Jean Akers;
the designer was Wanda Siedlecka;
the production supervisor was Richard A. Ausburn.
The photo editor was Elyse Rieder.
Von Hoffmann Press, Inc., was printer and binder.

Cover photos: Top left, Peter Bryon/Monkmeyer; center left, MacDonald/The Picture Cube; bottom left, Sullivan/TexaStock; right, Bob Daemmrich/The Image Works.

Library of Congress Cataloging-in-Publication Data

Gregory, Hamilton.
    Public speaking for college and career / Hamilton Gregory. — 3rd ed.
       p.   cm.
    Includes bibliographical references and index.
    ISBN 0-07-024701-3
    1. Public speaking.   I. Title.
PN4121.G716   1993
808.5′1—dc20   92-37916

Contents

Chapter 6

Finding Materials   101

Chapter 7

Supporting Your Ideas   129

APPENDIXES

Preface

In a recent survey of 200 U.S. corporate vice presidents, 40 percent of the executives admitted that they have dozed off during speeches, and 44.5 percent said the average business presentation is "boring" or "unbearable."[1]

This depressing research item poses a challenge to those of us who teach public speaking: How can we help our students become dynamic speakers who give clear, interesting, and meaningful speeches that *nobody* sleeps through? The answer, I believe, is twofold. We must show our students the basic principles of speech communication and simultaneously teach them to apply those principles to the speeches they give in the classroom, in their careers, and in their communities.

In this book I have tried to fulfill these goals. While presenting thorough coverage of basic principles, drawn from contemporary research and from the accumulated wisdom of over 2,000 years of rhetorical theory, I have endeavored to show students the real-life applicability of those principles by providing copious examples and models from both student and professional speeches.

Many of the career and community examples come from my interviews in recent years with over 100 people in business, professional, and technical fields. Not surprisingly, their views reinforce the basic concepts that public speaking instructors have been teaching for years. I discovered, for example, that they consider outlining to be a vital part of preparation, and they dislike hearing speeches that are read from a prepared manuscript.

In addition, I drew from my own experiences in giving speeches to civic clubs, professional organizations, college forums, and parent-teacher associations on such topics as "How Mentally Retarded Citizens Can Be Integrated into the Work Force," "How to Help Refugees Learn English and Get Jobs," and "How Parents Can Help Their Children Develop Effective Study Skills."

The major themes of this book are the same ones that most public speaking instructors stress in the classroom. For example, audience-centered communication is emphasized throughout the book: how to analyze the listeners; how to be sensitive to their needs and interests; and how to talk *to* and *with* them, not *at* them. Students are urged to communicate ideas to real people rather than merely stand up and go through the motions of "giving a speech."

A rule of thumb in American seminaries is that ministers should spend an hour in the study for each minute in the pulpit. Since this ratio is a good one for any speaker, I devote ten chapters to showing students how to go through the preliminary stages systematically—analyzing the audience, selecting a topic and specific purpose, devising a cental idea, finding verbal and visual support material, organizing the material into a coherent ouline, and practicing effectively.

At every stage of preparation and delivery, students are encouraged to engage in critical analysis, asking themselves such questions as these: "What are the attitudes and interests of my audience?" "How can I adapt my subject to their special needs and concerns?" "How can I make my ideas understandable and persuasive?" By the time students finish this book, they will realize that they have been trained not only in public speaking but in critical thinking as well. These skills will be useful to them in the future as tools for their own speeches, and as a means for analyzing the persuasive appeals of politicians and advertisers.

Because many students are troubled by a lack of self-confidence, I have tried to show how speakers can possess and project confidence in themselves and in their ideas. Chapter 3 provides a reassuring discussion of nervousness and shows students how to turn their nervousness into an asset by using it as constructive energy.

New Features

Three major changes have been made in this edition:

▶ To help students cope with career situations, I have nearly doubled the number of Tips for Your Career.

▶ To give students more tools for the task of persuasion, I now devote two chapters to persuasive speeches (as opposed to only one chapter in previous editions). The new Chapter 15 explains types of persuasive speeches and patterns of organization. Advice has been added on how to encourage an audience to take action on a speaker's proposals. The new Chapter 16 has a much fuller treatment of persuasive techniques: analyzing the audience (with the help of a persuasion scale), building credibility, providing strong evidence, using sound reasoning, appealing to motivations, and arousing emotions. Because many students struggle with the concepts of deduction and induction, I have reworked the sections that explain these terms. In the "Fallacies in Reasoning" section, I have changed the label "begging the question" to "building on an unproven assumption." My own students had experienced difficulty in understanding the old term; when I read an article by *New York Times* language columnist William Safire concerning *his* readers' difficulty with the term, I knew it was time to devise a more understandable label.

▶ More emphasis is placed on credibility and ethics at various points throughout the book, especially in Chapter 12 (in a new section on double-speak) and Chapter 16 (in new guidelines on using emotional appeals ethically).

Other new features of this edition:

▶ The chapter preview at the beginning of each chapter has been expanded.

▶ In Chapter 1 (Introduction to Public Speaking), I show the real-life relevance of the speech communication process by describing a new trend in America's courtrooms—letting jurors take notes, make suggestions, and even sometimes question a witness.

▶ In Chapter 5 (Selecting Topic, Purpose, and Central Idea), I have revised the section on the central idea to make this concept clearer and to distinguish it from the specific purpose statement. A new Tip for Your Career urges students to examine ulterior purposes that sometimes sabotage their avowed purpose.

▶ In Chapter 6 (Gathering Materials), I have inserted information on a new research tool widely used in libraries—the CD-ROM player—and I have spotlighted the growing use of electronic databases.

▶ In Chapter 7 (Supporting Your Ideas), I have revised the explanations of averages, percentages, and correlations to make these concepts easier for students to grasp.

▶ In Chapter 8 (Visual Aids), several sections have been renovated to reflect current trends in business and professional presentations (such as the popularity of dry erase boards and the increased use of videotape). In the Tips for Your Career, I have added (1) a warning against a growing problem—the overuse of visuals, especially glitzy video shows that some presenters use as a substitute for a well-organized, well-reasoned speech, and (2) a suggestion that students appeal to the senses of hearing, smell, taste, and touch whenever possible.

▶ Chapter 11 (Outlining the Speech) includes a new option for speaking notes—using visual aids as prompts—that has become popular in career settings.

▶ In Chapter 12 (Wording the Speech), a new section (Beware of Double-speak) has been created to clarify the proper and improper usage of euphemisms and inflated language.

▶ In Chapter 13 (Delivering the Speech), the section on impromptu speaking has been augmented because this method of speaking is often required in business and professional situations, and sixteen new items have been added to the list of common pronunciation mistakes.

▶ In Chapter 17 (Special Types of Speeches), new examples are given of the speech of tribute and the speech of inspiration.

▶ New sample outlines (plus transcripts of the speeches as delivered) have been placed at the end of Chapters 11, 14, and 15. In addition, Appendix B has two new items: a prize-winning persuasive speech and an entertaining speech.

Overview of the Book

Most instructors have their own ways of organizing and presenting information for this course. I have tried to make each chapter as self-contained as possible so that it can be adapted to any instructor's syllabus.

Part One, Foundations of Effective Communication, contains basic introductory material. Chapter 1 describes the benefits of a public speaking course, including advantages in the job market. It also explains the speech communication process and discusses speakers' responsibilities toward their audiences.

Chapter 2 guides students in improving their effectiveness as listeners and discusses the listener's responsibilities toward the speaker.

Chapter 3 is a comprehensive treatment of nervousness, with suggestions on how speakers can convert nervous tension into positive energy. Students should be heartened to learn that stage fright is a common problem that most speakers experience and learn to control.

Part Two, Preliminary Stages, guides students through the difficult but crucial tasks of choosing and refining a topic and gathering materials. Chapter 4 emphasizes a major theme of the book—the need to focus on the listeners at every stage of preparation and delivery. Students are shown how to analyze the audience and how to adapt their remarks accordingly.

Chapter 5 is a practical guide to selecting a topic and narrowing it to manageable proportions. For students who have trouble finding topics, two worksheets—one for exploring personal interests, the other for brainstorming—are explained and illustrated. After students refine their topics, they are shown how to devise a general purpose, a specific purpose, and a central idea.

Chapter 6 explains how to research a topic using several sources, including personal experiences, libraries, computer databases, and interviews. It also discusses taking notes and finding the right materials quickly and efficiently.

Chapter 7 discusses verbal materials that can be used to support ideas: definitions, descriptions, examples, narratives, comparison and contrast, testimony, and statistics. Special attention is given to the use and misuse of statistics.

Chapter 8 examines visual supports for ideas. Various types of visual aids—graphs, charts, drawings, photographs, computer graphics, objects, and models—are discussed, along with media for visual aids: boards, posters, flip charts, handouts, overhead transparencies, slides, and videotapes. Also included are guidelines for using visual aids effectively.

Part Three, Organizing the Speech, explains time-tested methods for arranging materials for a speech. Chapter 9 deals with the body of the speech—how to select main points and organize them in a logical pattern. A section called "Creating the Body" helps students who get lost in their notes and can't distinguish main points from subpoints. Attention is also drawn to using transitions to carry the listener from one part of a speech to another.

Chapter 10 focuses on introductions and conclusions. Introductions are explained as a two-part process: first, capturing attention and interest, and second, preparing the audience for the body of the speech. In the section on conclusions, the emphasis is on reinforcing the central idea.

Chapter 11 provides a step-by-step guide for developing an outline and then preparing speaking notes based on the outline. Included in the chapter is a full-length sample of a student's outline and speaking notes followed by a transcript of the speech as it was delivered.

Part Four, Presenting the Speech, examines verbal and nonverbal dimensions of speechmaking. Chapter 12 deals with the need for speakers to use language that is appropriate, accurate, clear, and vivid. One section also shows the differences between oral and written language.

Chapter 13 is a comprehensive treatment of delivery, including how to practice. It also discusses how to handle question-and-answer periods.

Part Five, Types of Public Speaking, focuses on the major kinds of speeches that students are likely to give in the classroom and in their careers. Chapter 14 provides guidelines on informative speaking. A sample informative speech, with commentary, is printed at the end of the chapter.

Chapters 15 and 16 are devoted to persuasive speaking. In Chapter 15, two popular types of persuasive speeches—the speech to influence thinking and the speech to motivate action—are examined, followed by a discussion of patterns of organization. A sample persuasive speech, with commentary, is featured at the end of the chapter. Chapter 16 focuses on principles of persuasion: knowing your audience, building credibility, using evidence, employing sound reasoning, appealing to motivations, and arousing emotions.

Chapter 17 covers special types of speeches: the entertaining (or after-dinner) address and speeches of introduction, presentation, acceptance, tribute, and inspiration.

Chapter 18 deals with group discussions, with special emphasis on the reflective-thinking method for solving problems, and team presentations (symposiums and panels).

Appendix A gives pointers on how to speak in front of the camera. In many different college courses, students produce or participate in videotaped demonstrations or discussions. More and more businesses and professions are using videotapes for instructions, sales pitches, and in-house communications.

Appendix B is a selection of sample speeches that illustrate and reinforce concepts taught in the text.

Resources for Instructors

Ancillary materials for instructors include the following:

▶ *How to Build an Outline* is a set of 27 overhead transparencies that show students how to create an outline. Two outlines (one for an informative speech, the other for a persuasive speech) are constructed step by step so that students can see the process in action. Both outlines are completely new—they do not appear in the text.

▶ The *Instructor's Manual* provides dozens of ready-to-reproduce worksheets and forms for use in the classroom, including two handouts that list over 100 topics for informative and persuasive speeches, several sample outlines of speeches, and exercises on outlining. A blank outline "skeleton," or template, helps students see the overall structure of an outline and makes it virtually impossible for them to skip or overlook key parts. Tips are given on how instructors can videotape student speeches. The manual also includes sample speeches not printed in the text itself, including a reproducible transcript of Martin Luther King's famous "I Have a Dream" speech. The manual now features three ready-to-reproduce tests for each chapter: Forms A and B have true-false and multiple-choice questions; Form C contains short-answer questions.

▶ *Supplementary Readings* in the form of photocopy masters can be reproduced and distributed to students at appropriate points during the course. A handout on speech phobia, for example, gives tips for self-therapy to those students whose fear goes far beyond the normal range discussed in Chapter 3. This handout has proved valuable in many colleges and universities in encouraging phobic students not to drop out of public speaking class. Other handouts are "A Quick Guide to Public Speaking" (to help students with their early speeches), "Self-Introduction Speech," "Evaluating Speeches," "Using a Personal Computer for Research," "Oral Interpretation of Literature," "Job Interviews," "Voice Production," and "Public Speaking Tips for ESL Students."

Acknowledgments

In preparing this edition, I received valuable suggestions from the following people who reviewed the book: Joel L. Bailey, Mountain Empire Community College; Melvin H. Berry, Nicholls State University; Darlene Bock, Western Oklahoma State College; Dawn O. Braithwaite, New Mexico State University; Rodney M. Cole, University of Maine at Augusta; Jackie Ganschow, Del Mar College; John Robert Greene, Cazenovia College; D. E. Jukes, Community College of Allegheny County; Sara J. Kataoka, Berkshire Community College; Chris Kennedy, Western Wyoming Community College; Harold J. Kinzer, Utah State University; Leonard Madzy, Berkshire Community College; Charles R. Newman, Parkland College; LeRoy Pavés, Queensborough Community College of the City University of New York; David J. Robinson, Youngstown State University; Mike Wartman, Normandale Community College; and Charles W. Weedin, Yakima Valley Community College.

Though space does not permit a listing of names, I also remain indebted to the reviewers of earlier editions.

I wish to acknowledge, with gratitude, the valuable assistance of the following members of the editorial and production staff at McGraw-Hill: Roth Wilkofsky, Hilary Jackson, Fran Marino, Cynthia Fostle, Jean Akers, Kathy Bendo, Wanda Siedlecka, Rich Ausburn, and Mary Farrell.

I am also grateful to the following individuals: Dr. Olin Wood, for urging me to write this book; Tom Gaffigan and Dr. Celia Miles, for giving me encouragement and support; Calvin Allen, John Barber, Emily Gean Bergere, Sandy Cagle, David Holcombe, and Peggy Ryan for supplying ideas for the text and the instructor's manual; Helen Camp, Billie Dalton, Maretta Hensley, Terry Holt, and Peggy Kyle, for ordering research materials for me; Richard Babb, Alan Willcox, C. L. Satterfield, and Jim Cavener, for providing ideas in the early stages of the book; D. Michael Frank, past president of the National Speakers Association, for giving me an entrée to most of the professional speakers who contributed to this book; Attorney Paul Rifkin, for putting me in touch with Mr. Frank; Bob Sampson of Central Piedmont Community College, for contributing two of his class handouts to the instructor's manual; Dr. William Anixter of Mountain Psychiatric Center, for providing me with information on speech phobia; and Larry Schnoor, executive director of the Interstate Oratorical Association, for giving permission to reprint speeches from *Winning Orations*.

I am indebted to the hundreds of students in my public speaking classes over the years who have made teaching this course a pleasant and rewarding task. From them I have drawn most of the examples of classroom speeches.

And for their support and patience, special thanks to my wife Merrell and to our children, Jess, Jim, and June.

Hamilton Gregory

Introduction to Public Speaking

▶ **Benefits of a Public Speaking Course**

▶ **The Speech Communication Process**

Speaker / Listener / Message / Channel / Feedback / Interference / Situation / The Speech Communication Process in Action /

▶ **The Speaker's Responsibilities**

Respect Your Audience / Take Every Speech Seriously / Be Ethical /

I f you are smart and hard-working, can you expect to succeed in a business, professional, or technical career?

Not necessarily, says Midge Costanza, a nationally known business entrepreneur from Escondido, California. "You may have brilliant ideas that you want to share, but if you don't develop and use your speaking skills, then you have all this knowledge locked up within a body that cannot communicate [your ideas] to someone else."

To succeed in any field, she says, you must have "the ability to stand on your feet, either on a one-to-one basis or before a group, and make a presentation that is convincing and believable."[1]

This book and your public speaking course are designed to help you deliver effective speeches with confidence and vigor—not only in college but in your career as well.

Benefits of a Public Speaking Course

Many college graduates look back on all the courses they took in college and say that public speaking was one of the most valuable.[2] Here are some of the reasons why this course is considered so important:

1. *You learn how to speak to a public audience.* Knowing how to stand up and give a talk to a group of people is a rewarding skill that you can use throughout your life. Imagine yourself in these public speaking scenarios:

- ▶ In court you explain to a jury why a traffic accident was not your fault.
- ▶ At the monthly meeting of your club, you give a treasurer's report.
- ▶ You talk to a gathering of neighbors about your ideas for curbing crime in the neighborhood.
- ▶ You teach softball techniques to thirty boys and girls on the team you coach.

Throughout your life you will encounter many such occasions that require public speaking ability.

2. *You learn skills that apply to one-on-one communication.* Though the emphasis of this course is upon speaking to groups, the principles that you learn also apply to communication with individuals.[3] Throughout your lifetime you will be obliged to talk in situations such as these:

- ▶ In a job interview, the personnel manager says, "We've got fifty applicants for this job. Why should we hire you?" If you know how to give a reply that is brief, interesting, and convincing, you obviously improve your chances of getting the job (assuming, of course, that your qualifications are as good as those of the other forty-nine applicants). In a public speaking course, you learn how to organize and present persuasive messages.

▶ You sit down in front of a bank executive to ask for a loan so that you can buy a new car. The skills of nonverbal communication (such as eye contact and facial expression) that you learn in a public speaking class should help you convey to the executive that you are a trustworthy and reliable person who will repay the loan.

After taking a public speaking course, many students report that their new skills help them as much in talking to one person as in addressing a large audience.

3. You develop the oral communication skills that are prized in the job market.   When you go to a job interview, which of the following is most likely to influence the employer when he or she decides whether to hire you?

▶ The reputation of your school
▶ Your grade-point average
▶ Letters of reference
▶ Technical knowledge in your field
▶ Oral communication skills—speaking and listening
▶ Written communication skills—reading and writing

Communicating clearly and effectively is an important skill in all fields. In a hospital, it can mean the difference between life and death.

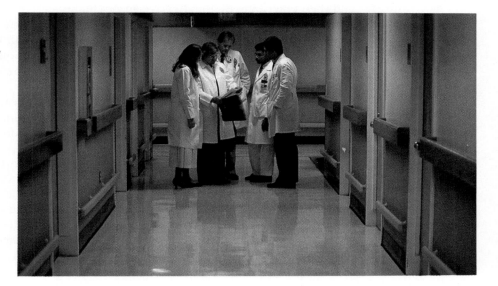

Research shows that "oral communication skills" is the correct answer.[4] Employers generally rank the ability to speak well and listen intelligently as the most highly prized of all skills when it comes to hiring—and promoting—employees. These are precisely the skills that you can develop in a public speaking class.

The answer to the above question is surprising to many students. Surely "technical knowledge in the field" is the most important factor for jobs in science and technology, isn't it? Not according to employers. Consider engineers, for example. They work mainly with numbers, designs, and materials, so one might assume that communication skills would be less important than technical skills. But according to a survey by *Engineering Education* magazine, 500 leaders in the field of engineering said that the most important capability for civil and electrical engineers was communication skills. *All the technical skills were ranked second in importance.*[5]

Whatever field you are in, it does no good to have technical skills and brilliant ideas if you can't communicate them to others. "No one who aspires to success in any profession," says Jack Valenti, president of the Motion Picture Association of America, "can neglect the art of communication. . . . It is not enough to be intellectual, gorged with facts, smart, competent in administration or in designing strategy. You must be able to speak reasonably, believably, engagingly."[6] Gerald Ford, former President of the United States, says, "If I went back to college again, I'd concentrate on two areas: learning to write, and learning to speak before an audience. Nothing in life is more important than the ability to communicate effectively."[7]

4. You practice and gain experience in an ideal laboratory. Just as carpenters become masters of their trade by learning woodworking skills and then practicing them, effective speechmakers become adept by learning certain skills and then practicing them. The classroom is a good laboratory for practicing your skills because (1) it is an unthreatening setting—no one will deny you a job or a raise based on the way you perform in class and (2) your audience is friendly and sympathetic—made up of students who must go through the same experience.

Extremely valuable to you are the critiques given by your instructor (and, in some cases, by fellow students). If, for example, you say "er" or "uh" between every sentence, you can get help in breaking yourself of this habit.

5. You gain self-confidence. Giving a public speech is one of the most difficult tasks in life, and if you learn to do it well, you gain an extraordinary amount of self-assurance. It is similar to Outward Bound, the program that teaches urban citizens to climb mountains and survive in the wilderness. "After Outward Bound," one graduate of the program told me, "I can take on any challenge." Many students have the same feeling of pride and self-worth after completing a public speaking class.

The Speech Communication Process

A mistake made by some speakers is to think that when they have given a speech, communication has *necessarily* taken place. It often does take place, of course, but it sometimes does not, for this reason: *Speaking and communicating are not the same thing.* You can speak to a listener, but if the listener does not understand your message in the way you meant it to be understood, you have failed to communicate.[8] Here's an example:

> At one hospital's fitness clinic for persons recovering from heart attacks, Brenda Shapiro, a staff nurse, gave a speech on cholesterol. "To decrease your cholesterol level," she told the audience, "you should stop eating red meat."
>
> A couple of months later, when she checked the cholesterol levels of the participants, she discovered that one man's cholesterol level had failed to drop. In fact, it had gone up slightly.
>
> "Did you stop eating red meat?" Shapiro asked.
>
> "Yes," said the patient. "I used to eat my steaks medium-rare, but now I cook them until they are brown through and through."
>
> Most people know that *red meat* refers to meats such as beef and mutton that are red before they are cooked. Because the patient had the mistaken notion that a thoroughly cooked steak was no longer considered red meat, he continued to eat the very food he was supposed to avoid.

This incident illustrates that speaking and communicating are not synonymous. The nurse (in the role of speaker) gave instructions, but true, effective communication failed to take place because the patient (the listener) interpreted the message incorrectly. According to Hitachi, Ltd., of Japan, "Communication is not simply sending a message. It is creating true understanding—swiftly, clearly, and precisely."[9]

Let us examine how speech communication works, using Figure 1.1 as our guide.

Speaker

When you are a *speaker*, you are the source, or originator, of a message that is transmitted to a listener. Whether you are speaking to a dozen or to 500, you bear a great responsibility for the success of the communication. The key question that you must constantly ask yourself is not "Am I giving out good information?" or "Am I performing well?" but rather "Am I getting through to my listeners?"

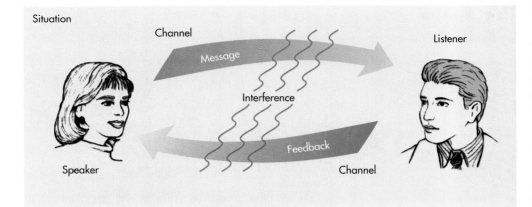

FIGURE 1.1
A model of the speech communication process. In the context of a particular situation, the speaker sends a message via a channel to the listener, who in turn gives feedback via a channel to the speaker. Interference is whatever impedes the flow back and forth.

Listener

The *listener* is the recipient of the message sent by the speaker. As we saw in the red meat incident, the true test of communication is not whether a message is delivered by the speaker but whether it is accurately received by the listener. "A speech," says management consultant David W. Richardson of Westport, Connecticut, "takes place in the minds of the audience."[10] In other words, no matter how eloquent the speaker, no matter how dynamic the speaker's delivery, if the listeners' minds don't receive and interpret the message correctly, the desired communication has failed to take place.

Who is to blame for such failure—the speaker or the listener? Depending on the situation, the blame could be placed on either, or both. While speakers share part of the responsibility for communication, listeners also must bear some of the burden. They must try hard to pay attention to the speaker, fighting off the temptation to daydream or think about personal concerns. They must listen with an open mind, avoiding the tendency to prejudge the speaker or discount a speaker's views without a fair hearing.

Message

The *message* is whatever the speaker communicates to the listeners. The message is sent in the form of *symbols*—either *verbal* or *nonverbal.*

Verbal symbols are words. It's important for you to recognize that words are not things; they are symbols of things. If you give me an apple, you transfer a solid object from your hand to mine. But if you're making a speech and you mention the word *apple*, you are no longer transferring a concrete thing. You are transferring a symbol, which may be interpreted by your listeners in ways that are quite different from what you had in your mind. When you say *apple*, one listener may think of a small green fruit, while another conjures an image of a big red fruit. One listener might think of crisp tartness, while another thinks of juicy sweetness.

Nonverbal symbols are what you convey with your tone of voice, eyes, facial expression, gestures, posture, and appearance.

Everything that you express in a message is in the form of symbols. If, for example, you want to tell me about your headache, you cannot transfer the ache and pain from your head to mine. You must transmit a symbolic description of it. The symbols you use might be verbal ("My head feels as if it's splitting apart") and nonverbal (a grimace).

When listeners receive messages, they must interpret the symbols—that is, make sense out of the speaker's verbal and nonverbal symbols. This can cause misunderstanding and confusion because symbols are only an approximation of reality. The listener who hears of your headache might interpret the words "My head feels as if it's splitting apart" in a way that you did not intend. For example, persons who have never had a headache (there are a few such lucky people in the world) might have trouble imagining the pain. Some listeners might misinterpret the symbols "splitting apart" and think that you had a psychotic break with reality.

As a speaker you should strive to use symbols that will cause the listener to arrive at a meaning that is as close as possible to the one in your mind. Don't say, "Smoking may cause you a lot of trouble." The vague verbal symbols at the end of the sentence—"a lot of trouble"—might be interpreted by some listeners to mean "coughing," by others to mean "stained teeth," or by still others to mean "cancer." Be specific: "Smoking may cause lung cancer."

When you use abstract words like *socialism, feminism,* and *censorship,* you must be especially careful to define precisely what you mean because listeners often have their own widely varying interpretations. The term *censorship* might mean "stamping out filth" to some listeners or "total government control of the press" to others.

Ideally, the two types of symbols, verbal and nonverbal, are harmonious, but if they are not, the listeners receive a mixed message. Suppose you say to an audience, "I'm delighted to be here tonight," but as you say these words, your face has a mournful expression and your tone of voice is regretful. The listeners are getting a mixed message. Which will they believe, your words or your nonverbal behavior? In most instances of mixed messages, listeners accept the nonverbal behavior as the true message. In this case, they will believe that you are not delighted to be there. This is an example of how your intended message is not always the same as the actual message received by listeners.

The solution to this problem is to make sure the nonverbal part of your message reinforces, rather than diminishes, the verbal part. In other words, smile and use a friendly tone of voice when you say, "I appreciate the opportunity to speak to you tonight."

Channel

The *channel* is the medium used to communicate the message. A speech can reach you by means of a variety of channels: radio, television, a public address system, or direct voice communication.

For public speaking in the classroom, you have the best channel of all—direct face-to-face contact. For some speeches in the community, you may have a public address system. This can be a very effective channel (if the system works well and the acoustics in the room are good) because you can speak in an easy, conversational style without having to raise your voice.

Feedback

Feedback is the response that the listeners give the speaker. Sometimes it is *verbal*, as when a listener asks questions or makes comments during a lecture. In most public speeches and certainly in the ones you will give in the classroom, listeners refrain from giving verbal feedback until the question-and-answer period at the end of the speech.

Listeners also give *nonverbal* feedback. If they are smiling and nodding their heads, they are obviously in agreement with your remarks. If, on the other hand, they are yawning and looking at you with a glazed expression, they are probably bored or weary. ("A yawn," wrote English author G. K. Chesterton, "is a silent shout.")

If you are a speaker and you receive negative feedback, try to help the listeners. If, for example, you are explaining a concept, but some of your listeners are shaking their heads and giving you looks that seem to say, "I don't understand," try again, using different words, to make your ideas clear.

While some audience feedback, such as a bewildered look, is easy to understand, there are times when audience behavior is difficult to decipher. If a couple of listeners are dozing, it does not necessarily mean that your speech is boring. It could mean that they stayed up late the night before and are quite drowsy.

Interference

Interference is anything that blocks or hinders the communication of a message. There are three types:

> ▶ *External* interference arises outside the listener: someone coughing, a baby crying, or people talking loudly in the hall. It could be an air

FOR YOUR CAREER

TIP 1.1: Seek Feedback*

One college professor had the habit of using his pipe as a dramatic tool while lecturing. "He thought the pipe made him impressive," recalls Dr. Jerry Tarver of the University of Richmond, but many students found it distracting. When they evaluated the class, "one of the most forceful suggestions was 'Get rid of the pipe.' "

Distracting mannerisms and foibles can mar your speechmaking without your realizing it. You may, for example, develop the unconscious habit of smoothing your hair or straightening your clothes as you talk. The best way to discover these quirks is to do what the professor did: Get feedback (in the form of an evaluation) from your listeners.

While feedback is valuable for pinpointing delivery problems, it is even more important as a way of assessing the *content* of your speech: Are your remarks enlightening or confusing to the listeners?

You don't need an evaluation of every speech in your career, but you should seek one occasionally. Strive to get both positive and negative input so that you can keep the good while eliminating the bad. Here are four good methods.

1. Ask several friends or colleagues to critique a speech. Don't make an imprecise request like "Tell me how I do on this" because your evaluators will probably say at the end of your speech, "You did fine—good speech," to avoid hurting your feelings. Instead give them a specific assignment: "Please make a note of at least three things that you like about the speech and my delivery and at least three things that you feel need improvement." Now your listeners have an assignment that they know will not hurt your feelings, and you are likely to get some helpful feedback.

2. Pass out evaluation forms to all your listeners. Ask them to make comments anonymously and then drop the forms in a box near the exit. The form can contain the requests mentioned above or you can create your own items.

3. Invite a small but representative group of listeners to join you after a meeting to sit down and share their responses to your speech. This is especially useful in finding out whether the listeners understood and accepted your message. Try to listen and learn without being argumentative or defensive.

4. Have a presentation videotaped. Then invite a colleague to watch the tape with you and help you evaluate it. Because many people are *never* pleased with either themselves or their speech on videotape, the colleague can often provide objectivity (for example, an introduction that now seems dull to you might strike your colleague as interesting and captivating).

* The sources for Tips are cited in the Notes section in the back of the book.

conditioning breakdown that leaves the listeners hot and sticky and preoccupied with their discomfort.

▶ *Internal* interference comes from within the listener. Some listeners might be daydreaming or worrying about a personal problem. Some might be too tired or sleepy to expend mental energy on listening. As a speaker, you can help listeners overcome internal distractions by making your speech so lively and interesting that the audience feels compelled to listen to you.

▶ *Speaker-generated* interference occurs when the speaker uses words that are unfamiliar to the audience or uses words that are interpreted in a way that the speaker did not intend. If the speaker wears bizarre clothing, some listeners might scrutinize the attire instead of concentrating on the speech.

Sometimes listeners will fight to overcome interference—for example, straining to hear the speaker's words despite a truck roaring down the street outside the room. At other times, though, some listeners will fail to make the extra effort and no communication takes place.

When you are a speaker, watch for any signs of interference and, if possible, take steps to overcome the problem. For example, if a plane roars in the sky and you see your listeners leaning forward to hear your words, you can either speak louder or pause until the plane's noise has subsided.

Situation

The *situation* is the context—the time and place—in which communication occurs. Different situations call for different behaviors. For example, one who delivers a eulogy in the stately hush of a cathedral would not crack jokes. On the other hand, jokes would be quite appropriate for an entertaining after-dinner speech at a convention.

Time of day plays a part in how receptive an audience is. Many listeners, for example, tend to be sluggish and sleepy between 3 and 5 P.M.; if you give a speech during that period, you need to have an especially lively presentation, perhaps using colorful visual aids to "jazz" up your speech. If your speech is a long one, you might invite the listeners to stand up and stretch at the midpoint of your speech so that they can shake off their sleepiness.

When you prepare a speech, find out as much as possible about the situation: Where will the speech be given, indoors or outdoors? What is the nature of the occasion? How many people are likely to be present? By assessing these variables in advance, you can adapt your speech to make it appropriate to the situation.

The Speech Communication Process in Action

To examine the speech communication process in action, let's look at a dramatic transformation taking place in America's courtrooms.

In the past, two opposing sides argued a case in front of twelve jurors, who were forbidden to take notes or ask questions. They simply sat and watched and listened (and sometimes slumbered), and then later met in private to deliberate and reach a verdict.

Today, in a movement called "jury liberation," more and more juries are being permitted to actively participate in trials. Jurors can take notes, make suggestions, and in some cases even question the witnesses. Here is an example of how this new system works:

> In a trial in the Wisconsin circuit court of Judge Mark Frankel [*situation*], a prosecutor [*speaker*] spoke directly [*channel*] to jurors [*listeners*]. She argued that the defendant in the case had stabbed the victim [*verbal message*]. Because the trial was in the late afternoon, she realized that some of the jurors might be mentally sluggish [*interference*], so she employed a dramatic visual aid [*overcoming interference*]: she held up the victim's bloody jacket and sweater, pointing out the rips where the knife had entered [*nonverbal message*]. In rebuttal, the defense attorney [*speaker*] maintained that the defendant was merely acting in self-defense [*message*]. On a hunch, one juror [*listener*] made a suggestion [*feedback*] to the judge: have the victim put the garments on. The judge agreed [*response to feedback*] and a dramatic revelation unfolded: the rips lined up with the stab wounds only when the victim curled into a self-protective crouch [*nonverbal message*]. It was obvious that the victim had been curled up when the stabbing occurred and could not have been attacking the defendant. The jury convicted the defendant [*feedback*].[11]

If the jury had been required to sit passively, as in the old days, the verdict might have been different. Letting jurors become part of the process meant that justice was served.

As you can see, the speech communication process becomes a dynamic, two-way transaction when listeners give feedback and then speakers respond to the feedback.

The Speaker's Responsibilities

A speaker who stands before an audience has certain responsibilities which a conscientious person should accept. Here are some guidelines:

Respect Your Audience

As a speaker, you should respect your listeners, no matter who they are or why they have come to listen to you. Consider this case of a speaker who failed to show respect:

> A retired military officer confided that he "blew it" in the first civilian job he held after leaving the service—teaching math in a college. "I was very gruff with the students," he said. "In the classroom I would yell at them, make sarcastic comments, and ridicule them if they made a mistake. I didn't really mean to hurt anybody's feelings. I was just trying to stimulate them and get them to think. But

it was a disaster: three-fourths of the students dropped my class within a couple of weeks, and my contract was not renewed. In looking back, I realize I should have been courteous and patient and helpful."

Not only does a disrespectful attitude alienate your audience, but it also diminishes you. It deprives you of meaningful communication with your fellow human beings.

Never patronize your listeners or talk down to them. If you say, "I know I won't change anybody's mind today, but . . .," it is almost the same as saying, "I know you idiots are all closed-minded and won't listen to me intelligently." You are insulting your audience. One professor closed each of his lectures by gathering up his notes and declaring, "Well, I've finished casting my pearls." The statement was clearly an insult, since it was an allusion to the Biblical verse, "Neither cast ye your pearls before swine." When you insult or antagonize listeners, you do more than make them angry or defensive; you reduce the possibilities of reaching them with your ideas.

When Michelle Cuomo tried to persuade an audience that smoking should be banned in restaurants, she knew that some of her listeners smoked. She could have given them a stern tongue-lashing: "Don't you smokers have any common decency? How do you think the rest of us feel when you blow your foul smoke into the air that we must breathe?" If she had berated her audience in this fashion, how do you think the smokers would have reacted? With anger and defensiveness, of course. Wisely, Cuomo used a more respectful approach. She said, "I know that some of you smoke, and I know that when you go out to eat at a restaurant with your friends, it's very enjoyable to have a cigarette at the end of the meal. I normally would not want to do anything to take away from your enjoyment, except that I have asthma, and I'd like to explain what smoke does to me." Notice how friendly and reasonable Cuomo was. She refrained from attacking the intelligence or morals of the smokers; she merely presented her case in a respectful, but assertive manner that should have prevented any listener from getting angry or defensive. And who knows? She might have convinced some smokers to accept her views.

Take Every Speech Seriously

Contrary to what some students think, your classroom speeches are as important as any speeches that you may give in your career, and they deserve to be taken seriously. Here is why: (1) Speech class is an ideal place to practice, and as with any endeavor in life, you get the maximum benefit from practice if you exert yourself to the fullest. High jumpers who win gold medals in the Olympics do so by trying as hard in practice as they do in Olympic competition. (2) Although the classroom is a laboratory for speechmaking, the speeches are not artificial. They deal with real human issues and they are given by real human beings. As a teacher, I look forward to classroom speeches, not only because they are interesting, but also because they are highly instructive. I learn a great deal from them. To cite just a few examples from recent years: I have learned how to save the life of a person choking on food, I have learned the correct way to cut down some decaying trees in my backyard, and I have modified my views on gun control because of the persuasive talents of several students.

Some speakers think that if an audience is small, or a great deal smaller than they expected, they need not put forth their best effort. This is a mistake; you should try as hard to communicate with an audience of five as you would with an audience of 500. At conventions, there are usually a number of speakers scheduled at the same time in different meeting rooms. I have seen some speakers get so angry at seeing only a handful of people show up for their talk (while hundreds are crowding in to hear the speaker across the hall) that they let their disappointment color their speech. They give their speech in a peevish mood. Isn't it ironic? They are irritated at the people who did not come, but their negative "vibrations" go out to the people who honored them by attending. They impatiently hurry through their presentation, or even cut it short; their attitude seems to be: Why should I take pains with just a handful of people?

Now, for contrast, observe Nido R. Qubein, a professional speaker who was scheduled to give a talk at a convention of the Associated General Contractors of America. Because of some last-minute scheduling changes, he found that his competition was none other than the President of the United States! Instead of having an audience of hundreds, he found himself with only about thirty listeners. "It would have been easy for me to assume that . . . it was a hopeless situation," he said. "But I realized that those people who came really wanted to hear my message, and I tried twice as hard to please them. I called them up to the front of the room, seated them around a large table, and we had a group discussion. They got so involved that it was hard to break it off at the appointed time."[12]

Professional speakers have learned to take every audience seriously, even if it is an audience of only one. James "Doc" Blakely of Wharton, Texas, tells of a colleague who traveled to a small town in the Canadian province of Saskatchewan to give a speech, but found that only one person had showed up to hear him. He gave the lone listener his best efforts, and later that listener started a national movement based upon the speaker's ideas.[13]

Be Ethical

Being ethical means being honest and straightforward with your listeners, avoiding all methods and goals that are deceitful, unscrupulous, or unfair.[14]

As an ethical speaker, you should follow two important principles:

1. Be as well-informed as possible.   Speak on a subject only after you have thoroughly investigated it. If, for example, you are planning to speak on electronic monitoring of convicts so that they can live at home instead of in prison, you should carefully collect data and analyze the statements of the experts—both proponents and opponents. Sometimes, of course, there will be gaps in your knowledge of a subject; you should be willing to admit this to the audience (for example, "I was unable to find any studies on whether convicts are able to trick the electronic system and slip away from home.")

    2. Be honest with facts and figures.   Don't fabricate information to prove a point. Refrain from distorting data to fit an argument. But, you might ask, isn't it all right to bend the facts if one's cause is noble and good? No, for the principled speaker, the ends never justify the means. Let's say that you sincerely believe that a synthetic molecule, rCD4, is the miracle cure for AIDS (acquired immune deficiency syndrome) that the world has long awaited. You come across an article that reports that twelve out of the sixteen doctors interviewed by the authors favored legalization of the drug on an experimental basis even though they all predicted that the medicine would prove to be worthless. Would it be ethical to say in your speech, "Three out of four doctors surveyed support legalization of rCD4"? This would of course be an outrageous distortion of statistics. Your statement would make it sound as if three-fourths of all doctors in America favor legalization, when in fact only sixteen doctors were involved in the poll. Furthermore, you would be withholding a vital piece of information from your audience: the fact that all the doctors predicted that the drug would prove to be worthless. Even if you could get away with this kind of dishonest reporting (that is, not being challenged by anyone in the audience), it would be unethical to pursue it, regardless of how admirable you think your goal is. Distorting facts or figures in the service of a good goal is always unethical.

Summary

A public speaking course helps you develop the key oral communication skills (speaking well and listening intelligently) that are highly prized in business, technical, and professional careers. You gain both confidence and experience as you practice these skills in an ideal speechmaking laboratory— the classroom—where your audience is friendly and supportive.

    The speech communication process consists of seven elements: speaker, listener, message, channel, feedback, interference, and situation. Communication does not take place just because a speaker transmits a message; the message must be accurately received by the listener. When the speaker sends a message, he or she must make sure that the two components of a message—verbal and nonverbal—don't contradict each other.

As a speaker, you should hold your listeners in high esteem. Respect them and treat them courteously, no matter who they are or how large the audience is. In every aspect of your speech, maintain high ethical standards, making sure that you are as well-informed as possible and that you are honest with your facts and figures.

 FOR YOUR CAREER

TIP 1.2: Avoid the Five Biggest Mistakes Made by Speakers

In a survey I asked sixty-four business and professional speakers to cite what they considered to be the most common mistakes made by public speakers in America today. Here are the mistakes that were most often listed.

1. Failing to tailor one's speech to the needs and interests of the audience. A *poor* speaker bores listeners with information they already know or have no use for. A *good* speaker sizes up the listeners in advance and gives them material that is useful, relevant, and vital.

2. Being poorly prepared. A good speech does not just "happen"—the speaker must spend hours researching the topic, organizing material, and rehearsing the speech before he or she rises to speak. Jock Elliott, chairman emeritus of Ogilvy & Mather advertising agency, spends about 28 hours preparing each of his speeches. Many ministers recommend 8 to 10 hours in the study for every hour in the pulpit.

3. Trying to cover too much in one speech. Some speakers are so enthusiastic and knowledgeable about their topic that they want to tell you everything they can. So they try to cram a huge amount of material into a short speech. As Arnold "Nick" Carter, a corporate executive in Chicago, puts it: "They try to put ten pounds of information in a one-pound bag."

Covering too much material causes the listeners to suffer from "information overload." They simply cannot absorb huge quantities of information in one sitting. A wiser approach is to give the listeners one big idea with a few main points to back it up.

4. Failing to maintain good eye contact. Listeners tend to distrust speakers who don't look them in the eye. Yet some speakers spend most of their time looking at their notes or at the floor or at the back wall.

One good way to maintain eye contact with your listeners is to think of your speech as a conversation with them. Hope Mihalap, a professional humorist from Norfolk, Virginia, says that she tries to "make the audience feel that we're all sitting together in a living room, having a warm, one-on-one conversation."

5. Being dull. A dull speech can be caused by poor content or by poor delivery. To avoid being dull, you should (1) choose a subject about which you are enthusiastic, (2) prepare interesting material, (3) have a strong desire to communicate your message to the audience, and (4) let your enthusiasm shine forth during your delivery of the speech.

Review Questions

1. Why are communication skills important to your career?
2. Name five personal benefits of a public speaking course.
3. What are the seven elements of the speech communication process?
4. Why is speaking not necessarily the same thing as communicating?
5. If there is a contradiction between the verbal and nonverbal components of a speaker's message, which component is a listener likely to accept as the true message?
6. What are the three major responsibilities of a speaker, as discussed in this chapter?

2

Listening

ailing to listen effectively can have comical results, as evidenced by an episode related by Professor Morris K. Holland of the University of California, Los Angeles:

A congressman once publicly criticized the Department of Agriculture for wasting the taxpayers' money in printing useless pamphlets. According to the congressman, they printed pamphlets about everything except the love life of the frog.

Following the congressman's speech, the Department of Agriculture began to receive orders for *The Love Life of the Frog*. Since the orders continued to arrive, the department eventually had to make a public announcement stating emphatically that there was no such pamphlet on the love life of the frog. After the public denial, letters requesting *The Love Life of the Frog* began to arrive by the hundreds. Finally, the Secretary of Agriculture, in a national address, stated that the department had never printed such a pamphlet and had no intention of doing so. Following the broadcast thousands of orders for the pamphlet arrived in the mail.[1]

This story illustrates the difference between hearing and listening. *Hearing* occurs when your ears pick up sound waves being transmitted by a speaker. *Listening* involves making sense out of what is being transmitted. As Keith Davis put it, "Hearing is with the ears, listening is with the mind."[2] When some listeners heard the words "love life of the frog" and "Department of Agriculture," they took note, but they failed to accurately process the entire message.

We may snicker at these befuddled listeners, but most of us are just as ineffective at listening.[3] According to Dr. Lyman K. Steil of the University of Minnesota in St. Paul, "Tests have shown that immediately after listening to a 10-minute oral presentation, the average listener has heard, understood, properly evaluated and retained approximately half of what was said. And within 48 hours, that drops off another 50% to a final 25% level of effectiveness. In other words, we quite often comprehend and retain only one-quarter of what is said."[4]

Society pays a heavy price for our poor listening, Dr. Steil says. "With more than 100 million workers in this country, a simple $10 mistake by each of them, as a result of poor listening, would add up to a cost of a billion dollars. And most people make numerous listening mistakes every week. Letters have to be retyped, appointments rescheduled, shipments rerouted. Productivity is affected and profits suffer."[5]

Poor listening also hurts us at home. Many marriages, for example, are weakened by the absence of real listening. "Most couples never truly listen to each other," says Dr. M. Scott Peck, a psychiatrist and author of several best-selling books on mental health. "When couples come to us for counseling or therapy, a major task we must accomplish . . . is to teach them how to listen."[6]

Effective listening is taught not only by marriage counselors but by many American businesses as well. To boost productivity and sales, giant corporations such as 3M, AT&T, and General Electric routinely send employees to special listening-skills classes. One of New England Telephone Company's divisions was losing $874,800 a year because 20 percent of its operater-assisted calls were delayed by listening problems. After the company developed a program to teach effective listening, it recovered about $500,000 of its annual loss.[7]

How to Listen Effectively

If you are reading a book, you can put it aside when you become weary or distracted, and then come back to it later. If the book contains complicated material, you can reread passages until you extract the meaning.

Not so with a speech. Unlike a book, which is stable and enduring, a speech is transitory and short-lived—"written on the wind," as someone once said. If you listen to a speech and fail to get the message the first time around, there's usually no way to go back and retrieve it. For this reason, listening is more difficult than reading.[8]

Though listening is a difficult task, here are some skills that you can develop to maximize your understanding and retention of material:

Don't Fake Attention

If you are like most people, you have indulged in fake listening many times. You go to history class, say, and sit in the third row and look squarely at the instructor as she speaks. But your mind is far away, floating in the clouds of a pleasant daydream. Occasionally you come back to earth: the instructor writes an important term on the chalkboard, and you dutifully copy it in your notebook. Every once in a while the instructor makes a witty remark, causing others in the class to laugh. You smile politely, pretending that you heard the remark and found it mildly humorous. You have a vague sense of guilt that you are not paying close attention, but you tell yourself that you can pick up the material from the textbook or from a friend's notes. Besides, the instructor is talking about road construction in ancient Rome and nothing could be more boring. So, back you go to your private little world.

You should never fake attention, for two main reasons: (1) you miss a lot of information, and (2) you can botch a personal or business relationship. Writer Margaret Lane relates an embarrassing instance of such fakery:

Years ago, fresh out of college and being interviewed for a job on a small-town newspaper, I learned the hard way . . . [that] the ability to listen and respond can make all the difference in any relationship. . . . My interview had been going well, and the editor, in an expansive mood, began telling me about his winter ski trip. Eager to make a big impression with a tale of my own about backpacking in the same mountains, I tuned him out and started planning my story. "Well," he asked suddenly, "what do you think of that?" Not having heard a word, I babbled foolishly, "Sounds like a marvelous holiday—great fun!" For a long moment he stared at me. "Fun?" he asked in an icy tone. "How could it be fun? I've just told you I spent most of it hospitalized with a broken leg."[9]

If you fake listening, you will rarely be so painfully exposed, but this does not mean that you can get away with deception most of the time. Many speakers are sensitive to facial cues and can tell if you are merely pretending to listen. Your blank expression, your unblinking gaze, and the faraway look in your eyes are the cues that betray your inattentiveness.

Even if you are not exposed, there is another reason to avoid fakery: it is easy for this behavior to become a habit. For some people, the habit is so deeply ingrained that they automatically start daydreaming the moment a speaker begins talking on a subject that seems complex or uninteresting. This causes them to miss a lot of interesting and valuable information.

Be Willing to Expend Energy

When you listen to a comedian cracking jokes on TV, do you have to work hard to pay attention? No, of course not. You simply sit back in a comfortable chair and enjoy the humor. It is easy, effortless, relaxing.

If you are like many listeners, you assume that when you go into a room for a lecture or a speech on a difficult subject, you should be able to sit back and absorb the content just as easily as you do in listening to a comedian's jokes. This is a major misconception because the two situations are quite different. Listening to light, entertaining material requires only a modest amount of mental effort, while listening effectively to difficult, complex material requires arduous work. You must be alert and energetic, giving total concentration to the speech, with your eyes on the speaker, your ears tuned in to the speaker's words, and your mind geared to receive the message.

"Listening is hard work," says Dr. Ralph G. Nichols, who did pioneering work on listening skills at the University of Minnesota. "It is characterized by faster heart action, quicker circulation of the blood, and a small rise in body temperature."[10]

If you tend to drift away mentally whenever a speaker begins to talk about unfamiliar or difficult material, try to break yourself of the habit. Vow to put as much energy as necessary into paying attention.

Prepare Yourself

Since listening to difficult material is hard work, you must prepare yourself as thoroughly as a runner prepares for a race.

Prepare yourself *physically*. Get plenty of sleep the night before. If necessary, exercise right before the speech or lecture. Let's suppose that you will be sitting in a warm room in midafternoon and therefore likely to become drowsy and lethargic. You could take a brisk walk before entering the room to make yourself alert and keen-minded.

Prepare yourself *intellectually*. If the subject matter of the speech is new or complex, do research or background reading beforehand. In this way, the speech will be much easier to understand. As the American philosopher Henry David Thoreau once said, "We hear and apprehend only what we already half know." The truth of this statement is shown in the way one student prepared for listening:

> Margaret Edney, a student nurse, planned to attend a lecture by an expert on Alzheimer's disease, a crippling disorder affecting many elderly persons. Edney realized that unless she did some background reading, the lecture would probably be too difficult to understand because of the unfamiliar medical terms that would be used. So she went to the library and found two recent articles on the disease. As she read the articles, she looked up definitions of some of the more important clinical terms associated with the disease—*cholinesterase, acetylcholine, physostigmine,* and so on. Later, when she went to the lecture, she was able to make sense out of the expert's remarks—thanks to her advance research.

This technique is of course what all good students do in preparing for their classes. They read the relevant textbook pages before attending a lecture so that they can gain maximum understanding of the instructor's remarks.

Resist Distractions

Concentrating on a speech is always hard work, but the task is made even more difficult by distractions. The four most common types of distractions are (1) *auditory* (a fly buzzing near your ear, an air conditioner that creates a racket, people coughing or whispering), (2) *visual* (cryptic comments on the chalkboard from a previous meeting, a nearby listener who is intriguing to look at, birds landing on a windowsill), (3) *physical* (headaches or stuffy noses, seats that are too hard, rooms that are too hot or too cold), and (4) *mental* (daydreams, worries, and preoccupations—we think about tomorrow or evaluate yesterday when we should be paying attention to the present moment).

Mental distractions are often caused by our minds running faster than the speaker's words. In most speeches, we as listeners can process information at about 500 words per minute, while most speakers talk at 125 to 150 words a minute. This means that our brain works three or four times faster than the speed needed for listening to a speech. This creates a lot of mental spare time. Dr. Nichols says, "What do we do with our excess thinking time while someone is speaking? If we are poor listeners, we soon become impatient with the slow progress the speaker seems to be making. So our thoughts run to something else for a moment, then dart back to the speaker. These brief side excursions of thought continue until our mind tarries too long on some enticing but irrelevant subject. Then, when our thoughts return to the person talking, we find he's far ahead of us. Now it's harder to follow him and increasingly easy to take off on side excursions. Finally we give up; the person is still talking, but our mind is in another world."[11]

How can you keep your mind from wandering? By using rigorous self-discipline. Shortly before a speech, prepare yourself for active listening by arriving in the room a few minutes early and getting yourself situated. Find a seat that is free from such distractions as blinding sunlight or friends who might want to whisper to you. Make yourself comfortable, lay out paper and pencil for taking notes, and clear your mind of personal matters. When the speech begins, concentrate all your mental energies on the speaker's message. There are two things you can do to aid your concentration—listen analytically and take notes. We will discuss both of these techniques in the sections below.

Listen Analytically

Analyze a speech as it is being presented, both to help you concentrate and to help you understand and remember the speaker's message. There are two elements that you should examine analytically: the main points and the support materials. Let's examine each in turn.

▶ Focus on Main Ideas

Some listeners make the mistake of treating all of a speaker's utterances as being equal in importance. This causes them to "miss the forest for the trees"—they spend so much time looking at individual sentences that they fail to see the "big picture" or larger meaning.

Try to distinguish the speaker's primary ideas from the secondary material—such as facts, figures, and stories—that are used to explain or prove the primary ideas. If a speaker tells an interesting story, for example, ask yourself, "Why is the speaker telling me this? What main idea is the speaker trying to get across to me by telling this story?"

In the following passage, taken from a speech by Rick Ballard, see if you can identify the main idea:

> Cocaine can kill you. Without warning, it can cause a fatal reaction at any time with any kind of user. Not just heavy users, but also light, so-called recreational users who snort only at weekend parties and ingest only a small amount of cocaine during any given evening. Two years ago, one of these recreational users, a 20-year-old woman in Miami, went to a party, drank some wine, snorted some cocaine, and then told friends she needed to lie down. A few moments later she experienced a violent seizure—caused by cocaine, not by epilepsy. The seizure was so strong that it threw her off the bed. An ambulance was called, but before it arrived, she was dead. She had used cocaine on previous occasions; for some reason her body—without warning—had suddenly developed an intolerance for the drug. Drug-abuse experts say that there is no way of predicting who will die from cocaine—it could be a regular user or a first-time user. Miami, Florida, has two cocaine deaths each month. Washington, D.C., had 88 last year. We should all remember that cocaine is a poison; cocaine used pharmaceutically in hospitals has the familiar poison warning—a skull and crossbones—on the bottles.

After hearing the above passage in a speech, some unskilled listeners might remember only that cocaine bottles in hospitals have a skull and crossbones on them or that a young woman in Florida died after using cocaine. But these items are *not* the main ideas of the passage. A careful listener would concentrate on, and try to remember, one idea above all else: Cocaine can randomly kill any user—light or heavy—without warning.

▶ Evaluate Support Materials

Most speakers use support materials such as stories, statistics, and quotations to explain, illustrate, or prove their main points. As a listener, you should evaluate each support as it is being presented: Is it accurate? Are objective sources used? Is enough support given? Am I getting an accurate picture of reality or a distorted one? As an example of how to evaluate support materials, let's suppose that a speaker tries to convince us that most Americans fail to get enough sleep, causing accidents, inefficiency, and irritability. Let's evaluate the evidence as the speaker gives it to us:

> Medical researchers have found that the average human needs about eight hours of sleep each night in order to function well on the job, on the highway, in school, and in the home. But according to a cover story in *Time* magazine, the majority of Americans try to get by on less than eight hours; in fact, 80% get six hours of sleep or less each night.

So far, we have a generalization but we are not convinced that a problem exists. We need more evidence.

Dr. Charles Pollak, head of the sleep-disorder center at Cornell University's New York Hospital, says, "Sleepiness is one of the least recognized sources of disability in our society. It doesn't make it difficult to walk, see, or hear. But people who don't get enough sleep can't think, they can't make appropriate judgments, they can't maintain long attention spans."

This quotation from an expert adds credence to the speaker's argument, but we still need specifics.

The U.S. Department of Transportation estimates that 200,000 traffic accidents each year may be sleep-related and that 20 percent of all drivers have dozed off at least once while behind the wheel. In 1988, there was a head-on collision between two freight trains near Thompsontown, Pennsylvania, with four people killed. Investigators think that the cause of the crash might have been the drowsiness of the engineer and crew.

Now we have some solid evidence from a government agency. But does this problem afflict only drivers and train engineers?

David Dinges, a biological psychologist at the University of Pennsylvania, says, "Human error causes between 60 percent and 90 percent of all workplace accidents . . . and inadequate sleep is a major factor in human error." *Time* reports that doctors at hospitals routinely work 120-hour weeks, including 36 hours at a stretch. A California surgeon fell asleep while sewing up a woman's uterus—and toppled onto the patient. In another California incident, a sleepy physician forgot to order a diabetic patient's nightly insulin shot and instead prescribed another medication. The man went into a coma.

By quoting the statistics of an authority and by giving vivid examples, the speaker continues to build a credible argument. Are there other problems caused by sleep deprivation?

Time says, "Perhaps the most insidious consequence of skimping on sleep is the irritability that increasingly pervades society. Weariness corrodes civility and erases humor, traits that ease the myriad daily frustrations, from standing in supermarket lines to refereeing the kids' squabbles. Without sufficient sleep, tempers flare faster and hotter at the slightest offense."

By providing a variety of statistics, quotations from authorities, and examples, the speaker has given us a convincing picture of a major problem in our society.

Take Notes

I strongly urge you to take notes whenever you listen to a speech—for the following reasons:

1. Note taking gives you a record of the speaker's most important points. Unless you have superhuman powers of memory, there is no way you can remember all of a speaker's key ideas without taking notes.

2. Note taking sharpens and strengthens your ability to listen analytically. When you take notes, you force your mind to scan a speech like radar, looking for main points and evidence. You end up being a better listener than if you did not take any notes at all.[12]

3. Note taking is a good way to keep your attention on the speaker and not let your mind wander. This is why I recommend taking notes on *all* speeches—not just on important lectures at school. A colleague explains why he takes notes at every meeting he attends, even though he usually throws them away soon afterward:

I take notes at any talk I go to, whether it's a business briefing, a professional seminar, or an inspirational speech. I usually review the notes right after the

Taking notes helps listeners pay attention, and it provides a useful record of the speaker's main ideas.

meeting to solidify the key points in my mind. Afterwards, I may save the notes for my files or for some sort of follow-up, but usually I drop them in a trash can on my way out of the room. This doesn't mean that I had wasted my time by taking notes. The act of writing them helped me to listen actively and analytically. It also—I must confess—kept me from daydreaming.

When taking notes, don't try to write down the speaker's exact words because you could easily fall into the habit of transcribing without evaluating. As much as possible, put the speaker's ideas into your own words, so that you make sure that you understand what is being said.

There are many different ways of taking notes, and you may have already developed a method that suits you. Whatever system you use, your notes should include major points, with pertinent data or support materials that back up those points. You may also want to leave space for comments to yourself or questions that might need to be asked. One effective method for taking notes is to list main ideas in one column, support materials in a second column, and listener responses in a third column. Here's a sample of the top of a sheet as it would look at the beginning of a speech:

Main Ideas	Support Material	Response

Using this method, let's examine some notes based on the first part of the speech (about sleep deprivation) discussed in the preceding section:

Main Ideas	Support Material	Response
Avg. person needs 8 hours sleep	80% of Americans get 6 hours or less	
Sleepiness—a source of disability	Trouble thinking, making judgments, keeping long attention span	
May cause accidents	D.O.T.:—200,000 traffic accidents a year—20% of all drivers have dozed off	Most at night?

The response column is designed to help you interact with the speaker and ask questions that arise in your mind during the speech. When the question-and-answer period begins, you can scan the response column and ask questions. If a question that you jotted down gets answered later in the speech itself, no harm has been done; having raised the question will cause you to listen to the explanation with extra-special interest. The response

FOR YOUR CAREER

TIP 2.1: Take Notes in Important Conversations and Small-Group Meetings

Whenever your superiors and colleagues talk to you (either one-on-one or in a group meeting) about work-related matters, take notes. Not only does this give you a written record of important discussions, but it also creates a favorable impression. You show that you are a good listener who values the advice and opinions of the speaker. It is a nonverbal way of saying, "Your ideas are important to me—so important that I want to make sure I get them down correctly." Contrary to what some may think, taking notes does *not* signify to others that you have a poor memory.

One of the most common gripes of employees is that "the boss never listens to what we say."

So, if you are ever in a supervisory position, take notes whenever one of your subordinates comes to you with a suggestion or a complaint. It shows that you value the employee's comments and are prepared to take action if necessary. Even if you can't take action, the employee's morale is boosted because you have shown you truly listen and truly care.

Can you ever rise so high in your career that you no longer need to take notes? Not if you're Robert Stempel, chairman of General Motors. Though he heads one of the world's largest corporations and could hire a platoon of secretaries to take notes for him, Stempel takes his own notes at management meetings.

column also enables you to plan follow-up research (for example, a response note for a lecture might be a reminder to yourself: "Look up additional info in library"). Notice that the response column does not require an entry for each of the speaker's points. In other words, use the response column only as needed.

If you have taken notes on a class lecture or some other complex presentation, review your notes soon afterward and expand them if necessary while the speaker's words are still fresh in your mind. If any parts of your notes are vague or confusing, seek help from another listener (or the speaker, if available).

Avoid Prejudgments

Prejudging a speaker is an unfortunate tendency that many listeners have. Some people reject a speaker even before he or she stands up to speak. They dislike the speaker's looks or clothes or the organization the speaker represents. Let's say that a Catholic priest speaks on marriage; some people in the audience might say to themselves, "Why should I listen to him? What does a priest, who is celibate, know about marriage?" What is unfortunate about this reaction is that such listeners cut themselves off from gaining skills and insights. A priest might offer some excellent advice based on years of counseling couples.

Don't reject speakers because their delivery is ragged or because they seem shaky and lacking in confidence. Their ideas might be worth paying attention to. Professor Wayne Austin Shrope gives a good example of the value of concentrating on the message rather than on delivery:

> When I was in college I took a history class from an instructor who was generally considered a very dull lecturer. He sat behind his desk and read his notes in a dull monotone. The other students I knew approached the lectures with the attitude that they would be bored by his dull delivery, and that they would learn nothing. This turned out to be a self-fulfilling prophecy: they *were* bored, and they *did* learn nothing. I, on the other hand, approached the lectures determined to get something from them—perhaps because I found that if I listened carefully I didn't have to read the text. At any rate, I found the lectures to be the best organized I have ever heard, and I thought the examples, details, facts, and language were fascinating. I liked the course better than any history course I ever took. I learned a great deal about history and particularly the people who made it. My classmates, who apparently listened only to the monotone and nothing else, were amazed at how well I did in the course despite little time spent studying, just by listening well in class.[13]

Give every speaker a fair chance. You may be pleasantly surprised by what you learn.

Don't Mentally Argue with the Speaker

Some people avoid prejudging a speaker, but as soon as he or she starts talking about a controversial topic, such as sex education or gun control, they immediately have a powerful emotional reaction that seems to cut off intelligent listening for the rest of the speech. Instead of paying attention to the speaker's words, they "argue" with the speaker inside their heads or think of ways to retaliate in the question-and-answer period. They often jump to conclusions, convincing themselves that the speaker is saying something that he or she really is not.

One speaker argued against the death penalty for armed robbery (although she did believe that capital punishment should be used for first-degree murder). Her reasoning: "An armed robber will know that if he's caught and convicted, he's going to be executed, so he has an incentive to kill his victim. He will say to himself, 'If I let this person live, he'll be a witness against me. So I may as well kill him because the penalty for armed robbery is the same as the penalty for murder."

In the question-and-answer period, some listeners accused the speaker of being soft on crime. They missed hearing her say that she was in favor of the death penalty for murder. And they failed to grasp that the speaker's ideas were aimed at saving victims' lives rather than coddling criminals.

When you are listening to speakers who seem to be arguing against some of your ideas or beliefs, make sure you understand exactly what they are saying. Hear them out, and *then* prepare your counterarguments.

The Listener's Responsibilities

As we discussed in Chapter 1, the speaker who is honest and fair has ethical and moral obligations to his or her listeners. The converse is also true: the honest and fair listener has ethical and moral obligations to the speaker. Let's examine three of the listener's primary responsibilities.

Avoid Rudeness

If you were engaged in conversation with a friend, how would you feel if your friend yawned and went to sleep? Or started reading a book? Or looked at the floor the entire time? You would be upset by your friend's rudeness, wouldn't you?

There are many people who would never dream of being so rude to a friend in conversation, yet when they sit in an audience, they are terribly rude to the speaker. They fall asleep or read a newspaper or study for a test or carry on a whispered conversation with their friends. Fortunately, a public speaking class cures some people of their rudeness. As one student put it:

> I had been sitting in classrooms for 12 years and until now, I never realized how much a speaker sees. I always thought a listener is hidden and anonymous out there in a sea of faces. Now that I've been a speaker, I realize that when you look out at an audience, you are well aware of the least little thing somebody does. I am ashamed now at how I used to carry on conversations in the back of class. I was very rude, and I didn't even know it.

If you are seated in the audience and you turn to whisper to a friend, your movement is as noticeable as a red flag waving in front of the speaker's eyes. If you do more than whisper—if you snicker or grin—you can damage the morale and confidence of inexperienced speakers, for they may think that you are laughing at them.

Think of a speech as nothing more than *enlarged* conversation, and show the speaker the same politeness you would show your best friend during a chat.

Provide Encouragement

A good philosophy to follow is summed up in the Golden Rule of listening: "Listen unto others as you would have others listen unto you." When you are a speaker, you want an audience that listens attentively, courteously, and enthusiastically. So when you are a listener, you should provide the same response.

Encourage the speaker as much as possible—by giving your full attention, taking notes, leaning slightly forward instead of slouching back in your seat, looking directly at the speaker instead of at the floor, and letting your face show interest and animation. If the speaker says something you particularly like, nod in agreement or smile approvingly. (If the speaker says something that offends you or puzzles you, obviously you should not give positive feedback; I am not recommending hypocrisy.)

The more encouragement a speaker receives, the better he or she is able to speak. Most entertainers and professional speakers say that if an audience is lively and enthusiastic, they do a much better job than if the audience is sullen or apathetic. From my own experience, I feel that I always give a better speech if I get encouragement. Maybe it is just a few people who are displaying lively interest, but their nods and smiles and eager eyes inspire and energize me.

When we cause a speaker to give a good speech, we are doing more than an act of kindness; we are creating a payoff for ourselves: the better the speaker, the easier it is to listen. And the easier it is to listen, the better we will understand, remember, and gain knowledge.

Listeners exert a tremendous power over the speaker. At one college, some psychology majors conducted an experiment to prove that professors can be as easily manipulated as laboratory rats by means of positive reinforcement. In one political science class, if the professor walked to the left side of the classroom during his lecture, the students would give him approving looks, nod their heads in agreement, and enthusiastically scribble notes in their notebooks. But when he stayed in the middle or walked to the right side of the class, they would lay down their pencils and look away from the professor with glum expressions on their faces. Before long the professor spent the entire hour standing on the left side of the room. Carrying their experiment a step further, the students "rewarded" the professor with encouraging looks and nods only if he stood on the left side next to the window and absent-mindedly played with the lift cord of the venetian blinds. Soon the professor was spending all his lecture time holding the lift cord, blithely unaware that he was the "guinea pig" in a behavior-modification experiment.[14]

I tell this story not to suggest that you manipulate a speaker but to show the power that you as a listener exert. Use that power wisely. Use it to encourage and uplift the speaker.

Find Value in Every Speech

There will be times when you are forced to hear a speech you feel is boring and worthless. Instead of tuning the speaker out and retreating into your private world of daydreams, try to exploit the speech for something worthwhile. Make a game of it: see how many diamonds can be extracted from the mud. Is there any new information that might be useful to you in the future? Is the speaker using techniques of delivery that are worth noting and emulating?

What if a speech is complicated and over your head? Listen anyway, and try to broaden your knowledge. Dr. Steil gives some good advice on this point:

> The listener who responds to complex material by "tuning out" can be missing a great opportunity to learn, to discover, to broaden himself. We have all had the experience of mastering a body of information, and then—when the material has become entirely familiar—using it as a foundation for understanding additional, even more complex information. It is a heady feeling—one of the joys of learning. And it can only be felt if we as listeners greet the arrival of complex information with anticipation. Not with anxiety.[15]

If a speech is so bad that you honestly cannot find anything worthwhile in it, you can always look for a how-not-to-do-it lesson. Ask yourself, "What can I learn from this speaker's mistakes?" Here is an example of how one business executive profited from a poor speaker:

> At a convention recently I found myself in an extremely boring seminar (on listening, ironically enough). After spending the first half-hour wishing I had never signed up, I decided to take advantage of the situation. I turned my thought "This guy isn't teaching me how to run a seminar on listening" into a question: "What is he teaching me about how *not* to run a seminar?" While providing a negative example was not the presenter's goal, I got a useful lesson.[16]

"Turn your lemons into lemonade," some wise person once advised. If you look for value or a how-not-to-do-it lesson in every poor speech, you will find that the sourest oratorical lemon can be turned into lemonade. "Know how to listen," the Greek writer Plutarch said twenty centuries ago, "and you will profit even from those who talk badly."

Summary

Listening effectively is often a difficult task, but it can be rewarding for the person who is willing to make the effort. The guidelines for effective listening include the following: (1) Avoid fakery. Don't pretend to be listening when in fact your mind is wandering; this kind of behavior can settle into a hard-to-break habit. (2) Be willing to put forth energy. Since listening is hard work, especially if the material is new or difficult, you must have a strong desire to listen actively and intelligently. (3) Prepare yourself for the act of listening. Do whatever background reading or research that is necessary for gaining maximum understanding of the speech. (4) Resist distractions, both external and internal. Use rigorous self-discipline to keep your mind concentrated on the speaker's remarks. (5) Listen analytically, focusing on main ideas and evaluating support materials. (6) Take notes, not only for a record of key points but as a way of keeping your mind from wandering. (7) Avoid prejudgments. Don't dismiss a speaker even before he or she starts the speech.

(8) Don't mentally argue with a speaker: you might misunderstand what he or she is really saying.

As a listener you have three important obligations to a speaker: to avoid all forms of rudeness, to provide encouragement, and to find value in every speech. The more support you give a speaker, the better the speech will be, and the more you will profit from it.

Review Questions

1. What is the difference between *hearing* and *listening*?
2. Why is listening to complex material in a speech more difficult than reading the same material in a book?
3. List several ways in which you can prepare yourself both physically and intellectually to listen to a speech.
4. List five possible distractions that can keep a listener from concentrating on a speech.
5. What are the advantages of taking notes during a speech?
6. When you are a listener, how can you encourage a speaker?

3

Controlling Nervousness

▶ **Reasons for Nervousness**

▶ **The Value of Fear**

▶ **Guidelines for Controlling Nervousness**

In the Days and Weeks before Your Speech / During Your Speech /
Additional Hints /

A U.S. Marine Corps general who had won a Congressional Medal of Honor, the nation's highest military decoration, for his heroism in combat was scheduled as a guest on a national television show. But five minutes before airtime, with his face looking ashen, the general told the show's producer, Roger Ailes, that he had decided not to appear. "He was clearly terrified by the prospect of appearing on a national television show," recalls Ailes.[1]

"If he didn't go on, the show would be a disaster," said Ailes. "I had to think quickly. I finally said, 'General, let me put it this way. In just a few minutes you will be introduced and either you're going to walk out there and talk or I'm going on in place of you and tell everybody you're chicken.' There was a long pause. He was huge, and I thought he was going to pound me into the floor. But then he smiled . . . and went on the show. He was shaky starting. His throat was tight and he gave one-word answers. But after the first couple of minutes, he was fine."[2]

If you experience nervousness as a public speaker, you are not alone. Most people—even war heroes like the general—suffer from stage fright when called upon to speak in public. In fact, when researchers ask Americans to name their greatest fears, the fear of speaking to a group of strangers is listed more often than fear of snakes, insects, lightning, deep water, heights, or flying in airplanes.[3]

With the tips offered in this chapter, you will be able to control your nervousness and—like the Marine general—step forward and do fine.

Reasons for Nervousness

Is it foolish to be afraid to give a speech? Is this fear as groundless as a child's fear of the boogeyman? I used to think so, back in the days when I first began making speeches. I was a nervous wreck, and I would often chide myself by saying, "Come on, relax, it's just a little speech. There's no good reason to be scared." But I was wrong. There *is* good reason to be scared; in fact, there are *four* good reasons.

1. Fear of being stared at. In the animal world, a stare is a hostile act. Dogs, baboons, and other animals sometimes defend their territory by staring. Their hostile gaze alone is enough to turn away an intruder. We human beings have similar reactions; it is part of our biological makeup to be upset by stares. Imagine that you are riding in a crowded elevator with a group of strangers. Suddenly you realize that the other people are staring directly at you. Not just glancing. *Staring.* You probably would be unnerved and frightened because a stare can be as threatening as a clenched fist—especially if it comes from people you don't know. That is why public speaking can be so frightening. You have a pack of total strangers "attacking" you with unrelenting stares, while you are obliged to stand alone, exposed and vulnerable—a goldfish in a bowl, subject to constant scrutiny.

2. Fear of failure.   Most speakers worry about botching their speech: What if I make a fool of myself? What if my mind goes blank and I forget everything I was planning to say? What if I stumble or stammer? Any normal person, especially if he or she is an inexperienced speaker, is apt to have this fear. Indeed, a person who never has self-doubts is probably foolish and vain.

3. Fear of rejection.   What if we do our best, what if we deliver a polished speech, but the audience still does not like us? It would be quite a blow to our ego because we want to be liked and, yes, even loved. We want people to admire us, to consider us wise and intelligent, and to accept our ideas and opinions. We don't want people to dislike us, reject us, or worst of all, consider us foolish.

The most terrifying speaking situation of my life occurred in high school when I decided to telephone a girl to invite her to a dance. I was attending an all-boys' school, I was shy around girls, and it was my first date. Before I called her, I was afraid that I would fail to think of clever things to say, so I made note cards with sentences written out in full—things like "What is your favorite subject in school?" and "What kind of music do you like?" Even with these cue cards, I was choked with fear when I finally gathered enough courage to call her; my heart was thumping so furiously that it leaped up into my throat, and I could barely get my words out. She did say yes, but when I hung up the phone, I realized that I was now faced with a fresh terror: I would have to talk to her on our date, and I would have no cue cards to guide me through. What made this event so excruciating, of course, was my fear of rejection.

4. Fear of the unknown.   Throughout our lives we are apprehensive about doing new things, such as going to school for the first time, riding a bus without our parents, or going out on our first date. We cannot put a finger on exactly what we are afraid of because our fear is vague and diffused. What we really fear is the unknown; we worry that some unpredictable disaster might occur. When we stand up to give a speech, we are sometimes assailed by this same fear of the unknown because we cannot predict the outcome of our speech. Fortunately, this fear usually disappears as we become experienced in giving speeches—we have enough confidence to know that nothing terrible will befall us, just as our childhood fear of riding in a bus by ourselves vanished after two or three trips.

All four of these fears are as understandable as the fear of lightning. There is no reason why you should be ashamed of having them.

The Value of Fear

Because the fears engendered by public speaking are real and understandable, does this mean that it is impossible to get rid of nervousness? If you are like many of the students who come into my public speaking class, this is your primary concern: to completely eliminate all traces of nervousness. My response may surprise you as much as it surprises my students: *You should not try to banish all your fear and nervousness. You need a certain amount of fear to give a good speech.*

You *need* fear? Yes, fear energizes you; it makes you think more rapidly; it helps you speak with vitality and enthusiasm. Here is why: When you stand up to give a speech and fear hits you, your body goes on "red alert," the same biological mechanism that saved our cave-dwelling ancestors when they were faced with a hungry lion or a human foe and had to fight or flee in order to survive. Though not as crucial to us as it was to our ancestors, this system is still nice to have for emergencies. If you were walking down a deserted street one night and someone tried to attack you, your body would release a burst of adrenalin into your bloodstream, causing fresh blood and oxygen to rush to your muscles, and you would be able to fight ferociously or run faster than you have ever run in your life. The benefit of adrenalin can be seen in competitive sports: athletes *must* get their adrenalin flowing before a game begins. There is one high school football coach who looks at his players' hands before the kickoff. Any player without sweaty palms is benched; he is obviously not fired up enough to play well. The great home-run slugger Reggie Jackson said during his heyday, "I have butterflies in my stomach almost every time I step up to the plate. When I don't have them, I get worried because it means I won't hit the ball very well."[4]

Public speakers often have the same attitude. Don Beveridge of Barrington, Illinois, has spoken professionally for 20 years to audiences ranging in size from 15 to 5000. "No matter what the speaking situation, my hands sweat before each and every presentation, and frankly that's what makes me a good speaker . . . . The day my palms stop sweating, I'll quit!"[5]

In public speaking, adrenalin infuses you with energy; it causes extra blood and oxygen to rush not only to your muscles but to your brain as well, thus enabling you to think with greater clarity and quickness. It makes you come across to your audience as someone who is alive and vibrant. Elayne Snyder, a speech teacher, uses the term *positive nervousness*, which she describes in this way: "It's a zesty, enthusiastic, lively feeling with a slight edge to it. Positive nervousness is the state you'll achieve by converting your anxiety into constructive energy . . . . It's still nervousness, but you're no longer victimized by it; instead you're vitalized by it."[6]

If you want proof that nervousness is beneficial, observe speakers who have absolutely no butterflies at all. Because they are 100 percent relaxed and cool, they give speeches that are dull and flat, with no energy, no zest. There is an old saying: "Speakers who say they are as cool as a cucumber usually give speeches about as interesting as a cucumber." Most good speakers report that if they don't have butterflies before a public appearance, their delivery is poor. One speaker, the novelist I. A. R. Wylie, said, "I rarely rise to my feet without a throat constricted with terror and a furiously thumping heart. When, for some reason, I *am* cool and self-assured, the speech is always a failure. I need fear to spur me on."[7]

There is another danger in being devoid of nervousness. Some years ago, before I learned the value of controlled nervousness, I tried to talk myself into being completely relaxed for a speech. I told myself, "There's nothing to be afraid of. Be calm, play it cool." On one particular occasion it worked— for a while. I was an after-dinner speaker at a banquet. For once, I was able to eat food before a speech without having it taste like cardboard. I congratulated myself on being completely relaxed as I sat at the head table and listened to the master of ceremonies introduce me. There was not a single butterfly in my stomach. I got up confidently, strode to the lectern, looked out at my audience, and then—WHAM!—I was suddenly struck by a lightning bolt of panic. I got a huge lump in my throat, my heart pounded, and I had so much trouble breathing that every word had to be wrestled from my suffocating larynx and forced out of my mouth. My face turned red and I started sweating heavily. It was a nightmare. Somehow I got through the speech and sat down, humiliated and angry at myself. But I learned a lesson I would never forget: to avoid last-minute panic, I must be "psyched up." Nowadays I never go into a speech without encouraging my butterflies to flutter around inside, so that I can be poised and alert.

Other speakers have come to the same conclusion. If they aren't "pumped up" for a speech, they either suffer the kind of panic that hit me, or else they give boring speeches that have no fizz and sparkle.

Guidelines for Controlling Nervousness

We have just discussed how a complete lack of nervousness is undesirable. What about the other extreme? Is *too much* nervousness bad for you? Of course it is, especially if you are so frightened that you forget what you were planning to say or if your breathing is so labored that you cannot get your words out. Your goal is to keep your nervousness under control, so that you have just the right amount—enough to energize you, but not enough to cripple you. How can you do this? Here are some ideas that have helped my students.

In the Days and Weeks before Your Speech

▶ Choose a Topic You Know a Great Deal About

Nothing will get you more rattled than speaking on a subject about which you know little. If you are asked to talk on a topic that you're not comfortable with, decline the invitation (unless, of course, it is an assignment from a boss who gives you no choice in the matter). Choose a topic you know a lot about (or can learn about by doing extensive research). This will give you enormous self-confidence; if something terrible happens (for example, you lose your notes on the way to the meeting), you can always improvise because your head is filled with information about the subject. Also, you will be able to handle yourself well in the question-and-answer period after the speech.

▶ Prepare Yourself Thoroughly

Here is a piece of advice given by many experienced speakers: *The very best precaution against excessive stage fright is thorough, careful preparation.*[8] You have heard the expression, "I came unglued." In public speaking, the best "glue" to hold you together is good, solid preparation. Joel Weldon of Scottsdale, Arizona (who quips that he used to be so frightened of audiences that he was "unable to lead a church group in silent prayer") gives his personal formula for controlling fear: "I prepare and then prepare, and then when I think I'm ready, I prepare some more."[9] Weldon recommends five to eight hours of preparation for each hour in front of an audience.[10]

Start your preparation far in advance of the speech date, so that you have plenty of time to gather ideas, create an outline, and prepare speaking notes. Then practice, practice, practice. Don't just look over your notes—actually stand up and rehearse your talk in whatever way suits you: in front of a mirror, into a tape recorder, before a family member or friend. Don't rehearse just once—run through your entire speech at least four times. If you "give" your speech four times at home, you will find that your fifth delivery—before a live audience—will be smoother and more self-assured than if you had not practiced at all.

▶ Never Memorize a Speech

Giving a speech from memory courts disaster. As a young man, Winston Churchill—considered one of the greatest orators of modern times—used to write out and memorize his speeches. Then one day, while giving a memorized talk to Parliament, he suddenly stopped. His mind went blank. He began his last sentence all over. Again his mind went blank. He sat down in embarrassment and shame. Never again did Churchill try to memorize a speech. This same thing has happened to many others who have tried to commit a speech to memory. Everything goes smoothly until they get derailed, and then they are hopelessly off the track.

Even if you avoid derailment, there is another reason for not memorizing: you will probably sound mechanical, like a robot with a tape recorder in its mouth. In addition to considering you dull and boring, your audience will sense that you are speaking from your memory and not from your heart, and they will question your sincerity.

▶ Think of Communication, Not Performance

Regard your task as *communication* rather than *performance*. Dr. Michael T. Motley of the University of California, Davis, says that speakers who suffer from excessively high levels of anxiety make the mistake of thinking they are *performing* for listeners, whom they see as hostile evaluators. According to Dr. Motley, such people say, "The audience will ridicule me if I make a mistake. I'll be embarrassed to death." But in fact, says this authority, audiences are more interested in hearing what you have to say "than in analyzing or criticizing how [you] say it." Audiences "usually ignore errors and awkwardness as long as they get something out of a speech."[11]

When speakers stop worrying "How well am I performing?" and start thinking "How can I share my ideas with these people?" two things usually happen: (1) their anxiety level comes down to a manageable level, and (2) their delivery improves dramatically. By treating speechmaking as more like one-on-one communication than as a stage exhibition, they tend to talk *with* people, instead of orate *at* them; they tend to speak conversationally rather than in a stiff, unnatural way.

When one of my students, Maxine Jones, began her first classroom speech, her voice sounded artificial and cold, but after she got into her talk, she sounded animated and warm, as if she were carrying on a lively conversation. This caused her to become more interesting and easier to follow. Later she explained her transformation: "At first I was scared to death, but then I noticed that everyone in the room was looking at me with curiosity in their eyes, and I could tell that they really wanted to hear what I was saying. I told myself, 'They really *care* about this information—I can't let them down.' So I settled down and talked to them as if they were my friends. I got so involved with explaining things to them that I didn't worry too much about being scared."

If you stop thinking of a speech as performance, you can rid yourself of the idea that you *must* give a perfect, polished speech. Such a notion puts enormous—and unnecessary—pressure on you, and it causes you to concentrate your energies on yourself rather than on what should be your real target—your listeners. Remember that they don't care whether your delivery is perfect; they simply hope that your words will enlighten or entertain them. Think of yourself as merely a telegram messenger; the audience is interested in the telegram, not in how well you hand it over.

▶ Imagine Yourself Giving a Good, Strong Speech

Let yourself daydream a bit. Picture yourself going up to the lectern, nervous but in control of yourself, then giving a forceful talk to an appreciative audience. Does this sound silly? It is a technique that has worked for many

TIP 3.1: Consider Your Speech as a Service

Larry McMahan has a good technique that helps him control nervousness: "I think of a speech not as a chore but as a *service* to my audience—a way to help people." A speech does indeed enrich the listeners: informative and persuasive speeches can give them valuable knowledge or insights, sometimes even changing their lives for the better; an entertaining speech can divert them from their cares and troubles, and an inspiring speech can encourage and uplift them. If you like to help others, adopt McMahan's mental outlook. It will help you focus your energies on your audience instead of on yourself.

speakers and it might work for you. Whatever you do, don't let yourself imagine the opposite—a bad speech or poor delivery. Negative daydreams will add unnecessary fear to your life in the days before your speech, and sap you of creative energy—energy that you need for preparing and practicing. Actress Ali MacGraw says, "We have only so much energy, and the more we direct toward the project itself, the less is left to pour into wondering 'Will I fail?' "[12]

Notice that the daydream I am suggesting includes nervousness. You need to have a realistic image in your mind: Picture yourself as nervous, but nevertheless in command of the situation and capable of delivering a strong, effective speech.

This technique, often called "positive imagery," has been used by athletes for years. Have you ever watched professional golf on TV? Before each stroke, golfers carefully study the distance from the ball to the hole, the rise and fall of the terrain, and so on. Just before swinging (many of them report), they imagine themselves hitting the ball with the right amount of force and watching it go straight into the cup. Then they try to execute the play just as they imagined it. The imagery, many pros say, improves their game.

Positive imagery works best when you can couple it with *believing* that you will give a successful speech. Is it absurd to hold such a belief? If you fail to prepare well, yes, it is absurd. But if you spend time in good, solid preparation and rehearsal, you are justified in believing in success.

▶ Know That Shyness Is No Barrier

Some shy people think that their shyness blocks them from becoming good speakers, but actor and speechmaker Steve Allen says this is a mistaken notion. "I tend toward shyness, particularly in the presence of strangers in small social gatherings," he says, noting that many other Hollywood figures are shy and introverted, yet are excellent speakers. "Like stutterers who have no trouble singing, we shy introverts often blossom when placed on stage, in front of a camera, or next to a microphone," he says. "So whether you personally are a life-of-the-party type or are inclined to sit and listen to others means little so far as . . . public speaking is concerned."[13] (Other shy introverts in show business: Carol Burnett, Barbara Walters, Carly Simon, Garrison Keillor, and Michael Jackson.[14])

The truth of Allen's remark is demonstrated by Joe W. Boyd of Bellingham, Washington. "I used to stammer," says Boyd, "and I used to be petrified at the thought of speaking before a group of any size." Despite his shyness, Boyd joined a Toastmasters club to develop his speaking skills. Two years later, in 1984, he won the Toastmasters International Public Speaking Contest by giving a superb speech to an audience of over 2000 listeners.[15]

During Your Speech

Here are some important things to keep in mind as you deliver a speech.

▶ Deal Rationally with Your Body's Turmoil

If you are a typical beginning speaker, you will suffer from some or all of the following symptoms when you begin your talk:

- ▶ Pounding heart
- ▶ Trembling hands
- ▶ Shaky knees
- ▶ Dry, constricted throat
- ▶ Difficulty in breathing
- ▶ Quivering voice
- ▶ Flushed face

You usually suffer the greatest discomfort during the first few minutes of your speech, but then things get better. If, however, your symptoms get worse as you go along, it might be because your mind has taken the wrong path (see Figure 3.1).

If you take route A, you are trapped in a vicious circle. Your mind tells your body that disaster is upon you, and your body responds by getting worse. This, in turn, increases your brain's perception of disaster. If you take route B, however, your mind will help your body stay in control. You can remind yourself that your symptoms, rather than being a prelude to disaster, are evidence that you are keyed up enough to give a good speech.

▶ Concentrate on Getting Your Ideas Across

Before the kickoff, football players are nervous and tense—most are filled with butterflies. But what happens when the game actually starts? Though nervousness is still present, it recedes into the background as the players concentrate on catching the ball or making a tackle.

FIGURE 3.1
The alternative paths that a speaker might take.

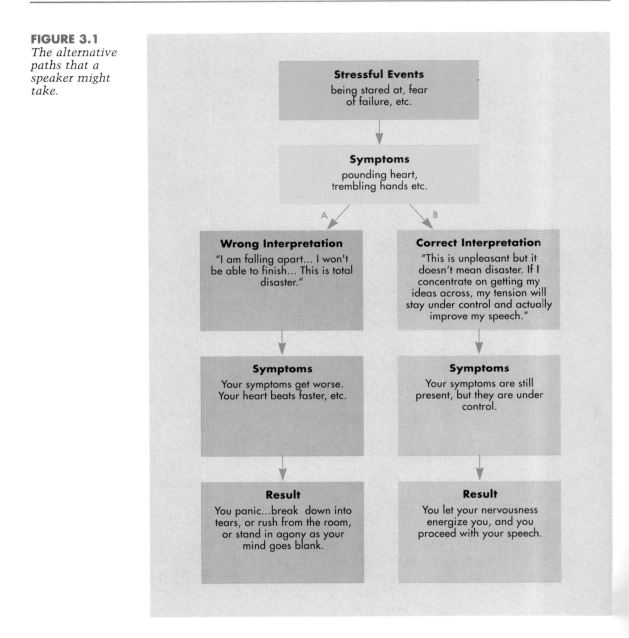

Public speaking is similar. You may experience terrible anxiety at the beginning, but once you get into your speech, if you focus all your attention on communicating your ideas to your listeners, your nervousness will recede into the background. It does not go away, of course; it simply simmers on a back burner, where it can remain an ongoing source of energy.

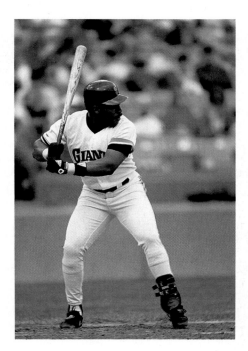

Most baseball players are gripped by nervous tension when they step up to the plate, but if they concentrate on hitting the ball, their tension recedes into the background. Likewise, public speakers may be filled with anxiety before a speech, but if they concentrate on communicating with the audience, their anxiety moves to a back burner, where it provides energy for the task.

When you concentrate on getting your message across to your listeners, you do more than quell your butterflies; you also give a better speech than you would if you were self-absorbed. Hugh Downs, the host of ABC's *20/20*, learned this lesson in dealing with his own nervousness problem. "Somehow when you give full attention to subject matter and audience," he said, "you wind up looking and sounding better than when you're focused on yourself."[16]

▶ Know That Most Symptoms Are Not Seen

Some speakers get rattled because they think the audience is keenly aware of their thumping heart and quaking hands. You, of course, are painfully aware of these symptoms, but believe it or not, your audience is usually oblivious to your body's distress. Remember that people are sitting out there wanting to hear your ideas. They are not saying to themselves, "Let's see, what signs of nervousness is this person displaying?" I have had students tell me after a speech that they were ashamed or embarrassed about their jittery performance, yet I and the other listeners in the class saw no signs of nervousness. We were listening to the ideas and failed to notice the speaker's discomfort. Various studies have found the same thing to be true: audiences simply are unaware of the signs that the speakers think are embarrassingly obvious.[17] In other words, you are probably the only one who knows that your knees are shaking and that your heart is pounding.

Dick Cavett, who spent many years as a TV talk-show host, says of stage fright on TV, "The best thing to do is tell yourself it doesn't show one-eighth as much as you feel. If you're a little nervous, you don't look nervous at all. If you're very nervous, you look slightly nervous. And if you're totally out of control, you look troubled. It scales down on the screen. Anybody who appears on a talk show should always remind himself that everything he's doing *looks* better than it *feels* . . . . Your nervous system may be giving you a thousand shocks, but the viewer can only see a few of them."[18] The same thing holds true for a speech: you look better than you feel.

▶ Never Call Attention to Your Nervousness or Apologize for It

Despite what I have said, there may be times when an audience does notice your nervousness—if, for example, your breathing seems labored. In such a case, resist the temptation to comment or apologize. Since everyone knows that most people get nervous when they talk in public, why mention it or apologize for it?

Commenting about nervousness can create two big dangers:

First of all, you might get yourself more rattled than you were to begin with. I remember listening to a teacher who was giving a talk at a PTA meeting one night. In the middle of her remarks she suddenly blurted out, "Oh, my God, I *knew* I would fall apart." Up to that time, I had not been aware of any discomfort or nervousness. She tried to continue her talk, but she was too flustered. She gave up the effort and sat down with a red face. I don't know what kind of internal distress she was suffering, of course, but I am certain that if she had said nothing about her nervousness, she could have dragged herself through the speech. When she sat down, I felt irritated and disappointed, because I had been keenly interested in her remarks. How selfish of her, I thought, to deprive me of the second half of her speech simply because she was nervous. I know that my reaction sounds insensitive, but it underscores an important point: your listeners don't care about your emotional distress; they only want to hear your ideas.

The second risk in mentioning symptoms: Your audience might have been unaware of your nervousness before you brought it up, but now you have distracted them from your speech and they are watching the very thing you don't want them to scrutinize—your body's behavior. If you say "I'm sorry that my hands are shaking," what do you think the audience will pay close attention to—at least for the next few minutes? Your hands, of course, instead of your speech. Keep your audience's attention focused on your ideas, and they probably will pay little or no attention to your emotional and physical distress.

▶ Don't Let Your Audience Upset You

Some inexperienced speakers get rattled when they look out at the audience and observe that most listeners are poker-faced and unsmiling. Does this mean they are displeased with your speech? No, their solemn faces have nothing to do with your performance. This is just one of those peculiarities of human nature: in a conversation, people will smile and nod and encourage you, but when listening to a speech in an audience, the same people will wear (most of the time) a blank mask. The way to deal with those stony faces is to remind yourself that your listeners want you to succeed; they hope that you will give them a worthwhile message. If you are lucky, you will notice two or three listeners who are obviously loving your speech; they are nodding in agreement or giving you looks of appreciation. Let your eyes go to them frequently, for they will give you courage and confidence.

If you are an inexperienced speaker, you may get upset if you see members of an audience whispering to one another. You may wonder, "Are these people making negative comments about me?" If the listeners are smiling, it's even worse: You ask yourself, "Did I say something foolish? Is there something wrong with my clothes?" If this happens to you, keep in mind that your rude listeners are probably talking about something other than the quality of your speech or your personal appearance. Most likely, they are just sharing some personal gossip. If by chance they *are* whispering about something you've said, it's not necessarily negative. They may be whispering that they agree with you 100 percent.

What if a listener stands up and walks out of the room? For some inexperienced speakers, this is a stunning personal setback, a cause for alarm. Before you jump to conclusions, bear in mind that the listener's behavior is not necessarily a response to your speech. He or she may have another meeting to attend or must visit the restroom or perhaps has suddenly become ill. But what if the listener is indeed storming out of the room in a huff, obviously rejecting your speech? In such a case, advises veteran speaker Earl Nightingale, "Don't worry about it. On controversial subjects, you're bound to have listeners who are not in agreement with you—unless you're giving them pure, unadulterated pap. Trying to win over every member of the audience is an impossible and thankless task. Remember, there were those who disagreed with wise, kind Socrates."[19]

▶ Accept Imperfection

If you give many speeches in your life, you are bound to make a few mistakes along the way. Don't worry; it happens to everyone. A few years ago a State Department official said during a speech, "We are dedicated to the prevention of peace." When he heard murmurs and chuckles in the audience, he realized his mistake and corrected himself: "We are dedicated to the *preservation* of peace."

If you completely flub a sentence or mangle an idea, you might say something like, "No, wait. That's not the way I wanted to explain this. Let me try again." If you momentarily forget what you were planning to say, don't let it defeat you. Pause a few moments to regain your composure and find your place in your notes. If you can't find your place in your notes, ask the audience for help: "I've lost my train of thought—where was I?" There is no need to apologize. In conversation, you pause and correct yourself all the time; to do so in a speech makes you sound spontaneous and natural.

If you make a mistake that causes your audience to snicker or laugh, try to join in. If you can laugh at yourself, your audience will love you—they will see that you are no "stuffed shirt." Some comedians deliberately plan "mistakes" as a technique for gaining rapport with their audience.

Additional Hints

Here are some extra tips that might be useful.

Use visual aids. Using a visual aid such as slides or overhead transparencies can help you in two ways: (1) you shift the audience's stares from you to your illustrations, and (2) you walk about and move your hands and arms, thereby siphoning off some of your excess nervous energy. Whatever illustrations you decide to use, make sure they are understandable, appropriate, and clearly visible to everyone in the room.

Check arrangements in advance. Long before you give your speech, inspect the place where you will speak and anticipate any problems: Is there an extension cord for the slide projector? Do the windows have curtains so that the room can be darkened for your slide presentation? Is there a chalkboard? Some talks have been ruined and some speakers turned into nervous wrecks because at the last moment they discover that the entire building lacks an extension cord.

Arrive early on the day of your speech and reinspect every aspect of the arrangements. Has the extension cord been laid out for you? Is there chalk in the chalkboard tray? Is there an eraser for the chalkboard? If you are using equipment for visual aids, set it up to make sure it is working. If there is a public address system, test your voice on it before the audience arrives so that you can feel at ease with it.

Devote extra practice time to your introduction. Since it is at the beginning of your speech that you are apt to suffer the greatest amount of distress, you should spend a lot of time practicing your introduction.

Most speakers, actors, and musicians report that if they can survive the first minute or two, their nervousness moves to the background and the rest of the event is relatively easy. Ernestine Schumann-Heink, the German opera singer, once said, "I grow so nervous before a performance, I become sick. I want to go home. But after I have been on the stage for a few minutes, I am so happy that nobody can drag me off." Perhaps happiness is too strong a word for what you will feel, but if you are a typical speaker, you will find the rest of your speech smooth sailing once you have weathered the first few minutes of turbulent waters.

Veteran speakers recommend checking a speech site in advance. Where will they stand? How large will their visual aids need to be? Will they need a microphone? If possible, they practice their speech in the room several times. On the day of the speech, they arrive early to get acclimated to the room and greet listeners as they enter.

Get acclimated to your audience and setting. It can be frightening to arrive at the meeting place at the last moment and confront a sea of strange faces waiting to hear you talk. It is a good idea to arrive early so you can get acclimated to the setting and, if possible, chat with people as they come into the room. In this way, you will see them not as a hostile pack of strangers, but as ordinary people who wish you well.

Dr. Henry Heimlich, a popular lecturer and creator of the famed Heimlich maneuver for rescuing people who are choking, says, "I am always a little nervous wondering how a particular audience will accept me and my thoughts. It is good to meet some of the audience socially before lecturing to them, in order to relate to their cultural and intellectual backgrounds. You are then their 'friend.' "[20]

Danielle Kennedy of San Clemente, California, says that when she began speaking ten years ago, she was so nervous she would hide out in a bathroom until it was time for her to speak. Now, she says, she mingles with the listeners as they arrive and engages them in conversation. "This reminds me that they are just nice people like anyone else who wants to be informed. I also give myself pleasant thoughts. Things like: 'Can you imagine these people drove 100 miles just to hear me. I am so lucky. These people are wonderful.' I get real warm thoughts going by the time I get up there."[21]

Use physical actions to release tension. We have seen that adrenalin is beneficial, providing athletes and public speakers with wonderful bursts of energy, but it also has a bad side. When your body goes on red alert, you get pumped up and ready for action, but you also get trembling hands and jittery knees. If you are an athlete, this is no problem because you will soon be engaged in vigorous physical activity that will drain off excess nervous energy. As a public speaker, you lack such easy outlets; nevertheless, there are several tension releasers you can use. Try one or more of these techniques *before* you stand up to speak:

▶ Take a few deep breaths. Inhale slowly and exhale slowly.

▶ Do exercises that can be performed quietly without calling attention to yourself. Here are some examples: (1) Tighten and then relax your leg muscles. (2) Push your arm or hand muscles against a hard object (such as a desk top or chair) for a few moments, then release the pressure. (3) Squeeze your hands together in the same way: tension, release . . . tension, release . . .

▶ Mingle with your listeners (as discussed above) for the side benefit of releasing tension. Bert Decker of San Francisco greets his listeners and shakes hands with them as they enter the room. "The physical movement and use of vocal cords right before the presentation," says Decker, "will keep the tension from your chest and your larynx."[22]

For siphoning off excess energy *during* the speech, you can use visual aids (as mentioned above) and these two tension releasers:

▶ *Let your hands make gestures.* You will not have any trouble making gestures if you simply allow your hands to be free. Don't clutch note cards or thrust your hands into your pockets or grip the lectern. If you let your hands hang by your side or rest on the lectern, you will find that they will make gestures naturally. You will not have to think about it.

▶ *Walk about.* Though you obviously should not pace back and forth like a caged animal, you can walk a few steps at a time. For example, you can walk a few steps to the left of the lectern to make a point, move back to the lectern to look at your cards for your next point, and then walk to the right of the lectern as you speak.

In addition to reducing tension, gestures and movement make you a more exciting and interesting speaker than someone who stands frozen in one spot.

Act poised. To develop confidence when you face an audience, act as if you already are confident. Why? Because playing the role of the self-assured speaker can often transform you into a speaker who is genuinely confident and poised. In various wars, soldiers have reported that they were terrified before going into combat, but nevertheless they acted brave in front of their buddies. During the battle, to their surprise, what started off as a pretense became a reality. Instead of pretending to be courageous, they actually became so. The same thing often happens to public speakers.

Pause a few moments before starting your speech. All good speakers pause a few moments before they begin their talk. This silence is effective because (1) it is dramatic, building up the audience's interest and curiosity, (2) it makes you look poised and in control, (3) it calms you, and (4) it gives you a chance to spread out your note cards and get your first two or three sentences firmly in mind.

Many tense, inexperienced speakers rush up to the lectern and begin their speech at once, thus getting off to a frenzied, flustered start. In the back of their mind they have the notion that silence is a terrible thing, a shameful void that must be filled up immediately. To the contrary, silence is a good breathing space or punctuation device between what went before and what comes next. It helps the audience tune in to the speaker and tune out extraneous thoughts.

Look directly at the audience as much as possible. If you are frightened of your audience, it is tempting to stare at your notes or the back wall or the window, but this will only add to your nervousness rather than reduce it.

Force yourself to establish eye contact, especially at the beginning of your speech. Good eye contact means more than just a quick, furtive glance at various faces in front of you; it means "locking" your eyes with a listener's for a couple of seconds. Locking may sound frightening, but it actually helps to calm you. In an article about a public speaking course that she took, writer Maggie Paley said, "When you make contact with one other set of eyes, it's a connection; you can relax and concentrate. The first time I did it, I calmed down 90 percent, and spoke . . . fluently."[23]

Don't speak too fast. Because of nervous tension and/or a desire to "get it over with," many speakers race through their speech. "Take it slow and easy," advises Dr. Michael T. Motley of the University of California, Davis. "People in an audience have a tremendous job of information-processing to do. They need your help. Slow down, pause, and guide the audience through your talk by delineating major and minor points carefully. Remember that your objective is to help the audience understand what you are saying, not to present your information in record time."[24]

To help yourself slow down, rehearse your speech in front of friends or relatives and ask them to raise their hands whenever you talk too rapidly. For the actual delivery of the speech, write yourself reminders in large letters on your notes (such as "SLOW DOWN"). While you are speaking, look at your listeners and talk directly to them in the same calm, deliberate manner you would use if you were explaining an idea to a friend.

Get audience action early in the speech.   I said earlier that it's a bit unnerving to see your listeners' expressionless faces. In some speeches, you can change those faces from blank to animated by asking a question. (Tips on how to ask questions will be discussed in Chapter 10.) When the listeners respond with answers or a show of hands, they show themselves to be friendly and cooperative, and this obviously reduces your apprehension. When they loosen up, you loosen up.

Welcome experience.   If you are an inexperienced speaker, please know that you will learn to control your nervousness as you get more and more practice in public speaking, both in your speech class and in your career. You should welcome this experience as a way of furthering your personal and professional growth.

One student told her public speaking instructor at the beginning of the course that she just *knew* she would drop out of the class right before her first speech. She stayed, though, and developed into a fine speaker. She later got a promotion in her company partly because of her speaking ability. "I never thought I'd say this," she admitted, "but the experience of giving speeches—plus learning how to handle nervousness—helped me enormously. Before I took the course, I used to panic whenever I started off a talk. I had this enormous lump in my throat, and I thought I was doing terrible. I would hurry through my talk just to get it over with." But as a result of the course, she said, "I learned to control my nervousness and use it to my advantage. Now I'm as nervous as ever when I give a speech, but I make the nervousness work *for* me instead of *against* me."

In your career, rather than shy away from speaking opportunities, seek them out. As the old saying goes, experience is the best teacher.

Summary

The nervousness engendered by stage fright is a normal, understandable emotion experienced by most public speakers. Instead of trying to eliminate nervousness, welcome it as a source of energy. Properly channeled, it can help you give a better speech than if you were completely relaxed.

The best way to avoid excessive, crippling nervousness is to pour time and energy into preparing and practicing your speech. Then, when you stand up to speak, deal rationally with your nervous symptoms (such as trembling knees and dry throat); remind yourself that the symptoms are not a prelude to disaster, but instead are evidence that you are keyed up enough to give a good speech. Never call attention to your nervousness and never apologize for it; the listeners don't care about your emotional state—they just want to hear your message. Concentrate on getting your ideas across to the audience

TIP 3.2: Use Self-Deprecating Humor

Benjamin Franklin was a speaker who was willing to poke fun at himself in a speech. For example, he liked to relate this incident:

> While in Paris, Franklin attended a public gathering that featured many speeches. He had trouble understanding French when it was declaimed, but wishing to appear polite, he decided that he would applaud whenever he noticed a distinguished woman, Mme. de Boufflers, express satisfaction. After the meeting, his grandson said to him, "But Grandpapa, you always applauded, and louder than anybody else, when they were praising you."

Many good speakers tell humorous anecdotes at their own expense because it's an effective way to build rapport with the audience—to create a bond of warmth, trust, and acceptance. Benjamin Franklin's listeners must have been delighted to learn that the Great Man was capable of committing a faux pas, just like everyone else, and they loved him all the more.

Self-deprecating humor has another virtue: it reduces your tension. You become lighter and more at ease. You banish the burden of having to be the *perfect* speaker giving the *perfect* speech. You can relax and be yourself: a human being with foibles and quirks just like the rest of us.

Poke fun at any aspect of yourself except your nervousness (remember what we discussed in this chapter about never calling attention to your jitters), and tie your humor to the speech or the occasion. In a speech on how to discipline children without crossing over into child abuse, Diana Perkins Hirsch, a family counselor, wanted to show her audience that she wasn't a judgmental person who considered herself morally superior to her audience. Such an image would have caused many listeners to be defensive and unreceptive to her ideas. Early in her talk, she said, in a self-teasing tone,

> I am the perfect person to talk to you about raising kids because I am the perfect mother. To show you just how perfect I am, let me tell you what happened a few years ago. One weekend we had three sets of relatives visiting us in our home. All together we had seven adults and eleven kids under the same roof. On Sunday morning, it was a madhouse as we all rushed around trying to get ready for church. Somehow we managed to get everyone bathed and dressed. We jumped into the cars and rushed off, and we walked into church a split second before the service began. During the opening hymn, my sister and I smiled at each other in triumph—we had pulled it off: we had managed to get this crazy tribe to church on time. But as I looked down the pew, I suddenly realized that two of the kids were missing! My sister and I hastily left the church and drove back home, and there they were—happily watching TV in a back room. In all the hustle and bustle, we had forgotten them.

Take your speech seriously, take your audience seriously, but don't take yourself too seriously. And if you can find a way to share self-deprecating humor with your listeners, you will help create an atmosphere of warmth and friendliness.

this will get your mind where it belongs—on your listeners and not on yourself—and it will help you move your nervousness to a back burner, where it can still simmer and energize you without hindering your effectiveness.

Review Questions

1. Why are fear and nervousness beneficial to the public speaker?
2. Why does extensive preparation help a speaker to keep nervousness within bounds?
3. Why is delivering a speech from memory a bad method?
4. Why should you never call attention to your nervousness?
5. Does an audience detect most of a speaker's nervous symptoms? Explain your answer.
6. How can you reduce excessive tension before and during a speech?

4

Reaching the Audience: Analysis and Adaptation

▶ **The Audience-Centered Speaker**

▶ **Analyzing and Adapting**

▶ **Attitudes**

▶ **Interest Level**

▶ **Knowledge**

▶ **Demographic Variables**

What Are the Listeners' Ages? / Are Both Sexes Represented? / What Is the Educational Background? / What Are the Occupations? / What Is the Racial and Ethnic Composition? / What Are the Religious Affiliations? / What Is the Economic and Social Status? /

▶ **The Occasion**

What Is Your Time Limit? / What Is the Purpose of the Occasion? / What Other Events Will Be on the Program? / How Many People Will Be Present? /

▶ **Getting Information about the Audience**

▶ **Adapting during the Speech**

When an advertising agency produces a 30-second commercial for TV, what do you think takes the longest time? Writing the script? Rehearsing the roles? Filming the scenes?

The answer is: none of the above. What takes the longest amount of time is *audience analysis.* "Before we sit down to write a commercial," says award-winning advertising executive Helayne Spivak of New York City, "we go through stacks of research to learn who our [target] audience is. How old are they? Where do they live? What are their buying habits? . . . We interview consumers to understand what they like and dislike, not only about the product we're selling but about all other competitive products. It's a painstaking process, but when it's over we know who we're talking to and exactly what to say to them."[1]

A successful speech is just like a successful commercial: it is based on a solid and shrewd understanding of who the listeners are.

The Audience-Centered Speaker

Which of the following kinds of speakers have you ever encountered?

Robots are lifeless speakers who have no energy and no desire to reach the audience. They prepare dull, uninteresting speeches, which they deliver without a trace of enthusiasm. They often read in a monotone from a manuscript and scarcely glance at their listeners, who are half asleep with boredom.

Fountains of Knowledge, who are enthusiastic and knowledgeable about their subject, expect the audience to absorb their ideas as easily as a sponge soaking up water. So they pour out a huge amount of information quickly. They seem unaware that listeners need help in processing information—a patient, unhurried delivery with plenty of explanations and examples.

Boors are thoughtless speakers who wrongly assume that listeners share their prejudices or their notions of what is funny. A few years ago a network anchor (for *CBS Morning News*) gave a talk to the San Francisco Press Club on AIDS (acquired immune deficiency syndrome). He made a crude joke about AIDS that angered and upset some listeners, especially those who had witnessed and written about the agonies of persons dying from the disease. In another speech, a male speaker began his answer to a female questioner with "Well, honey . . . ." This condescending response caused some members of the audience to turn against him.[2]

Performers at first seem to be perfect speakers; they have good eye contact, a strong voice, and confident posture. But they talk *at* their listeners, rather than *with* them. They perform rather than communicate, and they are oblivious to the listeners' needs and interests. I once knew a man who jumped at every chance to give a speech because he loved the sound of his own voice. It was indeed a deep, rich voice, and this man sounded brilliant with his grandiloquent phrases and poetic images. He always gave the same speech; I heard it several times, but I could never find any substance. It was all cream puff and no meat. He was just a glib show-off, with nothing to say.

What all four kinds of speakers have in common is a low sensitivity to their audience—a failure to understand and reach the people sitting in front of them.

When you stand up in front of an audience, is your goal merely to deliver a good speech and then sit down? If your focus is upon yourself or upon your speech, you will never be an effective speaker. Your goal should be to reach your listeners and change them, so that they walk away with new information or new opinions or a warm feeling in their hearts.

All good speakers are *audience-centered.* They truly want to make contact with their listeners—to inform, persuade, entertain, or inspire them. Carol Conrad, a student in one of my classes, typified this kind of speaker. In evaluating one of her speeches, another student said, "I had the feeling she was talking to me personally." How did Conrad achieve this success? She composed her speeches carefully, selecting examples, statistics, quotations, and visual aids that would capture the interest of her audience. And when she delivered a speech, she displayed a strong desire to communicate with her audience—she would look her listeners in the eye and speak directly to them. Her tone of voice and facial expression carried a clear message to the listeners: "I care about you and I want you to understand and accept my message."

Analyzing and Adapting

To be an audience-centered speaker, you need to carry out two important tasks: (1) *Analyze* the listeners to find out exactly who they are and what they know. (2) *Adapt* your speech to their particular needs and interests. Analyzing and adapting should be done at every step of your preparation—when you choose your topic, when you gather your material, and so on.

When I was a freshman in college, I signed up for Introduction to Astronomy. At the beginning of the course I was very excited because I wanted to learn some basic facts about the universe, and this particular class was to be taught by a visiting professor, a highly regarded astronomer from a leading observatory. My enthusiasm soon dissipated, however, when I sat through the first lecture. The professor was brilliant—no doubt about that—but he spent the first hour of class discussing complex ideas that only a graduate student in astronomy could have understood. We freshmen were hopelessly lost. Though his ideas were brilliant, the professor had failed in the most important task of any speaker: to communicate ideas in a way that can be understood by the listeners. He had concentrated on himself and his ideas rather than on his audience. He had wasted his time—and ours.

Now let's look at another astronomer, Dr. Carl Sagan, professor of astronomy and space sciences at Cornell University and host of the television series *Cosmos*, which has been viewed by 140 million people throughout the world. In one of the programs, Sagan is shown visiting an elementary school where he explains a few facts of astronomy to a class of sixth-graders. He speaks in language the children can understand. He draws, for example, an analogy that is beautifully clear but not insultingly simplistic: "A handful of sand contains about 10,000 grains, more than the number of stars we can see with the naked eye on a clear night. But the number of stars we can *see* is only the tiniest fraction of the number of stars that *are* . . . . The total number of stars in the universe is greater than all the grains of sand on all the beaches of the planet Earth."[3]

Notice the big difference in how these two astronomers handled analysis and adaptation. The first failed to analyze the audience to find out who we were, and he failed to adapt his ideas to our level of understanding. Dr. Sagan, on the other hand, shrewdly sized up his audience. He knew that to show sixth-graders the richness of the universe he would have to devise an analogy based on their own experience: every child has a good knowledge of a handful of sand, the size of a grain, and the vastness of beaches. Notice how he avoided the extremes of overestimating and underestimating his audience. In other words, he did not talk over their heads, nor did he talk down to them as if they were kindergartners. He pitched his remarks to their level.

Adapting does not mean being insincere or compromising one's principles. Suppose that because you are strongly opposed to the use of all illegal drugs, you have been invited to talk on drug abuse to a class of eighth-graders. Should you use the current slang of eighth-graders to show that you are one of the gang? No, that is not what is meant by adapting. That would be phony, and the students would resent your chummy approach. Should you water down your beliefs, dropping your opposition to marijuana in order to win audience support for your stand against cocaine? No, that is not what is meant by adapting, either. Such a tactic would be foolish; you would lose respect for yourself, and weaken your credibility with the audience (if you are perceived as inconsistent). How, then, can you adapt your ideas to the eighth-graders without being a phony? In the first place, use terms and concepts that all eighth-graders can understand; for example, say "pep pills" instead of "amphetamines." Second, relate your ideas to their lives and interests: "I know that sometimes you feel down in the dumps. Maybe you're making bad grades in one of your classes, or you're afraid that a certain person no longer likes you, or you're having constant hassles with your parents. In times like these, it's easy to be tempted by little pills that someone tells you will make you feel good."

Let us now look at the ways in which you can analyze your listeners and then adapt your speeches to their special needs.

Attitudes

Attitudes are the emotional baggage—the favorable or unfavorable predispositions—that the listeners bring to your speech. Are your listeners negative, neutral, or positive toward your ideas?

If they are negative toward your ideas, you should design your speech with their opposing arguments in mind. Suppose, for example, that you want certain industries to stop spewing toxic wastes into the atmosphere. You advocate the passage of laws that would force the plants to clean up their emissions. As you prepare your speech, you anticipate that your listeners will say, "But won't the cost of cleaning up the emissions be so great that the plants will go out of business, throwing thousands of people out of work?" To counter this argument, you find information showing that similar plants in other states were forced to stop polluting, without causing economic harm to the companies.

Don't become disheartened if you fail to win the support of an audience that is negative toward your ideas. Sometimes your ideas may be so far removed from what the audience believes that you have no realistic chance of persuading everyone. In such cases, the best you can hope for is to soften their opposition. Let's imagine that you give a speech in favor of raising the speed limit on interstate highways to 75 miles per hour. Everyone in the audience disagrees with you, but by the end of the speech many of the listeners admit that your argument has merit—it's not as crazy as they first thought. In this instance, a "limited" victory might be the best you can realistically hope to achieve.

If your listeners are apathetic or neutral, try to involve them in the issue and then win them to your side. For example, during times of peace, when there is no military draft, most listeners are neutral and apathetic about whether the country should bring back conscription. To win an audience to one side or the other, a speaker would have to paint a picture of imminent war and say something like, "Six months from now, all of you—male and female alike—could be standing in the ranks of the United States Army." Such a picture, if believed by the audience, could move them from neutrality and apathy toward the position you espouse. What you are trying to do, of course, is show that the issue is not a faraway abstraction but a real possibility that could affect their own lives.

If your audience is favorably disposed toward your ideas, your task is to reinforce their positive views and perhaps even motivate them to take action. For example, you give a pep talk to members of a political party in your community, urging them to campaign on behalf of the party's candidate in an upcoming election.

FOR YOUR CAREER

TIP 4.1: Try to Meet Audience Expectations

A well-known science writer was once invited to speak at a large university. Most of the 2000 people in the audience expected him to speak on a scientific topic; when he talked instead on a controversial political issue, many listeners were outraged. There were mutterings of discontent throughout the speech, and some people even walked out in anger.

For career and community speeches, find out in advance what expectations your listeners have. Are they expecting to be instructed, inspired, or amused? If you fail to act as expected, you may disappoint or anger them. For an after-dinner speech, for example, your audience would expect you to give a light, diverting talk. If instead you deliver a tedious, highly technical speech, they might groan inwardly and tune you out.

Interest Level

As you choose and develop a topic, you need to ask yourself how much interest your listeners will have in your material. Consider the following example:

> A student whom I'll call Calvin had an unusual hobby: collecting and firing muzzle-loading rifles, the kind used in George Washington's day. He gave a speech on how to clean such rifles. It was terribly boring; no one in the audience cared about technical things like patches and cleaning oil and ramrods. During the question-and-answer period, however, there was lively interest in the rifles: Why would anyone in the modern world want to fire antique rifles? Are they dangerous? Are they accurate? How quickly can you reload? It was clear that if Calvin had spoken on the rifles themselves, he would have had an interesting topic. He should have saved his "how to clean" speech for his fellow gun-club members, who would have loved all the technical lore.

Now contrast Calvin's failure with a successful speech:

> Ray Dillingham, a student speaker, knew how to train horses, and he planned to give a speech on how to train the Tennessee Walking Horse for competition. As he analyzed his audience, however, he realized that such a specialized talk would be uninteresting to anyone but a horse trainer, so he switched his focus to horses in general. He spoke on the different breeds of horses, showing color

slides to demonstrate their variety and beauty. The speech was well received by the listeners, who found it very interesting.

These two examples show that whenever you prepare a speech, you should ask yourself what aspect of your topic would be most interesting to your particular audience. In some cases, if your audience is not very interested in a topic before you speak, you can *generate* interest. Here is how one speaker generated interest by using a provocative introduction:

Melinda Sanchez, a sales representative for a company that manufactures home bread-baking machines, demonstrated one of the machines to a group of young professionals. From her audience analysis, she knew that most of the listeners were uninterested in her product because they assumed that her bread tasted no better than store-bought bread. So she began her talk by opening the machine and saying, "This machine has just finished baking a loaf of bread. All I did was dump in the ingredients four hours ago." Then she removed the loaf, sliced it, and passed pieces around for the listeners to sample. Soon there were murmurs of delight as listeners discovered that her bread tasted much more delicious than any bread available in a store. The audience listened to the rest of her talk with keen interest.

A good way to gain interest is to figure out which aspect of your topic would be most relevant to the personal lives of the listeners. Think back to your own experiences as a member of an audience. If you are like most people, you wanted to know "What's in it for me?" In other words, did the speaker have anything to say that you considered useful in your own life? People like to hear speeches that will help them reach their personal goals. They want to be healthy, feel secure, have friends, make money, solve problems, enjoy life, and learn interesting things. If you can talk about such things in an appealing way, people will listen to you with great interest. Here is an example of how one speaker related her topic to her audience.

Brenda Gudger wanted to convince her audience to use bargaining techniques in buying a used car. Since she knew that many of her listeners might find the subject boring and unrelated to their own lives, she began by saying: "A lot of people don't like to haggle over buying a car. They'd rather pay the sticker price than bargain with the salesperson. Well, a couple of months ago, I haggled over a used car, and I was able to get $500 knocked off the price of the car. Today I'd like to tell you how you can save yourself a lot of money by bargaining with salespeople."

By appealing to everyone's desire to save money, Gudger increased her audience's interest in her speech.

Knowledge

As you analyze your listeners, find out what they already know about the topic. Do they know a lot? A moderate amount? Nothing at all? Here are some tips on handling the different kinds of audiences.

Audiences that know a lot about the topic. Your audience will be bored and resentful if you give information that everyone already knows. Suppose that you have been asked to talk on computers. Is your audience a group of business executives who already own personal computers? If so, you don't need to define such basic terms as *default* and *booting up*. What you should do is give them new ideas and concepts.

Audiences that know little or nothing about the topic. Here are some hints on how to handle the audience that does not know much about your topic:

▶ Carefully limit the number of new ideas you discuss. People cannot absorb large amounts of new information in a short period of time. If you overwhelm them with too many concepts, they will lose interest and tune you out.

▶ Whenever possible, use visual aids to help listeners grasp the more complicated concepts.

▶ Use down-to-earth language; avoid technical jargon. If you feel that you must use a specialized word, be sure to explain it.

▶ Repeat key ideas, using different language each time.

▶ Give vivid examples.

Mixed audiences. What should you do if some listeners know a lot about your subject and others know nothing? Whenever possible, the solution is to start off at a simple level and add complexity as you go along. Suppose you are speaking on computers; you ascertain that some listeners know very little and some know a great deal. You can say something like this: "I hope the computer buffs here will bear with me, but I know that some people in the audience will be confused unless I spend a few moments explaining what a disk drive is." The computer buffs will not be upset, because you have acknowledged their presence and their expertise, and they will not mind a little review session (they might even pick up something new). The computer novices, meanwhile, will be grateful for your sensitivity to their inexperience.

Demographic Variables

Making a demographic analysis of your audience will give you many clues to the items we have just discussed—attitudes, interest, and knowledge. Let us take a look at the basic questions you should ask.

▶ What Are the Listeners' Ages?

If you have a variety of ages represented in your audience, be sensitive to the interests, attitudes, and knowledge of all your listeners, giving explanations or background whenever necessary. If, for example, you are talking about a musician who is popular only with young people, you may need to give some information about her music and lifestyle for the benefit of older members of the audience.

Here is an example of insensitivity to the ages of listeners:

> At the graduation exercises of a state university, the commencement speaker told the graduates, "Your parents are proud of you . . . . You are now gaining full citizenship . . . . You will soon enter the work force . . . . You will settle down and raise a family . . . ." The speaker was treating all the graduates as if they were in their early twenties—a big mistake because one-fourth of the graduates in front of him were over 30 and had been in the work force for years. Many of them had already raised a family. One middle-aged graduate said later, "I lost all respect for the speaker. Couldn't he just look at us and see that we were mature adults?"

This story illustrates that you need to find out the ages of your listeners ahead of time, and then adapt your remarks accordingly. Now let's turn to an example of effective adaptation:

> William Edwards, a minister, was well known in his community for conducting a special service on Sunday mornings for families with small children. His sermon was usually in the form of a parable—a simple story with an easily grasped moral, such as the story of the Good Samaritan. He would tell the story in a dramatic fashion so that the children were captivated by the narrative; in the meantime he would subtly point out the deeper allegorical meanings to the adult listeners. Thus, Edwards succeeded in adapting his sermon to the wide age span of the audience; he reached the 4-year-old and the 44-year-old, without talking down to anyone, without boring anyone. People of all ages went away satisfied.

▶ Are Both Sexes Represented?

The sex of your audience will give you some clues about their background knowledge. If, for example, you are talking on sex discrimination to an all-female audience, you might need to provide little or no explanation of what you mean by sex discrimination. They already know—some from firsthand experience—what you are talking about. If there are males in the audience, however, you might need to elaborate by giving anecdotes about the subtle ways in which women are sometimes treated unfairly.

Both male and female listeners become irritated when a speaker seems to exclude them because of their gender. Some male nurses, for example, say they are peeved when a supervisor uses the pronoun *she* in talking about the typical nurse; they feel as if they are being viewed as unwanted intruders in the nursing profession. And female executives have good reason to be annoyed at situations like the one described by Janet Elliott of Los Angeles: "A speaker at a seminar for men and women insurance agents turned off a portion of his audience when he began by saying, 'As you look at your face in the mirror each morning when you shave . . .' He did not choose his words carefully to avoid offending by exclusion all those in his audience who have never shaved their faces."[4]

▶ What Is the Educational Background?

Always consider the educational background of your listeners. Avoid talking over their heads, using concepts or language that they cannot understand. Likewise, avoid the other extreme: Don't talk down to your listeners. Find the happy medium. Albert Einstein, considered by many to be the most brilliant scientist of the twentieth century, could present his incredibly complex theories to his scientific peers in language that was appropriately sophisticated for their level of understanding, yet he could also adjust his speech for the benefit of the 99.9 percent of us who cannot begin to comprehend his theories. For example, he once made part of his theory of relativity understandable to the average person by using this analogy: "Time is relative. If you sit on a park bench with your girl friend for an hour, it seems like a minute. But if you sit on a hot stove for a minute, it seems like an hour." Thus did Einstein humorously and simply illustrate part of his theory—that time seems to slow down in relation to other events.[5]

Define terms whenever you think that someone in the audience does not know what you are talking about. Fred Ebel, past president of a Toastmasters club in Orlando, Florida, says that to one audience, "I told a joke which referred to an insect called a praying mantis. I thought everyone knew what a praying mantis was. But I was greeted by silence that would have made the dropping of a pin sound like a thunderclap. Several listeners came up to me and asked, 'What is a praying mantis?' It came as a shock to me until I realized that not everyone had taken a course in biology."[6]

▶ What Are the Occupations?

Adapt your speeches to the occupational backgrounds of your listeners. The best examples of this kind of adaptation can be found near election time when politicians size up the needs and interests of each audience they face. With steelworkers, for example, the typical politician may discuss competition from Japanese industries; with farmers, soil erosion; with truck drivers, highway speed limits; and with bankers, credit regulations. None of this is necessarily manipulative or unethical; it is simply good audience analysis and adaptation. Steelworkers don't want to hear about soil erosion, and farmers don't want to hear about Japanese steel imports.

▶ What Is the Racial and Ethnic Composition?

Find out the racial and ethnic composition of your audience so that you can adapt your remarks to their needs and interests. For example, in many college classrooms (and in other audiences as well), you will find a sprinkling of foreigners. As much as possible, include them in your adaptation. One student speaker, Mark Hopkins, was planning a speech on the kind of automobiles called hot rods. While conducting informal interviews with members of his speech class, he discovered that some of the foreign students did not know what a hot rod was. So he prepared a drawing of a hot rod on a large piece of poster board, and then displayed it at the beginning of his speech.

Most important of all, avoid material that might offend any racial or ethnic group. In this connection, a note of warning: some people think that if there are no members of a particular race or ethnic group present, it is all right to make insulting jokes. It is *never* all right. Such slurs are offensive and unfunny to many men and women who don't belong to the group being ridiculed, and they will automatically lose respect for the speaker.

Many audiences, such as these people attending a ceremony to become U.S. citizens, represent a wide range of ethnic and racial backgrounds. A good speaker will try to meet the needs and interests of all listeners.

▶ **What Are the Religious Affiliations?**

Knowing the religious affiliations of your audience will give you some good clues about their beliefs and attitudes. Most Seventh-Day Adventists, for example, are very knowledgeable about nutrition because of the strong emphasis the denomination places on health; many Adventists are vegetarians and nondrinkers. If you were asked to speak to an Adventist group on a health-related issue, you could assume that the audience had a higher level of background knowledge on the subject than the average audience has; you would therefore avoid going over basic information they already know.

While religious background can give you clues about your audience, you have to be cautious. You cannot assume that all members of a religious group subscribe to the official doctrines. A denomination's hierarchy, for example, may call for a stop to the production of nuclear weapons, while the majority of the members of that denomination may not agree with their leaders' views.

▶ **What Is the Economic and Social Status?**

Be sensitive to the economic and social status of your listeners so that you can adapt your speech accordingly. Suppose you are going to speak in favor of food stamps for the poor. If your listeners have low incomes, most of them will probably be favorably disposed to your ideas before you even begin. You might therefore want to aim your speech at encouraging them to support political candidates who will protect the food-stamp program. If your listeners are upper-middle-class, however, many of them will be opposed to your ideas and you will have to aim your speech at winning them over to your way of thinking.

The Occasion

Find out as much as you can about the occasion and the setting of your speech, especially when you are giving a speech in your community or at a career-related meeting. Here are some questions to ask; pay special attention to the first one.

▶ **What Is Your Time Limit?**

I have seen many public occasions marred by long-winded speakers who droned on and on, oblivious to the lateness of the hour and the restlessness of the audience. Always find out how much time has been allotted for your speech, and *never* exceed the limit. This rule applies when you are the sole speaker and most especially when you are one of several speakers. If four speakers on a program are supposed to speak for only 10 minutes apiece,

When a program features many presenters, it is important for a speaker to find out the exact nature of the occasion. How many people will be speaking? On what topics? For how long? If speakers exceed their time limits, they risk making the event so over-long and depriving other speakers of their full allotment of time.

imagine what happens when each speaks for 30 minutes. The audience becomes fatigued and inattentive.

Though many audiences will suffer through an interminable speech without being rude to the speaker, some will not. One speaker found this out the hard way when he gave a speech to a civic-club luncheon. At the hour when the meeting was supposed to be over, even though the speaker was still holding forth, the club members got up and walked out. It was explained later that all the members had to return to their jobs by a certain time.

Some speakers have absolutely no concept of time. For a 5-minute speech, some of my students talk for 20 minutes and then swear later that they could not possibly have talked for more than five—something must have been wrong with my stopwatch. As we will see later, practicing your speech at home (and clocking yourself) will help you keep within time limits.

People who give long-winded speeches might desist from this terrible vice if they knew what misery they cause their audiences. The poor listeners are forced to undergo an agony of boredom, as they squirm and fidget, stifle their yawns, and yearn for release from this windbag who is torturing them for what seems like an eternity. If you tend to be a garrulous speaker, follow the wise speechmaking formula of President Franklin D. Roosevelt:

▶ Be sincere.
▶ Be brief.
▶ Be seated.

FOR YOUR CAREER

TIP 4.2: Be Prepared to Trim Your Remarks

One of the most exasperating situations you as a speaker can face is this: Because of circumstances beyond your control, your speech comes at the end of a long, tedious meeting when listeners are weary and yearning to leave. Often the best response is to trim your speech. As the following incident shows, the audience will be grateful.

An all-day professional conference was supposed to end at 3:30 P.M. so that participants would have plenty of daylight time for driving back to their hometowns. Unfortunately, most of the speakers on the program exceeded their time limit, and the final speaker found himself starting at 3:18. Without commenting on the rudeness of the other speakers, he

started out by saying, "How many of you would like to leave at 3:30?" Every hand went up. "I will end at 3:30," he promised. Though it meant omitting most of his prepared remarks, he kept his promise. One of the participants said later, "We appreciated his sensitivity to us and his awareness of the time. And he showed class in not lambasting the earlier speakers who stole most of his time. He showed no anger or resentment."

Here's a technique to consider: When I am invited to speak at meetings where there are several speakers, I prepare two versions of my speech—a full-length one to use if the other speakers respect their time limits and a shorter version if events dictate that I trim my remarks.

▶ What Is the Purpose of the Occasion?

A leading television commentator, widely known for his probing questions during live TV interviews, was paid $25,000 to lead a panel discussion at a national computer show in Atlanta. His task, according to *PC Week* magazine, was to extract "pithy and provocative insights" from major computer industry leaders. He failed to carry out this assignment, however, because he "evidently misunderstood the show's business orientation." Instead of asking probing questions about how business can use computers, he "repeatedly hammered on the subject of home computing, to the apparent confusion and irritation of the panelists."[7]

Avoid this commentator's mistake by finding out in advance the purpose of the meeting. Suppose that you are an authority on the life and music of the late singer John Lennon, a member of the Beatles, who was murdered by a deranged fan, and you are asked to give a talk at a club meeting. To prepare your speech, it would be crucial for you to know the purpose of the occasion. Is the club meeting devoted to remembering Lennon's tragic death? If so, you would obviously want to prepare a somber eulogy to Lennon. Or is the meeting devoted to a celebration of the Beatles' music? In this case, you might want to give an upbeat talk on Lennon's personality, interlaced with tape-recorded selections of his music.

▶ What Other Events Will Be on the Program?

Find out all that you can about other events on a program. Are there other speakers on the agenda? If so, what will they speak on? It would be disconcerting to prepare a speech on the life of Martin Luther King and then discover during the ceremony that the speaker ahead of you is talking on the same subject.

Even more disconcerting is to come to a meeting and find out that you are debating someone on your topic. Obviously you need to know such information in advance, so that you can anticipate what the other speaker will argue and prepare your rebuttal accordingly.

▶ How Many People Will Be Present?

It can be unsettling to walk into a room, expecting an audience of 20 but instead finding 200. Knowing the size of your audience ahead of time will not only help you prepare yourself psychologically, but it will also help you plan your presentation. Will you need extra-large visual aids? Will you need a microphone?

Where your listeners sit in relationship to others can be important. If you have fifteen people scattered about in a large hall, it will be easier to make contact with them if you first have them move to seats at the front and center. Nightclub comedians are very sensitive to seating arrangements; they make sure tables are pushed close together because they know that patrons are more likely to laugh if they are jammed together in warm coziness. Some comedians would never dare tell jokes to an audience widely scattered in a large room; people feel isolated, and they are afraid that if they laugh, they will be conspicuous. (Have you ever noticed that funny movies are funnier if you see them in a packed theater than if you see them in a half-empty one?)

Getting Information about the Audience

Where can you get information about your audience? For classroom speeches, there are several ways to gain information. If your class has speeches in which students introduce themselves, you can make notes regarding their backgrounds, interests, and other features. Also, you can interview your fellow students directly.

For speeches in the community, your best source is usually the program director (or whoever invited you to speak).

If time permits, you may want to use a questionnaire to poll your future listeners on their knowledge, interests, and attitudes. If, for example, you were planning to argue against corporal punishment in schools, you could devise a statement like this—"Schools should not be permitted to spank children"—and ask your listeners to circle one of these responses: "Strongly agree," "Mildly agree," "No opinion," "Mildly disagree," "Strongly disagree." If most of your future listeners strongly disagree, you obviously should devote much of your speech to trying to change their minds. Another example: if you were planning to speak on computer viruses, you could devise a simple true-false quiz to determine how much accurate information the listeners already have.

Adapting during the Speech

Adapting to your audience—a vital factor in your preparation stages—must also take place during the actual delivery of the speech. You must be sensitive to their moods and reactions, and then make the necessary adjustments, if possible. Here is an example:

> Using a portable chef's stove, Lester Petchenik, a student speaker, was demonstrating how to cook green beans *amandine*. At one point he sprinkled a large amount of salt into his pan—an action that caused several members of the audience to glance at one another with looks of surprise. Noticing this reaction, Petchenik ad-libbed, "I know it looks like I put too much salt in, but remember that I've got three pounds of green beans in this pan. In just a moment, when you taste it, you'll see that it's not too salty." (He was right.)

Try to overcome any barriers to communication. John Naber of Pasadena, California, a former Olympic gold medalist in swimming, says that he once gave a speech in a room with poor acoustics. Realizing the audience would have trouble understanding him if he stayed at the lectern, he said, "I moved into the middle of the group and walked among them as I spoke."[8]

Be especially sensitive to the mood of the listeners. Are they bored, drowsy, or restless? Sometimes they are listless not because your speech is boring but because of circumstances beyond your control. It is eight o'clock in the morning, for example, and you have to explain a technical process to a group of conventioneers who have stayed up partying half the night.

If you ever need to "wake up" a listless audience, here are some techniques you can use: (1) Invite audience participation (by asking for examples of what you are talking about or by asking for a show of hands of those who agree with you). (2) Rev up your delivery (by moving about, by speaking slightly louder at certain points, or by speaking occasionally in a more dramatic tone). (3) Use visual aids.

Sometimes it is easy to read audience behavior. If some members of the audience are frowning when you mention a technical term, you know that you need to add a definition. In other cases, however, it is hard to interpret your listeners' faces. That man in the third row with a sour face—is he displeased with your speech? Before you jump to conclusions, pay heed to the astute observation of the well-known inspirational lecturer, Earl Nightingale:

> I've seen people in my audiences many times who appeared to be outright hostile to what I was saying, who seemed to be trying to tell me by their expressions that I was a blithering idiot, yet I have learned over the years that it's often these same people who come up to the head table afterwards with the most profuse compliments and expressions of gratitude. They just happen to look like that. They wear customary frowns and their mouths turn down at the corners as though they had just bitten into a dill pickle. That's the way they look.[9]

What if the frowns do mean disapproval? Should you alter your speech to make everyone in the audience happy? No, of course not. While trying to be sensitive to the mood of the audience, you should never compromise your principles or violate your personal integrity simply to win approval. Your goal in public speaking is not to have the audience like you, but to communicate your ideas to them as clearly and as effectively as possible.

Summary

To be an effective speaker, you must concentrate your attention and energies on your audience, and have a strong desire to communicate your message to them. You must analyze the listeners beforehand and adapt your materials and presentation to their needs and interests.

Analyze the listeners' attitudes, their level of interest in your subject matter, and their degree of knowledge about your material. Consider a variety of demographic factors: age, sex, educational levels, occupations, racial and ethnic composition, religious affiliations, and economic and social status. Also analyze the occasion to gather details about the time limit, the purpose of the meeting, other events on the program, and the number of people who will attend.

Be prepared to adapt to the needs of the listeners during the speech itself. Be sensitive to the cues that indicate boredom, restlessness, or lack of understanding.

TIP 4.3: Develop a Positive Attitude toward Each Audience

Have you ever seen this old comedy routine on TV? A nervous young man is waiting for a blind date to appear at a prearranged spot. As he waits, he fantasizes how she will react to him. The TV camera captures the fantasies: When she approaches him, she looks at him with disappointment bordering on disgust. When he introduces himself, she laughs at his name and says it is stupid. When he suggests that they go to a particular restaurant for dinner, she ridicules his idea of good food. When he tries to make small talk, she laughs at his accent. The fantasy goes on and on, from one humiliation to another. Finally, the fantasies fade away as the real, live date appears on the scene. By now, however, the young man is so outraged that he screams at the date, "Well, I didn't want to go out with you, either!" and storms away, as the startled date stands alone, blinking her eyes in confusion.

In like fashion, some speakers indulge in fantasies of audience rejection and when they actually stand up to speak, they act defensive, as if they *know* that everyone in the audience is going to reject them and their ideas. Their "body language"—tone of voice, facial expression, posture—is defensive, sometimes even angry and sullen. I saw one such speaker argue in favor of the sport of hunting animals. He knew that some members of the audience were opposed to hunting. From start to finish, he acted as if the audience had just insulted him. "We are not sadistic people who enjoy watching animals suffer," he said angrily. Who said he was sadistic? Who said he enjoyed watching animals suffer? Like

the young man waiting for his blind date, this speaker had worked himself into an unnecessary rage.

Don't prejudge your audience. Most listeners are kind and sympathetic to speakers. Even if they reject your ideas, they usually respect you, as long as you respect them.

Instead of nurturing gloomy fantasies, try to develop a positive attitude toward every audience. Professional speaker James "Doc" Blakely of Wharton, Texas, has an effective, audience-centered technique that he uses before each speech:

I learn everything I can about the organization I'm going to address as far in advance of the speaking date as possible. Then at least four hours prior to the actual speaking engagement, I review all the facts I know about the group, go over the points I want to make with them, and then concentrate on pouring positive thoughts into my mind about the group. I visualize them as accepting me as a friend, of being wildly enthusiastic about what I have to say to them, and I block out every negative emotion in my mind.

It helps to think of the audience not as an impersonal mass, but as a collection of individuals who are basically no different from you and your friends. "When I speak," says Rosita Perez of Brandon, Florida, "I communicate to the audience in the most personal way I am able to. In an auditorium of 3000, I speak as if to one."

Review Questions

1. What is an *audience-centered* speaker?
2. What is meant by audience analysis and adaptation?
3. What guidelines should be followed for a speech to an audience that knows little or nothing about your topic?
4. What demographic factors should you consider in analyzing an audience?
5. What aspects of the speech occasion should you examine before giving your talk?

Selecting Topic, Purpose, and Central Idea

▶ **Selecting a Topic**

Select a Topic You Care About / Select a Topic You Know a Lot about (or Can Learn About) / Choose a Topic That Will Interest the Audience / Narrow the Topic /

▶ **The General Purpose**

Informative Speech / Persuasive Speech /

▶ **The Specific Purpose**

Begin the Statement with an Infinitive / Include a Reference to Your Audience / Limit the Statement to One Major Idea / Make Your Statement as Precise as Possible / Make Sure You Can Achieve Your Objective in the Time Allotted / Don't Be Too Technical /

▶ **The Central Idea**

Devising the Central Idea / Guidelines for the Central Idea / Samples /

The best way to write a love letter, the Swiss-French philosopher Jean Jacques Rousseau once said, is to begin without knowing what you are going to say. Such a formula might be effective for the ecstatic outpouring of a love letter, but if applied to speechmaking, it is a recipe for failure. Yet I know some foolhardy individuals who insist that they have no more than a vague idea of what they are going to say to an audience until they stand up and "go with the mood of the moment" (as one of them expressed it). A couple of these people, I have to admit, are effective speakers, but most of them range from mediocre to devastatingly boring. Because their own minds are unfocused, their speeches are fuzzy. They ramble, fail to clarify ideas, and get bogged down in irrelevant matters.

The best speeches I have heard were given by men and women who sounded as if they were speaking spontaneously but who had in fact spent hours and days in careful preparation. In this chapter we will examine some of the most important steps in preparing a speech—selecting a topic, a general purpose, a specific purpose, and a central idea.

Selecting a Topic

For many of the speeches that you will give during your lifetime, your topic will be chosen by someone else. Your boss, for example, tells you to give a talk to your fellow employees on a new product. Or you are asked to speak to the Rotary Club on safe-driving skills because you are known in the community as an expert on the subject.

In most public speaking classes, on the other hand, students are permitted to choose their own topic, a freedom that causes some students a lot of grief. They spend days walking around with a dark cloud over their heads, moaning to friends, "I have to give a speech next week and I can't think of a *thing* to speak on." Don't let yourself get stuck at this stage. Choose your topic as far ahead of your speech date as possible because you will need to spend a great deal of time and energy on other important tasks, such as researching, outlining, and practicing. If you spend days and days stewing over which topic to select, you may find yourself without enough time to adequately prepare the speech.

As you read this chapter, keep a note pad handy and jot down ideas for topics as they come to you so that you will have a stockpile to draw from throughout the course. In the weeks ahead you can add to your list as you get more ideas.

Here are some important points to bear in mind as you look for a topic.

Select a Topic You Care About

Have you ever had something happen to you that was so exciting you could hardly wait to tell your friends? That's the way you should feel about your speech topic. It should be something you care about, something you are eager to communicate to others. Are you angry over air pollution in your town? Speak on air pollution. Are you excited about the wizardry of your personal computer? Speak on computers. Are you having so much fun baking pastries that you try a new recipe every week? Speak on how to bake pastries.

Enthusiasm is contagious; if you are excited, some of your excitement will infect your listeners. If, on the other hand, you are unexcited about your topic, you are apt to do a lackluster job in preparing the speech, and when you deliver it, you will probably come across as dull and unconvincing.

Here are two examples that illustrate how enthusiasm, or the lack of it, can make the difference between a good speech and a poor one:

A student whom I'll call Bob had trouble coming up with a topic for his speech class. At the last moment he grabbed a magazine article and used it as the basis for a talk on gun control. His speech was poorly constructed and tedious.

When choosing topics, speakers should talk about things that they find interesting and exciting. If they don't know much about the subject now, they can learn about it through observation and research.

Worst of all, he seemed to have no real enthusiasm for his subject. Normally, when a student talks on gun control, there is a lively response from the audience during the question-and-answer period, but Bob's listeners seemed as listless as he was; they had no questions or comments for him.

Theresa Schmidt gave a talk on doll collecting and brought along some of the dolls from her own collection. I was afraid that her talk would be boring to an audience of grown-ups, but she started off by telling why she, as an adult, still collected dolls. Then she related fascinating stories about how she got some of them from foreign countries and told of particular dolls' names and personalities. Her speech was a success, not just because of her well-told stories and colorful visual aids, but because she herself displayed a consuming, passionate interest in her subject. While she was speaking, I glanced around at the students in the class; their animated faces showed that they were fascinated.

Now look at these two speakers. Gun control is one of the most highly emotional subjects in our society today, as likely as any topic you can name to capture an audience's interest. But Bob succeeded in making it dull because he had a ho-hum-I-don't-really-care attitude. Theresa Schmidt, on the other hand, took a subject unlikely (at first glance) to appeal to adults and made it into a wonderful speech, mainly because she was imbued with a contagious enthusiasm. She *cared* about her subject.

Select a Topic You Know a Lot about (or Can Learn About)

Make things easy for yourself. Speak on something you are already thoroughly familiar with—or can learn about through research. If your listeners realize they know more about the subject than you do, they lose confidence in you. This can be especially painful if your speech is followed by a question-and-answer period. When I was in college, I was asked to give an oral report on a particular issue in a sociology class; I had no interest in the subject and did little research. After I gave my report, a student in the class (who knew a great deal about the subject) ridiculed my omissions and errors. I felt like an absolute fool. But I learned an important lesson: a person should *never* give a speech unless he or she knows the subject matter extremely well.

Here are several ways to probe for topics that you know a lot about (or can learn about).

▶ Personal Experiences

If you are permitted to choose your own topic, start your search with the subject on which you are the world's foremost expert—your own life.

"But my life isn't very interesting or exciting," you might say. You are wrong. Maybe you are not an international celebrity, but there are dozens of aspects of your life that could make colorful speeches. Let me give you some examples, all involving students:

Mitzi Stevens worked as a server in a restaurant. She gave a talk on the way customers treat servers, with some interesting insights. She reported, for example, that the most generous tippers are parents of small children, who apparently feel guilty for the fuss and mess their kids create.

Anthony Morgano worked as a stonemason for over a decade until a back injury forced him to abandon manual labor and go to college to seek an engineering degree. Drawing from personal experience, interviews with physicians, and magazine articles, Morgano told his listeners how they could avoid back injury by lifting properly and by doing special strengthening exercises.

Susan Peterson went to her first rock concert and discovered that the rock fans were as interesting as the band. She gave a speech about the different types of fans she observed, using vivid descriptions that amused her audience.

These students were *ordinary* people who chose to speak on *ordinary* aspects of their lives, but their speeches turned out the way all good speeches should turn out—interesting. When you are trying to come up with a topic, start with yourself and look for the interesting things in your own life. Figure 5.1 is an inventory that you can fill in to help you identify topics.

After you have filled in the inventory, go back and analyze the list for possible speech topics. If you are not sure which items would make good speeches, ask your friends for advice or consult your instructor. Figure 5.2 is an example of how one student, Karin Johansson, filled in the inventory. In Johansson's inventory, which items could make a good speech? All of them are potentially good speech topics. Which would be the best? That would depend on Johansson's current state of enthusiasm; her rafting trip on the Colorado River through the Grand Canyon sounds exciting, for example, but if it turned out to be a disappointing trip and Johansson is tired of telling about it, this would obviously be a poor topic for her.

▶ Exploring Interests

What if the personal inventory fails to yield a topic that you are happy with? Or what if you simply dislike talking about yourself? Don't despair! There are plenty of topics outside your personal life that can captivate your audience. Choose one that you have always wanted to know more about—something that intrigues you. The following case illustrates what I am talking about:

A few months before she enrolled in a public speaking class, Julia Lavage to saw a television documentary on UFOs (unidentified flying objects). This whetted her curiosity, and she yearned to read some books and articles on UFOs, but unfortunately she was too busy with her schoolwork. In her public speaking

FIGURE 5.1
This personal in-ventory can help you pinpoint speech topics from your own life

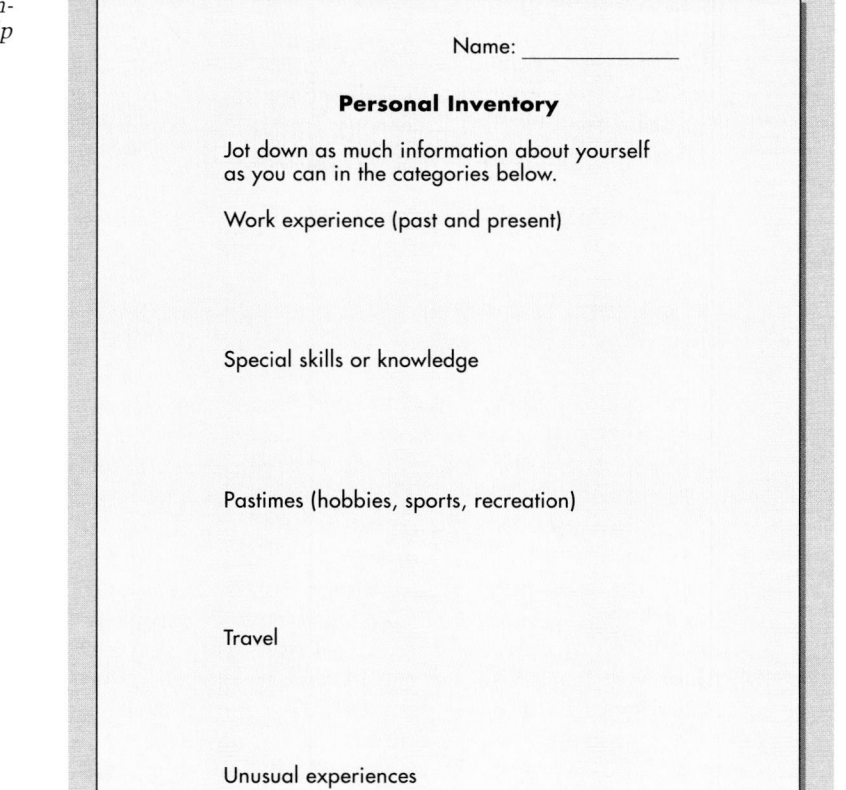

Name: _____

Personal Inventory

Jot down as much information about yourself as you can in the categories below.

Work experience (past and present)

Special skills or knowledge

Pastimes (hobbies, sports, recreation)

Travel

Unusual experiences

School interests (academic and extracurricular)

Concerns or beliefs (politics, society, family, etc.)

FIGURE 5.2
Personal inventory, as filled in by one student.

Name: *Karen Johansson*

Personal Inventory

Jot down as much information about yourself as you can in the categories below.

Work experience (past and present)

Emergency medical technician (paramedic)
Ambulance driver
Volunteer firefighter
Waitress

Special skills or knowledge

Cardiopulmonary resuscitation
Rescue from burning buildings
First aid

Pastimes (hobbies, sports, recreation)

Water skiing
Swimming
Cooking Chinese food
Restoring antiques

Travel

Quebec
Mexico
Colorado River (rafting)

Unusual experiences

Rescuing two children from a burning building
Rafting through the Grand Canyon

School interests (academic and extracurricular)

Nursing courses
Biology
Drama Club

Concerns or beliefs (politics, society, family, etc.)

We need to stop child abuse
Learning CPR should be a prerequisite for
getting a driver's license
Curtail sale of handguns (but not rifles)

course, Lavagetto realized that she now had the opportunity to meet her speech assignment and satisfy her intellectual craving at the same time. She read books and magazine articles on UFOs and gave an interesting speech.

Some students use their speech assignment as a vehicle for gaining vital information for their own lives. Here is an example:

Lloyd Feinberg still mourned the suicide of a close friend in high school. He deeply regretted that he had been unable to dissuade his friend from taking an overdose of pills. For his classroom speech, he decided to do research on suicide. He read books and magazine articles, and interviewed a suicide-prevention counselor. He ended up giving his talk on "How to counsel a person who threatens to commit suicide," a topic he chose because he wanted to know how to handle such a situation if it ever happened again. During his research he found tips and insights that were valuable not only for his audience, but for himself as well.

In the two cases just cited, the main point of this section—select a topic you know a lot about—still applies. If you don't know a great deal about the subject now, you can do some research and make yourself knowledgeable. Perhaps you will not qualify as an expert, but you will at least know more about the subject than most of your listeners.

▶ **Brainstorming**

If the suggestions already discussed don't yield a topic, try brainstorming (so called because it is supposed to create intellectual thunder and lightning). In brainstorming, you write down whatever pops into your mind. For example, if you start off with the word *school*, the next word that floats into your mind might be *algebra* and then the next word might be *equations*, and so on. Don't censor any words. Don't apply any critical evaluation. Simply write whatever comes into your mind. Nothing is too silly or bizarre to put down.

Using a sheet of paper (with categories like those in Figure 5.3), jot down words as they come to your mind. When you finish brainstorming, analyze your list for possible topics. Don't discard any possibility until you have chosen a topic.

Here is an example of how brainstorming might work: Under "Things," let's say you write *cars*. Then you think of the following: car payments . . . trips . . . highways . . . accidents . . . drunk drivers. . . . When you analyze the list, perhaps the word *trips* leads you to choose a trip to Mexico as your topic. Or the term *drunk drivers* causes you to realize that you feel strongly about the need for stronger laws against driving while intoxicated, so you choose drunk driving as your topic.

Figure 5.4 is a sample of one student's brainstorming notes. Under most categories the student's brainstorming was fairly straightforward. It is easy

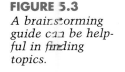

FIGURE 5.3
A brainstorming guide can be helpful in finding topics.

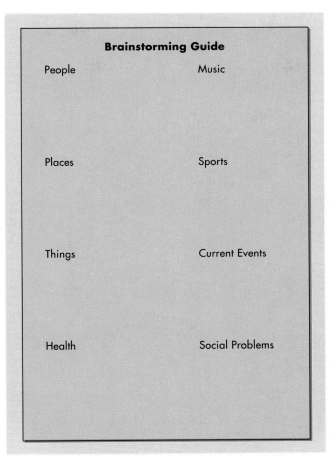

to see his train of thought. But under "Social Problems," he made some interesting jumps (which is okay; writing down whatever comes to mind is the way the "game" is played). He started with child abuse, a major problem in society. This led him to jot down "school dropouts," perhaps because abused children often do poorly in school and drop out early. This idea led to "violent crimes," which in turn caused "prison" to leap into his mind. The next two items—"overcrowding" (of prisons) and "parole" are social problems that stem from crime. Any of the thoughts in this list could be developed into a strong speech. The phrase "violent crimes," for example, could suggest many timely topics: gang warfare, assault weapons, handguns, armed robbery, and so on.

You may be wondering why you should put all this down on paper. Why not just let all your ideas float around in your mind? The advantage of writing

FIGURE 5.4
One student's entries on a brainstorming guide.

Brainstorming Guide

People
> David Letterman
> Jay Leno
> Bill Cosby
> Eddie Murphy
> stand-up comedians

Music
> heavy metal
> rap
> lyrics
> censorship
> music videos

Places
> Quebec
> Montreal
> Gaspé Peninsula
> Nova Scotia
> Newfoundland

Sports
> football
> Chicago Bears
> Super Bowl
> World Cup
> soccer
> indoor soccer

Things
> my car
> stereo
> speakers
> CDs
> tape
> digital tape

Current Events
> environment
> acid rain
> ozone layer
> global warmup
> greenhouse effect

Health
> headaches
> stress
> acupuncture
> herbal remedies
> Native American medicine

Social Problems
> child abuse
> school dropouts
> violent crimes
> prison
> overcrowding
> parole

thoughts down is that you end up with a document that can be analyzed. It helps you focus your thinking.

▶ Library Search

If the techniques discussed above fail to yield a topic, there is another method you can use. Go to the library and look through magazines or an encyclopedia or the *Reader's Guide to Periodical Literature* until you find something that appeals to you and should also appeal to your audience. Here is an example:

> Roosevelt Evans went to the library and picked up the most recent copies of several popular magazines. As he leafed through the magazines, he spotted an article on the foods one should eat in order to avoid cancer. This subject was so interesting to him that he read other articles on the same topic and decided to give his speech on it.

Choose a Topic That Will Interest the Audience

Choose a topic that listeners will consider timely, worthwhile, and interesting. Don't bore them with stale, commonplace, or trivial subjects. Instead of a dull speech on why people need to take vacations, give them a lively, fascinating talk on unusual getaway trips to exotic places.

In an informative speech, don't report facts that all the listeners already know. In a persuasive speech, don't try to convince people of what they already believe. Or, as the old saying goes, "Don't preach to the converted." Arguing in favor of a college education to a college class or to a roomful of successful lawyers is wasted effort. Everyone in the audience already agrees—or they wouldn't be where they are today.

Some students are unsure of their ability to determine whether a topic is worthwhile. "I'm excited about a topic," they say, "but how do I know whether it will be interesting to the audience?" Here are some ways to assess the interest level of a topic:

- ▶ Analyze the audience as thoroughly as you can, as suggested in Chapter 4. This should enable you to make good educated guesses about the topics that would be ideal for your audience.
- ▶ Consult your instructor for his or her suggestions.
- ▶ Ask your friends how much interest they would have in the subject if they were part of the audience.
- ▶ Several weeks beforehand, distribute a questionnaire to members of the audience to find out how interested they would be in several potential speech topics. Use a rating scale for each topic, such as "very interesting," "moderately interesting," and "not very interesting."

Narrow the Topic

Once you find a topic, you need to narrow it. Suppose that you want to give a speech on crime in America: 5 minutes—or 20—is not enough time to adequately cover such a broad topic. How about limiting yourself to just crimes of violence? Again, 5 minutes would be too short to do justice to the topic. How about one type of violent crime—rape? This subject perhaps could be handled in a 5-minute speech, but it would be advisable to narrow the topic down even more—to one aspect of the subject: "how to fight off a rapist" or "why some men rape."

Narrowing a topic helps you control your material. It prevents you from wandering around in a huge territory: You are able to focus on one small piece of ground. Instead of talking on the vast subject of Native Americans before Columbus, you can limit yourself to describing life in one of the oldest settlements in North America—Acoma, a town atop a mesa in New Mexico that has been inhabited by Pueblos since about 1100 A.D.

Ask yourself this question: Is my topic one that can be adequately and comfortably discussed in 5 minutes (or whatever your time limit is)? If the answer is no, narrow the scope, alter the focus.

Here are some examples of topics that can be narrowed:

Too broad: Environmental pollution
  Better: How and where to recycle paper, metal, and plastics in our community

Too broad: Nutrition
  Better: Finding healthy alternatives to salt

Too broad: Gambling
  Better: Arguments for (or against) legalizing gambling casinos

An important way to narrow your topic is to formulate a specific purpose, which will be discussed later in this chapter. First, let's take a look at your general purpose.

The General Purpose

Establishing a general purpose will help you bring your topic under control. Most speeches have one of the following purposes:

▶ To inform
▶ To persuade

There are other purposes—to entertain, to inspire, to stimulate, to introduce, to create goodwill, and so on—but to inform and to persuade are the most common. Let's take a closer look at them.

Informative Speech

In an informative speech, you are concerned about giving new information to your listeners, not with winning them to your way of thinking. The informative speech can take a variety of forms, such as defining a concept (feminism, for example), explaining a situation (why TV soap operas are so popular), demonstrating a process (the correct way to cross-country ski), or describing a person, place, object, or event (a volcanic eruption).

Your main concern in this kind of speech is to have your audience understand and remember new information. You are in effect a teacher—not a preacher, nor a salesperson, nor a debater. Here is a sampling of informative topics:

- ▶ Possible cures for AIDS (acquired immune deficiency syndrome)
- ▶ The major achievements of Martin Luther King
- ▶ How to make a home or apartment burglar-proof
- ▶ Taking a vacation on a cruise ship
- ▶ The upsurge of neo-Nazi violence in Germany

Persuasive Speech

Your aim in a persuasive speech is to convince the listeners to come over to your side, to adopt your point of view. You want to *change* them in one or both of these ways:

1. Change their minds.   You try, for example, to persuade them that Lee Harvey Oswald acted alone in the assassination of President John F. Kennedy.

2. Change their behavior.   You try to bring about a transformation in either a positive or negative direction; that is, you get your listeners to *start* doing something they normally don't do (such as using seat belts) or get them to *stop* doing something they normally do (such as sprinkling salt on their food).

Here are some examples of persuasion topics:

- ▶ Dumping of garbage and toxic chemicals into the world's oceans should be stopped.
- ▶ A parent who reneges on child-support payments should be forced to pay or be sent to prison.
- ▶ Consuming huge quantities of vitamins to prevent disease or slow down the aging process is a dangerous practice.
- ▶ Colleges should abolish letter grades and specify only "pass" or "fail."
- ▶ Couples should not go into debt on anything except a home.

The Specific Purpose

After you have chosen a topic and determined your general purpose, your next step is to formulate a *specific* purpose, stating exactly what you want to accomplish in your speech. Here is an example:

> *Topic:* Life on other planets
> *General Purpose:* To inform
> *Specific Purpose:* To inform my listeners of the three main reasons why some astronomers believe that life exists on other planets

The specific purpose serves two important functions: (1) It helps you narrow your topic to something that can be covered comfortably and effectively in the time allotted, and (2) it forces you to put your ideas into sharp focus.

If you chose a topic such as television and then did nothing to bring it into sharp focus, you might make the mistake of talking about a lot of different aspects of television. To target one specific idea concerning TV, you would need a statement such as this:

> *Topic:* Television
> *General Purpose:* To inform
> *Specific Purpose:* To explain to my audience how local TV weather reporters formulate their forecasts

Now you have a sharp focus for your speech. You have limited yourself to something that can be covered adequately in a short speech.

Here are some guidelines for writing a specific-purpose statement.

▶ Begin the Statement with an Infinitive

An infinitive is a verb preceded by *to*—for example, *to write, to read*. By beginning your purpose statement with an infinitive, you clearly state your intent.

> *Poor:* Pyramids in Egypt
> *Better:* To explain to my audience how the pyramids in Egypt were constructed

For informative speeches, your purpose statement can start with such infinitives as "to explain," "to show," "to demonstrate." For persuasive speeches, your purpose statement can start with infinitives such as "to convince," "to prove," and "to get the audience to believe."

▶ Include a Reference to Your Audience

Your specific purpose should refer to your audience by means of such phrases as "to my listeners" or "to the audience." This may seem like a minor matter, but it is important for you to keep your listeners in mind at every stage of your speech preparation. Writing them into your specific purpose helps remind you that your goal is not to stand up and talk, but rather to communicate your ideas to real flesh-and-blood human beings.

Poor: To explain how fast-food restaurants use colors and music to stimulate sales

Better: To explain to my listeners how fast-food restaurants use colors and music to stimulate sales

▶ Limit the Statement to One Major Idea

Avoid the temptation to try to cover several big ideas in a single speech. Limit yourself to only one.

Poor: To convince the audience that scenes of explicit sex and violence in prime-time television shows should be censored and that local TV stations should be encouraged to expand their local news coverage

Better: To convince the audience that scenes of explicit sex and violence in prime-time television shows should be censored

In the first example, the speaker tries to cover two major ideas in one speech. While it is true that censorship and local news both pertain to television, they are not closely related and should be handled in separate speeches.

▶ Make Your Statement as Precise as Possible

Strive to have a statement that is clear and precise.

Poor: To help my audience brighten their relationships

Better: To explain to my listeners three techniques people can use to communicate more effectively with loved ones

The first statement is fuzzy and unfocused. What is meant by "to help"? What is meant by "brighten"? And what kind of relationships are to be discussed—marital, social, business? The second statement is one possible improvement.

▶ Make Sure You Can Achieve Your Objective in the Time Allotted

Don't try to cover too much in one speech. It is better to choose a small area of knowledge that can be developed adequately than to select a huge area that can be covered only sketchily.

Poor: To tell my audience about endangered species

Better: To convince my audience that international action should be taken to halt poachers from slaughtering elephants

The first statement is much too broad for a speech; you would need several hours to cover the subject. The second statement narrows the topic so that it can be covered easily in a short speech.

▶ **Don't Be Too Technical**

You have probably sat through a speech or lecture that was too technical or complicated for you to understand. Don't repeat this mistake when you stand at the lectern.

> *Poor:* To explain to my listeners the different types of golf clubs and their uses
>
> *Better:* To tell my audience why golf is an enjoyable sport for millions of Americans

The first statement is too technical for the average classroom audience. Some listeners will probably never play golf. The second statement focuses on an aspect of golf that should appeal to *all* listeners.

The Central Idea

As the guest speaker in a college sociology class, a counselor at an alcohol rehabilitation center spoke on alcoholism, giving many statistics, anecdotes, and research findings.

Afterward, I overheard some of the listeners heatedly arguing about the speech. Several contended that the speaker's message was "Drink moderately—don't abuse," while others thought the speaker was saying, "Abstain completely." Still others said they were confused—they didn't know what the speaker was driving at.

If this happens to you—if you give a speech and people later wonder or debate exactly what point you were trying to make—you have failed to accomplish your most important task: to communicate your *central idea.*

The central idea is the basic message of your speech expressed in one sentence. It is the same thing as the *thesis sentence* or *controlling statement,* terms you may have encountered in English composition courses. If you were forced to boil your entire speech down to one sentence, what would you say? *That* is your central idea. If, one month after you have given your speecher, the audience remembers only one thing, what should it be? *That* is your central idea.

As we will see in later chapters, the central idea is a vital ingredient in your outline for a speech. In fact, it *controls* your entire speech—that is, everything you say in your speech should develop, explain, illustrate, or prove the central idea. Everything? Yes, everything—all your facts, anecdotes, statistics, and quotations.

If you are unclear in your own mind about your central idea, you will be like the counselor who caused such confusion: Listeners will leave your speech wondering, "What in the world was that speaker driving at?" CBS news correspondent Charles Osgood, who gives many speeches throughout America, says that if you lack a central idea, your speech will be unfocused and scattered "all over the place." Worst of all, "your audience will sit there with your message going in one ear and out the other."[1]

▶ **Devising the Central Idea**

Let's imagine that you decide to give a speech on why governments on earth should spend money to send powerful radio signals into outer space. The specific-purpose statement of your speech might look like this:

Specific Purpose: To persuade my listeners to support government funding of radio transmissions into outer space

How are you going to persuade your audience? Can you simply say, "Folks, please support radio transmissions into outer space?" No, listeners might say to themselves, "Big deal, I don't want my tax dollars being spent on some harebrained scheme to beam radio signals into the night sky." To convince them, you need to sell the audience on an idea that, if believed, might cause them to support your position:

Central Idea: Most scientists agree that radio transmissions are the best means for making contact with extraterrestrial civilizations (if any exist).

If you can sell this idea, you will probably succeed in your specific purpose—to persuade the listeners to support funding of radio transmissions. They will be persuaded because the central idea is so appealing. Most people like the notion of communication with aliens from faraway planets, and if most scientists back the idea, it cannot be considered far-out and impractical. Yes, the listeners will say, let's spend some of our tax dollars to explore the heavens.

After you decide upon a central idea, your task in preparing the rest of the speech is to find materials—such as examples, statistics, and quotations—to explain and prove the central idea. In this case, you would need to explain the technology and cite the testimony of eminent scientists who support radio transmissions into space.

Some students have trouble distinguishing between the specific purpose and the central idea. Is there any significant difference? The answer is yes. The specific purpose is written partially from your point of view—it is what *you* set out to accomplish. The central idea is written entirely from the listeners' point of view—it is the message *they* go away with.

In planning your speech, the specific purpose statement should be written first—before you start gathering material. In many cases, you will be able to write the central idea immediately afterward, but not always. In some cases you may need to postpone formulating the central idea until you have completed your research. Imagine that you are preparing a speech on the use of steroids by athletes and bodybuilders. From watching news on television, you know that coaches and health experts are warning people not to use steroids, and you feel certain that your investigation will confirm this view. So you start off with a specific-purpose statement like this:

> *Specific Purpose:* To inform my audience of the health risks of using steroids for developing muscles

You haven't done any research yet, so you can't really write a central idea. But after you spend a few days in the library studying articles on steroids, you are now able to put your central idea at the top of your outline:

> *Central Idea:* Persons who chronically use steroids run the risk of suffering kidney and liver damage and of developing serious mental disorders.

Now that you have a clear statement of the key idea of your speech, your task will be to show the audience that what you say about steroids is true by citing statistics, case studies, and the testimony of experts.

▶ **Guidelines for the Central Idea**

1. Every speech should have only one central idea. Why not two? Or three? Because you are doing well if you can fully illuminate one big idea in a speech. If you try to handle more than one, you run the risk of overwhelming the listeners with more information than they can comfortably absorb.

2. Put the central idea on paper. It is important that you actually write down your central idea—at the top of your outline—rather than have some vague notion floating around in your mind. Writing it down gives you a clear sense of direction.

3. Let the central idea determine the content of the entire speech. As you prepare your outline, evaluate every potential item in light of the central idea. Does fact A help explain the central idea? If yes, keep it. If no, throw it out. Does statistic B help prove the central idea? If yes, keep it. If no, throw it out.

Let's assume that you want to give a talk on the following:

> *Topic:* The metric system
> *General Purpose:* To persuade

Next you write down what you want to accomplish with your audience:

> *Specific Purpose:* To convince my audience that the metric system should be adopted by the United States

To carry out your specific purpose, you need to plant an idea in the minds of your listeners—one key idea:

Central Idea: Using the metric system gives a nation economic benefits in world trade.

Now you have your speech in a nutshell. As you decide what to put in the speech, let the central idea control the process. Let's say, for example, that you find an interesting story about how our present system of measurements got started—a *foot* was originally the length of an average person's foot, and so on. Fascinating information, but does it relate directly to your central idea about the value of the metric system? No, so discard it. Next you come across an estimate by the Secretary of Commerce that U.S. firms lose $4 billion a year in export trade because their nonmetric products are excluded from some international trade markets. This, of course, is a powerful argument for your central idea, so use it.

▶ Samples

Here are some additional examples. Study them carefully, noting the difference between the specific purpose and the central idea in each case.

> *Topic:* Homeless children
> *General Purpose:* To persuade
> *Specific Purpose:* To persuade my listeners to support increased funding for services to homeless children.
> *Central Idea:* A top national priority should be to provide homeless children with safe shelter, well-balanced meals, medical care, and good schooling.

> *Topic:* Genetic testing
> *General Purpose:* To inform
> *Specific Purpose:* To explain to my audience how genetic testing predicts illnesses
> *Central Idea:* Genetic testing has enabled many people to take action against a genetic disorder before it becomes disabling or life-threatening

> *Topic:* Testing of teachers
> *General Purpose:* To persuade
> *Specific Purpose:* To persuade my audience to support mandatory testing of all teachers in grades K through 12
> *Central Idea:* All teachers in grades K through 12 should be required to pass a competency test in basic reading, writing, and math skills before being allowed to teach in public schools.

Formulating your general purpose, specific purpose, and central idea may seem to take a lot of time and energy, but in reality, it can be a shortcut. Because these steps channel your thinking, they prevent you from scattering your efforts across too wide a field. They end up saving you time. More importantly, they help you give a better speech than you might otherwise give.

Summary

In choosing a topic for your speech, think of subjects that (1) you care a great deal about, (2) you know a lot about (either now or after you complete your research), and (3) your audience will find interesting.

After you choose a topic, decide upon your general purpose in speaking (such as to inform or to persuade) and then formulate your specific purpose— exactly what you hope to accomplish in the speech. Next, write out your central idea: the one big idea that you want your audience to remember if they forget everything else in the speech.

Though they may seem time-consuming, these preliminary steps will actually save time in the long run and they will help you organize your ideas in a coherent, understandable form.

Review Questions

1. When a speaker is enthusiastic about his or her ideas, how do listeners usually react?
2. How does one go about brainstorming ideas?
3. List three *general* purposes for speeches.
4. List the six criteria discussed in this chapter for writing a specific-purpose statement.
5. What is the central idea of a speech?
6. What is the difference between the specific purpose and the central idea?

FOR YOUR CAREER

TIP 5.1: Examine Hidden Purposes

In an essay in *Harper's* magazine, Professor Jane Tompkins confesses that earlier in her career, while teaching at Columbia University, she was more concerned about making a good impression than meeting students' needs. "I was . . . focused on: a) showing the students how smart I was; b) showing them how knowledgeable I was; and c) showing them how well prepared I was for class. I had been putting on a performance whose true goal was not to help the students learn but to act in such a way that they would have a good opinion of me."

If other speakers were as candid as Professor Tompkins, they would admit that they, too, often have hidden, unstated objectives that are far afield from listener-oriented purposes like "to inform" or "to persuade." If their purposes were written out they might look like this:

▶ To dazzle my boss with my presentation skills.

▶ To demonstrate that I am smarter and more eloquent than my colleagues.

▶ To prove that I can outshine the other speakers on the program.

▶ To get the listeners to like me and consider me a wise and humorous person.

Hidden objectives are not necessarily bad. All of us have unstated goals like looking our best and delivering a polished speech. But we should eliminate ulterior purposes that make us self-centered and insensitive to our listeners. If our true goal is to demonstrate how smart we are, and this causes us to use big words that the audience cannot understand, we have failed to meet the needs of our listeners.

We should also eliminate purposes that sabotage our avowed purpose. An architect told me that when he started out in his profession, he was determined to prove that he knew as much about designing houses as his older competitors, so he focused on impressing potential customers with his vast knowledge. "I would give people a long spiel instead of talking about what they wanted to know. Most of them, of course, took their business elsewhere." Once he realized that his hidden purpose (to impress potential clients) was thwarting his avowed purpose (to persuade people to use his services), he began focusing on his listeners' needs and was able to win customers.

6

Finding Materials

At a textile plant employing over 1000 people, many workers asked the company to provide in-plant day care for their preschool children. The company responded by assigning Gloria Lopez, the personnel manager, to study the request and make specific recommendations to the board of directors.

To prepare for her presentation, Lopez drew from her own experiences as a working mother. She went to a nearby university library and checked out books on day care. With the help of her company's research department, she tapped into a computer database and extracted fourteen recent articles from magazines and *The Wall Street Journal* on corporations that have instituted day care centers. She interviewed over a dozen workers to find out exactly what kind of day care they needed, and she sent questionnaires to all employees to determine how many needed this service and at what hours. Traveling to three different states, she observed the workings of day care centers that other corporations had already established, and she quizzed corporate executives: How much money were they spending on day care? Did employee morale and productivity improve? Would they recommend that her company establish a day care center? Finally, she interviewed employees at these other plants to find out whether they were satisfied with the quality of the day care they had.

By the time Lopez finished her investigation, she had accumulated a wealth of information, and it was easy for her to prepare a proposal that was thorough, well-substantiated, and persuasive. When she stood before the board of directors, she gave an authoritative presentation on the need for an in-plant day care center, and she asked the board for its approval. After a brief discussion, the directors approved the proposal.

Lopez was successful because she had researched her topic thoroughly. A good speech should not be a collection of vague ideas and unsupported opinions; rather, it should be like Lopez's—an interesting package containing a rich variety of solid, up-to-date information. In this chapter we will discuss where and how to find materials for your speeches.

Personal Experiences and Investigations

In gathering materials for a speech, some speakers overlook their personal experiences, which can be a gold mine of good material. If it is relevant, a story from your own life can be the most interesting part of a speech. Your personal experiences can be especially useful when they are used to amplify information you have gleaned from books or magazine articles, as in the case below:

> David Rhodes gave his audience tips on how to buy a good car at the lowest possible price. He presented information from *Consumer Reports*, supple

menting it with firsthand knowledge he had picked up in his job as a car salesperson the previous summer. An example of his "insider's" knowledge: "When the car salesperson gives you the price on a car," Rhodes advised, "tell him that you'll think about it and maybe call back the next day. Start to walk away. Before you leave the lot, the salesperson will give you a lower price— he or she doesn't want you to get away."

You can also undertake personal investigations to gather material for a speech. For a speech on acid rain, for example, you can visit a mountaintop that has been ravaged by pollutants, making observations and perhaps even taking color slides. For a speech on prison conditions, you can visit a county jail or state prison and then tell your audience what you have seen. For a speech on animal overpopulation, you can tour a local animal shelter and interview the director.

Another type of investigation is to conduct public opinion surveys. One student polled her classmates on their views concerning the death penalty. This survey not only helped her analyze and adapt to her audience, but it also provided interesting data to include in the speech itself.

Library Resources

A library is a wonderful treasury of resources for your speeches. Your campus library is the best place to begin, but don't forget that there are many other kinds of libraries. Your local newspaper has a *morgue*, a library of old news stories that are clipped and filed by subject matter. These clippings are usually limited to local and state affairs; no effort is made to collect national and international news articles. Most newspapers allow researchers to look at the files and photocopy any items they want. There are also specialized libraries maintained by historical societies, museums, professional associations, law firms, medical societies, and large businesses. To find the location of these libraries in your community, consult the *American Library Directory* (in the reference section of your college library), or ask people who are knowledgeable about the particular field.

Getting Help from Librarians

Rather than wander around inside a library hoping to stumble upon good information, seek help from librarians. Contrary to what some students think, a librarian's work is not limited to ordering, shelving, and checking out books. An important part of a librarian's job is helping patrons find materials, so don't be shy about asking for help.

FOR YOUR CAREER

TIP 6.1: Use Interlibrary Loan

If your college or public library lacks a book or magazine article that you need, don't despair—use interlibrary loan. To locate a book, librarians can make a search (often very quick and computerized) of other libraries in your state or region until they find it and borrow it for you. It often takes less than two weeks to get the book, and usually there is no charge. To locate a magazine article, the librarians will find a library that carries the publication and request a photocopy of the article. A photocopying fee (such as 10 cents per page) is sometimes charged.

Although interlibrary loan is a wonderful resource, you cannot count on your request coming quickly; some books and periodicals are hard to locate, and mail delivery can be slow. Ask your librarian for details.

When you start your research, introduce yourself to a member of the library staff and explain the nature of your project. A librarian will be designated to help you; in large libraries, there is usually a reference librarian whose sole job is to help people track down information.

Consulting Reference Works

The reference section of the library, with its encyclopedias, dictionaries, yearbooks, and other aids, is an important resource. In most libraries, reference books cannot be checked out, so you need to allow yourself ample library time when you delve into these books.

General encyclopedias. For some research projects, encyclopedias are a good place to begin because they can give you an overview of your subject—a general idea of the basic concepts and issues. They also list books and articles on your subject, saving you the time it would take to compile such a list on your own. If the library carries several editions of a particular encyclopedia, look for the most recent edition. Popular encyclopedias include *The New Columbia Encyclopedia, The New Encyclopaedia Britannica,* and *World Book Encyclopedia.*

Specialized encyclopedias. Many specialized encyclopedias offer technical information written in language that a nonspecialist can understand. One of the best and most popular of these is the *McGraw-Hill Encyclopedia of Science and Technology,* a fifteen-volume set that includes an index. Here is a sampling from among the dozens of other specialized encyclopedias:

Encyclopedia of Advertising, Encyclopedia of American History, Encyclopedia of Athletics, Encyclopedia of Psychology, and *Encyclopedia of World Art.*

Dictionaries.   For definitions of currently used words in the English language, consult dictionaries such as *The American Heritage Dictionary, The Random House Dictionary,* or *Webster's Third International Dictionary.* For the history of a word, look at *The Oxford English Dictionary.* Also available are specialized dictionaries such as *Dictionary of American Slang, Dictionary of Scientific and Technical Terms,* and *Dorland's Medical Dictionary.*

Almanacs and yearbooks.   Because they are published annually, almanacs and yearbooks provide a great amount of updated facts and statistics. A few of the more popular are *Facts on File, Information Please Almanac,*and *Statistical Abstract of the United States.*

Atlases and gazetteers   Atlases contain maps and other geographical information; gazetteers are geographical dictionaries. Here are some of the most widely used: *Britannica Atlas, Rand McNally Cosmopolitan Atlas,* and *Times Atlas of the World.*

Biographical sources.   Most libraries have many different biographical references, giving you information about the lives and careers of famous people, living or dead. Here is a sampling: *Current Biography, Dictionary of American Biography, Notable American Women, Who's Who in America,* and *Who's Who of American Women.*

Collections of quotations.   If it is appropriate and interesting, a quotation can enrich a speech. Here are some sourcebooks: *Bartlett's Familiar Quotations, Dictionary of Quotations, Peter's Quotations,* and *The Quotable Woman.*

Finding Books

To find books on your speech subject, the quickest method is to consult the library's *catalog,* which tells you which books the library owns. The two most popular types are the card catalog and the on-line catalog (your college may have either or both).

The card catalog.   Arranged on index cards in filing drawers (or on microfiche in some libraries), this catalog lists books alphabetically by (1) author's last name, (2) title, and (3) subject. (In some libraries, name and title cards are housed separately from subject cards.) Which type of card should you

FIGURE 6.1
Subject, title, and author cards of a typical library book.

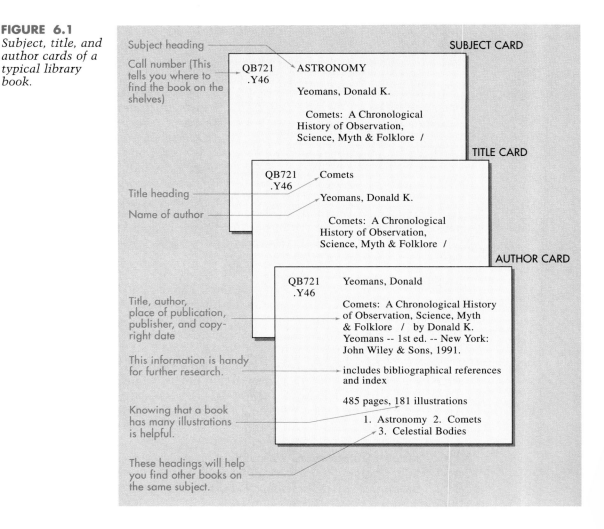

Subject heading

Call number (This tells you where to find the book on the shelves)

Title heading

Name of author

Title, author, place of publication, publisher, and copyright date

This information is handy for further research.

Knowing that a book has many illustrations is helpful.

These headings will help you find other books on the same subject.

SUBJECT CARD

QB721
.Y46   ASTRONOMY

        Yeomans, Donald K.

            Comets: A Chronological
        History of Observation,
        Science, Myth & Folklore /

TITLE CARD

QB721   Comets
.Y46
            Yeomans, Donald K.

                Comets: A Chronological
            History of Observation,
            Science, Myth & Folklore /

AUTHOR CARD

QB721   Yeomans, Donald
.Y46
            Comets: A Chronological History
            of Observation, Science, Myth
            & Folklore / by Donald K.
            Yeomans -- 1st ed. -- New York:
            John Wiley & Sons, 1991.

            includes bibliographical references
            and index

            485 pages, 181 illustrations

                1. Astronomy 2. Comets
                3. Celestial Bodies

consult? It depends on your situation. If you don't know much about your topic, the subject cards are very helpful. For example, if you want to do research on lasers but you don't already know the titles of any books in that field, begin by looking under the subject heading "Lasers." If, on the other hand, you know the name of an author in the field, you may want to go directly to the name in the "author" section and write down a list of his or her books. For example, if you know that Stanley Leinwoll is an expert on lasers, look under the author's last name, "Leinwoll." Finally, if you know of a book called *Laser Handbook* but you cannot recall the author's name, look for the title under "L" in the "title" section of the catalog. Sample cards are shown in Figure 6.1.

The on-line catalog.   In this system, a library compiles all its holdings on computer, which you can access via a computer monitor and keyboard. On-line catalogs vary from college to college in the way they display information, but they all offer the same basic information as card catalogs. As a bonus, many of them can do a few tricks that the card catalog cannot do: calling up on screen, for example, a list of all books in the library that contain the word *laser* in the title. Some on-line catalogs will indicate on screen whether a book is already checked out (saving you the time of hunting for it) and will permit you to place a *hold* on a checked-out book so that as soon as it is returned to the library, it is reserved for you.

In both types of catalogs, the most important item is the call number, for this tells you where to find the book in the library's stacks. The call number is based on the Library of Congress System or the Dewey Decimal System. Most libraries have a chart or map showing how to locate books in the stacks. If you have any problems, ask a librarian for help.

Finding Articles

Sometimes magazine and newspaper articles are better sources than books because they are more up-to-date and may even contain information that will never appear in book form. What is the best way to find magazine articles? If, for example, you want to find articles on modern aircraft carriers of the U.S. Navy, should you get a bunch of back issues of *Armed Forces Journal* and browse through until you find an article on aircraft carriers? No, this would be a waste of time. Go instead to one of many indexes that are available in most libraries.

Readers' Guide to Periodical Literature.   Your library is certain to have the *Readers' Guide to Periodical Literature*, a general index of over 170 popular magazines. Articles are listed alphabetically by author and subject. Each entry gives you all the information you need in order to track down the article. (If you don't understand any of the abbreviations, consult the key in the front of each *Readers' Guide.*)

Figure 6.2 gives some guidance on how to use the *Readers' Guide.*

Newspaper indexes.   Your library may have back issues of several newspapers on microfilm. Some newspapers are indexed, others are not; check with your librarian to find out what is available. If your library has only one newspaper on microfilm, it is likely to be *The New York Times* because of that publication's broad coverage of national and international events. *The New York Times Index* is a valuable resource because each entry contains a brief abstract of the story; if you are looking for a single fact, you can sometimes find it in the *Index* without having to go to the issue cited.

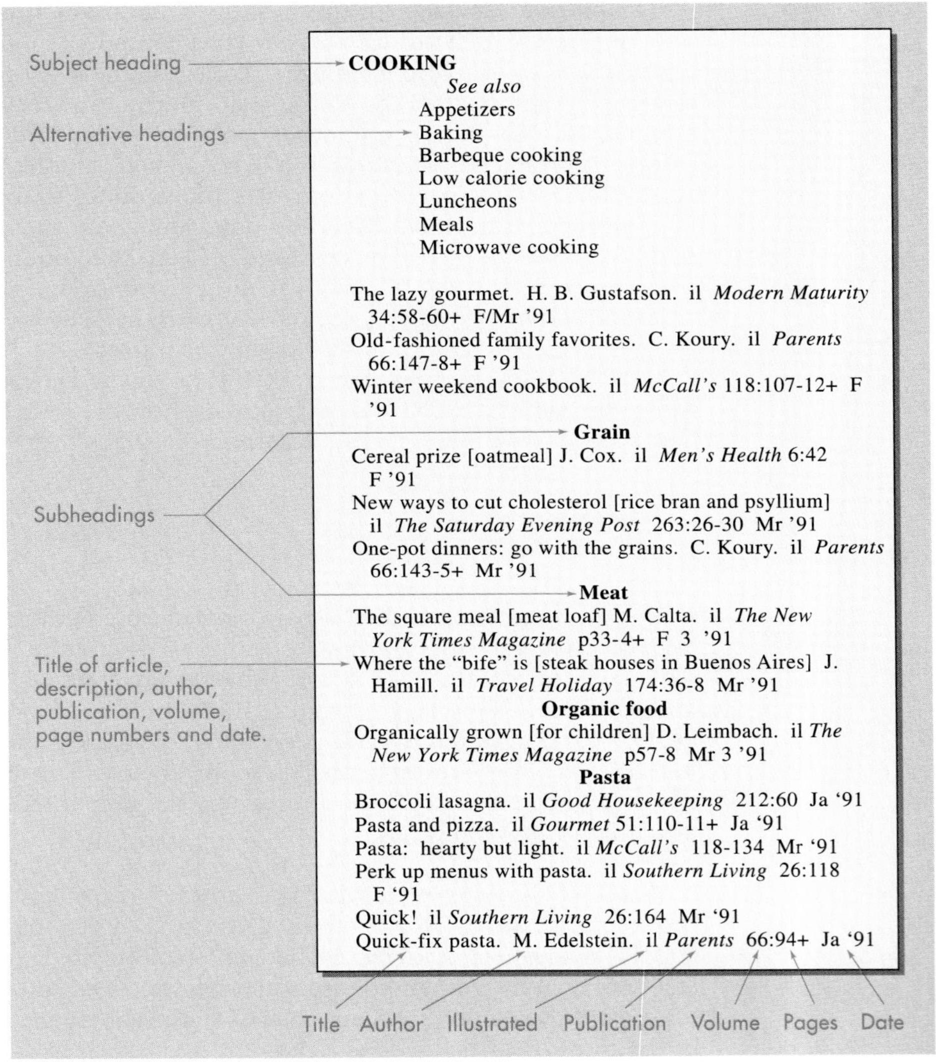

FIGURE 6.2
*Sample entry
from* Readers'
Guide to Periodi-
cal Literature.

Subject heading ──────→ **COOKING**
                 See also
                 Appetizers
Alternative headings ──────→ Baking
                 Barbeque cooking
                 Low calorie cooking
                 Luncheons
                 Meals
                 Microwave cooking

The lazy gourmet. H. B. Gustafson. il *Modern Maturity*
  34:58-60+ F/Mr '91
Old-fashioned family favorites. C. Koury. il *Parents*
  66:147-8+ F '91
Winter weekend cookbook. il *McCall's* 118:107-12+ F
  '91

──────→ **Grain**
Cereal prize [oatmeal] J. Cox. il *Men's Health* 6:42
  F '91
New ways to cut cholesterol [rice bran and psyllium]
  il *The Saturday Evening Post* 263:26-30 Mr '91

Subheadings ──────→ One-pot dinners: go with the grains. C. Koury. il *Parents*
  66:143-5+ Mr '91

──────→ **Meat**
The square meal [meat loaf] M. Calta. il *The New*
  York Times Magazine p33-4+ F 3 '91

Title of article, ──────→ Where the "bife" is [steak houses in Buenos Aires] J.
description, author,   Hamill. il *Travel Holiday* 174:36-8 Mr '91
publication, volume,   **Organic food**
page numbers and date. Organically grown [for children] D. Leimbach. il *The*
  New York Times Magazine p57-8 Mr 3 '91
              Pasta
Broccoli lasagna. il *Good Housekeeping* 212:60 Ja '91
Pasta and pizza. il *Gourmet* 51:110-11+ Ja '91
Pasta: hearty but light. il *McCall's* 118-134 Mr '91
Perk up menus with pasta. il *Southern Living* 26:118
  F '91
Quick! il *Southern Living* 26:164 Mr '91
Quick-fix pasta. M. Edelstein. il *Parents* 66:94+ Ja '91

Title Author Illustrated Publication Volume Pages Date

Another good resource is *Newsbank*, which not only indexes articles from 500 state and national newspapers, but also provides the news articles on microfiche.

    Special indexes. If you need information from specialized publications that are not covered by the above indexes, there are a number of other indexes you can consult. The *Social Sciences Index* lists articles from 270 periodicals in such fields as political science, psychology, sociology, medicine, law geography, anthropology, economics, and environmental science. In the *Humanities Index*, you can find listings for articles from 260 periodicals in history, philosophy, performing arts, language, literature, classical studies, and other areas of the humanities. Other indexes include *Applied Science and Technology Index*, *Biological Abstracts*, *Business Periodicals Index*, *Cumulative Index to Nursing and Allied Health Literature*, *Education Index*, *Environment Index*, *General Science Index*, and *Psychological Abstracts*.

Finding Audiovisual Materials

Most libraries have audiovisual materials that can be checked out or played in the library. These materials include videotapes, 16-mm films, audiotapes, phonograph records, filmstrips, and slide shows. These items may be listed in the card (or on-line) catalog or in a separate catalog. Ask your librarian for help.

Sometimes audiovisual materials that help you in your research can also be incorporated as aids in your speech (see Chapter 8).

Computer Databases

A spectacular change is taking place in libraries (and offices) throughout the world: computers are letting people find information with blazing speed and amazing ease. They are even saving lives:

> "I recently treated a woman who had gone into anaphylactic shock," says Dr. John Faughnan of Williamsport (Pennsylvania) Hospital. "Her heart wasn't functioning, and she wasn't responding to the usual treatment."
>
> If this had happened ten years ago, Dr. Faughnan would have combed through huge books listing articles written on anaphylactic shock. Then he would have ordered all available articles on the subject. In the meantime, the patient might have died.
>
> Fortunately, Dr. Faughnan had access (via telephone lines) to Medline, an electronic database of the national Library of Medicine in Bethesda, Maryland. Using a computer in his office, he was able to search the database and find—in a matter of minutes—the summary of an article that outlined a similar case that had occurred in England a few months before. "We followed the treatment outlined in the [summary]," says Dr. Faughnan, "and [the patient] came through."[1]

Computer databases are vast storehouses of information. Some of them duplicate the reference books we discussed above—complete encyclopedias and periodical indexes—while others offer information not available elsewhere. Your college library (or one in your community) might have computers that can tap into one of the more than 2000 databases currently available in the United States. Even if your library has no computers, it might be able to order a computerized search by an outside source on your behalf.

To demonstrate how computers help researchers, let's say you are researching "why elephants have become an endangered species."

Suppose that your library has the popular InfoTrac (Academic) computerized index to over 100,000 articles appearing in 390 scholarly and general-interest periodicals during the previous five years. Sitting in front of a computer terminal, you ask the computer to search for magazine articles on endangered species. Within seconds, InfoTrac informs you that it has listings for 1528 articles under the heading "Endangered" and 2090 articles under the heading "Species." Obviously, you don't have time to sift through these hundreds of citations. Next you ask the computer to search for articles on elephants. This time InfoTrac lists 389 articles. Still too many. Next you ask for a search of all articles that deal with all three words—"Endangered," "Species," and "Elephants." Now InfoTrac tells you that it has twenty-six references concerning all three items; in other words, it has narrowed the search down to your specific subject: the elephant as an endangered species.

You push a button and the computer displays a list of all twenty-six articles on your subject. The first one on the list looks like this:

```
1  Out of Time, Out of Space: Elephants. (includes related
   articles on elephant extinction, habitat, and evolution) by
   Douglas H. Chadwick il v179 National Geographic May '91 p2
   (45)
   LIBRARY SUBSCRIBES
```

This entry gives you (in order) the title of the article, an explanation of related articles, the author, the fact that the article is accompanied by illustrations (this is nice to know if you need visual aids for your speech), the volume number, the name of the magazine, the date, the page where the article begins (2), and the total number of pages (45). It also gives you a valuable tip: Your library subscribes to *National Geographic*. Now all you have to do is get the particular issue; your librarians can explain the correct procedure.

Computer databases offer these advantages as research tools: (1) They provide the fastest search available, spending minutes to find and compile information that might take a human several days of diligent labor in the library to locate. (2) They are updated more frequently than reference books; many of them receive new information every day. (3) Databases provide access to more magazines and technical journals than most libraries could possibly afford to subscribe to. For example, *Biosis Previews*—just one out of the 200 databases offered by Dialog Information Services—provides research information about the life sciences from 9000 medical and scientific journals published in the United States and abroad.

Two systems exist for extracting information from electronic databases: (1) *On-line searches* use telephone lines to tap into databases at a remote location; a library in Alaska can use (without a moment's delay) an on-line database in London, England. (2) *CD-ROM players* store databases on compact disks. CD-ROM (which stands for "compact disk-read only memory") uses the same kind of CDs that are popular for recorded music. One CD-ROM disk has enough space to contain an entire thirty-five–volume encyclopedia.

Does it make a difference which system you use? On-line searches tend to be faster; they provide access to a greater amount of data, and they are updated more often than CD-ROM. On the negative side, on-line searches are often costly (the cost of a typical 5-minute search ranges from $10 to $30). Since every minute on-line costs money, you feel pressured to work fast. CD-ROM services, on the other hand, are usually offered to library patrons at no cost; therefore, you feel free to explore a database without pressure.

Databases provide information in three forms (some databases offer only one of these types; some offer all three):

1. Citations.   This is a basic bibliographical reference, which usually gives the name of the article, the author(s), the name of the magazine, volume number, issue number, page numbers, and date.

2. Abstracts (or brief summaries) of an article.   An abstract is designed to give you enough information to decide whether you want to see the complete text of an article. Sometimes, however, the abstract itself gives you as much information as you need. For example, let's say you want to know if laetrile can cure cancer; you see the abstract of an article in *The New England Journal of Medicine* which examines ten years of research on laetrile and finds no efficacy in laetrile. Without reading the entire article, you can say in your speech, "According to a recent article in *The New England Journal of Medicine*, laetrile has been found to be ineffective in the treatment of cancer."

3. Complete texts.   A few databases offer complete texts of articles. You usually have three options: (1) You can read the text on the screen, making notes on paper as necessary; (2) you can print out the text on a computer-linked printer, or (3) you can pay the database owner to print out the text for you and mail it to you.

Interviews

Interviews with people who are knowledgeable about your subject can yield valuable facts and insights. Often these individuals can provide up-to-date information not yet available in magazines or books. In the world of computers, for example, change occurs so rapidly that a magazine article published three months ago on a particular kind of software can be hopelessly outdated today.

Where can you find experts to interview? Start with your own college; some faculty members may be well-versed on your speech topic. Then look at the larger community beyond the campus: Are any businesses, industries, or agencies involved in your subject? If so, telephone them and ask who is their most knowledgeable person on the topic. If you are speaking on snake-bites, for example, call the nearest zoo and ask to speak to the chief herpetologist. In some cases, you may want to interview fellow students. If you are preparing a speech on communication problems between males and females, for instance, you might want to collect the ideas, experiences, and observations of other students.

If you are lucky, there can sometimes be a wonderful bonus from an interview. You might develop a professional contact or personal friendship that will prove useful to you in later years. Consuela Martinez, an accounting

Interviewing a woman who experienced racial discrimination in the 1950s is a good way to gain information for a speech on the civil rights movement in the United States.

major in one of my classes several years ago, interviewed an official at a local bank to get information for a speech. The official was so impressed with Martinez that when she graduated and returned to the bank to seek a job, he hired her. Another student, Skyler MacPherson, interviewed a well-known poet in his community. After the interview, the poet asked MacPherson to come to his house for dinner, and a long-term friendship began, with the poet helping MacPherson to get some of his own poems published.

Don't let fear of rejection deter you from asking for an interview. Some students have the idea that the knowledgeable persons they want to interview are so important and so busy, they will certainly have no time for questions from a "lowly" student. This is a mistaken notion. I have sent hundreds of students into the community for interviews and have found that virtually everyone they approach loves to be interviewed. Does this surprise you? Think about yourself for a moment: When a friend asks you for advice (on such things as how to bake a cake or how to solve an algebra problem), don't you enjoy holding forth as an "expert?" The same is true of knowledgeable people in your community—they are flattered to be interviewed by a student.

Should an individual be interviewed in person or over the telephone? If you have only two or three short, easily answered questions, you could conduct your interview over the telephone, but if you want detailed answers to many different questions, you are more likely to get good responses if you conduct your interview in person. People tend to speak more freely and in greater detail during face-to-face encounters than they do on the telephone. There is also a greater chance of warmth and trust developing between you. Here are some guidelines for planning and conducting interviews:

Preparing for the Interview

Before the interview, there are a few things you should do:

Telephone in advance for an appointment.   To arrange a time that is convenient for the person you want to interview, telephone beforehand. Don't just drop by and expect the person to agree to an interview on the spot; you may catch him or her off-guard or during a hectic time of day. When you call to line up the appointment, explain briefly what you are trying to find out and why you think he or she can help you. Such an explanation gives the person time to get his or her thoughts together before talking to you.

Conduct research before the interview.   Read up on your subject *before* you go to an interview. Why? First of all, you need to know enough about the subject to ask intelligent questions. Suppose you are planning to interview a psychiatrist about schizophrenia. If you read articles and books on the mental disorder beforehand, you will know enough about the subject to ask an important question, such as "Do researchers feel that they are close to discovering a cure?" In addition to helping you ask intelligent questions, research will also help you avoid asking embarrassing questions like "How does the split in personality occur?" Such a question would be embarrassing because it would reveal your ignorance of what the term *schizophrenia* means. (It means "a psychotic break with reality," not a Jekyll-and-Hyde split in personality.)

Second, if you find something in your reading that you don't understand, the interviewee might be able to explain it. Suppose that while you are doing your library research on schizophrenia, you come across the term *folie à deux*. You look up the term in a dictionary but cannot make sense out of the formal definition. In your interview with a psychiatrist, you ask for a plain-English explanation of what the term means (it means "a psychotic delusion that one person persuades another person to share").

Finally, if you fail to find vital information in your library research, you can often get it from the interviewee. Suppose that you are investigating the effectiveness of automobile air bags in traffic accidents. You want to know, "Will air bags save a motorist's life if he or she is driving at 55 miles per hour and has a head-on collision with a car traveling at the same speed?" Your weekend spent in the library sifting through government studies failed to turn up the answer, but five minutes with a traffic safety expert may give you the information.

Prepare questions in advance. Decide ahead of time exactly what questions you want to ask, and write them down on a piece of paper, putting the most important ones first in case you run out of time.

Decide how to record the interview. It is a mistake to think that you can conduct an interview without a pencil or a tape recorder and then remember all the key information later when you are organizing your speech. Since human memory is highly fallible, you need a system for recording the interview. Most interviewers use either or both of these methods.

1. *Writing down key ideas.* Use a pencil or pen and a notepad. Jot down key ideas only; if you try to write down every word the person is saying, you will be completely absorbed in transcribing sentences instead of making sense out of what is being said. It is far more important to comprehend the interviewee's ideas than to get the exact words on paper.

2. *Using video- or audiotape.* A videocassette camcorder (on a tripod) or an audiotape recorder can be ideal when it is important to get a word-for-word record of the interview—you need not worry about forgetting key points or misquoting your source. Some interviewees, knowing they are being recorded, may try extra hard to be precise and accurate

in giving information. In some cases, you can use some of your video-tape in your actual speech (as did one speaker, who interviewed an engineer at the construction site of a bridge.)

There are some disadvantages in using recorders, however, according to Thomas Hunter, public relations director for Union Camp Corporation. "Recorders are mechanical beasts subject to malfunctions. And they can bog you down in hours of replay and transcription."[2]

If you want to use a recorder, seek permission from the interviewee beforehand. Most people will permit recording, but a few will refuse (because it makes them feel uncomfortable or intimidated). You should of course respect their wishes.

Important note: If you use a recorder, you should also take notes. At first glance it may seem silly to take notes while getting everything down on tape, but I recommend it for these reasons: (1) A mechanical foul-up might cause you to lose your entire tape; having notes would give you a backup record of the interview. (2) The act of making notes forces you to concentrate on the key ideas of your interview, thereby making you more alert in your questioning.

If you plan to take notes and make a recording simultaneously, you may want to have a friend accompany you to help with the recording. This frees you of all worry about operating the equipment.

Conducting the Interview

Here are some tips on how to conduct the interview.

Start the interview in a friendly, relaxed manner. Before you begin your questions, you need to establish rapport. You can make a statement of appreciation (for example, "Thanks for letting me come by to talk to you today") and engage in small talk on obvious topics (the weather, the beautiful painting on the wall, and so on). Small talk is an important lubricant in conversation, especially at the beginning of a dialogue, so you need not feel that it is a waste of time. You should also repeat the purpose of the interview; the person may have forgotten exactly what you are seeking. While these preliminary remarks are being made, you can set up your recorder (if you have previously received permission to use one).

Get biographical information about the interviewee. Since the person you are interviewing is one of your sources, you need to be able to tell your audience later why he or she is an authority on your subject. If you have not been able to get background information in advance, the early part of the interview is a good time to get it because it continues the building of rapport.

You could say, for example, "Where did you get your doctorate?" or "How long have you been working on this problem?"

Ask both prepared and spontaneous questions. Earlier we noted that you should decide ahead of time exactly what questions you want to ask. Make these questions as specific as possible. It would be ludicrous to walk into the office of an expert on robots and say, "Tell me what you know about robots." Such a question would probably draw a laugh and a comment like "Have you got two months to listen?" A better, more specific question would be something like this: "Will robots someday replace all automobile assembly-line workers?"

There are two types of questions that can be prepared in advance:

1. *Closed* questions require only yes or no responses or short, factual answers. Examples: "Do Democrats outnumber Republicans in this state?" "What percentage of registered voters actually voted in the last presidential election?" Closed questions are effective in getting specific data.

2. *Open* questions give the interviewee a wide latitude for responding. For example, "How do you feel about negative political ads?" The advantage of such a broad question is that the interviewee can choose the points he or she wishes to emphasize—points that it may not have occurred to you to ask about. The disadvantage is that sometimes an interviewee can wander off the subject into irrelevant side issues.

There are two other types of questions that cannot be prepared in advance but may need to be asked spontaneously during the interview:

1. *Clarifying* questions are used when you are confused about what the person means. Don't write down a murky response and say to yourself, "I'll study this in my notes later and try to figure it out." If you cannot make sense out of it during the interview, there is not much chance you will succeed later. Ask a question like this: "Could you explain that a little more?" or "Correct me if I'm wrong, but I understand you to say that . . . ." Some students shy away from asking clarifying questions because they are afraid to show their ignorance. This is illogical. You are there to interview the person precisely because you are "ignorant" in his or her area of expertise. So ask about any point that you don't understand.

2. *Follow-up* questions are designed to encourage the interviewee to elaborate on what he or she has been saying—to continue a story or to add to a comment. Here are some examples: "What happened next?" "Were you upset about what happened?" "Could you give me some examples of what you're talking about?"

Make the interview more like a relaxed chat than an interrogation. Be natural and spontaneous, and follow the flow of conversation. In other words, don't act as if you must plow through your list of questions item by item. The flow of conversation might lead to questions being answered "out of order." Simply check off the questions as they are answered. Toward the end of the interview, ask those questions that still have not been answered. Also, the person may bring up surprising aspects of your topic that you have not thought about; this should inspire you to ask spontaneous follow-up questions.

When the interviewee mentions things that are not on your checklist, write them down, even if they seem inconsequential at the time, because you may find a use for them later. This advice would not apply if the person goes off on a tangent, telling you things that are totally unrelated to the subject. In such a case, steer the conversation back toward the pertinent topic.

Maintain eye contact.   Show with your eyes that you are listening attentively and comprehending what is being said. You can do this even if you use a notepad (just jot down key ideas, keeping your eyes on the interviewee most of the time).

Ask the interviewee about other sources and visual aids.   Interviewees may know of other persons you can interview or library resources that you are unaware of. They may have a pamphlet or a book that they are willing to lend you. In some cases, they may even lend you a map or chart or some other kind of visual aid that you can use in your speech.

Near the end, ask if you've omitted any questions.   When you have gone through all the prepared questions, ask the interviewee if there are any items that you have failed to ask about. You may find that you have inadvertently overlooked some important matters.

End the interview on time.   Respect the amount of time that was granted when you set up your appointment; if you were allotted 20 minutes, stay no more than 20 minutes—unless of course the interviewee invites you to stay longer. If you still have questions when the time is up, you can ask for a second interview (perhaps a few extra questions can even be handled over the telephone).

Following Up

After you leave the interview, you have three important tasks:

Promptly expand your notes.   Immediately after the interview, go through your notes and expand them (by turning words and phrases into complete sentences) while the conversation is fresh in your mind. If you wait two weeks to go over the notes, they will be stale and you might puzzle over your scribbling or you might forget what a particular phrase means.

Evaluate your information. After you have expanded the notes, evaluate them to see if you got exactly what you were looking for. If you are confused on any points, or if you find that you need more information on a particular item, telephone the interviewee and ask for help. This should not be a source of embarrassment for you—it shows that you care enough about the subject and the interviewee to get the information exactly right.

Write a thank-you note. A brief note thanking the interviewee would be a classy finale.

Other Resources

You can often get literature and visual aids from companies and agencies in your community. One student, Rhonda Murchison, visited an office of the American Red Cross and told them she wanted to give a talk on CPR (cardio-pulmonary resuscitation); they lent her a portable dummy to use in her demonstration speech. Sometimes you can even get "freebies" from local sources. Student speaker Jerry Lipe was preparing a speech on stress; he went to a local mental health agency and got brochures and thirty stress detectors—small color-coded dots that can be placed on the skin to determine how much stress a person is under at that moment. He had enough tabs to give one to each listener at the end of his speech.

A vast amount of literature on a wide variety of subjects can be ordered at no charge (or for a very small fee) from thousands of corporations and associations. To get addresses of national groups, go to the library and consult reference books such as *The Encyclopedia of Associations* and *The Directory of Corporations.* Another good source is the U.S. government, which each year puts out 25,000 new publications on subjects ranging from rabid animals to gardening to solar heating. Your librarian can help you locate or order government documents.

A note of caution: Don't rely too heavily on requested material because it may not arrive in time for your speech. I remember one student telling me that she wrote requesting some interesting material, but it arrived *three months* after she gave her speech. Also, don't overestimate the value of material that you have not yet seen. One student felt certain that some pamphlets he ordered would give him all the information he needed for his speech; they arrived one day before his speech but turned out to be worthless. He had to race to the library to do some frantic research.

Finding the Right Materials Efficiently

Many students fail to come up with good material because they spend most of their time in unproductive research. They either fail to find the right kinds of information or they get more material than they have time to process. Here are steps leading to productive research.

Start Research Far in Advance

Running out of time is the most common reason students give for not doing adequate research. If you start your research well ahead of the speech date and budget your time sensibly, you should be able to do a thorough job. Keep in mind that most research takes longer than you anticipate. Leave yourself more time than you think necessary.

Turn Purpose Statement into Research Question

Your specific purpose should be decided before you start your research. Imagine that you had written the following specific-purpose statement: "To tell my audience how people can determine if they have a serious drinking problem." For research purposes, you can turn this into a question, "How can people determine if they have a serious drinking problem?" Why use a question? Because a question brings your research efforts into sharper focus than a statement does. If you write the research question at the top of the first page of your notebook or on your first index card—and keep it in front of you at each step of your research—it will be a constant reminder of precisely what you are searching for. It will prevent you from wandering off into areas that are not really related. Let's say you pick up an interesting book on alcoholism. It contains fascinating charts on the physiological effects of alcohol and fact-filled chapters on such things as cirrhosis of the liver and delirium tremens. But you notice that nothing in the book answers your specific question. So you put it back. No sense wasting your time on a book that will not contribute to your speech. (After you prepare and deliver your speech, you can always go back and read the book at your leisure.)

Establish a Research Strategy

Some people enter the library not knowing exactly what they are looking for and then drift from room to room, hoping to stumble on a helpful book or magazine. Rather than drifting about, spend a few minutes devising a research strategy; here are two ways to achieve this:

1. Talk to your librarians.   Explain your research question and get their advice. In your speech on alcohol, suppose that the librarian suggests that you start off by looking in the on-line (or card) catalog for some of the most current books on alcohol abuse with annotated bibliographies. These bibliographies might lead you immediately to the best materials. If this does not give you all that you need, the librarian might advise you to look in the *Readers' Guide to Periodical Literature* because popular magazines often run checklists such as "How to Tell If You Have a Drinking Problem."

2. Talk to an informed person on campus or in the community.   Suppose that you look in the *Yellow Pages* of the telephone directory and call the number of an alcohol abuse treatment center. The woman you talk to suggests that you come by and pick up some pamphlets on the subject. She also gives you the phone number of a member of Alcoholics Anonymous who has given talks in the community on the warning signals of alcoholism.

By this point you should be able to devise a firm research strategy involving a series of tasks. Assign dates for completion of each task, leaving yourself plenty of time in case you run into a delay or get sick or have some unforeseen crisis.

- ▶ Nov. 3—Call A.A. member to set up interview.
- ▶ Nov. 4—Go by alcohol abuse treatment center and get pamphlets.
- ▶ Nov. 5—On-line catalog—alcohol abuse—look for books with annotated bibliographies.
- ▶ Nov. 6—Look up the books and articles obtained from the above.
- ▶ Nov. 7—If still need information, see *Readers' Guide.*
- ▶ Nov. 9—Interview A.A. member

Post the schedule in a visible place in your room, or carry it around with you. Try to abide by it. With such a research strategy, you should be able to save time and avoid drifting.

Evaluate All Sources

Suppose that you find twelve books and nineteen magazine articles for your speech on alcohol abuse. Should you read through all the books and articles? No, of course not. That would take too long. What you need to do now is sift through your potential sources, choosing those which will help you and discarding those which are irrelevant or unimportant. To assist you in your task, here are some questions to ask yourself.

Is the source current?   In some fields, especially in the physical and social sciences, you need the most up-to-date materials on a subject. If you were doing research on robotics, for example, a book published last year would be far more valuable than one published 10 years ago because there have been hundreds of new developments in this field since the older book was published. Even in history and biography, more recent sources would generally be preferred because they might include previously undiscovered information; for example, a history of Native Americans published this year might report new evidence concerning how humans first migrated to the Western Hemisphere.

Is the source credible?   Decide whether your particular audience will consider a source believable. Suppose you are doing research on UFOs and you come across an article in one of the sensational tabloids (the kind sold at grocery store checkout counters) with this headline: FLYING SAUCER ABDUCTS FARMER AND COW. You would be wise to ignore the article because most audiences would consider such a source to be laughably unreliable. If, on the other hand, you read an article in a prestigious journal such as *Aviation Week and Space Technology* on the possibility of the existence of flying saucers, your audience would most likely respect the source and therefore give serious consideration to the source's ideas.

Is the source comprehensive?   If a magazine index shows that a particular article is only one-page long, you may want to skip it and look for a longer article. Longer articles usually contain more information, and you can save yourself time by concentrating on them.

Is the source understandable?   If you are researching volcanoes and you come across an article on the subject in the *Journal of Earth Sciences,* you might find (unless you are a geology major) that parts of the article are too complicated for you to understand. You would be wasting your time if you tried to struggle with it. If, on the other hand, you find an article on volcanoes in *National Geographic,* you can be sure that it is written in language that is understandable to the nonspecialist.

Can the source lead to other sources?   When you use the on-line (or card) catalog and you find a listing for a promising book, see if the book includes a bibliography (see Figure 6.1). A bibliography can save you an enormous amount of time if it cites the most important articles and books on your topic. Suppose you are interested in how people can interpret dreams. You find a book on the subject, and in the back is a long bibliography, giving you the names of dozens of magazine articles. You choose five of the most promising articles, look them up in the library, and subsequently find all the information you need for your speech. A bibliography can be especially helpful if it is annotated; that is, if the author gives a brief description of what is contained in each book or article cited. By the way, don't overlook your textbooks; they often have extensive bibliographies in the back.

Taking Notes

As you hunt for materials in the library, systematically record the key points that you find. Here are the steps you should follow.

Prepare Bibliography Cards

As you go through catalogs and indexes, jot down the names of books and articles that sound promising. Use 3 × 5 index cards (because they are easy to shuffle and place in alphabetical order). These cards help you locate materials, and will come in handy later when you put together the bibliography for your speech. In addition, if you need to consult a book or article again for clarification or amplification of facts, the data on your card should help you find it quickly. Figure 6.3 shows two sample bibliography cards.

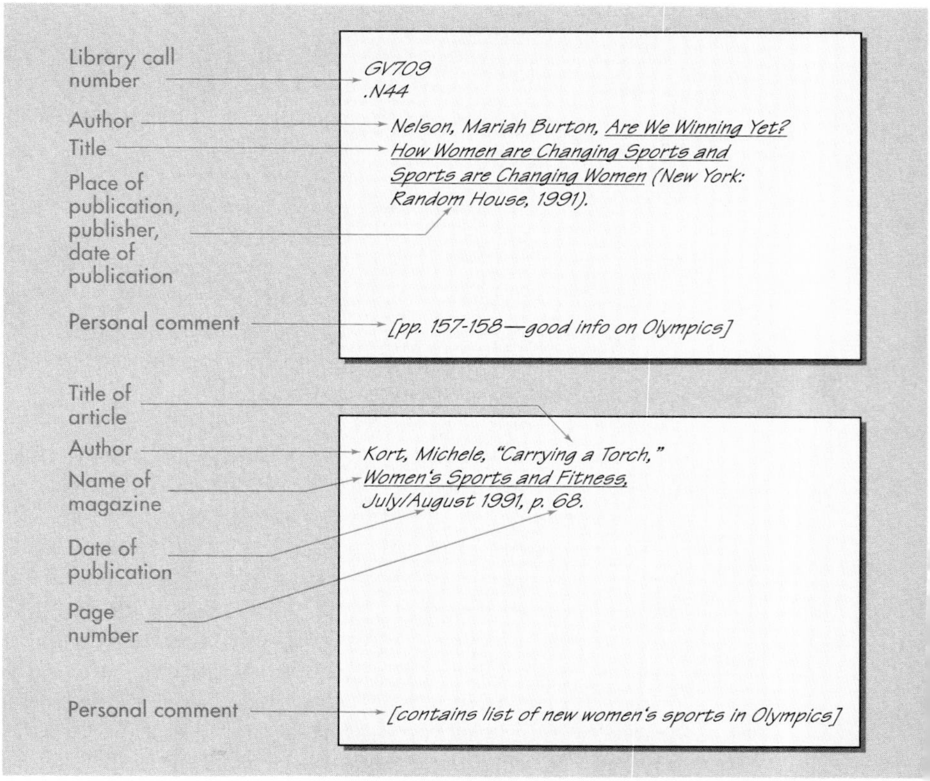

FIGURE 6.3
Sample bibliography cards for a book and a magazine article.

Library call number

Author
Title

Place of publication, publisher, date of publication

Personal comment

GV709
.N44

Nelson, Mariah Burton, *Are We Winning Yet?*
How Women are Changing Sports and
Sports are Changing Women (New York:
Random House, 1991).

[pp. 157-158—good info on Olympics]

Title of article
Author
Name of magazine

Date of publication

Page number

Personal comment

Kort, Michele, "Carrying a Torch,"
Women's Sports and Fitness,
July/August 1991, p. 68.

[contains list of new women's sports in Olympics]

Fill out a bibliography card for every book or article which you think might be helpful. You may end up with more sources than you have time to consult, but it is better to have too many sources than not enough. Leave space on each card for personal comments (see Figure 6.3), which can help you evaluate which sources are most likely to yield good information.

Make Note Cards

As you read through books and articles, make notes of key ideas on large cards (4 × 6 or 5 × 7). Using large cards will help you distinguish them from the smaller (3 × 5) bibliography cards and also give you ample room for note taking.

Put a subject heading at the top of each card, as shown in Figures 6.4 and 6.5. These headings will be valuable when you finish making your notes

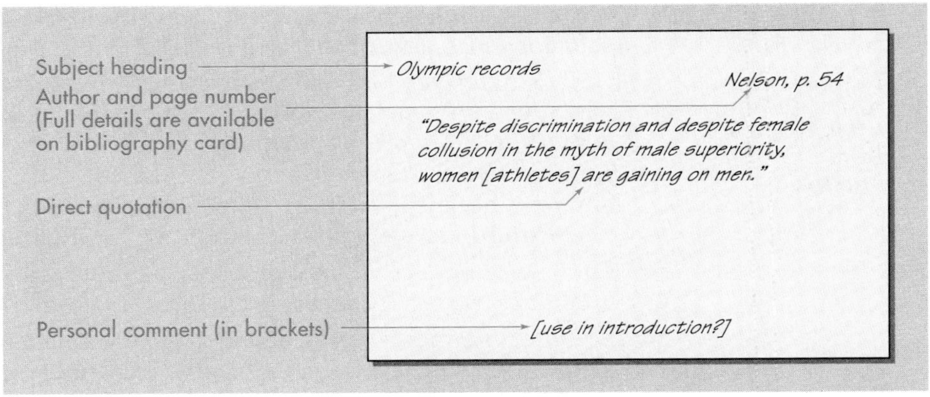

FIGURE 6.4
Sample index card for a direct quotation from a book.

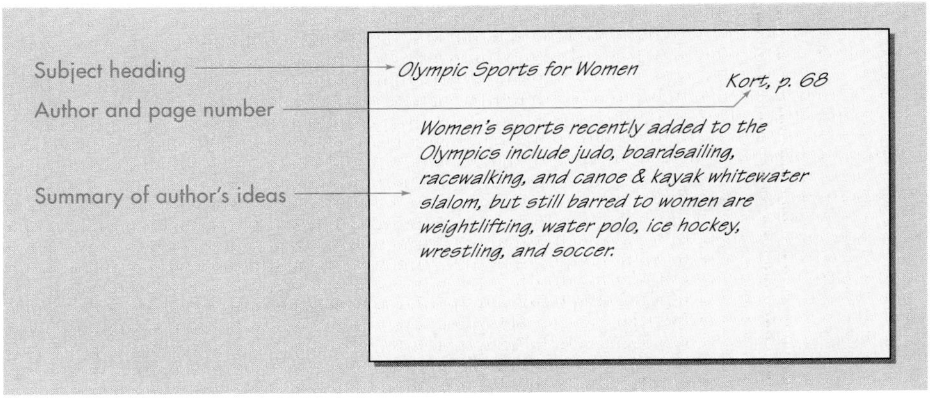

Subject heading ————————→ *Olympic records*
                                                    Nelson, p. 54
Author and page number
(Full details are available
on bibliography card)

                          "Despite discrimination and despite female
                          collusion in the myth of male superiority,
                          women [athletes] are gaining on men."

Direct quotation ————————

Personal comment (in brackets) ——————→ *[use in introduction?]*

FIGURE 6.5
Sample index card for a summary from a magazine

Subject heading ————————→ *Olympic Sports for Women*
                                                    Kort, p. 68
Author and page number ——————

                          Women's sports recently added to the
                          Olympics include judo, boardsailing,
                          racewalking, and canoe & kayak whitewater
Summary of author's ideas ————→ *slalom, but still barred to women are*
                          weightlifting, water polo, ice hockey,
                          wrestling, and soccer.

because you can then group the cards into related batches. Identify each card with the author's name. There is no need to write down full bibliographical information because those details are already on your bibliography cards.

In making notes, follow these steps:

▶ Quickly read through the material to see if there is anything worth noting.

▶ If there is, reread the material, this time very carefully.

▶ Try to summarize the key points in a few simple sentences. Avoid the temptation to copy down huge chunks of undigested information. Your task is to interpret, evaluate, and boil down ideas, not convey a text verbatim.

▶ While striving for brevity, you must make sure that you put summarized information in a coherent form. If you jot down a phrase like "schizophrenic—Jesus Christ or Napoleon," and then wait five days before organizing your notes, you may forget the meaning of that note. Write out a coherent sentence such as this: "Schizophrenics who have delusions often think they are Jesus Christ or Napoleon."

▶ Occasionally, you will find an arresting phrase or a short, vivid sentence which you will want to convey to your listeners in the form of a direct quotation. Be sure to put quotation marks around such passages in your note cards. Don't use too many direct quotations in your notes, however, because you may fall into the trap discussed above—copying down large blocks of text without proper evaluation and condensation.

▶ Take more notes than you probably will need. It is better to have too much raw material than not enough.

▶ Personal comments can be added to the bottom of note cards to provide ideas on how to use the note or how to connect it to other notes (see Figure 6.4). You can also express a personal reaction, such as "This sounds implausible—check other sources." Use square brackets or some other device to distinguish between your own comments and the text that you are summarizing.

▶ Use a separate card for each idea. This will make it easy to sort your cards by subject headings.

Giving Credit

If you have gathered information from sources, you should use oral footnotes in your speech; for example, "According to the *CBS Evening News* of March 15th of this year . . ." or "In the words of Thomas Jefferson . . . ." An oral footnote is the equivalent of a footnote in a written document and its purpose is the same: to give credit for information or ideas that did not originate with you. Oral footnotes also give credibility to your remarks. You are saying, in effect, "I didn't pull this out of thin air; I got this information from someone who is an authority on the subject."

If you got information from an interview, you could say something like this: "According to Elizabeth Smith, director of advertising for our city's biggest department store, ..."

For material from books or magazines, you could say, "In an article in the latest issue of *Scientific American,* Dr. Paul Rhodes says that . . ." or "The graph on this slide is based on data I found in the current issue of *World Almanac.*"

When you are quoting verbatim, use "oral" quotation marks such as the following: "To quote Abraham Lincoln . . ." on "In the words of Plato . . . ." Expressions like these are a little smoother than "Quote" at the beginning of a statement and "Unquote" at the end. A slight pause at the end of the quotation should be an adequate signal that you have finished quoting.

Summary

Your quest for speech material should begin with yourself. What personal experiences or observations can you draw upon? After you have looked inward, you can look outward—at the books, magazines, and audiovisual holdings of college and local libraries. Some of these libraries may have computer databases that can be tapped for quick retrieval of a vast amount of information.

Interviewing knowledgeable people on your campus or in your community can yield valuable, up-to-date information in many fields. To prepare for an interview, do extensive research on the topic and then draw up a list of questions to be asked. Conduct the interview in a relaxed, conversational manner.

Whatever sources you draw from, start your research far in advance, devise a research strategy, and then carry out that strategy in a systematic way. Make all your notes on cards, with a subject heading at the top, and with only one idea per card. These cards can later be shuffled and arranged systematically as an aid to the writing of your outline.

Review Questions

1. What is interlibrary loan and how can it help you?
2. What are three main advantages of using computer databases?
3. Why should a student not feel hesitant about asking a local expert for an interview?

4. Why should most of your speech be done *before* you call someone for an interview?

5. What are the advantages and disadvantages of using a video- or audio-tape recorder in an interview?

6. What steps should you take after an interview is completed?

7. In your research, why should you take more notes than you probably will need?

TIPS FOR YOUR CAREER

TIP 6.2: Develop a Lifetime Filing System for Important Ideas

Marie Judson, a computer programmer for a large manufacturing company, takes notes at every speech, training session, and seminar she attends and then files the notes under appropriate headings in her filing cabinet. She also clips and files articles from professional journals and newsletters.

Wherever Judson is required to write a memorandum or prepare a talk, her files provide a gold mine of good resource material. When her superiors want information about the latest developments in computers, they consult Judson first because of her extensive files. These superiors have come to regard Judson as an indispensable, "got-it-together" person who keeps up with developments in her field.

Like Judson, you should develop personal files on topics that are relevant to your career. Such files will obviously come in handy for preparing speeches and for writing memos and reports. Also, as in Judson's case, they can be useful in establishing yourself as a valuable, up-to-date employee.

Even if you are not yet employed in your chosen field, you should begin to keep files so that when you do enter the field, you will have a wealth of professional information at your fingertips.

What should you file? In addition to clipping or photocopying articles, I suggest that you keep a pack of index cards or a legal pad handy so that you can jot down notes of important ideas that you encounter. These ideas may come from your own thoughts, or they may come from books, TV programs, speeches, lectures, workshops, and interviews. Since many of your instructors are experts in their fields, you may want to file lecture notes from some of your college classes. Don't worry that you might accumulate too many notes. You can always go through your files later and discard deadwood.

How should you file information? Devise whatever method works best for you. A popular arrangement is to place items in manila file folders that are labeled by topic. You might want to start with some broad categories and then later create subcategories when a folder starts overflowing. For articles that you clip or photocopy, be sure to write down the name of the publication and the date. For notes of interviews or speeches, write down the speaker, date, place, and occasion. You can start off by putting your file folders in a cardboard box; later, when your files become bulky, you can store them in a filing cabinet.

7

Supporting Your Ideas

▶ **Reasons for Using Support Materials**

▶ **Types of Support Materials**

Definitions / Description / Examples / Narratives / Comparison and Contrast / Testimony / Statistics /

In a classroom speech, a student whom I'll call Sam made an interesting point. "Violence on television," he contended, "causes some viewers to commit violent acts."

The reaction of the audience was undoubtedly skeptical. Some of the listeners were probably saying to themselves, "I don't believe it—prove it" or "Says who?" or "How do you know that?"

After making his assertion, Sam made these comments: "When people see violence night after night, they are going to become violent themselves. It's just common sense: seeing violence encourages people to act violently. How can you let impressionable children and teenagers watch murder, robbery, and brutality every night and then expect them not to imitate what they see?"

Do you think Sam's remarks convinced the audience that TV violence causes some viewers to become violent? Probably not. His remarks did nothing to bolster his contention. He offered no proof, no illustration, no support. All he did was repeat his original point.

Now imagine how the audience might have reacted if Sam had substantiated his assertion with these items:

▶ Following the telecast of the film *The Deer Hunter*, which showed a character playing a game of Russian roulette with a revolver, twenty-nine Americans killed themselves while "playing" Russian roulette, according to Dr. Jon M. Shepard, professor of sociology at the University of Kentucky.[1]

▶ A TV show depicted an alcoholic "bum" being doused with gasoline and set on fire; the next day three "winos" in three different American cities were murdered in similar fashion by youths who had seen the show, according to The Associated Press.[2]

▶ The National Institute of Mental Health evaluated 2500 studies on TV violence conducted over a 10-year period and concluded that "violence on television does lead to aggressive behavior."[3]

These items, which are samples of *support materials*, help back up the contention that TV violence causes some viewers to commit violent acts. The first two provide vivid examples, while the last item brings in testimony from a prestigious source. If Sam had used these support materials, his audience would have seen that his argument had merit.

Examples and testimony are just two of the kinds of support materials that we will discuss in this chapter. The others are definitions, descriptions, narratives, comparisons, contrasts, and statistics.

Reasons for Using Support Materials

Support materials enable you to move from general and abstract concepts, which are often hard for audiences to understand and remember, to specific and concrete details, which are easily grasped. Support materials add spice and flavor to a speech, but they are more than just seasonings; they are basic nourishment that is absolutely essential to the success of a speech. Below are five reasons why support materials are so important:

1. Support materials develop and illustrate ideas. In a speech on sharks, Austin Fitzgerald pointed out that unlike most creatures of the sea, sharks behave unpredictably. To develop and illustrate his point, he said:

> In his book on sharks, Jacques-Yves Cousteau, the famous oceanographer, says that he has seen sharks flee from an almost naked, completely unarmed diver, but soon afterward hurl themselves against a steel diving cage and bite furiously at the bars. Sometimes a diver can scare off a shark by waving his or her flippers at it, while at other times sharks are so determined to attack that they are not deterred by the sight of five divers with spears. The terrifying thing, Cousteau says, is that sharks never give clues as to what kind of behavior they will exhibit.

Without these examples, Fitzgerald's contention that sharks behave unpredictably would have been weak. With the examples, the listeners got a clear picture of sharks' volatile nature. Notice, too, that Fitzgerald enhanced the credibility of his remarks by attributing his information to a well-known authority.

2. Support materials can clarify ideas. Helping the listener make sense out of your ideas is one of the main reasons for using support material. Years ago I was taught a valuable fact about statistics by a professor who used a good example to make his point. He was trying to show the class why professional pollsters interviewed only 1000 registered voters in all of America in order to predict a presidential election. Why not interview 10,000? or 100,000? Would not a larger sample produce a more accurate prediction? No, said the professor, a small sample is just as accurate as a large one. To make his idea clear and understandable, he gave us a hypothetical example: Imagine that you place 100,000 coins in a rotating drum. Of that number, 70,000 are gold coins and the remaining 30,000 are silver coins. In another rotating drum you place 1000 coins, using the same proportion: 700 gold coins and 300 silver coins. You spin both drums, thoroughly mixing up the coins, and then you get a blindfolded man to reach in and randomly select 100 coins from each drum. The man will pull out 70 gold coins and

30 silver coins (or come very close to these numbers) every time he tries, even though one drum has a hundred times more coins than the other. This hypothetical example makes clear why a small sample in a public-opinion poll can be as accurate as a large one.

3. Support materials can make a speech more interesting. In a speech on how explorers from earth would experience life on Mars, Diane Weber said,

> Most of the time Mars is much colder than the coldest regions of earth, with summer temperatures dipping down as low as 126 degrees below zero and winter temperatures twice that cold. Sometimes, however, at the equator of Mars, the temperature does warm up to an earthly level of comfort. For a few minutes, the temperature can climb to a high of 68 degrees—sort of like a pleasant October afternoon in New England.

Instead of merely reciting statistics, which would have been boring, Weber made her subject interesting by comparing and contrasting the climate of the two planets, using images (such as the October afternoon in New England) that her listeners could appreciate.

4. Support materials help listeners remember key ideas. Jeffrey Scott, a high school English teacher, says that his students are more apt to remember the meanings of a word in a vocabulary lesson if they are told the story of the word's origin. For example, he tells his students that we get the word *tantalize* from the god Tantalus in Greek mythology: "As punishment for betraying Zeus, Tantalus was sentenced to hang from the branch of a fruit tree that spread out over a pool of water. Whenever he got hungry and reached for fruit, the wind would blow it out of his reach. Whenever he got thirsty and leaned over to drink from the pool, the water would recede." This story, Scott says, helps his students to remember that when we tantalize people, we torment them by showing something that is desirable but unattainable.

5. Support materials help prove an assertion. When you want to prove a point, you must have evidence. If, for example, you wanted to prove that more counterfeiters are being caught today than ever before, you could quote a Secret Service official who states that the number of counterfeiting convictions this year is ten times the number of convictions in any previous year. Such a statistic from a reliable source is solid proof of your statement.

But a note of caution: Not all support materials constitute proof. Suppose a speaker argues that flying saucers from alien planets visit the earth regularly, and to prove his claim, he cites fifteen eyewitness accounts from different parts of the country. Is this proof? No. While it may be true that flying saucers do indeed visit the earth, the fifteen eyewitness accounts do not constitute proof. Some of the people could have seen explainable phenomena, such as weather balloons or swamp-gas apparitions. Some of the individuals could have experienced hallucinations caused by drugs or psychosis.

Types of Support Materials

In this chapter we will look at *verbal* support materials, reserving *visual* supports for the next chapter. The cardinal rule in using verbal supports is that they must be relevant; they must develop, explain, illustrate, or reinforce your message. They cannot be thrown in simply to enliven a speech.

Let's examine seven categories of verbal supports.

Definitions

One of the biggest obstacles to successful communication is the assumption that your listeners define words and phrases the same way you do. If you are speaking on gun control, it is not enough to say, "I'm in favor of gun control." Exactly what does "gun control" mean? To some members of your audience, it may mean that citizens must surrender all their firearms. To others, it may mean that citizens must give up only their handguns. To still others, it may mean that citizens can keep their guns if they register them with the authorities. If you say that you are in favor of gun control without giving your definition of the term, some listeners might misunderstand your position and angrily reject everything that you say on the subject. So define your terms at the outset; for example: "When I talk about gun control, I'm not talking about confiscation of all guns; I'm talking about citizens registering the serial numbers of their guns with the authorities." Now you and your audience have a common basis for an evaluation of your views.

Define any jargon or specialized words that some listeners might not know. Don't assume, for example, that everyone knows military lingo such as KP and AWOL. Even though there have been dozens of movies and TV shows about military life, some people might not know that KP means "kitchen police" and AWOL means "absent without leave." If you are a computer buff, you must be careful to define concepts like RAM (random-access memory) and ROM (read-only memory) that are well-known to you but not to the general public.

Avoid dictionary definitions, if possible. They tend to be tedious and hard to grasp. Instead, use informal definitions that can be easily understood by the audience. Here is an instructive case: *Chutzpah*, a slang word that the English language has borrowed from Yiddish, is defined by the *Random House College Dictionary* as "unmitigated effrontery or impudence." I once heard a speaker give a humorous, informal definition of the word: "*Chutzpah* is the kind of audacity and gall that a youngster would show if he killed both of his parents and then demanded that the court be lenient to him because he was an orphan." This informal definition drives home the point that *chutzpah* is more than ordinary gall; it is the *ultimate* form of gall. Such a definition not only helps the listeners understand the meaning of the word; it also helps them remember it.

Description

Descriptions are verbal pictures created by using lots of details about objects, animals, people, places, or situations. Of his visit to a tropical rain forest in Brazil, environmental activist Don Campbell said:

> The forest had so many layers of vegetation that I couldn't see the top canopy of trees. Almost no light filtered down to the forest floor. It was unlike anything else on earth: almost all the vegetation was *above* me—lush thickets of ferns, vines, and orchids entwined in the trees. The animals were all *above* me—not only brightly colored birds but sloths hanging upside down from limbs, monkeys scampering from branch to branch, and snakes as big as the barrel of a tank. Once a quick and violent thunderstorm occurred directly overhead. I could hear the thunder but I couldn't see lightning. I could hear rain falling but it was so far above me, and there was so much vegetation, that it sounded faint. No water fell on top of me until about 10 minutes after the storm had ended. It took that long for the water to work its way down through the dense layers of leaves and plants.

Notice that Campbell used specific details to paint his word picture. Details are the brush strokes that provide richness, color, and vividness.

Examples

Examples are instances or facts that illustrate a statement or back up a generalization. In a speech on counterfeiting, Bob Lanelli made the following point:

> Sophisticated counterfeiters are careful not to pass bills that are crisp and new looking.

If Lanelli had said no more on the subject, he would have forced his listeners to guess for themselves just how counterfeiters go about aging their bogus money. Fortunately for the audience, he gave examples:

To get their phony money to look old, counterfeiters might put the bills in a washing machine with a combination of water and coffee. Or they might run them through a homemade device that crinkles them up and rubs in dirt at the same time. Or they might crumple each bill by hand and tear off a corner.

In some speeches you may want to give many examples. In a speech extolling the resilience and creativity of elderly people, newspaper columnist Gloria Santiago cited these accomplishments of men and women over the age of 65:

- ▶ Boris Pasternak, the Soviet novelist, won the Nobel Prize for Literature at the age of 68.
- ▶ Golda Meir became Prime Minister of Israel at 70.
- ▶ Colette, the French writer, published her famous novel *Gigi* at 71.
- ▶ Grandma Moses, the famous painter, had her first exhibition at 80.
- ▶ Barbara McClintock, an American scientist, won the Nobel Prize for Medicine at 81.
- ▶ Benjamin Franklin helped frame the Constitution of the United States at 81.
- ▶ Arturo Toscanini of Italy was a vigorous orchestra conductor at 86.
- ▶ Pablo Picasso, the Spanish artist, painted several masterpieces at 87.
- ▶ Konrad Adenauer was Chancellor of West Germany at 87.
- ▶ Helen Keller, who lost her hearing and sight at age 2, wrote and lectured until her death at 88.

How many examples do you need to develop a point? In some cases, one example is sufficient, while other situations might require a series of examples. Ask yourself, "If I were those people sitting out there, how many examples would I need in order to understand, remember, or be convinced?"

Narratives

Narratives, which are stories that explain or illustrate your message, are audience favorites, lingering in the mind long after a speech has ended. People *love* stories, and even a sleepy or distracted member of the audience finds it hard to resist listening. As with all support materials, narratives must be relevant to your message. Never tell a story, even though it is a spellbinding tale, if it fails to develop, explain, illustrate, or reinforce your key ideas.

Dr. Barbara Wilensky, a psychiatrist who specializes in mood disorders, gave a speech on bipolar disorder (often known as manic-depressive illness) and included this story:

A barber whom I'll call Jones was in his mid-forties when he had his first episode of manic behavior. He woke up early one Sunday morning and threw on his clothes in a frenzy. Too agitated to eat breakfast, he told his wife that he was going to his shop to make major changes. He said he was going to become a millionaire within a few months and that the two of them could spend the rest of their lives traveling around the world in grand style. When he drove away, his wife noticed that he was traveling at a dangerously high speed. A few hours later, she went to his barber shop and found him with a sledgehammer, tearing down walls. "I'm expanding," he shouted. "Two chairs aren't enough for me. I'm going to put in twenty-five chairs and cut everybody's hair in town. I'll be a millionaire!" He laughed loudly and began to sing with feverish gusto. Unable to "talk sense" to him, Mrs. Jones telephoned relatives for help. When Mr. Jones' brother-in-law arrived, he tried to take away the sledgehammer, but this enraged Jones and a fistfight ensued. Finally, the police were called. Jones resisted arrest, and three officers were needed to subdue him. He was taken to jail and then transferred to a psychiatric hospital.

Notice that Dr. Wilensky's narrative was filled with details, giving you a sense of what this illness is like. Details give richness and color to narratives, painting a picture that listeners can see.

While Dr. Wilensky's story was factual, there are occasions when you may want to use a narrative that is *hypothetical*, that is, about an imaginary situation. Here is an example from a speech by Coretta Johnson:

You are riding along the highway when you see a two-car collision 50 yards in front of you. You pull over and park, and then run to offer help. You realize that you're the first to arrive at the scene of the accident, and you hear a person inside one of the cars screaming for help. What should you do?

By means of this hypothetical story, Johnson made her point—that all citizens need to know what to do if they arrive first at the scene of an accident. By putting her listeners squarely in the middle of her narrative, Johnson increased the audience's curiosity and involvement. Then, of course, she gave the steps that should be taken: Don't move the victims unless there is an imminent danger of the car's exploding, keep them calm and comfortable, administer first aid if they are bleeding or choking, and call an ambulance.

Comparison and Contrast

Sometimes the best way to explain a thing or a concept is to make a *comparison*, that is, show how it resembles something else. In a lecture on the development of the English language, a speaker noted the following similarities:

Just as scientists use the technique of comparison and contrast in the laboratory, a public speaker can help listeners understand a concept by showing similarities and differences between two or more things.

The Frisian language, spoken by 300,000 Frisians in the marshy headlands of northern Holland, is more closely related to English than any other language. Our *glass of milk* is their *glass milk*, our *butter* is their *butter*, our *dream* is their *dream*, our *boat* is their *boat*, our *green* is their *grien*, our *house* is their *hus*, our *cow* is their *ko*, our *goose* is their *goes*, our *sunshine* is their *sinneskine*. . .

By giving many points of comparison, the speaker strongly illustrated how similar the two languages are.

While a comparison shows how things are similar, a *contrast* shows how they are different. In the lecture just cited, the speaker made a contrast between the early insignificance of the English language and its current preeminence as a global language:

In his TV series *The Story of English*, Robert MacNeil points out that when Julius Caesar and his Roman troops landed in Britain 2000 years ago, English did not exist. Move forward in time 500 years—to the time of the fall of the Western Roman Empire—and you find an early form of English spoken by only a few thousand people. Move forward 1000 more years—near the time of Shakespeare—and you find English spoken by only 6 million people, all of them living in England. Move forward 500 more years—to the present day—and the contrast is amazing. English is used in all parts of the globe as the mother language of 400 million people and as the second language of another 400 million. It has become the language most often used for international business, science, medicine, and transportation.

Sometimes it is helpful to use both comparison and contrast. For example, comparing and contrasting Japanese and American cars could help the listener understand more fully the features of each.

Testimony

Suppose for a moment that one of your fellow students gives a speech on America's jury system, and she tells you that the method of selecting and using jurors in most communities is inefficient, overly expensive, and demoralizing to the jurors. Would you believe her? Probably not, if all she gave was her personal opinion—after all, she is not a lawyer or a judge. But what if she quoted the Chief Justice of the U.S. Supreme Court saying the exact same thing? Now would you believe her? You probably would, because the Chief Justice is one of the nation's experts on what happens in our courts.

When you use what knowledgeable people have to say on your subject, you are using *testimony* to back up your assertions. The main advantage of using testimony is that it gives you instant credibility; quoting an expert is a way of saying, "I'm not the only one who has this idea; it has the backing of a leading authority on the subject."

There are three ways of using testimony:

1. Quote verbatim.   Sometimes it is effective to quote a source word for word. For example, Lorraine Vallejo made the following point in a speech on dreams:

> For all of us, dreams are weird, chaotic, and crazy. An expert on dreams, Dr. William Dement says: "Dreaming permits each and every one of us to be quietly and safely insane every night of our lives."

Quoting the expert verbatim was very effective because the statement was phrased in a colorful way that would have been weakened if it had been paraphrased.

2. Summarize.   When a statement is lengthy, quoting it verbatim can bore the audience, and so it is best to summarize any quotation that is more than one or two sentences. In another part of Vallejo's speech, she took long quotation and boiled it down into one brief sentence:

Sigmund Freud believed that dreams reflect unconscious wishes and urges that we are afraid to think about during our daytime waking hours.

3. *Paraphrase.* If a quotation has archaic or technical language or is laced with jargon, you should paraphrase it. If, for example, you are speaking on computers and you want to quote an expert who says, "Don't buy a software package that doesn't have help menus," you can paraphrase this jargon into plain English by saying, "Don't buy a program for your computer unless it has lists of options on the screen to keep you from getting lost or confused."

Here are four guidelines for using testimony:

1. *Make sure quotations are accurate.* If you are not careful with a quotation, you can unwittingly change its meaning. For example, Ralph Waldo Emerson is often quoted as saying, "Consistency is the hobgoblin of little minds." That is an unfortunate misquotation. What he really said is quite different in meaning: "A foolish consistency is the hobgoblin of little minds." With the misquotation, consistency itself is condemned, but with the correct quotation, only a *foolish* consistency is deemed stupid.

2. *Use testimony from unbiased sources.* Ethical speakers avoid using sources that are biased. Suppose you are researching the question of whether polygraphs (lie detectors) are accurate, and you come across glowing pro-polygraph statements by two "experts" who are on the payroll of a firm that manufactures polygraph machines. Could you expect such sources to be unbiased? Of course not. They would probably lose their jobs if they said anything negative about the machines. Reject such "evidence" and look instead for statements by people who have no vested interest in the issue.

3. *Use testimony that your audience will respect.* As part of your pre-speech audience analysis, ask yourself, "What kind of expert would this particular audience believe?" If you are speaking on foreign policy, for example, and you have a good quotation from a movie star, would your audience consider the star's views irrelevant? If so, quoting the star might weaken, rather than strengthen, your case.

4. *State the credentials of your source.* If you quote a famous person like Abraham Lincoln, you obviously don't need to give any background information about the person. But for authorities who are not well known, be sure to give some biographical data to establish their credibility. For example, "Jack Smithson, who spent 25 years as a research scientist for NASA, says that . . . ."

Statistics

For a speech explaining the immense distances of space, Paula Schiller began with some mind-boggling facts:

> Proxima Centauri, the star that is closest to our solar system, is only 4.28 light years away. That doesn't sound like a very great distance, does it? Is there any chance that we can reach that star—or one of its planets—in our lifetime? Before you start fantasizing about being the first human to travel to our nearest star, consider this fact: if you traveled to Proxima Centauri in the fastest spacecraft now in existence, it would take you *40,000 years* to make the trip.

Schiller was using *statistics*, which are numerical ways of expressing information. As illustrated in this example, statistics don't have to be dry and boring. They can be made interesting and even exciting.

Statistics can be especially effective in persuading an audience to accept a particular point. In our society, people put a lot of trust in statistics. If a television commercial says that 78 percent of physicians prefer Cure-All pain reliever over all competing brands, many consumers will rush out to buy Cure-All.

In a speech in which she tried to persuade her audience to drive their cars less and walk more, Carol Morris wanted to prove that the fitness of Americans has been weakened by the automobile. She could have made a vague statement such as: "Because of the automobile, we Americans are getting soft and flabby." Instead, she gave a fascinating statistic to prove her point: "Since the advent of the auto, the average waistline of American adults has increased one inch every generation." That single statistic, short and surprising, was one of the most persuasive parts of her speech.

▶ **Understanding Statistics**

Although statistics can provide powerful support for ideas, they can be easily misused, either willfully or through carelessness or ignorance. Unfortunately, there is much truth in the old statement, "You can prove anything with statistics." To understand how statistics are used (and abused), let's look at several of the more popular varieties.

Averages. The most popular kind of statistic is the average. It can provide interesting views of a subject, as when one speaker pointed out, "On an average day, twenty-four mail carriers in the U.S. receive animals bites." Giving the average in a case like this is much more interesting than simply stating the annual total.

Though averages seem like straightforward pieces of statistical data, there are pitfalls. Most people are unaware that there are actually three differen kinds of averages—the mean, the median, and the mode. To understand these terms, consider the following numbers:

49   32   24   23   18   18   18

The *mean*, which is what most people use when they are asked to compute an average, is derived by adding the numbers (for a total of 182) and dividing by how many numbers there are (7). This gives us 26 as the mean.

The *median* is derived by listing the numbers, ranging from highest to lowest, and then locating the number that falls in the middle. In this case 23 is precisely in the middle, so it is our median.

The *mode* is simply the figure that occurs most frequently, in this case 18.

Since all three of these can be called an "average," problems arise in communicating information. Suppose a company is made up of a president with an annual salary of $290,000; a vice president with a salary of $170,000; three managers with salaries of $50,000 each, and twenty workers with wages of $20,000 each. What is the average income of the people who work at this company? If one uses the *mean* as the average, the answer is derived by totaling the salaries and dividing by 25 (the total number of figures)— $40,400. The *median* is derived by listing the salaries in a column, ranging from highest to lowest, and then locating the salary that falls in the middle: $20,000. The *mode* is simply the figure that occurs most frequently: $20,000.

Now suppose that the company had a labor-management dispute. In an interview with the press, the president could say, "I don't see what the workers are complaining about. The average income in this company is $40,400." And she would be correct, since she chose to use the *mean* as her version of average. A representative of the workers, on the other hand, could say "We are paid an average of only $20,000," and this would be correct, since the *median* is also a kind of average.

Percentages.   Giving a percentage (a portion of one hundred) can be a useful way to make a point. For example, suppose that you find that 2 percent of the 1000 employees in a company are physically handicapped, and yet only 1 percent of the parking spaces have been designated for the handicapped. With these figures, you can make a good argument for increasing the number of spaces for the handicapped.

Unfortunately percentages can be misleading. A television commercial might say, "Eighty percent of the doctors interviewed said they recommend Feel Good medicated tablets for their patients." How many doctors were involved? If only ten doctors were interviewed, and eight of them gave the endorsement, the commercial is accurate (eight out of ten amounts to 80 percent) but misleading.

The following statement is true: In one recent year Switzerland experienced a 50 percent jump in unemployment, causing that nation to rank number one in the world in the percentage increase of unemployed over the previous year. Sounds terrible, doesn't it? Sounds as if the prosperous little country is sliding toward economic catastrophe. But here is another way of reporting the facts: In the year cited, there were fifty-one jobless persons in Switzerland as compared to thirty-four in the previous year. This represents a 50 percent increase, but when you look at the actual number of people involved, there is obviously no reason for the Swiss to be alarmed.

Correlations.   The term *correlation* is used to show the relationship between two sets of data. Let's say that I have two sets of data concerning you and twenty of your friends: I have the scores (or IQs) from an intelligence test that all of you took, and I also have your grade-point averages. When I compare the two sets of data, I find that for most of you, the higher the IQ, the higher the grade-point average. I can now state that there is a high correlation between the two sets of data. This should be no surprise: For most people in our society, the higher the IQ, the greater the level of academic achievement. Statisticians would say that IQ scores and grade-point averages are highly correlated.

Now let's suppose that I compare the IQ scores with the shoe sizes of you and your friends. Will I find that the larger the foot, the higher the IQ? No, of course not. Will I find that the smaller the foot, the higher the IQ? Again, no. There is absolutely no pattern to observe—no correspondence between foot size and intelligence. In the language of statisticians, there is no correlation at all.

Correlation is a handy statistical device because it can help us predict outcomes for individuals. Because we know that a high correlation exists between amount of daily, vigorous exercise and longevity, medical experts can predict that a person who jogs regularly will probably live longer than someone who doesn't exercise.

Correlation, however, is often misunderstood and misused because some people think that it proves a cause-and-effect relationship. Just because two sets of data are correlated does not necessarily mean that one causes the other. For example, some medical researchers once thought that drinking milk might cause cancer because they found a high correlation between milk consumption and the incidence of cancer in some European countries, while finding a rarity of that disease in Asian nations where milk consumption is low. When the researchers analyzed their data, however, they found that third factor was involved: Cancer most often strikes people who are over 4 years old; most of the people studied in the poor Asian nations did not live long enough to get the disease. So a correlation between milk consumption and cancer does exist (people who drink a lot of milk have high cancer rates) but there is no cause-and-effect relationship (the milk is not what cause cancer).

▶ Guidelines for Using Statistics

Here are some guidelines to consider when you are evaluating statistics for possible use in a speech:

Use statistics fairly and honestly.   Sometimes a statistic is true, but it is cited in such a way as to leave a false impression. A favorite ploy of unethical politicians is to make an accusation like this: "While my opponent has occupied the office of governor, state tax revenues have shot up 30 percent." To many voters hearing that statistic on TV (and seeing the accompanying graph), it sounds as if the governor has hiked their taxes. The truth is that tax revenues have gone up because they are tied to rising income— not because the tax *rate* went up. In reality, the governor should be cheered for the dramatic rise in personal income, but her opponent has used a clever 20-second TV commercial to discredit her. Notice that the statistic is true; the opponent cannot be charged with falsifying information.

When you prepare a speech, be sure to analyze a statistic for its true significance. For example, if you look at employment figures and notice a big drop in employment from December to January, does that mean the country is headed for depression and ruin? No, it does not. If you look at previous years, you will see that because of the Christmas shopping season, employment always goes up in December and then dips down in January. It would be unethical, then, for you to cite the one-month drop as an indication of economic decline.

Make sure that your sources for statistics are unbiased. If a pharmaceutical company comes out with a new drug which it claims is 100 percent effective in eliminating migraine headaches, you would be wise to treat the claim with skepticism. Look for an evaluation by a source that has no vested interest in the product—such as a university medical school.

Use statistics sparingly.   If you use a large number of statistics, it is hard for the audience to absorb them. Be very selective, and choose only a few to make a point.

Poor: The United States has a population of 260 million people. California has 29 million, 900 thousand; New York has 18 million, 100 thousand; Texas has 17 million, 100 thousand; Florida has 13 million, 100 thousand; Pennsylvania has 12 million; Illinois has 11 million, 600 thousand; Ohio has 11 million; Michigan has 9 million, 400 thousand, and New Jersey has 7 million, 800 thousand. These nine states have half of the total U.S. population.

Better: The United States has a population of 260 million people. Half of these people live in just nine states. In rank order, these nine states are California, New York, Texas, Florida, Pennsylvania, Illinois, Ohio, Michigan, and New Jersey.

The statistics in the first version would be fine in a written essay, but in a speech all those figures would be hard for the audience to follow. The second version, streamlined and simple, would be easier for the audience to digest.

Round off long numbers.   In print, a long number is no problem, but in a speech, it is hard for the listener to absorb the information. A rounded-off number is easy to say and easy for the audience to grasp.

> *Poor:* Attendance at major league baseball games last year was 44,587,874.
> *Better:* Attendance at major league baseball games last year was about 45 million.

Translate your statistics into vivid, meaningful language.   If you have a statistic that would be meaningless to most listeners, translate it into language they can understand. If you are explaining disk drives to a group of listeners who know very little about computers, don't just say that a particular fixed-disk drive has a storage capacity of 20 megabytes. Convert that into information the listeners can easily grasp: "On a 20-megabyte fixed disk, you can store the equivalent of over 10,000 double-spaced typewritten pages." The listeners can visualize 10,000 sheets of paper; now they understand that you are talking about a huge amount of storage space.

One speaker, Diane McDaniel, found a fascinating way to illustrate how cutting down on a few calories each day can result in substantial weight losses:

> If you want to lose weight, you don't have to go on a crash diet; you can shed a lot of pounds by altering your eating habits in very small ways. For example, if you eat just one pat less of butter every day, you will lose three and a half pounds in one year. If you cut out one piece of cake a week, you will lose five pounds in a year. If you omit two slices of bacon from breakfast each week, you will lose one and a half pounds in a year.

This interpretation of statistics was much more interesting to the audience than a recital of calories per food would have been.

Adapt statistics to your particular audience.   Whenever possible, adapt your statistics to the needs and interests of your particular audience. Imagine that you are planning a speech on Alaska, and you want to give your audience an idea of that state's immense size. All you need to do is take a pocket calculator with you to the library, look up the areas of states in a reference work like the *World Almanac*, and make a few simple calculations. If you live in California, for example, you could give your audience a sense of Alaska's size by saying, "You can put three Californias inside Alaska's borders and still have room left over for Oregon."

Relate statistics to familiar objects.   One way to make statistics dramatic is to relate them to something familiar. In a speech on bats, Sally Ingle wanted to give the audience an idea of the incredible smallness of one variety of bat. Instead of giving its weight in grams, which would have meant little to most of the audience, she said, "One variety of bat is so tiny that when it is full-grown, it weighs less than a penny." Knowing the lightness of a penny, the audience could easily get a notion of the smallness of the bat.

Since everyone in America has a clear visual image of the width and length of a football field, it is convenient to use the field as a point of reference for size and distance. To show that a baseball diamond uses more space than one would suspect from its appearance, you could say, "The distance that a homerun hitter travels around the bases is 60 feet more than the length of a football field." To show the smallness of a basketball court, you could say, "A regulation court, if placed on a football field, will extend from the goal line to the thirty-one-yard line; its width will cover less than a third of the field."

Summary

Verbal support materials are vital to the success of a speech. They develop, illustrate, and clarify ideas; they make a speech more interesting and meaningful, and they can help prove an assertion. Some of the more popular types of verbal supports are definitions, description, examples, narratives, comparisons, contrasts, testimony, and statistics.

Of all these types, the narrative (or story) is the favorite of most audiences. People love to hear stories and are more apt to remember them than most other parts of your speech. As with all support materials, you must make sure that a narrative explains, illustrates, or reinforces the message of your speech. Telling a story that is irrelevant to the subject is not appropriate in informative and persuasive speaking.

Statistics such as averages, percentages, and correlations can be useful in a speech, but you must be careful to use them accurately and fairly. Adapt statistics to your particular audience, making them as interesting and as meaningful as possible.

Review Questions

1. List five reasons why support materials are important in a speech.
2. Why are informal definitions usually superior to dictionary definitions in a speech?

3. "The human brain is like an incredibly sophisticated computer." Is this sentence an example of a comparison or a contrast?

4. What is the main advantage of using testimony in a speech?

5. The boss of a small firm has an annual salary of $100,000. Each of his thirteen employees makes $12,000 a year. Give the average salary of the firm in terms of *mean*, *median*, and *mode*.

6. Whenever tar on asphalt roads gets hot enough to bubble on a summer day, the incidence of heat exhaustion among citizens goes up. In other words, there is a strong correlation between bubbling tar and heat exhaustion. Does the correlation prove that tar fumes cause people to pass out? Explain your answer.

TIPS FOR YOUR CAREER

TIP 7.1: Let Your Subconscious Mind Help You Prepare Speeches

Many speechmakers rely upon their subconscious mind to help them prepare speeches. The subconscious is the part of the mind that simmers beneath the surface of awareness. It is especially active at night, when it creates dreams, but it is also active during the day, when it occasionally floats an idea up to the surface of our minds. You probably have had the experience of wrestling with a problem, then later, while you were taking a walk or driving your car and not consciously thinking of the matter, a good solution suddenly appeared in your mind like a flash of light—your subconscious mind had continued to work until it found a solution.

The subconscious mind can provide you with topics, support materials, and organizational patterns, but unfortunately it cannot be ordered to perform like a trained dog. It is unpredictable, often mysterious, and usually requires a lot of time. Nevertheless, there are four things you can do to take advantage of this creative process.

1. Supply raw materials. The subconscious cannot spin cloth out of thin air. You must fill your mind with information. Read, do research, conduct interviews.

2. Allow time to elapse. Sometimes you must allow a few days—or even a few weeks or months—to give the subconscious ample time to incubate your ideas. This is where the subconscious is most unpredictable—it's hard to forecast how long the process will take. (*Note:* In order for the subconscious to work for classroom speeches, choose your topic and do your research far in advance of your speech date.)

3. Get away from deliberate mental activity. For some reason the subconscious transmits its ideas when your mind is disengaged from rational, conscious work. In other words, don't sit at your desk and flog your brain for ideas.

Go for a walk or take a ride in your car. Forget about whatever you've been working on. Once you "let go," you will often be happily surprised to have an idea suddenly well up from your subconscious. Relaxation seems to unlock the subconscious. Thornton Wilder, a Pulitzer Prize–winning playwright, reported that his best ideas came to him on hikes or in the shower, but never at his desk. Joe W. Boyd, a professional speaker from Bellingham, Washington, says, "I get my best topics when I'm exercising (running) or driving long distances. The topics just seem to flow into my mind."

4. Be prepared to record ideas. Because ideas from the subconscious often come at odd times (when you are climbing out of bed, driving to work, or walking across campus between classes), keep paper and pen with you at all times to get these ideas down. If you don't seize an idea at once, it might slip away and be gone forever.

Margaret McFadden, a business executive, uses her subconscious in a process she calls "living with" a speech. "As soon as I receive an invitation to speak," she says, "I choose my topic and do whatever research I need to do. Then I 'live' with my speech for a few weeks. Wherever I go—to work, to the store, to the beach—I find myself thinking about the speech. Not fretting or brooding, just playing with ideas. I carry a pad with me and jot down the ideas as they come to me. At the end of each day, I drop the notes into a manila folder. After a few weeks, I sit down at my desk, pull out the folder of notes, and organize my material into an outline. Usually everything just falls into place."

Everything falls into place because her subconscious mind has been busy for weeks, sorting and editing the materials.

Visual Aids

▶ **Reasons for Using Visual Aids**

▶ **Types of Visual Aids**

Graphs / Charts / Drawings / Photographs / Computer Graphics / Objects / Models / Yourself /

▶ **Media for Visual Aids**

Boards / Posters / Flip Charts / Handouts / Overhead Transparencies / Slides / Videotapes /

▶ **Guidelines for Using Visual Aids**

Choose Visual Aids That Truly Support Your Speech / Prepare and Practice Far in Advance / Don't Use Too Many Visuals / Make Visual Aids Simple and Clear / Make Sure Everyone Can See Your Visuals / Explain Visual Aids / Don't Let Visuals Distract from Your Message / Don't Talk to Your Visual Aid / Use Progressive Revelation / Plan for Emergencies /

For several months, Megan Kennerly, a dental hygienist, tried telling her patients how to floss their teeth correctly, but "most of them didn't really catch on." Then she began coupling her instructions with a demonstration, using a string (to represent dental floss) and a large model of a row of teeth. As a result, her patients were able to understand, remember, and apply her instructions.

What Kennerly discovered is that oral instructions alone are not as effective as oral instructions combined with a visual aid. This insight has been confirmed by the research of Robert Craig, chief of the U.S. Public Health Service audiovisual facility. He found that people who were taught orally could remember only 10 percent of the information three days later, but people who were taught orally and visually could recall 65 percent of the information three days later.[1]

Because most people have grown up with television and therefore are conditioned to learn things by means of visual images, visual aids are considered a vital part of most business and professional presentations today. The attitude throughout society is: "Don't tell me, show me."

Reasons for Using Visual Aids

While Chapter 7 dealt with *verbal* supports, this chapter will examine *visual* supports for a speech. Let's examine some reasons for using visual supports.

Visual aids can make your ideas clear and understandable.   Mary Callahan gave a speech on how the United States government, when printing paper currency, uses complicated techniques that prevent counterfeiters from producing perfect imitations. Using a slide of a greatly enlarged dollar bill, she pointed out intricate designs and clever nuances that most people never would have dreamed existed. Without the blown-up dollar, her explanations would have been hard to follow. With the slide, her remarks were lucid and easy to grasp.

Visual aids can make your speech more interesting.   Li Yang, a foreign student from Mauritius, showed slides to supplement his talk on his native country, which is an island in the Indian Ocean. To illustrate the geographical diversity of Mauritius, Yang showed beautiful views of sparkling beaches and majestic mountains. To illustrate the racial and ethnic diversity of the island, he showed slides of citizens in a marketplace. There were also pictures of wind surfing and dancing. All in all, the slides took the audience on a vicarious trip to an exotic land and enhanced the speech.

Visual aids can help the audience remember facts and details.   Research shows that visual aids help a listener retain ideas.[2] During his speech on Mauritius, Yang showed a map of the world, on which he pinpointed his tiny country's location in the Indian Ocean. As we all do with visual aids, I took a mental snapshot of the map, which will help me remember where Mauritius is located.

Visual aids can make long, complicated explanations unnecessary.   If you watch professional basketball on TV, you see a coach call a time-out to set up one last play, with only seconds remaining in the game. He does not have time to explain to each player the complex pattern of the play, but he uses a miniature basketball court with little magnetic buttons representing the players. He moves the buttons about to show the players where they should run and what they should do. The players nod their assent, walk out onto the court, and execute the play as they saw it on the miniature board. The coach's visual aid saves time and makes a long, complicated explanation unnecessary.

Visual aids can help prove a point.   A representative of Leica, the German camera manufacturer, once gave a talk to a group of photographers. He maintained that the body of the Leica (not the lens) could be dropped on a concrete floor without suffering any damage; in fact, he said, it could be dropped out the window (the group was on the third floor) to the sidewalk below and it would still function as well as ever. To prove his point, he sent the entire audience down to the sidewalk. The group formed a semicircle and watched as he dropped the camera from the third floor to the sidewalk. Sure enough, the camera was undamaged. He challenged the photographers to take pictures with the camera if they doubted his claim. Most speakers don't have such dramatic visual aids, but even simple aids like graphs and drawings can help prove a point. As the old saying goes, "Seeing is believing."

Visual aids can add to your personal credibility.   When you display good visuals during a speech, the audience is impressed, for it is obvious you have spent time and energy in order to make the speech interesting and understandable. Researchers at the University of Pennsylvania found that presenters who used visual aids were rated by listeners as "better prepared, more professional, more persuasive, more credible, and more interesting" than presenters who used no visuals.[3] But other research also needs to be mentioned as a warning. If listeners think that your visual aids are poor, their confidence in you falls off.[4] In other words, you are better off using no visual aids at all than poor ones.

Types of Visual Aids

► Graphs

Graphs help audiences understand and retain statistical data. The *line graph* should be a familiar form to all college students because it is widely used in textbooks. It uses a horizontal and a vertical scale to show the relationship between two variables, as in Figure 8.1.

The *bell-shaped curve* for normal distribution is a feature known to many people through such statistical graphs as IQ scores in the general population. This curve can be used in symbolic ways (instead of being expressed only in mathematical terms), as Figure 8.2 demonstrates.

A *bar graph* is an easy way to show a great deal of data in a clear, easily comprehended manner. This kind of graph enables you to show comparisons within groups, as in Figure 8.3.

A *pie graph* is a circle representing 100 percent. It is easy for the audience to understand as long as there are not too many different "pieces" of pie. A textbook could have a pie graph with twenty different pieces because the reader would have ample time to analyze them, but a pie graph in a speech

TIPS FOR YOUR CAREER

TIP 8.1: Never Let Visuals Substitute for a Speech

Because visual aids are so powerful, some speakers let them dominate a speech—the visuals become the real show, with the speaker acting as a mere technician. It is easy for this to happen, especially if you have some dazzling slides or a spectacular video. The punch and glitz of the visuals make you feel inadequate, and you think you ought to step aside and let the graphics take command. This attitude is a mistake, as is shown by the experience of Preston Bradley, vice president of Graystone Corporation:

Several years ago I made a presentation in which I used a commercially produced videotape. Thinking that the audience would prefer animated, full-color images to my words, I let the videotape take up most of the time; I merely added a few comments at the end and fielded a few questions. Later, several listeners told me that the videotape had been far less helpful than my remarks, and they recommended that in the future I talk more and use videotape less. The reason: during my informal talk I was able to explain tough concepts and interact with the audience. The videotape, on the other hand, zipped along, incapable of sensing whether the audience was absorbing the information.

People can see electronic bedazzlements on television at any hour of the day, but a speech has a dimension that TV lacks—a living, breathing human engaged in the stimulating act of direct communication. Don't let visuals rob your speech of aliveness and rapport.

FIGURE 8.1

In a speech on opportunities for women a speaker used a line graph to show that the number of Ph.D. degrees earned by women is expected to exceed those earned by men in the year 2000. (Source: The speaker adapted the graph from one that appeared in *U.S. News & World Report*, Jan. 1, 1990)

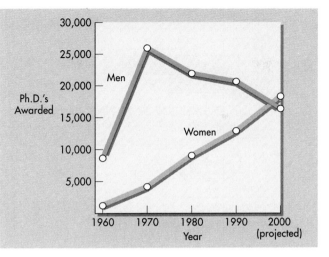

FIGURE 8.2

This is a graphic representation of the Yerkes-Dodson law in psychology. One speaker used this graph to discuss the anxiety that students experience in taking tests. At point A, people are asleep—no nervousness or anxiety, no mental performance. At point B, people are alert because they have a small amount of tension; their performance on tests is moderately good. At point C, people have a moderate amount of nervousness, and so their performance is at its peak. At point D, the nervousness is acute and the test-taking performance is beginning to falter. At point E, panic and mental disorganization have set in and performance is zero. The purpose of the graph is to show that a moderate amount of nervousness or anxiety while taking a test is desirable. (This graph could also be used to demonstrate the point made in Chapter 3: A moderate amount of nervous energy during a speech is ideal for effective speechmaking.)

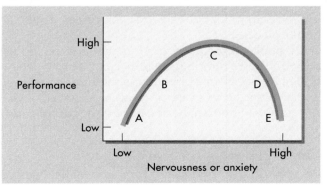

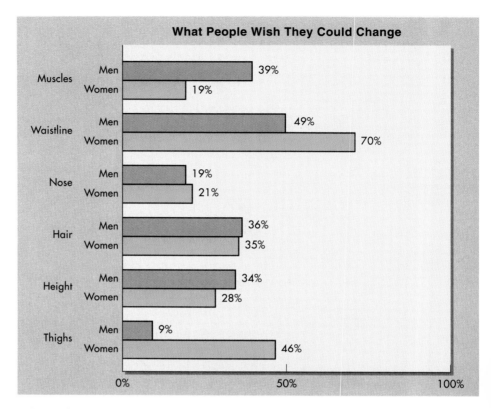

FIGURE 8.3

In a survey on self-esteem, pollster Louis Harris found that the vast majority (96 percent) of the American people were unhappy with their physical appearance and wished they could change the way they looked. This bar graph shows the percentages of men and women who cited various aspects of their appearance that they would change if they could. (Source: Louis Harris, Inside America, *New York, Random House, 1987)*

should have no more than six or seven pieces. Figure 8.4 shows a pie graph with four pieces.

Of all graphs, a *pictorial graph* is perhaps the easiest to read, because it visually translates information into a picture that can be grasped instantaneously. Figure 8.5 is an example of a pictorial graph.

You need not be an artist to create a pictorial graph. Anyone can draw a representation of human figures, even if they are as primitive as those shown in Figure 8.6.

▶ **Charts**

Charts provide information in a compact, easily digested form. An *organization chart* can be used to show a hierarchy in a business or agency. We are

FIGURE 8.4
This pie graph shows how much sleep adult Americans get each night, according to a Harris Survey. The most surprising finding is that one person out of four sleeps 6 hours or less per night. (Source: Louis Harris, *Inside America,* New York, Random House, 1987)

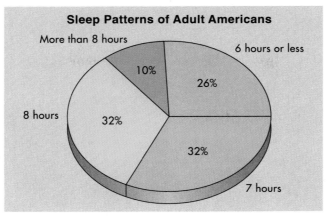

Sleep Patterns of Adult Americans

More than 8 hours — 10%
6 hours or less — 26%
8 hours — 32%
7 hours — 32%

familiar with charts that show the president of the company at the top and lines of authority going downward. A *flowchart* shows the flow, or sequence, of related events. (See Chapter 3, Figure 3.1, for a flowchart showing two possible sequences of events that can happen to a nervous speaker.) Figure 8.7 shows a flowchart that explains the collection of radio waves from outer space.

FIGURE 8.5
To show that elephants in Africa are endangered, one speaker used this pictorial graph. When listeners were told that each elephant figure represented 100,000 elephants, they were able to grasp the immensity of the deaths caused by poachers and ivory hunters. (Source: United Nations Environment Program)

Elephant Population of Africa

1980	1990	2000 (projected)

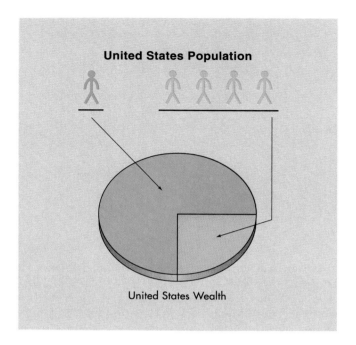

FIGURE 8.6
*One speaker used five humans to represent the popula-
tion of the United States and pointed out that the rich-
est one-fifth of the population (one person out of five)
owns or controls three-quarters of the wealth of the nation. The other four-fifths of the population (four out of
five persons) share the remaining one-fourth of U.S.
wealth. These simple stick figures demonstrate that one
need not be an artist to make pictorial graphs. (The
speaker used statistics from the U.S. Bureau of Census,
1991.)*

FIGURE 8.7
*A speaker used this flowchart to show how radio waves from outer space are col-
lected and analyzed. She needed no labels because she explained the flowchart
during her speech. Starting on the left, distant stars emit electromagnetic radiation—or radio waves (shown by wavy lines)—which is collected by the radio tele-
scope dish. The waves are processed by a radio receiver (first box shown) and
converted into electrical signals (the final box shows a graph of signal strength).*

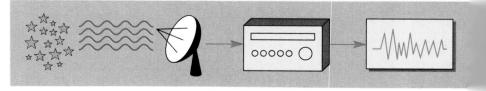

An *information chart*, also called a *list of key ideas*, is a convenient way to show main points or steps in a process. Figure 8.8 shows a good technique for presenting a list.

While the main advantage of a list is obvious—it helps the audience follow your speech and remember salient points—there is a less obvious advantage: a list stimulates audience involvement. "Audiences love lists," says advertising executive Ron Hoff. "Tell people you have six things for them to do and they will instinctively pick up their pencils and start writing. It must be a carryover from high school. Or some kind of deep-rooted association of lists with matters of substance. A list . . . communicates nonverbally, 'Here's something you'd better remember.' "[5] Hoff recommends that you tell the listeners how many items are on your list (for example, "Here are the three

FIGURE 8.8

A list of key ideas can be placed on transparencies, slides, or posters. If possible, display only one item at a time so that listeners stay with you and don't read ahead.

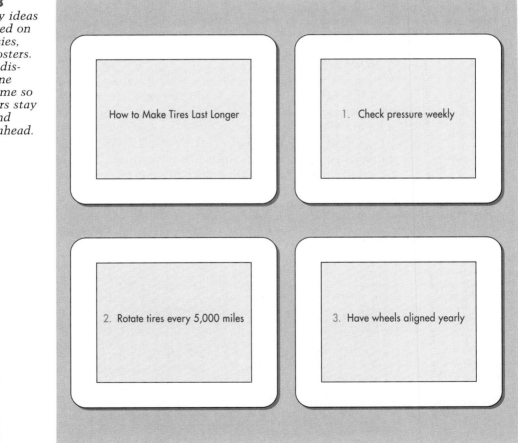

How to Make Tires Last Longer

1. Check pressure weekly

2. Rotate tires every 5,000 miles

3. Have wheels aligned yearly

steps to follow when you give first aid to a burn victim"). "It's magic," Hoff says, "Note-taking will accelerate like crazy. You'll *feel* the activity in the room—bodies moving forward in their chairs, pages of notepads being flipped, papers being rustled in the search for pencils and pens. The place comes *alive*."[6]

An information chart can sometimes be created in the form of a *table*, which presents information in rows and columns. Figure 8.9 shows how easy to understand a table can be.

For lists or tables, here are some suggestions:

Read the item to the audience. Reading the item aloud ensures that the listeners stay with you. Also, it gives them time to jot down the item if they are taking notes.

Don't distribute a handout with a lengthy list or table on it *during a speech.* A detailed handout, warns Hoff, "gets people involved in reading instead of being led by you. It's often difficult to get their attention back."[7] (A fuller discussion of handouts will be given later in this chapter.)

▶ **Drawings**

Drawings make good visual aids because they can illustrate points that would be hard to explain in words. For example, telling an audience how to jump-start a dead battery would be difficult without a drawing, such as that in Figure 8.10.

One kind of drawing that is highly effective is a map. By sketching a map yourself, you can include only those features that are pertinent to your speech. If you were speaking on the major rivers of America, for example, you could outline the boundaries of the United States and then draw heavy blue lines for the rivers, leaving out extraneous details, such as cities. Figure 8.11 shows a map.

FIGURE 8.9

A table is an effective information chart. When the speaker points out that walking burns 250 calories an hour—the equivalent of one piece of chocolate cake—the listener can easily see how one column in the table is related to the others.

Activity	Calories Per Hour	Food Equivalent
Sleeping	65	1 orange
Walking	250	1 piece, chocolate cake
Bicycle Riding	300	6 chocolate chip cookies
Running	650	2 cups, ice cream

FIGURE 8.10
This drawing shows how to jump-start a car with a dead battery. The speaker would, of course, explain the steps while the audience looked at the drawing.

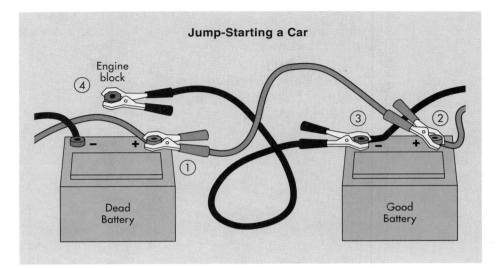

FIGURE 8.11
This drawing shows the five most visited national parks in the United States. (Source: National Park Service)

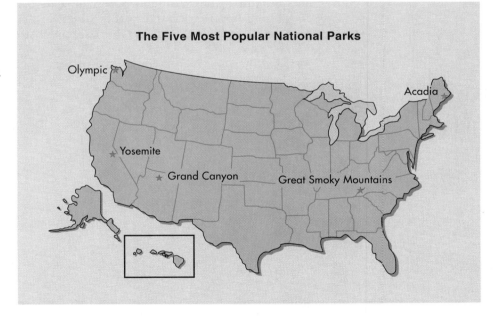

► **Photographs**

Photographs have a high degree of realism; they are very good for proving points. Lawyers, for example, often use photographs of the scene of an accident to win a case. In a speech, use photographs only if they are enlarged to poster size. If you have a small photograph that you think would make an important visual aid, have your school's audiovisual department make a 35-mm slide from it, if possible, and then project it so that everyone in the audience can see it.

▶ Computer Graphics

Computers can create all kinds of graphs, charts, maps, and drawings, which can then be printed (sometimes in color) either on paper or on transparencies for overhead projection. Slides can also be made from computer graphics. Your college may have a computer that generates graphics. More and more businesses are producing visual aids by this means because computers can create graphics much more quickly than an artist can. Such graphics are highly accurate and easily updated.[8]

▶ Objects

Three-dimensional objects make good visual aids, provided they are large enough for everyone in the audience to see. You could bring such things as a blood pressure gauge, a hibachi, handmade pottery, mountain climbing equipment, and musical instruments. Living objects could also be used, but be sure to get your instructor's approval in advance. You could use a friend, for example, to illustrate self-defense methods against an attacker.

Speakers can use themselves as visual aids—a technique used at a historic site by a tour guide dressed in a colonial American costume.

▶ Models

A model is a representation of an object. One speaker used a model of the pyramids to discuss how the ancient Egyptians probably built their famous pyramids. If you were discussing space travel, you could use a model of a space shuttle. One advantage of a model is that you can move it around. If you had a model airplane, for example, you could show principles of aerodynamics more easily than if you had only a drawing of a plane. One speaker used a homemade "lung," the interior of which consisted of clean cotton. When cigarette smoke was sucked through a tube, the lung turned from white to a sickening yellow-brown.

▶ Yourself

Using yourself as a visual aid, you can demonstrate yoga positions, judo holds, karate chops, stretching exercises, relaxation techniques, ballet steps, and tennis strokes. You can don native attire, historical costumes, or scuba-diving equipment. One student came to class dressed and made up as a clown to give a speech on her part-time job as a clown for children's birthday parties.

Media for Visual Aids

Some of the types of visual aids we looked at above—charts, graphs, drawings, and so on—can be conveyed to the audience by means of a variety of different media. Here are some of the more popular media:

▶ Boards

The two most popular types of presentation boards used today are chalkboards and dry-erase (or "white") boards. The latter type has a white surface, on which the presenter writes with a special pen available in many different colors. The pen writes as liquid, but the result is erased as if it were chalk. You must be sure to use the special pen: If you use an ordinary magic marker, the writing might not come off.

Because chalkboards are so common, they are generally considered rather dull as presentation media. Dry-erase boards are more exciting because the white background makes bright colors highly visible and attractive.

Either type of board makes a good tool for visual aids if you have a few technical words that you need to write for your audience. If you use a big word like *transmogrification* (which means changing into a different, sometimes bizarre, form), you can step over to the board and write it down in big letters. A board is also effective if you have complex drawings that require constant insertions and erasures—for example, the diagraming of plays for a soccer team.

Boards have some disadvantages. If you put your visual—a graph, say—on a board during your speech, you have to turn your back on the audience; while you're drawing, their attention drifts away from you, and you may find it hard to regain it. Would it be a good idea to put your graph on the board before the speech begins? No, because the audience would be distracted by it; they would scrutinize it before you are ready to talk about it. (It would do no good to say, "Don't pay any attention to this until I get to it." Such an admonition would make the graph all the more interesting—and therefore distracting.) There is one possible solution: Cover the part of the board on which you have written, but this can be awkward. You would have to find something large enough to do the job but not distracting. Another problem is that speakers preceding you may also be planning to use the board, and they might erase your visual aid.

Both types of boards sometimes have a problem with glare, so you need to study the lighting in the room beforehand. Put your visual on the board and then sit in various parts of the room; if some listeners would be unable to see your visual, make necessary adjustments or choose another approach such as posters.

▶ Posters

You can put many kinds of visual aids—such as graphs, drawings, and charts—on posters. They do the same work as chalkboards, but they are usually a lot neater and more visually appealing.

The size of the poster should depend upon the size of the audience. Ask yourself: Can the person in the back row see the words or artwork clearly? For huge audiences, posters obviously would be unsuitable; you would have to use slides.

Make sure there is a reliable place to put your posters. If you prop them against a chalkboard or tape them on a wall, they might fall to the floor during the middle of the speech. Using thumbtacks might work if there is a suitable place for tacking. One technique is to put posters on a desk near the lectern and take one at a time from the pile and hold it up. If you follow this technique, be sure to hold your posters steady. Another method is to put your poster on an easel (your school's audiovisual department may be able to provide one). Even with an easel, however, some posters tend to curl and resist standing up straight. To make a poster firm, tape a second (blank) poster to the back of it. (*Tip:* An even better solution to the problem of curling is to buy posters that are sturdier than the standard poster stock sold at drugstores. Art supply stores carry *illustration boards* and *foam-core boards*. Though more expensive than standard posters, they will not sag or curl.)

▶ Flip Charts

A flip chart is a giant writing pad glued or wired at the top. It can be mounted on an easel. When you are through with each page, you can tear it off or flip it over the back of the easel.

You can prepare the visuals on each page in advance, or you can "halfway" prepare them—that is, lightly pencil in your sheets at home; then during the speech, with a heavy marker, trace over the lines. (Since the audience is unaware that you are tracing, not drawing, you come across as crisp and professional.) With some flip charts, the paper might be so thin that ink will seep to the next page, so you might need to have a blank page between each drawn-on sheet.

▶ Handouts

In a survey, 1267 corporate executives were asked what format was most often used by their companies in presenting business graphics. The winner was paper handouts, with 40 percent (overhead transparencies placed second, with 38 percent, and 35-mm slides came in third, with 11 percent).[9]

At a time when businesses can use dazzling electronic media, it is surprising to see handouts used so frequently. Or perhaps it is not so surprising when you consider that handouts are easy to prepare, can be updated quickly at the last moment, and provide a permanent document that listeners can take with them when they leave a presentation.

Though handouts are popular, they are often misused. I have witnessed the following fiasco dozens of times: A presenter distributes stacks of handouts at the beginning of a talk. While he or she discusses each handout, the room is filled with the sound of rustling papers, as the listeners race ahead, reading handouts that the presenter has not yet come to, ignoring or only half-listening to what he or she is saying. (Some speakers try to solve this problem by imploring the audience to stay with them and not read ahead, but this is futile; humans are naturally curious, and their eyes cannot resist reading.)

Because handouts are so often misused, some instructors forbid them in classroom speeches, so be sure to find out your instructor's policy.

Whenever you use handouts, here are some recommendations:

- ▶ If a handout is short and simple (that is, a one-page document with an easy-to-understand graphic or a *small* amount of text), you may distribute it *during* a speech.
- ▶ Never give a handout until you're ready to talk about it. A premature handout is a distraction, and it grows stale before it is discussed.
- ▶ Avoid talking about a handout while you are distributing copies. Wait until every listener has a copy, and then start your explanation.
- ▶ A lengthy or complex handout—one that has many different graphics or lots of words or more than one page—should *not* be distributed during the speech (because your listeners would be tempted to study it rather than pay attention to you). If, however, you want your listeners to have a copy to take home with them for further study or review, you can distribute it *after* the question-and-answer period. (For classroom speeches, check with your instructor; he or she may prefer that you

wait until the end of the class period; if you give out material at the end of your speech, students might read it instead of listening to the next speaker.)

▶ Overhead Transparencies

Overhead projectors are illuminated boxes that project images from transparencies onto a screen. There are five advantages in using overhead transparencies:

1. The transparencies are simple to produce.
2. You can easily make last-minute changes in artwork or statistics.
3. You don't need another person to operate the machine for you.
4. The room usually doesn't need to be darkened, so you and the audience can see each other at all times (also, this means that if you are using notes and if some listeners are taking notes, there is enough light).
5. When you want to point to an item on your visual, you don't have to turn your back to the audience by going to the screen; you can simply point to the proper place on the transparency with a pencil or pen.

Prepare transparencies well ahead of time. You can reproduce photos or illustrations from magazines and books, or you can create original graphics. Using a variety of color pens, you can write directly on the film, or you can make a master copy on plain white paper and then use certain kinds of office copiers to make your transparency. (Your college's audiovisual department may be able to help you produce transparencies for a small fee, or a print shop in your community can make the transparencies from your master copy.)

Make your artwork and letters larger than you think necessary. Don't try to use a typewriter to make the master copy because the letters are too small. Even large typefaces, such as IBM's Orator, are too small to be seen by people in the back of a room.

During a speech, you can use your pen to circle key words, draw arrows, or insert updated statistics. But don't try to create an entire visual aid from scratch during the speech because you might lose your audience's attention while you write or draw.

When you create transparencies in advance, you must make sure that you use a marking pen especially designed for overheads. If you use an ordinary marker to prepare a transparency the night before your speech, the graphics might look fine at the time, but by the next day ink may evaporate, leaving you with only thin traces. Avoid storing transparencies directly against one another. The ink may transfer from one to another. Put them in file folders or store them with a piece of paper between each one.

If you use transparencies frequently in your career, it is worth mounting them in cardboard frames for easy handling and storing. Frames also elimi nate unnecessary projector light at the edges, making the visuals look crisper. You can number each frame for quick sorting and write brief speaker's notes on the margins to remind yourself of what you want to say as you present each transparency.

▶ Slides

Slides are popular in business, government, and military presentations. They allow a great deal of flexibility: You can insert and delete slides quickly and easily, thus adapting a slide show to meet the needs of different kinds of audiences. As an example, if during a recent trip to Mexico, you took 245 slides, including 35 at an ancient Mayan excavation site, you might want to show all 35 of the Mayan slides in a talk to an archaeological society. But if you are giving a talk to a civic club, you might want to show only three or four of those slides because a general audience may not be interested in detailed information on archaeology.

Slide projectors are easy to operate. You can set your own pace, lingering over a slide that requires long explanation, while hurrying through slides that need little or no commentary. If you have a remote-control device on a long cord, you can stand next to the screen and point out items without having to walk back and forth between projector and screen.

If you have a photograph, chart, drawing, magazine ad, or cartoon that is too small for the audience to see, consider making a slide of it. If you create a chart or graph from scratch (to be photographed as a slide), limit yourself to only two or three bold, contrasting colors (too many colors would be garish), and don't use too many words. Keep the slide simple and vivid.

To be seen clearly, slides must be shown in a completely darkened room. This situation is both good and bad. Good because your listeners' eyes cannot wander and become distracted—they are concentrated on the screen. Bad because you and your listeners lose eye communication with each other; you have to rely solely on your voice to make contact. To solve this problem, some speakers show slides in a semidark room, but this makes the slides appear washed out and therefore hard to see.

Once you have finished discussing a slide, don't leave it on the screen. If you are not yet ready to go to the next slide, project a light-colored blank slide on the screen while you talk, or turn off the projector and turn on the lights until you are ready for the next slide.

▶ Videotapes

Consider the power of videotapes:

> ▶ In a speech on the importance of wearing seat belts, Maureen Tener showed, in slow motion, a videotape of the high-speed crash of a car in which a human-size dummy not wearing a seat belt was viciously hurled and crushed.

▶ To show her listeners how clog dancing looks and sounds, Erika Rogers videotaped cloggers performing at a dance festival.

▶ To demonstrate how paratroopers jump out of airplanes, Mark Gowing showed a videotape of himself and other U.S. Army Rangers parachuting from a plane during a training exercise.

If you videotape your interviews, you may be able to use some excerpts in your speech. In a community speech on unsanitary conditions in which some children are forced to live, Linda Morales, a social worker, included videotaped interviews of children who pointed at the cockroaches and other insects in their apartment. The videotape was much more powerful than verbal description would have been.

You can show a commercially produced videotape, or if you have access to a videocassette camcorder, you can make your own. Because of the ease in rewinding and advancing a videotape, you can show key segments of a tape, eliminating irrelevant or redundant parts.

As discussed earlier, it is a mistake to let a visual dominate your speech, so don't play a videotape for your entire allotted time. Use it only at carefully selected moments. Perhaps a brief segment could serve as an appetizer at the beginning—something to whet the taste buds for the main course, your speech. If you have detailed, technical material to cover, you might use video in the middle of your speech to break the monotony. Or you could use a segment at the end if it will motivate the audience to take action on your proposals.

A videotape shown on a television set is usually suitable for only a small audience, so don't try to show a videotape to a large audience (unless you are lucky enough to have access to a large-screen TV or a special projection device—expensive equipment which more and more businesses and convention centers are buying).

Guidelines for Using Visual Aids

Here are some guidelines for using visual aids effectively in your speeches:

▶ Choose Visual Aids That Truly Support Your Speech

Before using a visual aid, ask yourself: Will it help clarify or illustrate an important idea in my speech? If the answer is no, discard it. Your job is not to dazzle people with pretty colors on a screen or to impress them with your creative artwork. A beautiful drawing of an airplane, for example, would not really contribute to a speech on touring the castles of Europe.

"Visual aids are too often used as a crutch and a substitute for thorough preparation," says speech consultant Sandy Linver. "When they're added a the last minute, or used just to fill time or give a touch of slickness to the presentation, they merely distract the audience's attention away from you and your message."[10]

Beware of using a visual that is ugly, confusing, or incomprehensible. As we discussed earlier, a poor visual aid is worse than none at all because it can weaken your credibility with the audience. Take a candid, realistic look at your visuals. Are they really worth displaying?

▶ Prepare and Practice Far in Advance

If you wait until right before your speech to prepare your visuals, they may turn out sloppy and unpolished, and when you show them during the speech, you may fail to use them smoothly. Even worse is waiting until you are actually giving the speech: Few people can write or draw effectively while speaking to an audience.

The best approach is to prepare your visuals far in advance so that you have ample time to design them well. Then it is important to practice using them as you rehearse your speech. If you will be using unfamiliar equipment such as overhead projectors or videotape machines, rehearsals will help prevent fumbling or faltering during your speech.

▶ Don't Use Too Many Visuals

Some speakers believe that the more graphics they display while talking, the better the speech. This notion is untrue: If there are too many visuals, the listeners could suffer "sensory overload" and become blinded to the speaker's true message.

"Too much sight and sound" can befuddle an audience, says Laurel Griffith, a management consultant in Birmingham, Alabama, who tells of a physician who went from one extreme (no visuals at all) to the other extreme (too many). At first the physician was giving over fifty speeches a year to nonmedical audiences on cardiovascular disease, but in every speech he was disheartened to notice several people falling asleep midway through his remarks. To enliven his talks, he began using visuals, "certain that no one would fall asleep this time." He was right. Now his listeners stayed awake, but they found the talk bewildering because of the huge number of slides, posters, and overhead transparencies. "Instead of making cardiovascular disease and its treatment easier to understand, he took a complex topic and made it more confusing by using too many visual aids. His audience left the auditorium feeling overwhelmed by the multitude of pictures and diagrams he had loaded into a relatively short presentation."[11]

How many visual aids should you use in a speech? Only the number necessary to clarify or illustrate your key ideas. No more, no less.

▶ Make Visual Aids Simple and Clear

Make each visual aid so simple that your listeners can quickly grasp its meaning—either at a glance or after minimal explanation by you. Avoid complexity. Too much information can confuse or overwhelm the listeners. They might spend so much time and energy trying to make sense out of your visual that they stop listening to you.

If you take graphs or charts from books, be careful. Some visual aids in books are jam-packed with fascinating details; they are suitable for publication in a book because the reader has a lot of time to analyze them, but they're too complex for a speech.

Visual aids should be attractive, clear, neat, and uncrowded. In aids such as graphs, make all labels horizontal (in a textbook, many labels are vertical because readers of a book can turn the visual sideways, but listeners should not be forced to twist their necks to read vertical lettering). You need not label every part of your visual, as you are there to explain the aid.

▶ Make Sure Everyone Can See Your Visuals

If a visual aid cannot be seen easily and vividly by a person in the back row, *don't use it*. It is better to use no visual aids at all than to use aids that can't be seen by everyone. The listeners who are shut out by a too-small aid feel frustrated, even angry, and their opinion of you and your speech declines. In their eyes you look amateurish and insensitive.

You would think that such an obvious error would be avoided by almost all speakers, but, alas, it occurs quite frequently. I have seen the head of a large corporation show an overhead transparency to an audience of over a thousand, with only three or four hundred people close enough to actually read the words on the screen.

When you prepare graphics, make your letters and sketches much larger than you think necessary. Before the date of your speech, go to the room where you will be speaking, display your visual aid in the front of the room, and then sit in the back row and determine whether you can see it clearly. (Or even better, have a friend sit in the back row to pass judgment.) If your visual cannot be seen vividly, discard it. You can create another or simply not use one.

Right before a speech, move any objects or furniture that might block the view of some listeners. If you're using equipment such as an overhead projector, make sure it doesn't obstruct anyone's vision. If, despite your best efforts, there will be some listeners who are blocked from seeing your visuals, ask them (before you start your introduction) to shift their chairs or move to a different part of the room.

If you have a multidimensional object, be sure to turn it during your talk so that everyone can see all sides of it.

▶ Explain Visual Aids

No matter how simple your visual aid is, you should explain it to your audience. Some speakers slap a transparency of a graph onto an overhead projector, talk about it for a moment, and then whisk it off. To such speakers the graph is simple and obvious; they don't stop to think that the listener have never seen it before and need time to analyze and absorb the visual information.

As you discuss a part of your visual aid, don't wave your hand in the general direction of the aid and assume that the audience will know which feature you are pointing out. Be precise. Point to the specific part that you are discussing. For pointing, use a finger, ruler, pen, or extendable pointer. To avoid twisting your body, use the hand nearer the aid.

▶ Don't Let Visuals Distract from Your Message

What's wrong with the following scenario? For your next speech, you bring five posters on which are handsome bar graphs, pictorial graphs, and lists of key ideas. At the beginning of the speech, you proudly display all five posters at the front of the room.

Here's why this approach is bad: As you talk about your first poster, many of your listeners aren't paying attention, for they have already scrutinized it and now they are studying your fourth and fifth posters. Since they are being distracted from your remarks, they miss some of the key points you are making.

The cardinal rule for visual aids, says business writer Kirsten Schabacker, "is that they should complement your presentation, not distract the audience from what you're saying."[12] Here are some hints:

Show one visual at a time, and don't leave it on display. To keep the eyes and minds of your listeners focused on your speech, show a visual as you discuss it—don't pull it out early or leave it on display after you have talked about it. If you have five posters, show poster 1 when it is time; then cover it up or turn it over; display poster 2 and talk about it, and so forth. If you have an object to show, keep it covered or in a box. When you do bring an aid out, don't just show it briefly and leave the audience wishing for more time to see it. Let the audience have a good look before you put it away.

There is one exception to this rule: If you have a visual aid that can provide a simple, undistracting backdrop or evoke a mood, you may leave it on display during the entire speech. One speaker kept a bouquet of flowers on the front table throughout her speech on gardening; the flowers provided a pleasing complement to her remarks. Another speaker left a giant photograph of the majestic Swiss Alps on exhibit throughout his speech on mountain climbing in Switzerland. In both cases, the visual aids were not distracting—in fact, they enhanced the speeches—so the speakers did not err in keeping them visible.

Beware of using animals or children as visuals. Exotic pets and cute kids can easily draw the attention of your listeners away from your ideas, so you should use them carefully, if at all. One speaker brought in a ferret to demonstrate what great pets they make. The only trouble was that the ferret did cute impromptu stunts all during the speech, causing the audience to

FOR YOUR CAREER

TIP 8.2: Appeal to as Many Senses as Possible

While the visual channel is powerful, don't overlook the other senses:

▶ **Sense of hearing.** To accompany a slide presentation on dolphins, marine biologist Jennifer Novak played an audiotape of the clicks, whistles, and other sounds that dolphins use to communicate with one another.

▶ **Sense of taste.** In a speech on Korean cuisine, chef Chong Man Park cooked and served rice and vegetable dishes while explaining Korean culinary techniques to listeners.

▶ **Sense of smell.** Floral designer Charlene Worley gave a speech on how flowers provide not only messages of love and consolation, but also medicine and food. At the end of her talk, she invited the audience to sniff a bouquet of flowers she had created. She also appealed to the sense of taste by serving crackers on which she had spread jam made from violets.

▶ **Sense of touch.** Wishing to disprove the notion that snakes have slimy skin, herpetologist Jeanne Goldberg invited listeners to come forward and stroke the nonpoisonous king snake she was holding. Many listeners were surprised to find the skin dry and firm, with a texture like glass beads tightly strung together.

laugh at its antics rather than listen to the speech. Since some instructors disapprove of using animals in speeches, be sure to get permission before bringing an animal into the classroom.

Watch for misspelled words. Bloopers can cause listeners to smile (as when a speaker wrote FRIST for first) or even roar with laughter (as when a poster extolled the United States Marine CORPSE instead of Corps). Double-check the spelling of all words in time to correct any mistakes.

Never circulate a visual aid. Let's say that you have a visual aid, such as a magazine illustration or a piece of jewelry, that is too small for listeners to see from their seats. Should you pass it around the room? No, because people will look at it instead of listening to you. And there's likely to be distraction, perhaps even whispered comments, as it is being passed from one person to another. Some speakers try to handle this problem by walking from listener to listener, giving each person a close-up view. But this is poor technique; the listeners who are not seeing the visual aid may get bored or distracted, and they may start whispering comments to their friends. Also the listeners who are looking at the aid may ask questions that mean nothing to the rest of the audience. In a case like this, you can easily lose your audience's attention and interest.

Is there anything you can do with a small aid? Here are some options: (1) Leave it in the front of the room and invite the audience to see it *after* the speech. (2) Create a blowup drawing of the item on a poster, slide, or transparency—for example, an enlarged view of a piece of jewelry—that every listener can see clearly; discuss the enlargement during the speech and then permit listeners to take a look at the real object after the speech. (3) If the item is a small photo or drawing, consider duplicating it on handouts that can be distributed to each listener (but heed the warnings given in our earlier discussion of handouts).

▶ Don't Talk to Your Visual Aid

Many speakers are so intent on explaining a visual aid that they spend most of their time talking to it instead of to the audience. You should stand next to your aid and face the audience during most of your discussion. Look at the aid only in two situations: (1) When you introduce it, look at it for several seconds—this is long enough to draw the listeners' attention toward it. (2) Whenever you want to redirect the audience's attention to a new feature, look at the aid for one or two seconds.

▶ Use Progressive Revelation

Whenever possible, reveal only one part or item at a time—especially with lists, bar graphs, flowcharts, and drawings. If, for example, you are presenting a bar graph on a transparency, use a sheet of paper to cover everything except the top bar; discuss it, and then pull the sheet down to reveal the second bar, and so on. Or if you have five steps in a process, reveal one step at a time.

Progressive revelation creates suspense, making the listeners curious as to what comes next, and it prevents them from reading or studying ahead of you. Another bonus: when you walk over and reveal a new item, you create movement and action, which serve to "nudge" the listeners, keeping them alert and breaking up the monotony of a speech.

▶ Plan for Emergencies

With visual aids, there is always a chance of a foul-up, especially if you are using electronic media, so you should plan carefully how you will handle any problems that might arise. Sometimes the problem is simple but nevertheless frustrating. If you plan to sketch on the chalkboard, make sure there is chalk. It is disruptive to have to send someone to another room to find chalk.

Before you use any electronic media, talk with your instructor or the program chairperson to make arrangements (for darkening the room, getting an extension cord, and so on). Always check out the location of your speech in advance. Is there an electrical outlet nearby? If not, can you get an extension cord? Can the room be darkened for slides? Is there a place to put your posters? Is there a chalkboard?

Be prepared for the unexpected—slides appearing upside down, the bulb in the overhead projector burning out, videotape breaking in the middle of the program. Some of these disasters can be mitigated by advance planning. For example, carry a spare bulb for the overhead projector; if the videotape breaks, be ready to fill in the missing information. If equipment breaks down and cannot be fixed quickly, continue with your speech as best you can. Try to keep your poise and sense of humor.

Summary

Visual aids can enrich and enliven your speech in many ways. They can make your ideas clear and understandable, they can make your speech more interesting and memorable, they can help prove a point, and they can add to your personal credibility.

Types of visual aids, including graphs, charts, drawings, photographs, computer graphics, objects, models, and yourself, can be conveyed via the following media: boards, posters, flip charts, handouts, overhead transparencies, slides, and videotapes.

Whatever aids you choose, consider the following guidelines: (1) Choose visual aids that truly support your speech. (2) Prepare and practice far in advance. (3) Don't use too many visuals. (4) Make your aids as simple and clear as possible. (5) Make sure everyone can see your visuals. (6) Explain each aid, regardless of how simple it is. (7) Make sure the aids don't distract from your message. (8) Don't talk to your aids. (9) Use progressive revelation (10) Plan for emergencies.

Review Questions

1. List at least six types of visual aids.
2. List at least five media for visual aids.
3. Why would it be a mistake to circulate a small photograph during your speech?
4. Why should a graphic in a speech be less complex than a graphic in book?
5. What are the disadvantages of using a chalkboard for visual aids?
6. What is progressive revelation?

TIPS FOR YOUR CAREER

TIP 8.3: Use a Friend to Assist You

For speeches that you give on the job or in the community, you may want to ask a friend to assist you. Here are five ways in which an assistant can be useful:

1. An assistant can help you set up and operate audiovisual equipment, turn lights off and on, or search for a missing extension cord. Such assistance will free you to concentrate on getting your message across to the audience.

2. If you are speaking to strangers, the presence of your friend can give you a psychological boost—you have an "ally" in the room.

3. An assistant might be able to handle any distractions or emergencies that arise. If, for example, a group of people start a loud conversation right outside the door of the room where you are speaking, the assistant can open the door and whisper a request for silence.

4. Your assistant can stand or sit in the back of the room while you are speaking and give you signals that the two of you have rehearsed. For example:

▶ "Slow down—you're talking too fast."
▶ "Speak louder—I can barely hear you."
▶ "You're looking at your notes too much."
▶ "You've reached the time limit—wrap things up and sit down."

5. An assistant can give you a critique of your speech afterward, so that you can learn from any mistakes you have made. Sometimes the assistant can mingle with the audience in the hall after your speech and find out how listeners responded to the presentation, so that you can learn about your strengths and weaknesses.

9

The Body of the Speech

I once heard a naturalist give a talk on why the leaves of hardwood trees change colors in autumn. As he talked (without notes), it was obvious that he had no coherent plan for his speech. He rambled from one item to another, without tying things together. He would talk for a while about the chemical makeup of leaves, then throw in a few comments about rainfall and temperature, and then go back to chemistry. He gave his information in random order, not following a logical sequence. He backtracked a great deal ("Oh yeah, when I was talking about rainfall, I forgot to mention . . ."). For me, the speech was confusing rather than enlightening. I failed to get what I came for: an understanding of the chemical process by which leaves change colors. I think I would have understood the process, however, if he had organized his material in a logical, easy-to-follow pattern, such as: "Here's how leaves change colors: First . . . , Second . . . , Third . . . ," and so on.

Organizing material logically and intelligently is important in all types of communication, but especially oral communication. If readers of an essay find themselves confused, they can easily go back a few paragraphs and study the material until they make sense out of it, but people who listen to a speech don't have this option. If they fail to understand what a speaker is saying, they are out of luck. There is no instant replay. As a speaker, you must organize your ideas clearly and logically, so that your listeners will understand you. Here are some advantages of a well-organized speech over a poorly organized one:

1. A well-organized speech is easier to understand. As in the case of the naturalist, many speakers have interesting, important ideas, but their speeches are so poorly organized that the audience fails to grasp the ideas. Studies have shown that a well-organized speech is much easier for a listener to understand than a poorly organized one.[1]

2. A well-organized speech is easier for the audience to remember. Imagine that you need to remember to buy the following items at the store:

▶ bagels	▶ butter
▶ frozen spinach	▶ tomatoes
▶ milk	▶ hamburger buns
▶ lettuce	▶ carrots
▶ rolls	▶ frozen peas
▶ frozen squash	▶ yogurt

In a number of experiments, psychologists[2] have shown that your chance of recalling all the items increase if you revise your list to look something like this:

Breads	**Dairy products**
▶ bagels	▶ butter
▶ rolls	▶ yogurt
▶ hamburger buns	▶ milk

Frozen foods	**Fresh produce**
▶ spinach	▶ lettuce
▶ squash	▶ tomatoes
▶ peas	▶ carrots

The reason the second list is easier to remember is that items are grouped in meaningful clusters. You can, for example, get a mental picture of the bread section of your grocery store, and then tell yourself that you need to pick up only three things in that section—bagels, rolls, and hamburger buns. In a good speech, you should apply the same principle: Group your ideas in meaningful clusters that are easy to comprehend and recall.

3. A well-organized speech is more likely to be believed. Studies show that if you present a poorly organized speech, your listeners will find you less believable at the end than they did at the beginning of the speech.[3] But if your speech is well-organized, you will come across as someone who is in full command of the facts, and therefore believable.

All good speeches are made up of three parts: introduction, body, and conclusion. You might think it logical to formulate your introduction first, but most speakers find it easier to begin with the body of the speech and then prepare the introduction. If you stop and think about it, this makes a lot of sense: How can you introduce the body until you know its full nature?

In this chapter we will discuss how to organize the body of the speech. In the next chapter we will look at introductions and conclusions. Then, in the chapter following, we will examine how to put all these parts together in an outline.

Creating the Body

Before we scrutinize the different parts of the body of a speech, let's look at the overall picture.

Overview of the Process

To create the body of a speech, start with your *specific purpose*, which is the goal of your speech, and with your *central idea*, which is the key concept that you want to get across to your audience. (If you are unsure about these terms, please review Chapter 5 before proceeding in this chapter.)

Suppose you want to argue against the sport of boxing, and you come up with the following purpose statement:

Specific Purpose: To persuade my listeners that the sport of boxing should be outlawed

Next, ask yourself, "What is my essential message? What big idea do I want to leave in the minds of my listeners?" Your answer, of course, is your central idea. Here is one possibility:

Central Idea: Boxing should be banned because it is uncivilized and brutal.

This central idea is your speech boiled down to one sentence. It is what you want your listeners to remember if they forget everything else.

The next step is to ask yourself this question: "How can I get my audience to believe my central idea?"

The best way to get the central idea across to your audience is to firmly implant in their minds a few *main points* that are based on the central idea. In our boxing example, here are three main points that could be made:

I. Boxing can cause permanent brain injury.
II. Boxing sometimes leads to death.
III. Boxing is the only sport in which inflicting injury is the primary goal.

Next, ask yourself, "How can I make these main points stick in the minds of my listeners?" The answer is to back up each main point with supporting materials such as narratives, examples, and statistics. For example, here is how you could develop main point II:

II. Boxing sometimes leads to death.
  A. According to the American Medical Association, 439 boxers have died from boxing injuries since 1918.
  B. Willie Classen was knocked unconscious in the tenth round of a middleweight bout at Madison Square Garden and died 5 days later of massive brain damage.
  C. Duk Koo Kim, a young Korean, was killed in a televised match with lightweight champion Ray "Boom Boom" Mancini in 1982.

If you arrange a speech in this way, you will have an easy time getting your message across. Your listeners will know your central idea—that boxing should be outlawed because it is brutal—and they will know *why* boxing is brutal, thanks to your well-developed main points.

In chart form, here is what the body of a typical speech would look like:

Central idea

> Main point
>
> > Support material
> > Support material
> > Support material
> > Support material
>
> Main point
>
> > Support material
> > Support material
>
> Main point
>
> > Support material
> > Support material
> > Support material

In this chart, note the three levels of importance: Your central idea is supreme; it is developed by main points, which in turn are buttressed by support material. All three levels are necessary: Your listeners will not believe your central idea unless you have some strong main points, and they will not believe your main points unless your support material is convincing.

How to Develop Material

I've heard people say something like this, "When I'm putting together a speech, I get lost in my notes. How do I know which are main points and which are subpoints? How do I know what to put in and what to leave out?" To develop your material, here are the steps to follow:

► **Cluster Your Research Notes**

Your first step is to group your research notes into piles or clusters, according to subject matter. Suppose that you are preparing a speech on the claims that vitamin C is a "miracle" substance for colds and cancer. You conduct extensive research and come up with a thick stack of notes. For brevity's sake, let's examine only eleven of your notes:

1. All researchers agree that vitamin C helps maintain and repair connective tissue and bones and promotes healing of wounds.
2. Since the eighteenth century, it has been known that humans must consume modest amounts of vitamin C (60 milligrams a day) to avoid the deficiency disease called scurvy.
3. Vitamin C is contained in citrus fruits and in potatoes, tomatoes, and other vegetables.

4. Dr. Linus Pauling, a Nobel Prize winner, believes that taking large amounts of vitamin C supplements can reduce the number of colds a person gets.
5. Dr. Pauling has won the Nobel Prize for his work in chemistry.
6. Dr. Pauling won a Nobel Peace Prize for working to reduce the risks of nuclear war.
7. Dr. Pauling says large doses of vitamin C can improve a cancer patient's chances of survival.

8. On the basis of several tests conducted over a 10-year period, the prestigious *New England Journal of Medicine* concluded that vitamin C does not help a person to contract fewer colds.
9. Dr. Terence W. Anderson, a Canadian investigator who conducted three studies on more than 5000 adults, found no reduction in the frequency of colds during winters when vitamin C was taken, as compared with winters when the vitamin was not taken.
10. According to the *Harvard Medical School Health Letter*, two investigations at the famous Mayo Clinic found that cancer patients receiving vitamin C did not show any more improvement than patients not taking the vitamin.
11. Researchers have concluded that although smokers have lower blood levels of vitamin C than nonsmokers, they don't need to take extra vitamin C.

Notice that the notes have been placed into clusters—the first three items contain background information that all scientists agree on. The next four items (4 through 7) are concerned with Dr. Linus Pauling. The last four items deal with recent research on vitamin C. Grouping your research notes into clusters is an important way to gain control of your material.

▶ Create Main Points and Support Them

Your next step is to create main points and then back them up with support materials. You can do this by systematically answering the following questions:

1. What is the specific purpose of my speech?
2. What is my central idea—the key concept that I want my listeners to understand, believe, and remember?
3. What main points can I present to drive home the central idea?
4. What support material (narratives, statistics, quotations, etc.) will I need under each main point to explain or prove it?

Let's apply these four questions to your speech on vitamin C.

1. *What is the specific purpose of my speech?* Here is one possibility:

Specific Purpose: To inform my audience of the latest research findings about vitamin C's influence on health

Note that you have narrowed your topic to something that can be managed in a short speech. If you had tried to cover all the different kinds of vitamins, you would have created too broad a topic.

2. *What is my central idea—the key concept that I want my listeners to understand, believe, and remember?* From studying the above notes, you can see that Dr. Pauling, despite his prestige as a scientist, has formulated hypotheses about vitamin C that have been disproved by researchers. How do you know that Dr. Pauling is wrong? Because you have evidence from highly esteemed sources: The *New England Journal of Medicine* is one of the most respected medical journals in the world; the Mayo Clinic and Harvard Medical School are famous for their careful, reliable research in medicine. Armed with testimony from such highly credible sources, you can formulate the following as the gist of your speech:

Central Idea: Contrary to claims by Dr. Linus Pauling, vitamin C is not a miracle substance for colds and cancer.

3. *What main points can I present to drive home the central idea?* Put yourself in the place of the listeners. What would they say in response to your central idea? They would probably say, "How do you know that?" Based on your notes, you can create two main points—two key reasons why Dr. Pauling is wrong:

I. Research shows that vitamin C cannot decrease a person's chances of catching colds.

II. Research shows that vitamin C cannot increase the chances of recovery of a cancer patient.

Why these particular points? If you examine the central idea again, you will see that these are the points that are needed to explain and develop it. These are the points that summarize the findings of researchers. Our notes are important, but they are not main points. How about item 9—Dr. Anderson's research? That looks important. It *is* important, but it is not what you want your audience to remember. It would be nice if they could remember Dr. Anderson's name and the number of persons studied—5000—but is it realistic to expect an audience to remember such details a month after your speech? No, but you do hope they will remember the gist of Dr. Anderson's research, as expressed in main point I.

What about items 1 through 3? Aren't they worthy of being main points? No, because they merely give background information; they are not items that drive home the central idea. They can be included in the speech (in the introduction, as we will see in the next chapter), but not as main points.

4. What support material (narratives, statistics, quotations, etc.) will I need under each main point to explain or prove it? By themselves, your main points would be unconvincing to the audience. Take a look at main point I above. If you made this statement by itself, the listeners would say to themselves, "Says who?" So you would need to substantiate it by using items 8 and 9 from your notes. Here is how it would look in outline form:

I. Research shows that vitamin C cannot decrease a person's chances of catching colds.
   A. On the basis of several tests conducted over a 10-year period, the prestigious *New England Journal of Medicine* concluded that vitamin C does not help a person contract fewer colds.
   B. Dr. Terence W. Anderson, a Canadian investigator who conducted three studies on more than 5000 adults, found no reduction in the frequency of colds during winters when vitamin C was taken, as compared with winters when the vitamin was not taken.

You could substantiate your other main point in the same fashion. (If this were a "real" speech, you obviously would have more notes than the samples above.)

▶ Discard Irrelevant Material

In any speech, you need to be selective, choosing only those items that directly relate to the central idea. If you include irrelevant information, you risk confusing your listeners or overloading them with too much information.

In our vitamin C example, should all the research notes above be used? Let's examine items 5 and 6 from our list. Item 5—the Nobel Prize in chemistry—is important in this speech because it establishes that Dr. Pauling has credentials that should be taken seriously in the field of medicine. But item 6—the Nobel Peace Prize for working to reduce the risks of nuclear war—is irrelevant to this speech. Discard it.

How about item 11—the findings about smokers? Let's say you jotted down this research note because you thought that it might be pertinent to your speech. By now, however, you realize that although it is an interesting piece of research, it has no bearing on the narrow scope of your speech. Discard it.

Devising Main Points

"Do I need more than one main point?" some students ask. Yes. If you have only one main point to develop your central idea, you have a weak structure, like a bridge that has only one pillar to hold it up. If you provide only one main point, your listeners have only *one* reason to believe your central idea. If you give them two or three main points, you multiply your chances of convincing them.

"How many main points should I have?" you may be asking. To answer this and other questions, let's examine some guidelines for refining main points.

Limit the Number of Main Points

A common mistake of public speakers is to cram too many points into a speech. They do this because they are approaching the speech from their own personal viewpoint and not from the viewpoint of the listeners. If you ask yourself, "How much information can I squeeze into the 5 minutes allotted?" you are approaching from your own viewpoint. To approach from the audience's viewpoint, you should ask, "How much information can the audience comfortably pay attention to, understand, and remember?" Audiences simply cannot absorb too much new information. You should know this from your own experience; you can probably recall many speakers (including some teachers) who overwhelmed you with a barrage of ideas, facts, and figures. Don't be afraid to cut and trim your material.

Exactly how many main points should you have? In a short speech (5 to 10 minutes), you should limit yourself to two or three (or occasionally four) main points. That is as much as an audience can absorb. In a longer speech, you could have as many as five main points, but most experienced speakers cover only two or three, regardless of the length of their speech. It is a rare—and usually ineffective—veteran speaker who attempts six or more.

Restrict Each Main Point to a Single Idea

Each main point in a speech should focus on just one idea. The following example violates this rule:

> *Specific Purpose:* To convince my listeners that country life is superior to city life
> *Central Idea:* Living in the country is preferable to living in the city.
> *Main Points:* I. Country life provides more privacy than city life.
> II. Country life involves less stress than city life.
> III. Country life involves less pollution, and there is little crime.

The third main point covers two different ideas. The discussion of crime should be made into a separate point or perhaps used as supporting material for the second main point.

Use Parallel Language Whenever Possible

Parallel language means that you use the same grammatical forms throughout a sentence or paragraph. Read the following sentence aloud: "Joe enjoys hunting, fishing, and to camp." There is nothing wrong with the sentence grammatically, but it doesn't sound as pleasant to the ear as this version: "Joe enjoys hunting, fishing, and camping." Rather than the discord of *-ing*, *-ing*, plus *to*, our ears prefer the rhythm of *-ing*, *-ing*, *-ing*, as in the second sentence.

Suppose that you started with the following:

> *Specific Purpose:* To persuade my audience to swim for exercise
> *Central Idea:* Swimming is an ideal exercise because it dissipates nervous tension, avoids injuries, and builds endurance.

Now decide which set of main points would be most effective:

> *First set:* I. You can work off a lot of nervous tension while swimming.
> II. Muscle and bone injuries, common with other sports, are not a problem with swimming.
> III. Swimming builds endurance.

Second set: I. Swimming dissipates nervous tension.
II. Swimming avoids the muscle and bone injuries that are common with other sports.
III. Swimming builds endurance.

The second set is preferable because it follows a parallel grammatical form throughout (the noun *swimming* followed by a verb). Parallel language is not only pleasant to hear; it also helps listeners absorb your points. This consistent arrangement may not be practical in every speech, but you should strive for parallelism whenever possible.

Organizing Main Points

Main points should be organized in a logical, easy-to-follow pattern. Here are five of the most popular patterns speakers use:

Chronological Pattern

In the chronological pattern you arrange your main points in a *time* sequence—what occurs first, what occurs second, and so on. If, for example, you are describing a process, you can use this pattern to show how something is done step by step. Here is an illustration:

Specific Purpose: To tell my listeners how to revive a person who is in danger of drowning
Central Idea: To revive a person who is in danger of drowning, you should follow three simple procedures.
Main Points:
(First) I. With the victim on his or her back, tilt the head backward so that the chin juts upward.
(Second) II. Give mouth-to-mouth resuscitation until the victim breathes regularly again.
(Third) III. Place the victim on his or her stomach with the head facing sideways.

The chronological pattern is a logical choice for a speech dealing with periods of time in history. If, for example, you were speaking on the history of immigration in the United States, you could divide your subject into time periods—seventeenth century, eighteenth century, nineteenth century, twentieth century.

If you were speaking on the life of a person, you might want to divide the person's life into time periods, as in the following example:

Specific Purpose: To inform my listeners of the heroic life and example of Helen Keller

Central Idea: Helen Keller demonstrated the capacity of humans to live happily and creatively despite physical handicaps.

Main Points:

(Infancy) I. At an early age Keller was plunged into blindness and deafness.

(Youth) II. Keller was helped by a gifted teacher to develop her native intelligence and creativity.

(Adulthood) III. As an adult Keller became known internationally as a writer, lecturer, and champion of social justice.

Spatial Pattern

In the spatial pattern, you organize items according to the way in which they relate to one another in *physical space*—top to bottom, left to right, north to south, inside to outside, and so on. If you were speaking on the solar system, for example, you could discuss the sun first, then move outward in space to Mercury, Venus, Earth, Mars, and so on. Here is an example in which the speaker divides a car into space-related sections:

Specific Purpose: To tell my audience how to inspect a used car before deciding whether to buy it

Central Idea: If a person examines a used car carefully and critically, he or she can avoid buying a "lemon."

Main Points: I. Inspect the condition of the body of the car.

II. Inspect the condition of the motor.

III. Inspect the condition of the interior.

Another example of this pattern goes from bottom to top:

Specific Purpose: To describe to my audience the construction of the Leaning Tower of Pisa

Central Idea: The Leaning Tower of Pisa was crooked from the beginning, but it still stands after 800 years.

Main Points: I. The foundation and first story of the tower went crooked when the land settled soon after construction began in 1174.

II. The upper stories were designed with short pillars on the north side to compensate for the lean.

III. The bell tower on top was built at an angle to further compensate.

An instructor in anatomy and physiology uses the spatial pattern of organization, starting at the top of the skeleton's hand and working her way downward.

Causal Pattern

In some speeches, you are concerned with why something happens or happened—a cause-and-effect relationship. For example, some people refuse to ride in elevators because they have an inordinate fear of closed spaces. Their claustrophobia is the *cause*, and their refusal to ride in elevators is the *effect*. Here is a sample of a cause-and-effect pattern for a speech:

Specific Purpose: To inform my audience of how Americans are responding to the bombardment of telephone calls by businesses, charities, and politicians

Central Idea: Unwanted telephone solicitations by businesses, charities, and politicians are forcing many Americans to have unlisted telephone numbers.

Main Points:

(Cause) I. More and more businesses, charities, and politicians are using the telephone to solicit the public.

(Effect) II. A growing number of Americans are having the phone company change their telephone numbers from listed to unlisted.

Sometimes it is more effective to start with the effects and then analyze the causes, as in this case:

Specific Purpose: To explain to my listeners why people get headaches
Central Idea: Most headaches are caused by tension, psychological frustrations and conflicts, excessive alcohol consumption, or too much caffeine.

Main Points:
(Effects) I. Severe headaches create physical and psychological problems.
    A. They can make you short-tempered and irritable.
    B. They can keep you from sleeping.
    C. They can make you have difficulty thinking clearly.
(Causes) II. Headaches are caused by a variety of things.
    A. A build-up of tension is a primary cause of headaches.
    B. Psychological frustrations and conflicts can lead to headaches.
    C. Excessive alcohol consumption can create headaches.
    D. Too much caffeine from coffee, tea, and soft drinks can cause headaches.

In the above pattern, putting the effects first is good strategy because the listeners can nod in agreement and say to themselves, "Yes, that's exactly what headaches do." This puts them in the proper frame of mind to hear the causes. Their unspoken response will probably be something like, "Now tell me what causes headaches so I'll know how to avoid them."

Problem-Solution Pattern

A popular pattern in persuasive speeches divides the speech into two main parts: a problem and its solution. Here is an example:

Specific Purpose: To persuade my audience to support "pet therapy" for lonely elderly people in nursing homes
Central Idea: Having a pet can decrease the loneliness and improve the physical and emotional health of elderly people in nursing homes.

Main Points:
(Problem) I. Many elderly people in nursing homes are lonely and depressed—emotional states that harm their physical health.

(Solution) II. Researchers have discovered that having a pet improves the elderly person's physical and emotional health.

This pattern has the advantage of simplicity. You convince the listeners that a particular problem exists, and then you tell them how it can be solved.

Topical Pattern

In the topical pattern, you divide your central idea into components or categories, using logic and common sense as your guides. Thus, the federal government could be divided into three branches: executive, legislative, and judicial. You can divide according to whatever emphasis you wish to give; for example, politics could be divided into international, national, state, and local. Or it could be divided according to the people who practice it: liberals, moderates, and conservatives. Here is an example of the topical pattern:

Specific Purpose: To inform my audience of the two kinds of sleep that all persons experience

Central Idea: The two kinds of sleep that all persons experience at alternating times during the night are NREM (non-rapid-eye-movement) sleep and REM (rapid-eye-movement) sleep.

Main Points: I. NREM (non-rapid-eye-movement) sleep is the period in which a person does very little dreaming.
II. REM (rapid-eye-movement) sleep is the period in which a person usually dreams.

Another way of subdividing an idea is to show reasons for it, as in the following example:

Specific Purpose: To persuade my listeners to support the 55-mile-per-hour speed limit on interstate highways

Central Idea: The 55-mile-per-hour speed limit should be maintained and enforced on America's interstate highways.

Main Points: I. The 55-mile-per-hour speed limit saves thousands of lives each year.
II. The 55-mile-per-hour speed limit conserves fuel.

When you use the topical pattern, you can arrange your main points in whatever order suits the purpose of your speech. In the persuasive speech above, the speaker chose to use the stronger of the two points—that the 55-mile-per-hour limit saves lives—at the beginning of the speech. In some speeches, on the other hand, you may want to put your least important points first and build up to your most important points.

A note of caution: Some students make the mistake of thinking that the topical pattern is a formless bag into which anything can be dumped. Though you have a great deal of liberty to organize the points in whatever order you choose, you still must apply logic—for example, arranging points from least important to most important, or placing material under three major subdivisions.

Selecting Support Materials

In the preceding sections, we have concentrated on main points, but main points by themselves are not enough for the body of a speech. We also need support materials to develop and amplify our main points. These supports can be either verbal (as discussed in Chapter 7) or visual (as discussed in Chapter 8).

To see how support materials can be developed for main points, let's take a look at an outline by Janice Vogel:

General Purpose: To persuade
Specific Purpose: To persuade my listeners to protect themselves against permanent hearing loss
Central Idea: Loud music and other noises can cause permanent hearing loss unless individuals protect themselves.
Main Points: I. Permanent hearing loss can be caused by exposure to loud music and other noises.
II. People can prevent hearing loss by taking protective measures.

Using the problem-solution pattern, Vogel needs explanation and elaboration for both her first main point (problem) and her second main point (solution):

COMMENTARY

The speaker uses examples to help listeners understand decibel levels.

OUTLINE

I. Permanent hearing loss can be caused by exposure to loud music and other noises.
   A. The loudness of sound is measured in decibels.
      1. A normal conversation is 60 decibels, while a noisy restaurant is 70.
      2. Anything above 85 decibels is dangerous.
      3. Each of these is 110: A typical rock concert, a Walkman radio played loudly, and a jackhammer.
      4. Each of these is 130: A "boom car" (a car with big speakers installed) and a jet takeoff.

Testimony from a prestigious medical group is given.

B. Prolonged exposure to noise above 85 decibels can damage the sensitive hair cells lining the cochlea, the innermost part of the ear, according to the American Medical Association *Family Medical Guide.*

    1. Hearing loss caused by damage to the cochlea is irreversible—you can never regain it, says the AMA.

Statistics are used to show the extent of the problem.

    2. About 28 million Americans have suffered serious hearing loss, according to The National Institute on Deafness and Other Communication Disorders.

        a. Major groups with hearing loss are rock musicians, young people who listen to cassette players at high volume, and construction workers and others who use noisy equipment.

        b. Most endangered are young people with their personal stereos "blaring music into their skulls for hours, with blasts of 110 decibels or more into the ear," says *Time* magazine.

Testimony from an expert is effective.

        c. Dr. Jerome Goldstein of the American Academy of Otolaryngology says, "If you can hear the music from a Walkman someone next to you is wearing, they are damaging their ears."

    3. Most people have the false idea that as you get older, your hearing drops off dramatically.

        a. It is true that many Americans lose hearing as they get older, but it's because of abuse to their ears, not aging, says Dean Garstecki, head of the hearing-impairment program at Northwestern University.

The speaker uses a contrast to illustrate the problem.

        b. According to one study, the Mabaan people in Africa, who have never been exposed to industrial sounds, keep their hearing into old age.

II. People can prevent hearing loss by taking protective measures.

    A. If you work around noisy equipment, you should take protective measures, says the AMA.

       1. The best protection is heavily insulated earmuffs designed for construction workers.
       2. The second-best protection is earplugs made of foam, plastic, wax, or rubber.

B. Avoid loud music.

       1. Musicians who have suffered hearing loss are now recommending caution.

         a. Pete Townshend of the *Who* is spreading the message about the price of high-decibel rock, says *Time* magazine.

         b. Jeff Baxter of the Doobie Brothers says, "We teach kids to keep their hands off the hot stove. Let's do the same with their hearing."

       2. If you go to a rock concert, wear earplugs.
       3. If you use a personal stereo system, play it softly or moderately, and stay out of boom cars.

Examples of musicians who speak out against loud music add credibility to the speaker's advice.

If possible, distribute your supporting materials evenly. In other words, don't put all your support under point I and leave nothing to bolster point II. This does not mean, however, that you should mechanically place the same number of supporting points under every main point. In some speeches, it may turn out that you need five supports for one point and only two for another. You have to consider *quality* as well as *quantity*. A single powerful anecdote may be all that is required to illustrate one point, whereas five minor supports might be needed for another point.

When you are trying to decide how many supporting points to place underneath a main point, use this rule of thumb: Have enough supporting points to adequately explain or bolster the main point, but not so many that you become tedious and repetitious.

Supplying Transitions

Transitions are words, phrases, or sentences that show logical connections between ideas or thoughts. They help the listeners stay with you as you move from one part of your speech to the next. To get an idea of how transitions work, take a look at the following paragraphs and decide which is superior:

1. Mayor Smythe has been involved in graft for years. He is a capable administrator. I intend to vote for him.

2. Mayor Smythe has been involved in graft for years. Nevertheless, he is a capable administrator, so I intend to vote for him.

The second paragraph is obviously superior. The reason is that it contains two transitional words: *nevertheless* and *so.*

In a speech, transitions clarify the relationship between your ideas, thereby making them easy to comprehend. They serve as signals to help the listeners follow your train of thought. Here are just some of the many transitional words or phrases in the English language:

▶ To signal addition: *and, also, besides, furthermore, moreover, in addition*

▶ To signal time: *soon, then, later, afterward, meanwhile*

▶ To signal contrast: *however, but, yet, nevertheless, instead, meanwhile, although*

▶ To signal examples: *for example, to illustrate, for instance*

▶ To signal conclusions: *in summary, therefore, consequently, as a result*

▶ To signal concession: *although it is true that, of course, granted*

In public speaking, special types of transitions can be employed to help your listener follow your remarks. Let us look at four of them:

▶ Bridges

In crossing a bridge, a person goes from one piece of land to another. In giving a speech, the speaker can build "bridges" to tell the listeners of the terrain they are leaving behind and the terrain they are about to enter. It is a way of saying, "I've finished thought A; now I'm going to thought B."

Imagine that you had the following main points in an outline on "eating disorders":

I. Anorexia nervosa is an obsession with thinness and an extreme loss of appetite.

II. Bulimia nervosa involves recurring episodes of binge eating, followed by extreme efforts to disgorge food.

How can you go from point I to point II? You could simply finish with point I and begin II, but that would be too abrupt. It would fail to give the listeners time to change mental gears. One way to bridge the two points is with a sentence like this: "Well, that's all I have to say about anorexia nervosa; now let me tell you about bulimia nervosa." Such a sentence is better than no transition at all, but it is clumsy and artificial. A smoother way to make a bridge is to refer back to anorexia nervosa at the same time you are pointing forward to bulimia nervosa. Here is an example:

We have seen that anorexia nervosa is a very dangerous illness that can lead to death, but what about its close cousin, bulimia nervosa—is it also dangerous?

This is a successful bridge because it smoothly and gracefully takes your listeners from point I to point II. It also has the virtue of stimulating their curiosity about bulimia nervosa.

▶ Internal Summaries

At the end of a baseball game, announcers always give a summary of the game. But during the game itself, they occasionally give a summary of what has taken place up to the present moment ("We're in the middle of the fifth inning; Detroit is leading Milwaukee 4 to 3 on a grand-slam homer by . . . "). Though this is primarily designed for the viewers who have tuned in late, it is also appreciated by the fans who have been watching the entire game because it gives them a feeling of security and confidence—a sense of knowing the "main facts." You can achieve the same effect in a speech. When you finish an important point or group of points, you may want to spend a few moments summarizing your ideas so that they are clear and understandable. This device, called an *internal summary*, is especially helpful if you have been discussing ideas that are complicated or abstract. An internal summary can be combined with a bridge to make an excellent transition, as follows:

Internal summary: By now I hope I've convinced you that all animal bites should be reported to a doctor or health official immediately because of the possibility of rabies.

Bridge: While you're waiting for an ambulance or for an examination by a doctor, there is one other important thing you should do.

▶ Signposts

Just as signposts on a road tell motorists their location, signposts in a speech tell listeners where they are or where they are headed. If you gave a speech on how to treat a cold, you could say, "Here are three things you should do the next time you catch a cold." Then the audience would find it easy to follow your points if you said, "First, you should . . . Second, you should . . . Third, you should . . . ." Using these signposts is much more effective than linking your points by saying, "Also . . . " or "Another point is . . . ."

▶ Spotlights

Spotlights are transitional devices that alert the listeners that something important will soon appear. Here are some examples:

▶ Now we come to the most important thing I have to tell you.

▶ What I'm going to explain now will help you understand the rest of the speech.

▶ If you take with you only one idea from this speech . . .

Spotlights can build up anticipation and excitement: "And now I come to an idea that can mean extra money in your pocket . . . " or "If you want to feel healthier and happier, listen to the advice of Dr. Jonas Knudsen. . . . "

When you choose transitional devices, remember that your listeners are totally unfamiliar with your speech, so try to put yourself in their shoes at each juncture. Ask yourself, "How can I lead the listener from one point to another in a way that is logical and smooth?"

Summary

When you organize your speech, deal with the body first, leaving the introduction and conclusion for later. The best way to organize the body is to devise two or three (or sometimes four) main points based on your central idea. Arrange the main points in a logical pattern, such as chronological, spatial, causal, problem-solution, or topical.

Next, select support materials to back up the main points, and then supply transitions to help the listeners stay with you as you move from one part of your speech to the next. Common types of transitions are bridges, internal summaries, signposts, and spotlights.

Review Questions

1. How many main points should you have in a speech?
2. How many ideas should be represented in each main point?
3. Which pattern of organization would be best suited for a speech on the solar system?
4. Which pattern of organization would be ideal for a speech on food contamination and how the problem can be corrected?
5. Why are transitions important in a speech?

FOR YOUR CAREER

TIP 9.1: Test Your Material

Will your audience find your speech thorough, understandable, accurate, and believable? You can test the strength of your material in advance by using these techniques:

▶ In regard to each main point, think of the typical people who will be in your audience and ask yourself, "How will they react to this?" Then shape your material accordingly. If your imaginary listeners say, "How do you know this is true?" give the name and credentials of the expert from whom you derived your material. If they ask, "What do you mean by that?" give them an explanation. If they say, "Who cares?" show them the importance of your subject.

▶ Try out your material on friends or relatives. Victoria Vance, a hospital nutritionist who gives talks in her community on diet and nutrition, tests her ideas with her husband and teenage children at the dinner table. "I tell them, 'I'm going to give a speech at a high school next week. Here's what I plan to say.' Then I casually tell them the main points of my speech. Occasionally one of the kids will break in with something like, 'But, Mom, are you saying that *all* fast food is bad for you?' That tells me the places in the speech where I need to add some more explanations or examples."

▶ Do an "expert check"—that is, discuss your key ideas with someone who is knowledgeable about your subject matter, so that he or she can point out any errors or omissions.

10

Introductions
and Conclusions

 Introductions

Gain Attention and Interest / Orient the Audience / Guidelines for Introductions /

 Conclusions

Signal the End / Summarize Key Ideas / Reinforce the Central Idea with a Clincher / Guidelines for Conclusions /

 Sample Introduction and Conclusion

Nat McGill, manager of a large industrial plant in the Midwest, was alarmed. More and more accidents were occurring in the plant, causing injuries to workers and curtailing production. In an effort to solve the problem, McGill summoned all supervisors to a meeting. "We've got to stop these accidents—we've got to keep these workers from hurting themselves," he said. "I want each of you to give your crew a one-hour talk on safety. I want you to convince them to be more careful and to protect themselves from injury."

All the supervisors gave their speeches, but a few months later, the accident rate had failed to improve among all the crews—except one. This one crew suffered no accidents, no injuries. McGill summoned the crew's supervisor to his office, eager to know the man's public speaking secret. How was his speech different from those of the other supervisors?

Two strong elements of the supervisor's "secret," it turned out, were a dynamic opener—one that grabbed the attention of his crew and made "believers" out of them—and a strong ending.

He had begun by standing next to a heavy cast-iron cylinder and asking a volunteer to come forward. "Lift this and tell me how much you think it weighs."

"Over a hundred pounds," said the volunteer.

"Now, drop it on my toes."

The volunteer was reluctant, but the supervisor insisted. The cylinder hit the top of one foot.

"If I had on regular shoes, my toes would be crushed," said the supervisor, smiling, "but I'm not hurt because I'm wearing safety shoes with steel plates in the toes. All of you people can avoid being hurt on the job if you'll listen to what I'm going to tell you about protecting yourself."

Having captured his crew's attention and interest, he gave them tips on avoiding injuries. Then, at the end, he challenged every worker to show up the next day wearing steel-toe boots, shatterproof goggles, and other safety equipment.

Judging by accident rates, the supervisor's speech was highly successful, partly because of his fascinating introduction and forceful conclusion.

Some speakers give little thought to what they are going to say at the beginning of a speech and at the end. Some wait until the actual hour of delivery, preferring to let the mood of the moment determine what they will say. But these speakers are making a big mistake. A faltering or dull introduction can cause the audience to lose interest in both the speaker and the speech. A conclusion that is weak or clumsy can leave the audience with a bad opinion of what otherwise might have been a good speech.

Since both the introduction and conclusion are important to the success of any speech, you should take as much care and thought in devising them as you would in planning the body of the speech.

Introductions

The introduction to your speech has two parts: *attention material*, to capture and hold your audience's attention and interest, and *orienting material*, which prepares your audience intellectually and psychologically for the body of the speech. Here is a sample from the beginning of a speech by Jennifer Sheldon:

ATTENTION MATERIAL
Sheldon grabs the attention and interest of her listeners with two intriguing narratives.

I. Distraught over losing thousands of dollars on the stock market, a New York stockbroker went out one day with his American Express card and bought a gold Rolex watch costing $5000, a new video-and-sound system costing $20,000, and a set of golf clubs costing $7000. The problem was: he lacked enough money to pay for the credit-card charges. In Arizona, a secretary spent $36,000 in one afternoon, using her credit card to buy shoes, dresses, and furniture. She had the same problem as the stockbroker: not enough money to cover her purchases. In both cases, the merchandise had to be returned.

ORIENTING MATERIAL
The speaker prepares her audience for the body of her speech by giving background information, by revealing the central idea of the speech, and by telling the listeners what she will cover.

II. You have heard of alcoholism and compulsive gambling. Now psychologists are taking note of a new addiction—people who are unable to control their desire to go on wild shopping sprees. They are called shopaholics because their compulsive shopping disrupts their personal, business, and family lives and plunges them into a deep hole of debt. The credit card is to them what the bottle is to an alcoholic, according to Janet Damon, a New York City psychotherapist who has written a book called *Shopaholics*. From reading her book and several magazine articles, I believe that people go on shopping binges as a way of escaping from an emotional problem—whether it be depression, loneliness, or low self-esteem—so the best way for them to "recover" is to eliminate the problem or learn to cope with it constructively. To understand shopaholics, let's look at some details on who they are, why they go on binges, and what can be done to help them.

In the rest of her speech, Sheldon developed her central idea, giving examples and psychologists' insights.

Let's look at some techniques for gaining attention and interest (attention material) and for orienting your audience (orienting material).

Gain Attention and Interest

If you were sitting in an audience, would you want to listen to a speech that begins with: "I'd like to tell you about what I do in my spare time—writing paragraphs"?

Writing paragraphs? Sounds pretty dull. You might say to yourself, "Who cares?" and your mind might drift to something more interesting, such as the party you are planning to attend next weekend.

Now imagine that you were sitting in the audience when Jeanne-Marie Bellamy began a speech by holding up a $100 bill and saying, "How would you like to earn one hundred dollars by writing just one paragraph?" She went on to explain that magazines pay $100 to $400 for the little paragraphs used to fill up space at the end of a big article. "These 'fillers' are usually anecdotes about interesting or humorous things that have happened in a person's life," she said, adding that she earned an average of $700 per month in her spare time by writing paragraphs about "the amusing little things that happen to me and my family."

When Bellamy held up the $100 bill and asked her intriguing question, the listeners were hooked. How could they possibly turn their attention away? Bellamy's technique was to use attention material as a lure, just as a fisher dangles bait in front of a fish.

A lure needs to be dangled in front of listeners because of an unfortunate fact: Audiences don't automatically give every speaker their full, undivided, respectful attention. As you begin a speech, you may find that some listeners are engaged in whispered conversations with their neighbors (and they don't necessarily stop in midsentence when you start speaking). Some are looking at you but their minds are far away, floating in a daydream or enmeshed in a personal problem. Others are shifting in their seats to get comfortable; still others are thinking about what the preceding speaker said or looking about the room to see who they know. So your task is clear: Grab their attention when you start talking.

But grabbing their attention is not enough: Your introduction must also *keep* their attention, so that they will want to hear your entire speech. Your introduction must deprive them of any possible excuse to sink back into their private thoughts and daydreams. If you simply say, "I'm going to talk about 'writing paragraphs,'" you leave it up to the listeners to decide whether they want to listen to the rest of the speech. Don't give them a choice. Devise attention material that is so interesting that it is impossible for anyone *not* to listen to the entire speech.

Let us examine some common attention getters. Keep in mind that sometimes these can be combined.

▶ Relate a Story

Telling a story is one of the most effective ways to begin a speech because people love to listen to narrative accounts. Michelle Frady began a speech with this story:

> Three years ago, I was driving home late one night. Rounding a curve, I was blinded by the headlights of an approaching car. That's the last thing I remember. Two hours later I woke up in the hospital with three broken ribs, twenty-four stitches in my head, and several other injuries. The car had hit me head-on and since I wasn't wearing my seat belt, I was thrown through the windshield. I was very, very lucky. The police told me later that I could easily have been killed. They also told me that if I had been wearing a seat belt, I probably would have escaped injury.

Whatever story you tell must provide an easy and natural entry into the rest of your speech. Frady's story was an obvious prelude to a speech on the need for everyone to wear seat belts.

One kind of story you can use is the *hypothetical illustration*, as demonstrated by Jerome David Smith, an attorney, who said in a speech:

> One day you become angry over the nasty pollution of a river near your home, so you sit down and write a letter to the editor of your local newspaper. The letter is a scathing attack on a corporation that you believe is responsible for ruining the river. Two weeks later, you get a letter from the corporation's attorney informing you that you are being sued for $100,000 for "harming the reputation, prestige, and credibility of the corporation." Does this sound incredible? Can this happen in a country that celebrates freedom of speech? Yes, it can happen . . .

In the rest of his speech, he explained how lawsuits have become a popular way for companies and public officials to retaliate against criticism.

▶ Ask a Question

Asking a question can be an effective way to intrigue your listeners and encourage them to think about your subject matter as you discuss it. There are two kinds of questions that you can use as attention material: rhetorical and overt-response.

With a *rhetorical* question, you don't want or expect the listeners to answer overtly by raising their hands or responding out loud. Instead, you want to trigger an inner curiosity. For example:

Getting listeners to respond to a question is an excellent way to grab their attention and spark interest.

With powerful radio signals being beamed into outer space at this very moment, is there any realistic chance that during our lifetime we human beings will establish radio contact with other civilizations in the universe?

Not only does such a question catch the attention of the listeners, but it also makes them want to hear more. It entices them into listening to your speech for the answer to the question.

With an *overt-response* question, you want the audience to reply by raising their hands or answering out loud. Here is an example:

Mary Jo Adelberg began a speech by asking, "If you consider all the scientists who have ever lived on earth, what percentage do you think are alive today? Would anyone like to take a guess?"

"Twenty percent?" asked one person.

"No, it's more than that."

"Thirty percent?" asked another person.

"No, it's more than that."

"Fifty percent?" was the next guess.

"No, it's more than that. According to *Harper's* magazine, 85 percent of all the scientists who ever lived are alive today."

In this way Adelberg began her speech on the explosion of scientific knowledge in the past two decades. Note that she did not drag out the suspense too long. If listeners are forced to guess and guess and guess until the right answer is found, they might become exasperated, wishing that the speaker would get to the point.

Never ask embarrassing or personal questions such as, "How many of you have ever tried cocaine?" or "How many of you use an underarm deodorant every day?" An audience would rightfully resent such questions as intrusions into their private lives.

Never divide your audience into opposing camps by asking "loaded" questions like this: "How many of you are smart enough to realize that capital punishment is an absolute necessity in a society based on law and order?" By phrasing your question in this way, you insult those who disagree with you.

With some overt-response questions, you can try to get every member of the audience to participate, but this can be very risky, especially if you poll the audience in this way: "How many of you favor the death penalty? Raise your hands. Okay . . . now, how many of you are opposed to the death penalty? Okay, thanks . . . how many of you are undecided or unsure?" What if three people raised their hands for the first question, five for the second question, ten for the third, while the remaining sixty-seven people in the audience refused to cooperate? This can happen, and often does, much to the embarrassment of the speaker. Sometimes audiences are in a passive or even grumpy mood; this is especially true with "captive" audiences—that is, audiences that are required (at work or at school) to listen to a speech. In such a case, refrain from asking questions that require the participation of the entire audience.

Make sure the audience is clear as to whether you are asking a rhetorical question or an overt-response question. If you ask, "How long will Americans continue to tolerate shoddy products?" the audience knows you are not expecting someone to answer "Five years." It is clearly a rhetorical question. But suppose you ask a question like this: "How many of you have ever gone swimming in the ocean?" The listeners might be confused about whether you want them to raise their hands. Make it clear. If you want a show of hands, say so at the beginning: "I'd like to see a show of hands, please: How many of you have ever gone swimming in the ocean?" Alerting them in advance not only helps them know what you want, but is also makes them pay special attention to the question since they know that you are expecting them to respond.

▶ Make a Provocative Statement

An opening remark that shocks, surprises, or intrigues the listeners can certainly get their attention. Rhonda Ercolano, an attorney for a corporation, began a speech in the following way:

> Today each of you will be robbed of ten dollars. Tomorrow you will be robbed again of ten dollars. The next day, another ten dollars. In fact you will be robbed of ten dollars every day this year.

Then Ercolano explained:

> The robber will not be holding a gun, wearing a mask, and emerging from some dark alley. No, this robber will be well-dressed and well-to-do and possibly very polite. I am talking about so-called white-collar criminals, who steal billions from corporations and consumers alike, and plunder our national treasury through their tax frauds and evasions. The director of the FBI estimates that white-collar crime costs the average American about ten dollars per day in higher prices and taxes.

Ercolano used the technique of transforming statistics into a provocative statement. Here is another example of the technique: you could take the fact that 25 percent of all Americans will be afflicted by cancer and restate it in terms that can shock an audience:

> There are forty of you sitting out there in the audience. According to medical statistics, ten of you will someday be afflicted by one of the most dreaded of all diseases—cancer.

Such an opener is certain to draw your listeners in.

▶ Cite a Quotation

Quotations can provide a lively beginning for a speech. In a speech urging the audience to read good literature, librarian Mary Channing Russell began by saying:

> The semanticist and former U.S. Senator S. I. Hayakawa once said, "In a very real sense, people who have read good literature have lived more than people who cannot or will not read . . . . It is not true that we have only one life to live; if we can read, we can live as many more lives and as many kinds of lives as we wish." Let us look at what good literature is, and how we can use literature to add those extra lives to our time here on earth.

Quotations usually work best when they are short. Don't have a quotation that is so long that the listeners lose track of where the quotation ends and your remarks begin. The best way to indicate that you have finished quoting is to pause at the end of the quotation. The pause acts as an oral "punctuation" device, signaling the end of one thought and the beginning of another.

I don't recommend using the quotation as the first sentence of your opener. Consider the following:

> *Poor:* "The creative conquest of space will serve as a wonderful substitute for war." These words, by James S. McDonnell, builder of the Mercury and Gemini space capsules, offer a powerful reason for space exploration.

> *Better:* The builder of the Mercury and Gemini space capsules, James S. McDonnell, offers a powerful reason for space exploration. He said, "The creative conquest of space will serve as a wonderful substitute for war."

While the first version is better for a written composition, the second is better for a speech because the listeners need time to tune out distracting thoughts and tune in to you. If they fail to pick up the name of the expert, no harm has been done; what you want them to absorb is the quotation.

If a quotation is too concise, it may go by so fast that the audience fails to retain it. In such cases, it is a good idea to repeat it, as in this example:

> The great English ballerina Margot Fonteyn once said, "The one important thing I have learned over the years is the difference between taking one's work seriously and taking one's self seriously. The first is imperative and the second is disastrous." Think about that for a moment: "taking one's work seriously and taking one's self seriously. The first is imperative and the second is disastrous."

In print, the repetition looks silly, but in a speech the audience is grateful for the instant replay. It allows time for the idea to sink in.

▶ Arouse Curiosity

An effective attention getter is one that piques the curiosity of the audience. Brenda Johnson, a chef, began a speech by saying:

> I am addicted to a drug. I have been addicted to it for many years now. I feel like I need it to make it through the day. If I don't get this drug, my head aches. I'm nervous, irritable, and I begin to tremble. It's true—I am addicted.

Having aroused the curiosity of her listeners, Johnson continued:

> I am addicted to caffeine. Most people don't realize that caffeine is a drug— and that it is very addictive. It is present not only in coffee and tea and soft drinks but also in many legal drugs such as weight-control pills and pain relievers.

Johnson spent the rest of the speech giving details about caffeine and how listeners could reduce their intake.

▶ Provide a Visual Aid or Demonstration

Any of the visual aids we discussed in Chapter 8 could be used to introduce a speech, but you must be sure that while the aids get the audience's attention, they also are relevant to the main points of your speech. One student showed slides of sunbathers on a beach to begin a talk on sharks. Though there was a logical link (sometimes sunbathers who go into the water must worry about sharks), the connection was too weak to justify using these particular slides. In a case like this, it would be better to show a slide of a ferocious shark while describing a shark attack.

A demonstration can make an effective opener. Working with a friend, one student gave a demonstration of how to fight off an attacker, and then talked on martial arts. If you want to give a demonstration, get permission from your instructor beforehand. One note of caution: never do anything that might upset the listeners. Holding a revolver and firing a blank to start off a speech on gun control or suicide would upset some people and put them out of a receptive mood.

▶ Give an Incentive to Listen

At the beginning of a speech, many listeners have an attitude that can be summed up in these two questions: "What's in it for me? Why should I pay attention to this speech?" Such people need to be given an incentive to listen to the entire speech. So, whenever possible, state explicitly why the listeners will benefit by hearing you out. It is not enough to simply say, "My speech is very important." You must *show* them how your topic relates to their personal lives and their own best interests. If, for example, you were giving a talk on cardiopulmonary resuscitation (CPR), you could say, "All of you may someday have a friend or loved one collapse from a heart attack right in front of your eyes. If you know CPR, you might be able to save that person's life." Now each person in the audience sees clearly that your speech is important to his or her personal life.

It is a mistake to assume that listeners will always detect the connection between your speech and their lives. Spell it out. Here is how entrepreneur Don Aslett started a speech at a business convention on how to find a job:

> [Imagine that] everyone in here is fired as of right now. You have no job. You are unemployed.

Knowing that some listeners would think that the fantasy did not apply to them, Aslett continued:

> Some of you are smiling comfortably and saying to yourself, "It can't happen to me." Did you know that last month 28,000 people, secure in their jobs an

positions for sixteen years or more, were told to go with not much more than "thanks" and a good record?[1]

Now all the listeners should have realized that they could lose their job and that they ought to listen closely to Aslett's tips.

If you know some listeners have probably heard most of your speech material before, you can try to use incentives especially designed for them. Joel Weldon of Scottsdale, Arizona, gave a talk to over 700 business and industrial trainers at a national convention of the American Society for Training and Development. His speech consisted of tips on how to train people. In his introduction, he said:

> I know some of you are pros who have been involved in training for twenty years. When you hear some of these ideas, you're going to say, "I've heard all this before." I'm sure you have. But as you say that to yourself, ask yourself these two questions: Am I using this idea? And how can I improve it?[2]

Weldon's technique was effective because he acknowledged the presence and the experiences of the "pros," and then he challenged them to give his "old" ideas a fresh look.

Orient the Audience

Once you have snared the interest of your listeners by means of the attention material, you should go into the second part of your introduction, the *orienting material*, which gives an orientation—a clear sense of what your speech is about, and any other information that the audience might need in order to understand and absorb your ideas. The orienting material is a road map that makes it easy for the listeners to stay with you on the journey of your speech and not get lost and confused.

The orienting material does more than prepare the listeners intellectually for your speech; it also prepares them psychologically. It reassures them that you are well-prepared, purposeful, and considerate of their needs and interests. It shows them you are someone they can trust.

The three most common ways to orient the audience are: (1) preview the body of the speech, (2) give background information, and (3) establish credibility.

▶ Preview the Body of the Speech

Have you ever had trouble listening to a speech or lecture because the information seemed jumbled and disconnected and you couldn't grasp the significance of example A and statistic B? An effective way to avoid this problem is for the speaker to give the listeners a preview of the body of the speech. To help you see the value of a preview, consider this analogy:

Suppose you give a sack containing the 400 pieces of a jigsaw puzzle to a friend and ask her to complete the puzzle. She will have a hard time because she lacks a sense of how the puzzle is supposed to look when finished. Now imagine that you hand her a full-color picture of what the puzzle looks like when it is completely assembled—a panoramic view. Will her task be easier now? Yes, because the pieces "make sense"—she instantly recognizes that a light blue piece belongs to the sky in the upper part of the picture, a dark brown piece is part of a tree on the left side, and so on.

A speech is just like the puzzle. If you fail to give a preview, you are throwing out bits of information—pieces of the puzzle—without giving the listeners a clue as to how they all fit together. But if you give a preview, you are providing your listeners with a panoramic view of the speech. Then, as you progress through the body, you give details—the pieces of the puzzle— and the listeners are able to fit them into a logical, coherent picture in their minds.[3]

Your instructor may have specific requirements for what you must put in your preview. Unless he or she advises you otherwise, I recommend that you include your central idea and/or main points.

1. State the central idea.   Your audience can listen intelligently to your speech if you stress your central idea in the orienting material. For example, "Acid rain is killing all the trees on our highest peaks in the East. To prove this, I will give you evidence from leading scientists." (Occasionally, under special circumstances, it is best to withhold divulging your central idea until late in the speech; we will discuss this in Chapter 16.)

In a speech on losing weight, Mary E. McNair, a nurse, stated her central idea in this way:

> Fad and crash diets can actually backfire, causing a person in the long run to gain more weight than was originally lost.

This helped the audience listen with "the right set of ears." They knew they should pay attention to the counterproductive effects of fad and crash diets.

2. State the main points.   In most speeches listeners appreciate being given a brief preview of your main points. For example, Barbara LeBlanc said, "I believe that passive-solar heating should be used in every home—for two reasons: First, it's easy to adapt your house to passive solar. Second, the energy from passive solar is absolutely free. Let me explain what I'm talking about." By stating the main points, LeBlanc not only helped the audience listen intelligently but she also gave them an incentive to listen: she mentioned the possibility of saving money.

Giving a preview by stating the central idea and/or main points reassures the listeners that you are not going to ramble. In other words, you give th audience a message that says, loud and clear, "I'm well-prepared; I know exactly what I'm going to say; I'm not going to waste your time." This last "message" is important, because audiences like speakers who don't waste their time, and they resent speakers who do.

▶ Give Background Information

Part of your orienting material can be devoted to giving background information—definitions, explanations, and so on—to help your listeners understand your speech. In a speech on hypochondriacs, Lucinda Howard used her orienting material to define the term:

> Hypochondriacs are people who have a morbid preoccupation with disease. They usually think that they are ill in some way or another. I want to make clear that they are *not* malingering. *Malingerers* are people who fake illness; they know they're not really sick. *Hypochondriacs*, on the other hand, truly believe that they're ill.

Notice that Howard not only defined her term but she clarified her definition by contrasting hypochondriacs with malingerers to make sure that her audience did not confuse the two.

Sometimes it helps the audience if you explain the limitations of your speech. For example, assume that you are giving a speech on the notion that criminals should make restitution to their victims. If you are not careful, many people in your audience will reject your argument immediately by saying to themselves, "Restitution, baloney! How can a murderer make restitution to his victim?" So in your orienting material, you head off such objections by saying, "In this speech I will talk about criminals making restitution to their victims, but I'm only talking about nonviolent criminals such as swindlers, embezzlers, and bad-check writers. I'm not talking about rapists and murderers." By showing the boundaries of your subject, you increase the chances that members of the audience will listen with open minds.

▶ Establish Credibility

No one expects you to be the world's authority on your subject, but you can increase your audience's chances of accepting your ideas if you can give some credentials or reasons to show why you are qualified to speak on the subject. When student speaker Randy Stepp talked on how to escape a burning building, he enhanced his credibility by mentioning that he was a volunteer firefighter in a rural community and had fought many fires.

In the U.S. Congress, Representative Ben Nighthorse Campbell of Colorado arose recently to propose the construction of a memorial to Native Americans at the site in Montana where Gen. George Custer's troops fought "seven bands of the Teton Sioux and the Northern Cheyenne" in 1876. He strengthened his request by revealing his background: "It is an honor for me to stand before this body as the only American Indian in the U.S. Congress," he said. "My own great-grandfather was in that battle." By revealing these details, he showed his listeners that he could be trusted to say what Native Americans truly wanted concerning the memorial.[4]

Don't be shy about giving your credentials or background; the listeners appreciate information about your degree of interest and expertise. It helps them evaluate what you have to say. Be sure, however, to give this information in a way that is modest and tactful, rather than boastful and arrogant. In other words, if you are speaking on air pollution, say something like "I'm a chemist and I've analyzed in my lab the content of the air that we breathe in this community" instead of "I'm a professional chemist, so I know more about air pollution than anybody in this room."

Sometimes you can enhance your credibility by explaining how you arrived at your central idea. Student speaker Jimmy Williams said:

> Do you think electroshock treatment for mental patients is really just a form of torture? I certainly did when I chose this topic. I intended to argue for the abolition of shock treatments. I had seen the movie *One Flew over the Cuckoo's Nest*, and I thought electroshock was a sadistic form of punishment used by cruel people like Nurse Ratched in the movie. But after reading books and magazine articles on the subject and interviewing staff members at [a local psychiatric] hospital, I changed my mind. I now believe that electroshock treatment is humane, responsible, and very effective in relieving the agony of severely depressed patients.

By relating his change of mind, the speaker enhanced his credibility. He showed himself to be honest and open-minded, a person who could be trusted.

Guidelines for Introductions

Here are some points to keep in mind for introductions:

1. Don't prepare your introduction first. When you prepare a speech, i usually works best to complete the body of the speech and *then* work o your introduction. Once you have developed your main points, you are in stronger position to decide how to introduce them.

2. Make your introduction simple and easy to follow, but avoid makin it too brief. Your audience needs time to get into the groove of your speecl If the introduction is too short, it may go by too fast for the listeners t absorb. That is why effective joke tellers stretch out their introduction t give the listeners time to get "into" the joke. If the idea of stretching out a

TIPS FOR YOUR CAREER

TIP 10.1: Use an "Icebreaker" to Start Off a Community Speech

You have probably noticed that many speakers at business and professional meetings start off by saying something like this: "I'm glad to have a chance to speak to you today." They are giving what I call an *icebreaker*—a polite little prologue to "break the ice" before getting into their speech.

In outline form, here is how an introduction with an icebreaker would look:

  I. Icebreaker
 II. Attention material
III. Orienting material

An icebreaker is helpful because it eases your nervous tension and it lets the audience get accustomed to your voice. You don't need an icebreaker for classroom speeches because your audience has already settled down and is ready to listen (besides, most instructors would disapprove of using one), but when you give speeches in the community, you may want to use it.

I don't like "Hello, how are you?" as an icebreaker. It sounds too breezy and flip. It leaves a question as to whether the speaker wants the audience to roar a response like "Fine, thank you!" It is much better to say, "I appreciate the opportunity to speak to you tonight." But, you might object, phrases like this have been used so often, they are meaningless. Yes, they are. They are clichés. Nevertheless, they are valuable aids to smooth social relationships. When you engage in small talk with your friends, you use sentences like, "Hi, how are you?" Such expressions are trite but they are necessary because they lubricate the wheels of human discourse.

In addition to expressing appreciation for the invitation to speak, you can include a thank-you to the person who introduced you or a reference to the occasion ("I'm delighted to take part in the celebration of Martin Luther King's birthday"). Some speakers also use the icebreaker to formally greet the audience. This custom, however, has fallen out of fashion. In the old days, orators would begin speeches like this: "Madame President, Distinguished Members of the Paradox Society, Honored Guests, Ladies and Gentlemen, Greetings!" Such introductions are used today only in formal, traditional settings, such as a college commencement. In most of the speeches you will give in your life, a flowery greeting would sound pompous.

A note of caution: An icebreaker should be very brief—just a sentence or two. If you are too slow getting into your attention material, you may cause some listeners to tune you out.

introduction sounds wrong to you, it is probably because you have been taught in English classes to write concisely. While it is a sin in English composition to stretch out essays, it is a virtue to do so with a speech's introduction that might otherwise be too abrupt for an audience. A note of caution: don't let this tip cause you to go to the opposite extreme—being tedious and long-winded. Be brief, but not too brief. If you are unsure about whether you have achieved a happy medium, deliver your speech to relatives or friends and then ask them if they thought your introduction was too long or too short.

3. Make sure that your introduction has a direct and obvious tie-in with the body of the speech.   A common mistake is for speakers to give an introduction that has a weak or dubious link with the rest of the speech. This kind of introduction can be annoying and confusing to the listeners.

4. Never apologize.   You weaken your speech and hurt your credibility if you say things like "I didn't have much time to prepare" or "This may be too technical for you" or "I'm sorry I didn't draw a diagram."

Conclusions

When movies are made, the producers spend a lot of time and energy on getting a "perfect" ending because they know that if the ending is unsatisfying, the viewers will tend to downplay the film as a whole. As with the movies, the ending of a speech can either add to or subtract from the audience's opinion of the entire speech. So it is worthwhile to spend a lot of time working on your conclusion.

In your conclusion, you should do three important things: (1) signal the end of the speech to satisfy the audience's psychological need for a sense of completion, (2) summarize the key ideas of the speech, and (3) reinforce the central idea with a clincher. Let us discuss these points in greater detail.

Signal the End

Imagine that you are listening to your favorite song on the radio and letting your mind float freely with the music. Then suddenly, before the song is finished, the disk jockey cuts in with a commercial or a news bulletin. You missed only the last 10 seconds of the song, but you feel annoyed. Why? Because most people need to experience a sense of completion.

In listening to a speech, we have the same need for a sense of finality. We like to hear a conclusion that is psychologically satisfying, one that ties up all loose ends and wraps the speech into a nice, neat package. When a speaker ends a speech abruptly, we feel a vague dissatisfaction.

Just as a musical composition provides flourishes and other "signals" that indicate that the end is approaching,[5] a speech can give signals—both verbal and nonverbal. Use either or both of these signals instead of coming to an abrupt halt.

Verbal signals.   You can openly announce that you are coming to your conclusion by using such expressions as, "So, in conclusion, I'd like to say . . ."; "Let me end by saying . . . "; or "Let me remind you of the three major points I've been trying to explain today."

Nonverbal signals.   Whether or not you use verbal signals, you can always give two nonverbal cues: (1) say your conclusion with a tone of dramatic finality, and (2) subtly intensify your facial expression and gestures. These cues should come naturally to you, since you have observed numerous speakers use them in your lifetime. If you feel unsure of yourself, practice your conclusion in front of a mirror or, better yet, in front of a friend (who can give you feedback). You can also say it into a tape recorder and listen to see if you have the appropriate tone of finality in your voice.

Summarize Key Ideas

Because listening is often a difficult mental task, some people in the audience might get drowsy or inattentive toward the end of your speech. But when you signal that you are about to finish, listeners usually perk up. If they know they can rest soon, they may summon the mental energy required to stay alert for a few more minutes. Like runners near the finish line, they can bring forth an extra burst of energy.

This mental alertness of your listeners gives you a good opportunity to drive home your message one more time. One of the best ways to do this is to summarize your key ideas. There is a formula for giving a speech that has been around for over a hundred years. Sometimes it is attributed to a spellbinding country preacher, sometimes to a savvy Irish politician. The true originator will probably never be known, but the formula is worth heeding:

> Tell 'em what you're going to tell 'em.
> Tell 'em.
> Then tell 'em what you told 'em.

The first sentence refers to the introduction, the second to the body, and the third to a summary in the conclusion. The summary gives you a chance to restate the central idea and/or the main points.

If you are like a lot of people, you may say, "Why do I need to repeat my message? After all, in the body of my speech, I give the audience five minutes' worth of beautifully organized, forcefully delivered information. If I hit this stuff again in the conclusion, won't I be guilty of overkill?" No, research shows that a restatement of your main points will increase the likelihood that the listeners will remember them.[6]

A summary should be brief. Don't get bogged down in explaining each point a second time; do all your explaining in the body of the speech. The following summary, for example, succinctly boils down the body of a speech into a few brief sentences, reiterating how a person can prevent car theft:

> So remember, you can prevent your car from being stolen if you follow these guidelines: Always park in a well-lighted area. Always remove your key from the ignition. Always close all windows and lock all doors.

Listeners don't mind hearing this kind of information again; it helps them retain it.

Reinforce the Central Idea with a Clincher

In addition to providing a summary, close your speech with a clinching statement that reinforces the central idea—a finale that drives home the main theme of your entire speech.

Public speakers are like carpenters driving a nail into a floor, says Edward L. Friedman. They begin with a few preliminary taps in the introduction to get the speech started right. As they get into the body of the speech, they deliver one hammer blow after another to drive the nail into its proper place with carefully executed strokes. Then in conclusion they execute a powerful, clinching blow.[7]

Use a clincher that is memorable, that leaves a lasting impression with the listener. You can find clinchers by using some of the techniques mentioned earlier in this chapter for the introduction (such as a rhetorical question or a visual aid) or by using some of the following techniques.

▶ Cite a Quotation

A good quotation can dramatize and reinforce a speaker's central idea. After urging her audience to always buckle their seat belts, one speaker said,

> I would like to close with a quotation from Laura Valdez, an emergency medical technician in California who said, "I have driven my ambulance to hundreds of traffic accidents. I have found many people already dead, but I have yet to unbuckle the seat belt of a dead person."

At the end of a speech on why citizens should fight social ills rather than succumb to despair, Richard Kern said,

> Let me leave you with the words of Eleanor Roosevelt: "It is better to light one candle than to curse the darkness."

Eye contact is important at the end of your speech, so if you use a quotation, practice it so that you can say it while looking at the audience, with only occasional glances at your notes.

▶ Issue an Appeal or Challenge

In a persuasive speech, you can end by making an appeal or issuing a challenge to the audience. If you are trying to persuade the listeners to donate blood, you can end by saying:

> Next week the bloodmobile will be on campus. I call upon each of you to spend a few minutes donating your blood so that others may live.

One speaker tried to convince her audience to make out a will, and in her conclusion she issued a challenge:

> The simple task of writing a will can protect your family and give you peace of mind. It is a sad fact that three out of four Americans will die without a will. Are you going to be one of them? I hope not. Why don't you write your will before you go to bed tonight?[8]

▶ Give an Illustration

An illustration is a popular way to reinforce the central idea of a speech. For example, Angela Di Napoli gave a speech in which she urged her listeners to seek an evaluation of any old coins they possessed, and she concluded with a true story that illustrated her point:

> Several years ago a woman in New England was rummaging through a trunk in her attic when she came across a box full of old coins. She took them to a coin dealer and got an evaluation. All of the coins were worthless except one. It was a five-dollar gold piece issued in 1849. The coin dealer informed the woman of its present-day value—*five thousand dollars.* So if you have some old coins lying around your house, take them to a reputable coin dealer for an evaluation. You, too, may be the owner of a very valuable coin.

▶ Refer to the Introduction

Using the conclusion to hearken back to something said in the introduction is an effective way to wrap up your speech. One way of doing this is to answer a question asked at the beginning of a speech. Student speaker Daniel Hirata asked in his introduction, "Should we permit job discrimination on the basis of a person's weight?" In the conclusion, Hirata repeated the question and answered it: "Should we allow job discrimination against overweight people? From what I've said today, I hope you'll agree that the answer is 'no.' To deny a person a job simply because he or she is overweight is as wrong as to deny a person a job because of skin color or ethnic background."

Guidelines for Conclusions

There are four pitfalls to avoid in conclusions:

1. Don't drag out the ending.   Some speakers fail to prepare a conclusion in advance. When they reach what should be the end of their remarks, they cannot think of a graceful way to wrap things up, so they keep on talking. Other speakers signal the end of their speech (by saying something like, "So, in closing, let me say . . ."), but then they drone on and on. This gives false hope to the listeners. When they see that the speaker is not keeping the promise, they feel deceived and become restless.

2. Don't end weakly.   If you close with a statement such as, "I guess that's about all I've got to say," and your voice is nonchalant and unenthusiastic, you encourage your listeners to downgrade your entire speech. End with confidence.

3. Don't end apologetically.   There is no need to say: "That just about does it. I'm sorry I didn't have more time to prepare . . ." or "That's it, folks. I guess I should have looked up more facts on . . . ." Apologies make you look incompetent. Besides, some people may not have noticed anything wrong with your speech or your delivery; you may have done better than you realized. So why apologize?

4. Never bring in new main points.   It is okay to bring in fresh material for your conclusion; in fact, it is a good idea to do so, as long as the material does not constitute a new main point. For an illustration, look at the following conclusions, which are based on a speech about the advantages of swimming.

Poor: So if you're looking for a good sport to take up for fun and health, remember that swimming dissipates your accumulated tension, it builds up your endurance, and it gives you a good workout without putting a strain on your muscles and joints. And, oh yes, another good reason for swimming: it can prevent you from developing back problems in old age.

Better: So if you're looking for a good sport to take up for fun and health, remember that swimming dissipates your accumulated tension, it builds up your endurance, and it gives you a good workout without putting a strain on your muscles and joints. I go over to the Y for a twenty-minute swim three days a week, and I always come out feeling healthy and invigorated. I wouldn't trade swimming for any other sport in the world.

The first conclusion is faulty because it lets a whole new point (the issue of back problems) slip in. Since this is the first the listeners have heard of the matter, it could confuse them. "Huh?" they may say to themselves. "Did I miss something that was said earlier?" Some listeners would expect you to elaborate on this new main point, but if you did, you would drag out your conclusion and spoil the sense of finality. The second conclusion has fresh material, but this material is not a new main point. It is merely a testimonial that underlines the message of the speech.

Sample Introduction and Conclusion

To see how the principles discussed in this chapter can be applied to a speech, let us examine how one speaker, student Thomas Vandenberg, developed an introduction and a conclusion for a speech on consumer fraud.[9]

Consumer Scams

Specific Purpose: To persuade my audience to investigate gimmicks and prizes before getting involved with a company

Central Idea: To avoid being cheated, consumers should skeptically investigate companies that offer "free prizes."

ATTENTION MATERIAL
The speaker begins with an interesting narrative that gains the listeners' attention and interest.

INTRODUCTION

I. A few months ago, I received a letter that informed me that I had won a free cruise to the Bahamas. Sounds wonderful, doesn't it? I fantasized something like *Love Boat* on TV, a beautiful ocean voyage with dancing and dining and, of course, shipboard romances in the moonlight. I was skeptical, however, because I had done nothing to win a prize. But I was also curious, so I called the phone number listed in the letter. I was told that yes, I definitely had won a cruise. The catch was that in order to receive my ticket, I would have to buy $450 worth of vitamins. But this would still be a wonderful deal, they told me, because the cruise itself was worth far more than $450. I said I would think about it. Next, I called the Better Business Bureau, and they gave me the facts about this so-called cruise. Yes, the company would indeed give me a boat ticket from Miami to the Bahamas, but it would not be on a luxury liner—it would be on a commercial ferry. In other words, I would travel on a deck filled with cars and crates—a depressing scene when contrasted with my *Love Boat* fantasies. The Better Business Bureau said my ticket would be worth only $30, and in the meantime I would be stuck with vitamins that cost me $450 but would retail in drugstores for about $50.

ORIENTING MATERIAL

The speaker gives some background information on the subject.

The speaker gives a preview of the central idea and the two main points.

II. This "cruise" is just one of hundreds of scams that are cheating thousands of consumers every day. A subcommittee of the U.S. Senate estimates that consumer scams, especially health schemes, cost Americans $25 billion per year. I would like to tell you how these scams operate. Then I wish to convince you that you can avoid being a victim of a scam if you follow two guidelines: Number one, always remember the maxim that in life, you rarely get something for nothing. Number two, never get involved in a scheme unless the Better Business Bureau assures you that the company is honest.

[Using the problem-solution pattern, the speaker devotes the first half of his speech to describing the nature and extent of the problem. In the second half, he outlines the steps that a consumer should take to avoid being victimized.]

CONCLUSION

In the first part of the conclusion, the speaker summarizes the main points.

I. If you get a letter in the mail today offering you a fabulous free prize, I hope you will remember the two guidelines I have discussed: First, remind yourself that in life, you rarely get something for nothing. So don't be surprised if the "prize" turns out to be worthless junk, like the grandfather clock I told you about that was made of cardboard or the fishing boat that turned out to be a tiny plastic toy. Secondly, before getting involved with a company, investigate it by calling your local Better Business Bureau. If they have never heard of the company, you would be wise to avoid doing business with it; many scams operate for a few months and then quickly fold, to elude the authorities.

The speaker ends gracefully with a wry reference to the story told in the introduction.

II. If you follow these two guidelines, you can avoid being ripped off. Just imagine how you would feel if your *Love Boat* fantasy turned into the grim reality of a ferryboat ride with cars and crates as your unromantic companions.

TIPS FOR YOUR CAREER

TIP 10.2: Don't Let Early Success Lure You to Failure

Take a look at a man whom I'll call Joe, a sales representative who is giving a presentation to an audience of fifty-five potential clients. His opening jokes have the listeners roaring with laughter, his sparkling visual aids cause murmurs of appreciation, and he sees that everyone in the audience is "with" him. He is truly "on a roll."

This is a delicious moment for Joe. He feels the power and excitement of enthralling an audience. He had planned to talk for 40 minutes (the amount of time allotted by the host company), but things are going so well, he spontaneously extends his speech. He discusses some minor points that were not included in his original plan, and he relates some personal anecdotes that don't really pertain to his subject.

As he continues, stroking his ego in this pleasurable time of power and success, he fails to realize that his 40-minute talk has stretched to 60 minutes, and he fails to note that the mood of his audience has changed. Instead of smiles and excitement, the listeners' faces are showing weariness and their eyes have a glazed look. Joe has let his bright firework of a speech sputter out in a gray cloud of smoke.

Unfortunately this scenario is all too common. Advertising executive Ron Hoff calls it "stealing defeat from the jaws of victory." A speaker, he says, "can get so intoxicated by the laughs, smiles, chortles, and applause of even a small audience that all sense of time and purpose evaporates in a rising tide of euphoria." He or she then drones on and on until "everybody is . . . punchy."

No matter how triumphant your oratory seems to be, end your speech at the agreed-upon time, or perhaps even earlier. "The most welcome closing for the average business audience," says Tom Kirby, an executive in St. Petersburg, Florida, "is one that comes a little ahead of schedule. Don't rush to finish early; *plan in advance to do so.*" No speaker has ever been booed and hissed for ending a great speech on time—or for ending it early.

Summary

Much of the success of a speech depends upon how well the speaker handles the introduction and conclusion. The introduction consists of two parts: attention material (to gain the audience's attention and interest) and orienting material (to prepare the audience intellectually and psychologically for the rest of the speech).

For attention material, you can use one or more of the following techniques: tell a story, ask a question, make a provocative statement, cite a quotation, arouse curiosity, provide a visual aid or demonstration, and provide the audience with an incentive to listen. For orienting material, you can preview the body of the speech, give background information, and establish your credibility.

The conclusion of your speech should signal the end, summarize your key ideas, and reinforce the central idea with a clincher. Examples of clinchers are any of the techniques mentioned for attention material, an appeal or challenge, an illustration, and a reference to the introduction.

Review Questions

1. Why is it necessary to provide attention material at the beginning of a speech?
2. What is the purpose of the orienting material?
3. What is a rhetorical question?
4. Why is it a mistake to use a quotation as the first sentence of your speech?
5. Why is it a mistake to end a speech abruptly?

Outlining the Speech

n 1912, a new hotel was built in Baltimore—the New Howard Hotel. When the furnaces in the basement were fired up, a startling discovery was made. The builders of the hotel had failed to include chimneys![1]

This spectacular blunder illustrates the importance of using an architect's blueprint, or detailed plan, when constructing a building. The hotel builders had failed to follow a well-defined master plan.

Just as a blueprint helps a builder construct a building, an outline helps you construct a speech. An outline permits you to organize your thoughts into a logical sequence, and to see which points are irrelevant or improperly placed or poorly developed.

Some students dislike writing an outline because they consider it unnecessary, a total waste of time. As one student put it, "I know what I'm going to say—I've got the outline in my head." However, most people who shun written outlines discover sooner or later that their method hurts them. They may fail to present information in the clearest, most logical manner possible; they may annoy the audience with confusing or irrelevant material, or they may sit down after a speech and suddenly realize that they left out a very important point.

In a survey of sixty-four business and professional speakers for this book, fifty-nine (or 92 percent) said they use outlines, and they recommend that you do likewise. An outline will remind you to include chimneys, and it will help you construct solid, livable hotels that your audience will enjoy staying in.

So far, we have talked about gathering materials (Chapters 6, 7, and 8) and then organizing them in the body (Chapter 9) and the introduction and conclusion (Chapter 10). Now we will discuss how to put all these things together in an outline.

There are three steps in the outline-to-speech process: First, create an outline; second, use the outline to prepare speaking notes, and third, use the speaking notes to deliver the speech. (For your classroom speeches, your instructor may have guidelines that differ in some degree from this sequence; you should, of course, follow his or her rules.)

If you are confused at this point over the difference between an outline and speaking notes, don't worry. This will be explained shortly. For the time being, take a look at Figure 11.1, an overview of the three-step process. Study this chart and refer to it as you read the pages that follow. (Step 3, delivering the speech, will be discussed in Chapter 13.)

FIGURE 11.1
These are the three steps in the outline-to-speech process. (For classroom speeches, find out if your instructor wants you to use this system or some other plan.)

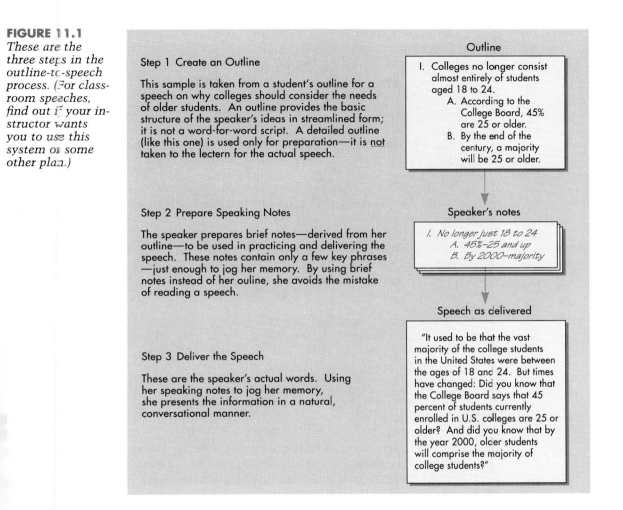

Step 1 Create an Outline

This sample is taken from a student's outline for a speech on why colleges should consider the needs of older students. An outline provides the basic structure of the speaker's ideas in streamlined form; it is not a word-for-word script. A detailed outline (like this one) is used only for preparation—it is <u>not</u> taken to the lectern for the actual speech.

Outline

I. Colleges no longer consist almost entirely of students aged 18 to 24.
   A. According to the College Board, 45% are 25 or older.
   B. By the end of the century, a majority will be 25 or older.

Step 2 Prepare Speaking Notes

The speaker prepares brief notes—derived from her outline—to be used in practicing and delivering the speech. These notes contain only a few key phrases —just enough to jog her memory. By using brief notes instead of her outline, she avoids the mistake of reading a speech.

Speaker's notes

I. No longer just 18 to 24
   A. 45%—25 and up
   B. By 2000—majority

Step 3 Deliver the Speech

These are the speaker's actual words. Using her speaking notes to jog her memory, she presents the information in a natural, conversational manner.

Speech as delivered

"It used to be that the vast majority of the college students in the United States were between the ages of 18 and 24. But times have changed: Did you know that the College Board says that 45 percent of students currently enrolled in U.S. colleges are 25 or older? And did you know that by the year 2000, older students will comprise the majority of college students?"

Guidelines for Outlining

Why use an outline? Why not just write out the entire speech?

A word-for-word script would create a sea of material that might overwhelm you. Even worse, you might be tempted to read the script, a method (as we will see in Chapter 13) that could put the audience to sleep.

An outline is better than a script because it shows the basic structure of your ideas in a streamlined form. It helps you see the relationship between ideas.

In essence, outlining is a commonsense way of arranging information in a logical pattern. The Federal Bureau of Investigation's Crime Index, for example, can be organized in the following way:

FBI Crime Index

I. Half of the eight crimes in the FBI Crime Index are considered *violent* crimes.
II. The other half of the eight crimes are considered *property* crimes.

Each of these major headings could be subdivided; for example, let's take the first one:

I. Half of the eight crimes in the FBI Crime Index are considered *violent* crimes.
   A. *Murder* means killing a person yourself, or hiring or manipulating someone else to do the killing for you.
   B. *Rape* means sexual assault or an attempt to commit sexual assault.
   C. *Robbery* differs from other forms of theft in that its victims are threatened with harm if they do not surrender their property.
   D. *Aggravated assault* means an attack on a person with intent to kill or cause injury.

If we wanted to, we could divide items A, B, C, and D into subcategories. For example, we could break murder down into categories of weapons used, with one category for guns, one for knives, and so on.

Here are some important points to keep in mind as you prepare your outlines.

Choose an Outline Format

The two most popular formats for outlines are the *topic outline* and the *complete-sentence outline*. Find out if your instructor prefers or requires one or the other. Some instructors and professional speakers recommend using both methods—the topic format in the early stages of preparation (when you are struggling to impose order on your material) and the complete-sentence format in the later stages (when you are refining and polishing your ideas)

▶ Topic Outline

In a topic outline, you express your ideas in key words or phrases. The advantage of this format is that it is quicker and easier to prepare than a complete-sentence outline.

At the beginning of this chapter, we saw a complete-sentence outline of the FBI Crime Index. If we put that information into a topic outline, it would look like this:

FBI Crime Index

I. Violent crimes
   A. Murder
   B. Rape

    C. Robbery
    D. Aggravated assault
  II. Property crimes
    A. Burglary
    B. Larceny/theft
    C. Motor vehicle theft
    D. Arson

▶ Complete-Sentence Outline

In the complete-sentence format, all your main points and subpoints are expressed in complete sentences. Unless your instructor tells you otherwise, I would recommend that you use complete sentences for your final outline. Here is why: (1) Writing complete sentences forces you to clarify and sharpen your thinking. You are able to go beyond fuzzy, generalized notions and create whole, fully developed ideas. (2) If another person (such as an instructor) helps you with your outline, complete sentences will be easier to understand than mere phrases, thus permitting that person to give you the best possible critique.

All the sample outlines in the rest of this book, including the one featured in this chapter, use the complete-sentence format.

A note of caution: the complete-sentence outline is not your speech written out exactly as you will present it. Rather, it is a representation of your key ideas; the actual speech should elaborate on these ideas. This means that your actual speech will contain many more words than the outline. See Figure 11.1 for an example.

Use Standard Subdivisions

In the standard system of subdividing, you mark your main points with roman numerals (I, II, III, etc.), then place the next level of supporting materials underneath in capital letters (A, B, C, etc.), then go to arabic numerals (1, 2, 3), then to small letters (a, b, c), and if you need to go further, use parentheses with numbers and letters. Here is the standard form:

  I. Major division
  II. Major division
    A. First-level subdivision
    B. First-level subdivision
      1. Second-level subdivision
      2. Second-level subdivision
        a. Third-level subdivision
        b. Third-level subdivision
          (1) Fourth-level subdivision
          (2) Fourth-level subdivision
    C. First-level subdivision

Notice that each time you subdivide a point, you indent. For most speeches you will not need to break your material down into as many subdivisions as illustrated here.

Avoid Single Subdivisions

Each heading should have at least two subdivisions—or none at all. In other words, for every heading marked "A," there should be at least a "B." For every "1" there should be a "2." The reason is obvious: How can you divide something and end up with only one part? If you divide an orange, you must end up with at least two pieces. If you end up with only one, you have not really divided the orange. One problem that arises is how to show a single example for a particular point. Below is the *wrong* way to handle the problem:

A. Many counterfeiters are turning to items other than paper money.
 1. Counterfeit credit cards now outnumber counterfeit bills.
B. . . .

This is wrong because item A cannot logically be divided into just one piece. There are two ways to correct the problem. One way is to simply eliminate the single item and combine it with the heading above:

A. Many counterfeiters are turning to items other than paper money: Counterfeit credit cards now outnumber counterfeit bills.
B. . . .

Another way of handling the problem is to not number the item but simply list it as "example":

A. Many counterfeiters are turning to items other than paper money.

 Example: Counterfeit credit cards now outnumber counterfeit bills.

B. . . .

Use Cards for Preliminary Outlines

One reason some students hate writing an outline is that they think the must sit down and write it all at once, then laboriously rewrite it wheneve a change is made.

Here is a technique that can save you a lot of time and labor: For you preliminary work (before you write your final outline), use extra-large (4 × 6 or larger) cards, putting one point on each card. Sit at a desk or table an display the cards containing your main points. Then underneath each mai point, place those cards which support it. (If you want to get fancy, you ca

FIGURE 11.2
Note cards such as these (on how to change a flat tire) can be used for a preliminary outline. This system provides flexibility, since you can add, delete, or rearrange cards before putting your outline into final form.

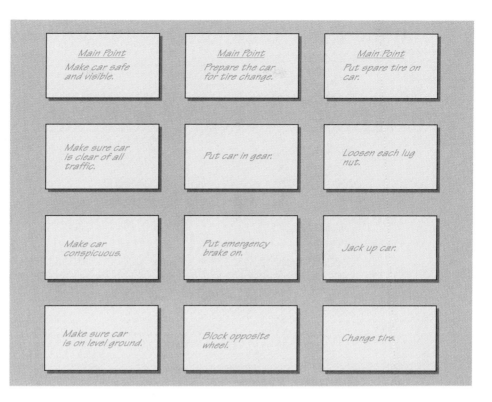

FIGURE 11.2
Note cards such as these (on how to change a flat tire) can be used for a preliminary outline. This system provides flexibility, since you can add, delete, or rearrange cards before putting your outline into final form.

use a color code—yellow cards, say, for main points and white cards for supporting points.) Figure 11.2 shows examples of cards for a preliminary outline on how to change a tire.

With this system, you can move cards about to try different sequences. As you develop your ideas, you can add or eliminate cards. After you have arranged the cards in logical sequences, you can number them according to the standard outline form, as discussed earlier in the chapter. Then you are ready to write out your final outline on a full sheet of paper.

Note to computer users: If you use word-processing software to create your outline, you will not need to use this card system because you can easily add, delete, and rearrange text on-screen.

Parts of the Outline

The parts of the outline discussed below are keyed to the sample outline that follows this section. Your instructor may have requirements for your outline that deviate somewhat from the description in these pages. (See Figure 11.3 for a schematic overview of a typical outline.)

FIGURE 11.3
This is a sche-matic overview of a typical outline. Although this out-line shows three main points, some speeches may have two or, occasionally, four.

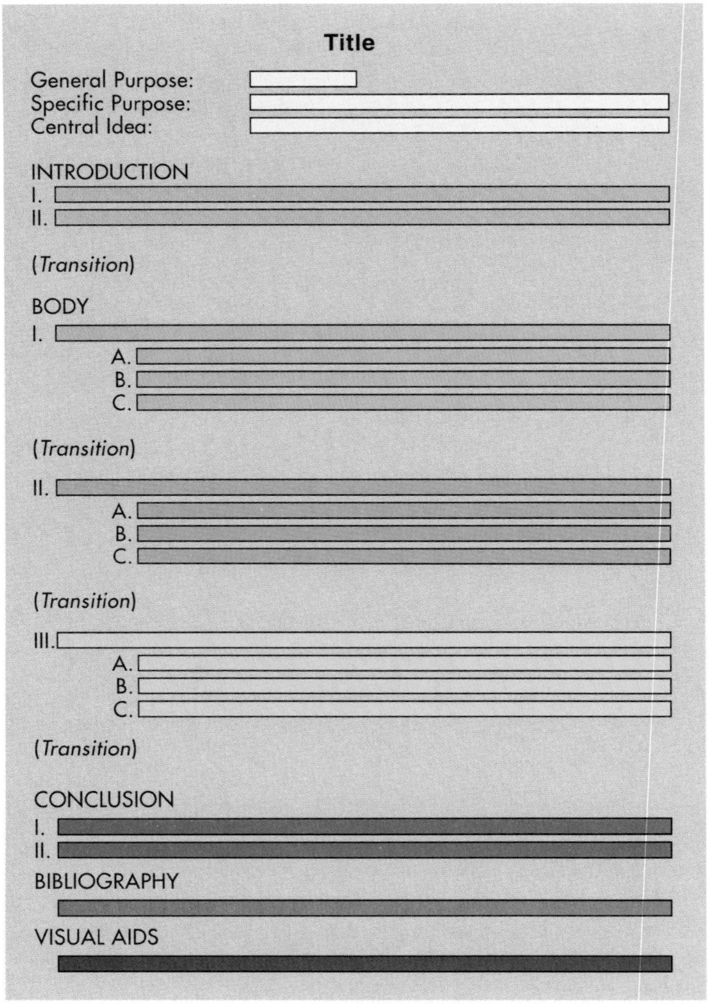

Title

General Purpose:
Specific Purpose:
Central Idea:

INTRODUCTION
I.
II.

(*Transition*)

BODY
I.
    A.
    B.
    C.

(*Transition*)

II.
    A.
    B.
    C.

(*Transition*)

III.
    A.
    B.
    C.

(*Transition*)

CONCLUSION
I.
II.

BIBLIOGRAPHY

VISUAL AIDS

1. Title. Your outline should have a title, but you *do not actually say it in your speech.* In other words, don't begin your speech by saying, "How to Lose Weight Permanently" or "The title of my speech is 'How to Lose Weight Permanently.' "

If you should not say the title, why have one? For classroom speeches your instructor may want you to write one simply to give you experience i devising titles. For some out-of-class speeches, a title might be requested s that your speech can be publicized in advance.

Your title should be brief and descriptive; that is, it should give a clea idea of what your speech is about. For example, "Why State Lotteries Shou

Be Abolished" is a short and helpful guide. If you want an attractive, catchy title, you can use a colorful phrase coupled with a descriptive subtitle—"A Lousy Bet: Why State Lotteries Should Be Abolished." Here are some other samples:

- ▶ War over the Wetlands: The Drive to Save Environmental Treasures
- ▶ Are You Being Ripped Off? How to Find an Honest Mechanic
- ▶ Ouch! What to Do When a Bee Stings You

2. Purposes and central idea. Having your general purpose, specific purpose, and central idea listed on your outline will help you bring into sharp focus the main points and supporting materials.

3. Introduction and conclusion. The introduction and conclusion are so vitally important in a speech that they deserve special attention and care. Some speakers recommend that you write out both of these items in full so you can make sure that they are well developed. Both sections should have their own numbering system, independent of the body of the speech.

4. Body. In the body of the outline, each main point should be identified by roman numerals. The body has its own numbering system, independent of the introduction and conclusion. In other words, the first main point of the body is roman numeral I.

5. Transitions. The transitional devices we discussed in Chapter 9 should be inserted in the outline at appropriate places. They are labeled and placed in parentheses, but they are not included in the numbering system of the outline.

While transitional devices should be placed wherever they are needed to help the listener, make sure you have them in three crucial places: (1) between the introduction and the body of the speech, (2) between each of the main points, and (3) between the body of the speech and the conclusion.

6. Bibliography. At the end of the outline, place a list of your sources—such as books, magazines, and interviews—which you used in preparing the speech. Give standard bibliographical data; for a book, for example, give the author, title, publisher, place of publication, date of publication, and the specific pages that you used. (Check with your instructor to see if he or she wants you to use a special format, such as that of the Modern Language Association.) If you used your own personal experiences, you should cite yourself as a source. The bibliography is useful not only to give your instructor a list of your sources, but also to provide you with a record if you ever give the speech again and need to return to your sources to refresh your memory or to find additional information.

7. *Visual aids.* If you plan to use visual aids, give a brief description of them. This will help the instructor to give you guidance on whether the visual aids are effective.

Sample Outline

Your outline should *not* include every word in your speech. It is merely the skeleton. Your actual speech will be longer.

Below is an outline by student speaker Patricia Clark Zarnowski.[2] Read it and then study the commentary in the left-hand column.

The Outline

COMMENTARY

Purposes and central idea should always appear at the top of the outline to help bring content into sharp focus.

The introduction is set off from the rest of the outline by its own heading and numbering system.

Part I grabs the listeners' attention and interest.

Part II previews the central idea and gives background information.

Many speakers find it helpful to write the introduction and conclusion in more detail than the rest of the outline.

Pumping Iron: A Necessity for Everyone

General Purpose: To persuade
Specific Purpose: To persuade my audience to lift weights
Central Idea: Every person, regardless of age, needs weight training in order to be fully fit and healthy.

INTRODUCTION

I. I am 54 years old. I am a grandmother. And I am a weight lifter. Does that sound freakish to you—a grandmother "pumping iron"? It sounded crazy to me when my doctor recommended weight lifting 2 years ago. But after 2 years of pumping iron, I feel better, I weigh less, and I am much stronger.

II. Health experts recommend weight training for everyone—men and women, young and old, athletes and nonathletes—as a way to stay healthy and strong. I hope to convince each of you to add weights to your exercise routine—not as a *substitute* for cardiovascular (or heart and lung) activities like running and swimming, but as a *supplement*. My information comes from several magazines and a book, and from an interview with Dr. Mark Gottlieb, a former medical advisor to the U.S. Olympic

Giving a prestigious source boosts the speaker's credibility.

team. The experts I read about and Dr. Gottlieb all agree that weight lifting is good for everyone.

Transitions are placed in parentheses and are not part of the outline's number system.

[Transition: Let's begin by looking at the health benefits you can get.]

The body contains main points, marked by roman numerals. Under each main point, subpoints are marked with capital letters (A, B, C).

BODY

I. Weight training can make you stronger, slimmer, and healthier.
  A. Weight training can make you stronger.
    1. Dr. Gottlieb says that most people lack upper-body strength.
    2. Some 65 percent of the body's muscles are above the hips.
    3. Most cardiovascular exercises do little to strengthen these muscles.
    4. When people neglect these muscles, their strength declines. Most middle-aged people can't carry a suitcase across an airport.
    5. Dr. Gottlieb says that after we have reached our full height, we start losing muscle mass if we don't exercise our muscles. By age 65, nonexercising persons have lost about 35 percent of their strength and 11 percent of muscle mass.
    6. Even when begun in your sixties or seventies, weight training can reverse the progressive withering away of muscles. Older people who develop their muscles are often stronger than younger people who never work out.
  B. Weight training can help you control your weight.
    1. As we get older, most of us lose muscle and gain fat. But this shift can be reversed.
    2. Dr. Gottlieb: Weight lifters lose fat as they gain muscle because of a change in body metabolism.
    3. Two groups of people went through an exercise program over an eight-week period. (*The New York Times*)

Subsubpoints are marked with arabic numerals (1, 2, 3).

Each level of subordination is shown by indentation.

a. The first group did only jogging; they lost an average of 3 pounds of fat but gained no muscle.

b. The second group did both jogging *and* weight lifting; they lost an average of 10 pounds of fat and gained 2 pounds of muscle.

C. Weight training can help you avoid disease and disability.

Research studies help substantiate a point.

1. One study showed that building strong muscles also builds strong bones. (*The New York Times*)

a. Researchers believe that weight training helps prevent osteoporosis, a disease of the bones.

b. People who start lifting weights in their late sixties are able to avoid developing brittle bones (the leading cause of hospitalization among the elderly is falling and breaking bones).

2. Strength training could prevent most back ailments.

Statistics are useful support.

a. Four out of five Americans will experience back problems at some point in their lives.

b. Dr. Gottlieb says that 80 percent of all lower-back problems are caused by muscular weakness, and that a weight training program can prevent most types of back injury.

D. Weight training can benefit everyone.

1. Weight lifting is good for old and young, male and female, athletes and nonathletes.

When a quotation is colorful, it is best to quote it verbatim rather than para-phrase it.

2. It is an ideal supplement to cardiovascular exercises like jogging. Dr. Gottlieb says: "I you run, walk, swim, or cycle regularly, you are doing wonderful things for your heart and lungs. Keep doing them. But these acti ities are not enough. To stay healthy and strong, and to enjoy your later years in life you must also strengthen your muscles."

The speaker antici-pates audience resis-tance and provides reassurance.

3. Don't worry about developing ugly, bulgin muscles.

a. To look like bodybuilders on TV, you would have to work out strenuously for several hours a day for years.

b. The average person who works out for 20 to 30 minutes three times a week will have increased muscular strength but will not develop massive, bulging muscles.

A transition is needed between main points.

(Transition: Now that we know the health benefits, let's talk about what you can do.)

II. You can easily create a weight training program for yourself.
   A. Weight training can be done by lifting so-called "free" weights—barbells and dumbbells—or by using resistance equipment.
      1. You can work out in the school's gym for free.
      2. You can work out at home. A set of barbells costs less than $40.
      3. If you can afford the fee, you can join a health club or spa.
         a. You get professional advice.
         b. Health clubs have high-tech weight machines.
   B. Weight training does not require much time.
      1. ACSM—The American College of Sports Medicine—recommends that you work out with weights 20 to 30 minutes three days a week.
      2. A day of rest is mandatory—to give muscles a chance to repair.
      3. ACSM suggests twelve repetitions of ten to fifteen different exercises for the large muscles of your chest, back, legs, and arms.
   C. You should learn to lift weights correctly.
      1. You can learn proper lifting techniques from instructors at a gym or spa.
      2. If you prefer to do your workouts at home, there is an excellent book that can teach you everything you need to know—*Getting Stronger*, by Bill Pearl.
      3. Heed some basic safety advice.

Specific details are helpful.

         a. Do light warm-up exercises and stretches before lifting.
         b. Never hold your breath while doing an exercise—this could cause you to pass out.
         c. To avoid back injury, lift with your legs—never bend over at the waist and lift with your back.

4. If you take these precautions, the risk of injury is small. Dr. James Graves, fitness director of the Center for Exercise Science at the University of Florida in Gainesville, says weight lifting exercises are low-impact: "There's no jarring of the skeletal system as there is in jogging."

The final transition prepares the audience for the conclusion.

(Transition: Let's review what we've discussed today.)

The conclusion has it own label and numbering system.

The speaker reviews the main points.

CONCLUSION

I. Weight training will make you stronger, it will help you stay trim and fit, and it can help ward off diseases such as osteoporosis and disabilities such as back pain. It does not require much time or money. It is easy to work out 20 to 30 minutes three times a week. If you don't want to join a health club, you can work out at home.

The clincher echos the introduction and appeals for audience action.

II. Is it silly for a 54-year-old grandmother to lift weights? No, and if I live to be 84, you will still find me pumping iron. I urge each of you to join me in this important form of exercise.

The bibliography lists all sources of information used in the preparation of the speech.

BIBLIOGRAPHY

Mark Gottlieb, M.D., former U.S. Olympic team advisor, personal interview, September 18, 1991.
Elizabeth Kaufman, "The New Case for Woman Power," *The New York Times Magazine*, April 28, 1991, p. S18.
Bill Pearl, *Getting Stronger* (Bolinas, CA: Shelter Publications, 1986), pp. 8–19.
"Strength Training," *Mayo Clinic Health Letter*, August 1990, p. 2.
Vic Sussman, "Muscle Bound," *U.S. News & World Report*, May 20, 1991, pp. 85–87.
Patricia Clark Zarnowski, personal experiences.

The speaker describes the visual aids.

VISUAL AIDS

Barbells and dumbbells
Posters showing main points
Handout giving details of the recommended book

Speaking Notes

After you have devised an outline, what do you do with it? Do you use it to practice your speech? No. Do you take it with you to the lectern to assist you in the delivery of your speech? No. The outline should be used only for *organizing* your ideas. When it comes to *practicing* and then *delivering* the speech, you should use brief speaking notes that are based upon the outline.

What is so bad about using your outline to give the speech? If you are using a complete-sentence outline, you might be tempted to read the outline, and nothing is duller than a read-aloud speech. As we will discuss in Chapter 13, you should deliver your speech extemporaneously; that is, in a conversational manner, looking at the audience most of the time, only occasionally glancing down at your notes. When you glance at your notes, you pick up ideas and then convey those ideas in whatever words come to mind at the moment. Thus you end up sounding natural and spontaneous.

While a complete-sentence outline is undesirable for delivery, the other extreme—using no notes at all—is equally bad. Without notes, you might forget important points, and you might fail to present your ideas in a logical, easy-to-follow sequence.

Notes bolster your sense of security. Even if you are in full command of the content of your speech, you feel more confident and self-assured knowing

Using brief notes (based on one's outline) is a good way to practice and then deliver a speech.

that you have notes as a safety net to rescue you if your mind goes blank and you fail to recall your next point.

By the way, some people have the idea that using notes is a sign of mental weakness or a lack of self-confidence, but this is unfounded. Most good speakers use them without losing the respect of an audience. After all, your notes represent a kind of compliment to your listeners. They show that you care enough about the occasion to spend time getting your best thoughts together in a coherent form. The kind of speaker that audiences *do* look down on is the windbag who stands up without notes and rambles on without tying things together.

Guidelines for Notes

As you read these guidelines, you may want to refer to the sample speaking notes in Figure 11.4.

▶ Make indentations in your speaking notes that correspond to those in your outline. This will help reinforce the structure of the speech in your mind. You may also want to repeat the numbering system; some speakers use only the roman numerals from their outline, and others use all the numbers and letters.

▶ Use only one side of a sheet of paper or note card because you might forget to turn the paper or card over.

▶ Write down only the minimum number of words or phrases necessary to trigger your memory. If you have too many words written down, you might overlook some key ideas, or you might spend too much time referring to your notes instead of looking at the audience. An exception to this rule would be long quotations or statistics that you would need to write out in full for the sake of accuracy.

▶ Write words in large letters that are neat and legible so that you have no trouble seeing them when you glance down during a speech.

▶ Include cues for effective delivery, such as "SHOW POSTER" and "PAUSE" (see the sample notes in Fig. 11.4). Write them in a bright color, so that they stand out. (By the way, some speakers use a variety of colors on their notes: black for main points, green for support materials blue for transitions, and red for delivery cues.)

▶ For speaking, use the same set of notes you used while rehearsing, so that you will be thoroughly familiar with the location of items on you prompts. I once practiced with a set of notes on which I penciled in so many editing marks that I made a fresh set of notes right before delivered the speech. This turned out to be a mistake because the note were so "new" that some of the key words failed to trigger my memor quickly, causing me to falter at several points. I should have staye

FIGURE 11.4
Here is how the speaker used note cards for the speech about weight lifting. Only the first two cards are shown.

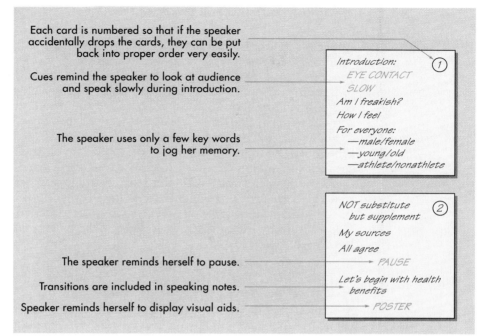

Each card is numbered so that if the speaker accidentally drops the cards, they can be put back into proper order very easily.

Cues remind the speaker to look at audience and speak slowly during introduction.

The speaker uses only a few key words to jog her memory.

Introduction:
    EYE CONTACT
    SLOW
Am I freakish?
How I feel
For everyone:
    —male/female
    —young/old
    —athlete/nonathlete

The speaker reminds herself to pause.

Transitions are included in speaking notes.

Speaker reminds herself to display visual aids.

NOT substitute
    but supplement
My sources
All agree
        → *PAUSE*
Let's begin with health
    benefits
        → *POSTER*

with the original notes. Even though they were filled with arrows and insertions and deletions, I knew them intimately; I had a strong mental picture of where each point was located. The new notes, on the other hand, had not "burned" an image in my brain.

▶ Don't put your notes on the lectern in advance of your speech. A janitor might think they are trash and toss them out. Or a previous speaker might accidentally scoop them up and walk off with them.

Options for Notes

Your instructor may require you to use one particular kind of note system, but if you have a choice, consider using one of three popular methods:

▶ Option 1: Use Note Cards

Your speaking notes can be put on note cards, as shown in Figure 11.4. Note cards (especially the 3 × 5 size) are compact and rather inconspicuous, and they are easy to hold (especially if there is no lectern to place notes on). Because of the small size of the card, you are forced to write just a few key words rather than long sentences that you might be tempted to read. If you use cards, be sure to number each one in case you drop them and need to reassemble them quickly.

▶ Option 2: Use a Full Sheet of Paper

If you use a full sheet of paper, you can have the notes for your entire speech spread out in front of you—you don't have to do any shuffling, as with cards.

There are, however, several disadvantages: (1) Because a whole sheet of paper is a large writing surface, many speakers succumb to the temptation to put down copious notes. This hurts them in speechmaking because they end up spending too much time looking at their notes at the expense of eye contact with the audience. (2) A full sheet of paper can cause a speaker's eyes to glide over key points because the "map" is large. (3) If sheets of paper are brought to the room curled up, they can curl up on the lectern, much to the speaker's dismay. (4) If no lectern is available, a hand-held sheet of paper tends to shake and rustle, causing a distraction to the listeners. (5) It is harder to make corrections on paper than on note cards. With paper, you may have to rewrite all your notes, whereas with note cards, you simply delete the card containing the undesired section and write your corrected version on a fresh card.

▶ Option 3: Use Visual Aids as Prompts

A popular technique in business and professional speeches is to use one's visual aids (such as transparencies, posters, flip charts, chalkboards, or dry-erase boards) as prompts. This not only provides the audience with a visual presentation of the key points, but it also helps the speaker stay on track (without having to look at notes on a lectern). One speaker, for example, put all her key ideas on a series of overhead transparencies. One graphic looked like this:

Longer School Year?	
Yes	62%
No	26%
Unsure	12%

As she showed this to the audience, she said, "In a recent poll, when parents were asked if they favored a longer school year for their children, 62 percent said yes, 26 percent said no, and 12 percent were undecided or unsure. I think this is a very strong mandate for extending the school year."

She proceeded from graphic to graphic in this manner. She had no note cards because the transparencies served as her cues.

This system "allows you to walk around the room, projecting greater confidence than you would if you remained riveted, eyes-to-paper, behind a lectern," according to media consultants Mike Edelhart and Carol Ellison.

If you use this strategy, here are some suggestions: (1) Avoid using a visual aid that is primarily a cue for yourself and has no value for the audience. In other words, a visual aid should always be designed for audience enlightenment, not for speaker convenience. The notes in Figure 11.4 are fine on note cards, but if they are displayed on a transparency, they are cryptic to the audience. (2) Avoid creating a deluge of text. Some speakers write a script and use virtually every sentence as a visual aid. This produces a tedious stream of words, causing the audience to become weary and irritated. Display only a few key words or numbers. (3) Don't use slides. In a darkened room with nothing but slides, you would lose eye contact with your audience. With other media (such as overhead transparencies), the room can remain undarkened so that you and your listeners can see each other clearly.

Some speakers put their main points and subpoints on a chalkboard or flip chart before a presentation begins, and as they speak, they assume that the listeners' eyes will automatically leap from point to point. This is not altogether bad, but there is a better way: Start with a clean board or chart, and as you come to each point, write a few key words (or use progressive revelation, as discussed in Chapter 8). This creates a bit of suspense and serves as a transition—a signal to the listeners that says, in effect, "Here comes a new point, so pay attention." Moreover, your physical activity makes you more interesting to the audience—it breaks up the potential monotony of a speaker standing in one spot.

Using visual aids as prompts is not a technique that must be used exclusively. You can combine it with note cards or a full sheet of paper.

Controlling Your Material

While preparing an outline and speaking notes, it is important that you control your material rather than let your material control you. Here are three things you can do to make sure that you stay in control:

1. Revise your outline and speaking notes whenever they need alterations. Some students mistakenly view an outline as a device that plants their feet in concrete; once they have written an outline, they think that they are stuck with it—even if they yearn to make changes. An outline should be treated as a flexible aid that can be altered as you see fit.

2. Test your outline. One of the reasons for creating an outline is to *test* your material to see if it is well-organized, logical, and sufficient. Here are some questions that you should ask yourself as you analyze your outline (in your career, you can ask colleagues to critique your outline, using the same questions):

▶ Does the introduction provoke interest and give sufficient orienting material?

▶ Do I preview the central idea and/or main points?

▶ Do the main points explain or prove my central idea?

▶ Are the main points organized logically?

▶ Is there enough support material for each main point? Is there too much?

▶ Do I have smooth transitions between introduction and body, between main points, and between body and conclusion?

▶ Have I eliminated extraneous material that doesn't truly relate to my central idea?

▶ Does my conclusion summarize the main points and reinforce the central idea?

▶ Is my conclusion strong and effective?

3. *Revise for continuity.* Often an outline looks good on paper, but when you make your speaking notes and start practicing, you find that some parts are disharmonious, clumsy, or illogical. A speech needs a graceful, even flow, carrying the audience smoothly from one point to another. If your speech lacks this smooth flow, go back and alter the outline and speaking notes until you achieve a continuity that you are comfortable with. (If you practice in front of friends, ask them to point out parts that are clumsy or confusing.)

4. *Make deletions if you are in danger of exceeding your time limit.* After you make your speaking notes, practice delivering your speech while you clock yourself to see how much time it takes. If the speech exceeds the time limit (set by your instructor or by the people who invited you to speak), you must go back to your outline and speaking notes and trim them down. Deleting material can be painful, especially if you have worked hard to get a particular example or statistic. But it is a job that *must* be done. Be ruthless. Be brave. Even if you exceed the limit by only 5 minutes, you must cut. A speech that exceeds its allotted time can spoil a program that features other speakers or events in a tight time frame.

Speech as Presented

The following is a transcript of the speech about weight lifting as it was delivered by Patricia Clark Zarnowski. Note that the wording is not identical to that used in the outline. The reason, of course, is that Zarnowski was delivering the speech extemporaneously, using the speaking notes shown earlier in this chapter. If she had read from her outline or from a complete text, she might have sounded stilted and artificial. By choosing her words as she went along, she made her speech vigorous, forthright, and easy to follow. If she gave this speech ten different times, the wording would be different each time, although the ideas would remain basically the same.

Pumping Iron: A Necessity for Everyone

Let me tell you something about myself: I am 54 years old. I am a grandmother. And I am a weight lifter. Does that sound weird to you—the idea of a grandmother "pumping iron"? It sure sounded crazy to me when my physician recommended weight lifting a couple of years ago. But after two years of pumping iron, let me tell you: I feel better, I weigh less, and I am much stronger.

Health experts recommend weight training for everybody as a way to stay healthy and strong. It doesn't matter whether you're male or female, young or old, athletic and nonathletic. Today I hope to convince you to take up weight lifting—not as a *substitute* for cardiovascular (heart and lung) exercises like running and swimming, but as a *supplement*. For this speech, I read a book and several magazine articles and I interviewed Dr. Mark Gottlieb, who was a medical advisor to the U.S. Olympic team a few years ago. Dr. Gottlieb and all the experts I read about agree that weight lifting is an important form of exercise for everyone.

Let's start off by looking at the health benefits. Weight training can make you stronger, slimmer, and healthier. First, strength: Dr. Gottlieb says that most people lack upper-body strength. This is true for people of all ages. About 65 percent of your body's muscles are located above your hips. Most cardiovascular exercises do little to strengthen these muscles. When you neglect these muscles, your upper-body strength declines. Most middle-aged people can't carry a suitcase across an airport. After we have reached our full height—Dr. Gottlieb says—we begin to lose muscle mass if we don't exercise our muscles. By age 65, if we haven't been exercising, we will have lost about 35 percent of our strength and 11 percent of our muscle mass. The good news is that weight training, even when begun in our sixties or seventies, can reverse the progressive withering away of muscles. Older people who lift weights are often stronger than younger people who never work out.

The next benefit is controlling our weight. As we get older, most of us lose muscle and gain fat, but this can be reversed. Most weight lifters lose fat as they gain muscle because of a change in body metabolism. The *New York Times* cites a study in which two groups of people went through an exercise program over an eight-week period. The first group did only jogging; at the end of the eight weeks, they had lost an average of 3 pounds of fat but gained no muscle. The second group did both jogging *and* weight lifting; at the end of the eight weeks, they had lost an average of 10 pounds of fat and gained two pounds of muscle.

Another benefit of weight training: it can help you avoid disease and disability. Recent medical research reported by the *New York Times* shows that weight lifting does more than build muscles: it also builds strong bones. Researchers believe that weight training may help prevent osteoporosis, a disease of the bones. People who start lifting weights in their late sixties are able to avoid developing brittle bones. This is important because the leading cause of hospitalization among the elderly is falling and breaking bones.

One of the greatest benefits of strength training is the prevention of most back problems. If you are typical Americans, four out of five of you will have a back problem sometime in your life. Dr. Gottlieb says that 80 percent of all lower back problems are caused by muscular weakness. So a weight training program that includes some exercises for the back can prevent most back injuries.

Please don't think that weight lifting is just for the young and athletic. Dr. Gottlieb says that weight lifting is good for young and old, male and female, athletes and nonathletes. It is a perfect supplement for cardiovascular exercises like jogging. Dr. Gottlieb says: "If you run, walk, swim, or cycle regularly, you are doing wonderful things for your heart and lungs. Keep doing them. But these activities are not enough. To stay healthy and strong, and to enjoy your later years in life, you must also strengthen your muscles."

Some people shy away from weight lifting because they're afraid of developing ugly, bulging muscles. This will not happen to you unless you want it. To look like the bodybuilders on TV, you would have to work out very hard for several hours a day for many years. If you work out for 20 to 30 minutes three times a week, you will never look like that. You will have stronger muscles but they won't be massive and bulging.

Now that we know the health benefits, let's talk about what you should do. It is very easy for you to create a weight training program for yourself. Weight training can be done very simply—by lifting "free" weights: barbells and dumbbells. Or you can use more sophisticated resistance equipment like Nautilus machines. You can work out in the school's gym for free. Or you can work out at home. All you need is a set of barbells—the cost is less than $40, a small investment considering the benefits you will receive. Another option, if you can afford the fee, is to join a health club or spa. Clubs have two advantages: you get professional advice and you can use high-tech weight machines that offer more variety than barbells.

Weight training does not require much time. ACSM—The American College of Sports Medicine—recommends that you work out with weights 20 to 30 minutes three days a week. You *must* have a day of rest after lifting weights to give muscles a chance to repair themselves. The ACSM suggests twelve repetitions of ten to fifteen different exercises for the large muscles of your body—chest, arms, back, and legs.

Wherever you work out, you should learn the proper way to lift weights. You can learn proper lifting techniques from instructors at a gym or spa. If you prefer to do your workouts at home, here is a good book that can teach you everything you need to know—*Getting Stronger* by Bill Pearl. Any bookstore can order it for you. I've got the information you need on a handout I'll pass out at the end of this speech.

You need to abide by a few basic safety precautions. First, do light warm-up exercises and stretches before lifting. Second, never hold your breath while lifting—this could cause you to pass out. Third, and most important of all, you can hurt your back unless you lift with your legs—never bend over at the waist and lift with your back. If you take these precautions, your chances of hurting yourself are small because lifting is a low-impact exercise. Here is a quote from Dr. James Graves, fitness director of the Center for Exercise Science at the University of Florida in Gainesville: "There's no jarring of the skeletal system as there is in jogging."

Now let's review what we've covered today. Everyone can profit from weight training, regardless of age or sex. Weight training will make you stronger, it will help you be lean and fit, and it can help prevent osteoporosis and back injury. It doesn't take much time or money. All you have to do is work out 20 to 30 minutes three times a week. You can join a spa or health club, or you can work out at home.

Do you think it's ridiculous for a 54-year-old grandmother to lift weights? I don't think so, and if I live to be 84, you'll still find me lifting weights. I urge all of you to join me in pumping iron.

▶ **For two other complete outlines (with transcripts), see the samples at the end of Chapters 14 (informative) and 15 (persuasive).**

Summary

An outline is as important to the speechmaker as a blueprint is to a builder. The outline provides a detailed plan to help the speaker organize thoughts into a logical sequence and to make sure nothing important is left out.

After you complete your outline, prepare speaking notes based upon it. You have three options—note cards, a full sheet of paper, or speaking notes displayed as a visual aid. Whichever you choose, avoid writing too many words because when you use notes in a speech, you want to be able to glance down quickly and retrieve just enough words to jog your memory.

Review Questions

1. Why is an outline recommended for all speeches?
2. What is the advantage of using complete sentences in an outline?
3. What are the parts of an outline?
4. Why should each subdivision of an outline have at least two parts?
5. What three options are available for speaking notes?

TIPS

FOR YOUR CAREER

TIP 11.1: When No Time Limit Is Set, Speak Briefly

We have already discussed the need to abide by the time limits placed on a speech, but what should you do when no time limit is set, that is, when you are invited to speak for as long as you like? The best advice I can give you is this: Be brief. Keep it short. In the words of Owen Feltham, a seventeenth-century English author, every person "should study conciseness in speaking; it is a sign of ignorance not to know that long speeches, though they may please the speaker, are the torture of the hearer."

How brief is brief? For a short speech, a good rule of thumb is to aim for about 5 minutes. Many clubs ask for 5-minute talks; many executives ask for 5-minute presentations, and all Toastmasters' clubs stipulate 5 minutes for their members' speeches. For longer speeches, such as after-dinner addresses, you would need to assess particular audiences and occasions. I would recommend no more than 20 minutes, although some after-dinner speakers go 45 to 60. In any situation, if you go over 60 minutes, you will usually see the audience become fatigued and fidgety.

Today audiences prefer—and are getting—shorter speeches, possibly because television has conditioned people to assimilate only short bursts of material. The demand for brevity is even being voiced in America's churches, which once featured sermons lasting well over an hour. Most ministers today preach for no more than 30 minutes. Donald Macleod, who teaches sermon preparation at Princeton Theological Seminary, tells his seminarians that 18 minutes is the maximum time for an effective sermon.

Whenever you are in doubt about length, remember that if one must err, it is always best to err on the side of brevity. If, when you finish a speech, the listeners are still hungering for more wisdom from your mouth, no harm is done. They will probably invite you to come back and speak again. But if you speak so long that they become bored, weary, and sleepy, they will resent you for wasting their time.

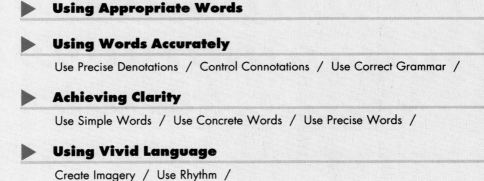

Wording the Speech

▶ **Using Appropriate Words**

▶ **Using Words Accurately**

Use Precise Denotations / Control Connotations / Use Correct Grammar /

▶ **Achieving Clarity**

Use Simple Words / Use Concrete Words / Use Precise Words /

▶ **Using Vivid Language**

Create Imagery / Use Rhythm /

▶ **Oral versus Written Language**

T he power of a single word is incredible. Take, for instance, the world of advertising. A book on automobile repair was once advertised under the headline "How to Repair Cars." When the advertising agency changed the headline to read "How to Fix Cars," sales jumped by 20 percent.[1] Why is *fix* more likely to garner sales than its synonym *repair*? No one is sure exactly why—perhaps it sounds easier to fix a car than to repair it. Whatever the reason, ad agencies know that while the right word can help an ad, the wrong word can hurt it. David Ogilvy, an advertising copywriter, once wondered why one of his ads failed to lure buyers. He conducted a survey, which showed that he made the mistake of using the word *obsolete* in the ad's headline. The survey revealed that 43 percent of consumers in the group targeted had no idea what "obsolete" meant.[2]

The producers of television commercials know that the right word can be worth millions of dollars in increased sales. They have learned, for example, that the words *new* and *improved* in a commercial will boost sales significantly. That is why TV viewers so often hear a product touted as "the new, improved . . . ."

While finding the right word is obviously vital in advertising, it is also important in public speaking. The difference between the right word and the *almost* right word, Mark Twain once observed, is the difference between lightning . . . and the lightning bug. The truth of Twain's remark can be seen in the following historical vignette: One of President Franklin Roosevelt's most famous speeches was his address to Congress asking for a declaration of war against Japan in the aftermath of the Japanese attack on the American fleet at Pearl Harbor. As written by an assistant, the speech began this way:

December 7, 1941: A date which will live in world history.

Before speaking, Roosevelt crossed out the words *world history* and substituted the word *infamy*. Here is what he ended up saying:

December 7, 1941: A date which will live in infamy.

This has become one of the most famous sentences in American history, along with such memorable statements as "Give me liberty or give me death!" And yet, if Roosevelt had used the original sentence, it never would have become celebrated. Why? Because *infamy*—a pungent word tinged with evil and anger—was the right description for the occasion; the term *world history*—dull and unemotional—was merely "almost right." Lightning . . . and the lightning bug.

In this chapter, we will look at how you can choose the right words for your speeches.

Using Appropriate Words

In choosing words for your speeches, your goal should not be to select the most beautiful or the most sophisticated, but to use the *right* words for the *right* audience. As you analyze your audience before a speech, ask yourself "How can I best express my ideas so that the audience will understand and accept them?" A word that might be ideal for one audience might be inappropriate for another.

Dr. Martin Luther King, the brilliant leader of the civil rights movement of the 1960s, was a master at using the right words with the right group. To a highly educated audience, for example, he would employ sophisticated language and abstract concepts, such as this sentence from his Nobel Peace Prize acceptance speech:

Civilization and violence are antithetical concepts.

Such a sentence, appropriate for an erudite audience, would have been incomprehensible if used in one of his speeches to poor, uneducated share-croppers in Mississippi. For them, he used simple words and down-to-earth illustrations. For example, in defending himself against accusations of being allied with communists, Dr. King used a simple, but vivid comparison that could be grasped by the least educated of his listeners:

There are as many communists in the freedom movement as there are Eskimos in Florida.

With either kind of audience, Dr. King was highly persuasive, but what did he do when he spoke to a group made up of both educated and uneducated people? He used inspirational messages designed to appeal to every listener. In his famous "I Have a Dream" speech, delivered to 200,000 people who had marched on Washington to demand equal rights for blacks, Dr. King used stirring words that appealed to everyone:

I have a dream that my four little children will one day live in a nation where they will not be judged by the color of their skin but by the content of their character.

There was nothing phony about Dr. King's adaptation to his audiences. All good speakers pitch their language to the appropriate level for their audience.

While considering your audience, you should also use words that are appropriate to the *occasion*. If you speak at a fund-raiser, your words should

FOR YOUR CAREER

TIP 12.1: Omit Salty Language

Some business and professional presenters use profane, obscene, or explicit language because (they say) it adds spice and "most people don't mind." While it may be true that most people aren't upset, it is a mistake to ignore the feelings of those who are genuinely offended. (By the way, coarse language isn't an age-related issue, with the young unbothered and the old bothered. There are people of *all* ages who feel slapped in the face.) Consider this:

Advertising executive Ron Hoff tells of a business presentation in which the speaker was trying to sell his company's services to a public utility firm. The speaker liberally sprinkled his talk with four-letter words, plus some five-letter varieties not often heard in public.

There were seventeen people in the audience, including one man "whose body actually convulsed a little every time he heard one of those words," says Hoff. "I watched him carefully. It was like somebody grazed him every few minutes with an electric prod. His body language attempted to cover these jolts he was receiving (he'd cross his legs, cover his face, slouch in his chair—nothing worked). He physically recoiled from the language he was hearing."

That man, it turned out, was the highest-ranking representative of the firm, so it came as no surprise when the firm declined to buy the services of the speaker's company.

Hoff later asked the speaker why he had used so much salty language.

"Oh, they love it," he said. "They talk just like that all the time."

Yeah, Hoff said to himself. All of them *except one*.

be uplifting and encouraging; at a funeral, solemn and respectful; at a pep rally, rousing and emotional.

Never make political, religious, racial, ethnic, or sexual references that might alienate anyone in your audience. Ask yourself, "Is there any chance at all that what I'm planning to say might offend someone in the audience?" If you cannot decide whether a word is appropriate, don't use it.

Stay away from sex-related stereotypical expressions such as *little old lady*, *broad*, *chick*, and *typical male brutality*. Try to eliminate sexism from sex-linked occupational terms. Here are some examples:

Original	*Preferred Form*
workman	worker
stewardess	flight attendant
fireman	firefighter
policeman	police officer
mailman	mail carrier
man-made	artificial
cleaning lady	housekeeper
foreman	supervisor

Janet Elliott of Los Angeles writes, "I recently attended a meeting in which nearly 80 percent of the audience was composed of young college women. The speaker was addressing the subject of career options for communications majors in business. Throughout his speech he used the term 'businessman' when referring to a business executive in general. Many members of his audience were offended by the exclusion."[3]

Using Words Accurately

To use words accurately, you need to be sensitive to two types of meanings—denotations and connotations—and also to the use of correct grammar.

Use Precise Denotations

The *denotation* of a word is the thing or idea that it refers to—its dictionary definition. The denotation of *chair* is a piece of furniture for one person to sit on. Complications arise when a word has more than one denotation. The word *verbal*, for example, means "in words, either spoken or written." If I asked you to give a verbal report, you would not know whether I wanted your words spoken or written. I would have to come up with a more precise word; *oral*, for example, would be clear and unambiguous.

Another complication is that words sometimes change their denotations. One middle-aged speaker used the word *aerobics* in the way it was used in the 1960s: denoting exercises, such as running and swimming, that are beneficial to heart and lungs. But his younger listeners misunderstood him. They thought that he was talking only about vigorous dance routines—the present-day denotation of "aerobics."

Sometimes a word has different meanings in different parts of the nation. If, for example, you say, "In considering your nutritional needs, pay special attention to dinner," what time of day are you referring to? You would need to give an explanation because not all Americans use the word *dinner* in the same way. While most people think of dinner as the third and final meal of the day, some Americans, especially those from rural areas and from certain geographical regions, picture dinner as the meal served in the middle of the day.

You should never use a word, advises Dr. Kenneth McFarland, a professional speaker, "unless you know . . . that it means what you think it means." Dr. McFarland tells of hearing a county agricultural agent make a speech on the problems of the farm surplus. "A dozen times in his discourse he spoke of the 'dearth of wheat' and the 'dearth of corn.' At first his audience was bewildered but eventually it became obvious to most of the hearers that the speaker thought dearth meant abundance or surplus. [Actually, *dearth* is the opposite of surplus—it means scarcity.] The misuse of this one word killed the effect of what could have been a good speech."[4]

Do you see why the county agent wounded his credibility? From the audience's point of view, how could they accept the ideas of a man who was so sloppy with language that he used a word in a sense that was opposite its true meaning?

Control Connotations

The *connotation* of a word is the emotional meaning that is associated with it. The words *slender, thin,* and *skinny* are synonyms; they have the same denotation, but the connotations are different: *slender* has a positive connotation, *thin* is neutral, and *skinny* has negative overtones. The words *fat, obese,* and *overweight* have similar denotations, but different connotations. Most fat people would prefer to be termed overweight, and if given a choice, they would rather be called fat than obese. Why? *Fat* sounds "fatter" than *overweight,* and *obese* suggests a gross fatness that is health-endangering. Other synonyms like *chubby* or *plump* have special connotations—*chubby* is often used to refer to children and suggests a healthy condition; *plump* suggests a pleasing roundness.

As a listener and as a speaker, you should be aware of how connotations express a person's attitude. Let's say that some filmmakers produce a documentary on Senator Sally Jones. If they want to remain objective about the senator, they can describe her with a word that has a neutral connotation—*legislator.* If they want to convey approval, they can choose a word that has positive connotations—*national leader.* If they want to express disapproval, they can use a word that has negative connotations—*politician.* If they describe one of her campaign events, they could call it a *gathering* (neutral), a *rally* (positive), or a *mob* (negative). When she travels to Central America, the *trip* (neutral) could be called a *fact-finding mission* (positive) or a *junket* (negative).

With some synonyms, the connotations are so subtly different that you have to be especially thoughtful in selecting the right one. If, for example, you wanted to speak on the need for individuals to get away from other people occasionally and be by themselves, which word would have the more positive connotations—*loneliness* or *solitude?* When people hear the word *loneliness,* they often think of feeling sad, being friendless, craving companionship. *Solitude,* on the other hand, conjures images of peaceful serenity—walking alone on the beach, curling up with a book in front of the fireplace on a wintry night, or relaxing in a bathtub. *Solitude,* then, is the word you would want for describing the joys of being alone.

In exploring connotations, you don't have to rely solely on your own judgment. Many dictionaries have synonym notes, which are usually located after a word's definitions. While I have found that the best synonym notes are in the giant *Webster's Third New International Dictionary* (which most libraries have), you can also find helpful notes in many abridged dictionaries.

Use Correct Grammar

Although I would never devalue a person for using incorrect grammar, many people downgrade individuals if they make serious grammatical mistakes. To these people, bad grammar is as offensive as body odor or food stains on the front of a shirt. For example,

▶ In North Carolina a corporation executive said, "I just can't stand to be around people who use bad English. I would never hire a person who said things like 'I done it.' "

▶ In California a man was passed over for a promotion (even though he was better qualified than the person who got the position) simply because he had the habit of saying "he don't" instead of "he doesn't."

▶ In New Jersey the head of a company wanted to promote a deserving part-time worker to full-time secretary, "but I can't get her to stop saying 'youse' [for the plural of 'you']," he said. "My customers just won't accept that because they're used to dealing with educated people. They might think that the sloppiness in language carries over to the way we handle their accounts."[5]

Poor grammar hurts you because it makes you sound (to some people) as if you are not very intelligent. To make matters worse, people will often refrain from telling you when your grammar offends them. A boss, for example, may be too ashamed to tell an employee that he or she uses unacceptable grammar; it is as embarrassing as telling friends that they have bad breath. So the employee is never told the real reason why he or she is being denied a promotion.

As for public speaking, "almost nothing discredits a speaker so totally as abuse of basic grammar," says lecturer Reid Buckley, brother of columnist William Buckley. "To fastidious ears, a glaring grammatical lapse is no less offensive than an obscenity."[6] Roy Fenstermaker, winner of the 1983 Toastmasters' International Speech Contest, says, "Careless syntax, ungrammatical expressions, or gross mispronunciation of common words are apt to be interpreted by listeners as evidence of lack of education or disrespect for the standards of the audience."[7]

From my observations, the following mistakes seem to be the ones that are most likely to cause some people to downgrade you:

Incorrect	Correct
He (or she) don't	He (or she) doesn't
You was	You were
I done it	I did it
Between you and I	Between you and me
I had went	I had gone
She's (He's) already went	She's (He's) already gone
I been thinking	I've been thinking
I've already took algebra	I've already taken algebra
hisself	himself
theirself	themselves
We seen it	We saw it
Her and me went	She and I went
Him and me went	He and I went
I come to see you yesterday	I came to see you yesterday
She ain't here	She isn't here
She don't love me no more	She doesn't love me anymore
He be late	He is late
I had wrote it	I had written it
Give me them apples	Give me those apples

If you make these or similar errors, I strongly urge you to learn how to correct your grammar and usage. Your school may have a tutoring service that can help you identify your grammatical mistakes and then correct them. Or perhaps you can find a book in a library or bookstore on improving one's English.

Achieving Clarity

To be clear in the words you use, you must first be clear in your thinking. Think about a word before you use it. Ask yourself, will it be clear to someone who is new to my subject? In this section we will examine how you can achieve clarity by using words that are simple, concrete, and precise.

Use Simple Words

A speechwriter for President Franklin D. Roosevelt once wrote, "We are endeavoring to construct a more inclusive society." President Roosevelt changed the wording to, "We're going to make a country in which no one left out."[8]

Roosevelt obviously believed in the value of the old public speakers' maxim: Never use a long word when a short one will do just as well. Some people think the best way to convey complex ideas is to use complex language—big words and weighty phrases. This is nonsense. If you examine great works of literature, you will see that profound thoughts can be expressed easily and beautifully by simple words. Some of the greatest pieces of literature in the English language—the King James version of the Bible and Shakespeare's works—use simple words to convey big ideas. For example, in Hamlet's famous soliloquy ("To be or not to be . . .") 205 of the 261 words are of one syllable. Citing an American literary classic, Abraham Lincoln's Second Inaugural Address, writer William Zinsser says, "Of the 701 words in [the address], 505 are words of one syllable and 122 are words of two syllables."[9]

Some speakers are pretentious, trying to show off instead of making sure that their ideas are clear to the audience. In contrast, audience-centered speakers will choose the simple word whenever possible because they want their listeners to understand what they are saying. A pretentious speaker or an audience-centered speaker—which would you prefer to listen to? Which would you prefer to be? Here are some examples of the contrasting styles:

> *Pretentious speaker:* It is incumbent upon the citizens of this country to find alternatives to the widespread distribution of discarded objects on the nation's roads and highways.
>
> *Audience-centered speaker:* People ought to throw their trash some place other than on the streets.
>
> *Pretentious speaker:* People who are experiencing intense negative emotions directed at a significant other would be well advised to disclose their condition to that individual.
>
> *Audience-centered speaker:* If you're extremely angry at a loved one, don't keep it bottled up—tell the person how you feel.

As these examples show, communicating with your listeners is more important than showing off with big words.

Use Concrete Words

Concrete words name or describe things that the listeners can see, smell, hear, taste, and touch—for example, *balloon, rose, gunblast, pizza,* and *chair.* They differ from abstract words, which refer to intangible ideas, qualities, or classes of things—for example, *democracy*, *mercy*, and *science*. While a certain amount of abstract language is necessary in a speech, you should try to keep it to a minimum. Whenever possible, choose concrete language because it is more specific and vivid, and therefore more likely to be remembered by your audience. Concrete words help you create the mental images that you want to convey to your listeners. Here are some examples:

Abstract	*Concrete*
She is wealthy.	She makes $400,000 a year, has a winter home in San Diego and a summer home in Switzerland, and owns four different sports cars.
It was a stormy day.	The sky was gray and gloomy, and the cold, moist wind stung my face.
Rattlesnakes are scary.	A rattlesnake is ominous-looking, with its beady eyes staring at you without ever blinking, and with its agile ability to slither through the brush without making a sound—until it suddenly coils and makes its terrible buzzing rattle.

Use Precise Words

The most commonly quoted authority in America is "they," as in the following sentences:

They say that too much salt is bad for you.

They say that the murder rate goes up during a full moon.

Who are "they"? Whoever they are, avoid using them as a source for information. Be specific. Be precise. For the first sentence above, find reliable sources: "Researchers at Johns Hopkins University have found that too much salt in one's diet can cause . . . ." For the second sentence, if you try to find who "they" are, you may discover, as did one student speaker, that reliable experts have concluded that the murder rate does *not* increase during a full moon, contrary to popular opinion. The mysterious "they" can be wrong.

Two kinds of words—doublespeak and misused jargon—rob a speech of precision. Let us examine each:

▶ Beware of Doublespeak

When some federal and state legislators raise taxes, they don't call it *raising taxes*—that term might anger taxpayers. No, timidly and sneakily they call it "revenue enhancement."

"Revenue enhancement" is an example of *doublespeak*, language that is deliberately misleading, evasive, meaningless, or inflated.[10] The term doublespeak has been made popular by the Committee on Public Doublespeak of the National Council of Teachers of English, which each year makes tongue-in-cheek "awards" for blatant examples of language abuse. Chairing the committee is Professor William Lutz of Rutgers University, who edits the journal *Quarterly Review of Doublespeak* and is author of the book *Doublespeak*.[11] Two of the most popular types of doublespeak, says Lutz, are euphemisms and inflated language.[12]

Euphemisms. These are pleasant, mild, or inoffensive words that are used to avoid a harsh or unpleasant reality. During the Persian Gulf war, some military leaders spoke of "incontinent ordnance." That doesn't sound as bad as what it means: bombs and artillery shells that fall wide of their targets and hit civilians.[13]

Euphemisms are not always undesirable. Lutz says:

When you use a euphemism because of your sensitivity for someone's feelings or out of concern for a recognized social or cultural taboo, it is not doublespeak. For example, you express your condolences that someone has "passed away" because you do not want to say to a grieving person, "I'm sorry your father is dead." When you use the euphemism "passed away," no one is misled. Moreover, the euphemism functions here not just to protect the feelings of another person, but to communicate also your concern for that person's feelings during a period of mourning.[14]

But when a euphemism is used to deceive, it becomes doublespeak. Here are some examples:

▶ A politician was caught lying, but instead of admitting his wrongdoing, he simply said that he "misspoke" earlier and that his previous statement was now "inoperative."[15]

▶ The Pentagon once concealed the fact that under one contract, a golf course was being constructed at taxpayer expense. Instead of referring to greens and bunkers, the design documents spoke of "land disposal areas" and "subzones" to keep Congress from knowing what was going on.[16]

▶ History shows that euphemisms are much used by demagogues and dictators. When Adolf Hitler and Joseph Stalin killed millions of innocent people in their respective dictatorships, they resorted to euphemisms: Hitler "liquidated undesirable elements" and Stalin "eliminated counterrevolutionary tendencies."[17]

While some euphemisms can be deciphered, others are confusing. If you heard that Chrysler "initiated a career alternative enhancement program," would you know that what really happened was that 5000 workers were fired? If a physician spoke of "a negative patient care outcome," would you know that the term means death?[18] If a general mentioned a "ballistically induced aperture in the subcutaneous environment," would you picture a bullet hole in a human being?[19]

Euphemisms become harmful when they mask a problem that should be dealt with. When a *slum* is called not a slum, but "substandard housing," does this help the public turn its eyes away from a problem that needs attention?

The bottom line is this: use euphemisms if tact and kindness require; avoid them if they serve only to deceive or confuse.

Inflated language. This kind of doublespeak, says Lutz, "is designed to make the ordinary seem extraordinary; to make everyday things seem impressive; to give an air of importance to people, situations, or things that would not normally be considered important."[20] Here are some examples:

▶ A used car is advertised as a "preowned car" or "preenjoyed automobile."

▶ A clothing store calls its salespeople "wardrobe consultants."

▶ One magazine referred to elderly people as "the chronologically gifted."[21]

▶ A national pizza delivery chain announced that its drivers wouldn't be called drivers anymore; henceforth they would be "delivery ambassadors."[22]

Some inflated language seems harmless. If garbage collectors prefer to be called "sanitation engineers," I may wince at the misuse of language but I cannot object too strenuously. If it makes them feel better about their valuable, but unglamorous work, if it increases their dignity and self-esteem, why should I criticize their term? But the problem is this: inflated language mushrooms to the point where it becomes hard to know what in the world is being discussed. If you saw an advertisement for a "grief therapist," wouldn't you envision a counselor for a mourning individual whose loved one has just died? That would be wrong, because a grief therapist is an inflated term for an undertaker. How are we to know that an "excavation technician" is a ditch digger? That a "communications monitor" is a switchboard operator? That an "architect of time" is a watchmaker? That a "traffic expediter" is a shipping clerk? That a "customer engineer" is a salesperson? That a "corrosion control specialist" is the person who sends your car through a car wash?[23]

An inflated term may begin in kindness, but it often ends in confusion. Avoid it unless you know that it is clearly understood and preferred by your audience. In other words, call a spade a *spade*—unless your audience is military personnel preferring the official name: "entrenching tool."

▶ Don't Misuse Jargon

Can you understand everything being said in the following sentence?

> During an attitude adjustment period, a government official explained to reporters that his department would effect a transformation in the preexisting regulations concerning domiciles for the lower socioeconomic bracket.

Translated into plain English:

> During a coffee break, a government official told reporters that his department would change the regulations concerning housing for the poor.

The government official was speaking in jargon, the specialized language of a group or profession. Some persons get so accustomed to using certain words at work that they fail to realize that people outside their field may be unaware of the words' meanings.

TIPS   FOR YOUR CAREER

TIP 12.2: Be Sensitive to Sexist Pronoun Usage

For centuries the masculine pronouns *he*, *his*, and *him* were used in the English language to designate an individual when gender was immaterial. In a sentence such as "Every driver should buckle *his* seat belt before *he* starts the engine," the pronouns *his* and *he* were understood to refer to drivers in general, both male and female. Today, however, according to Frederick Crews, a professor of English at the University of California, Berkeley, "many [people] find those words an offensive reminder of second-class citizenship for women."

To avoid offending anyone in your audience, you can handle this pronoun issue in one of three ways:

1. Use masculine and feminine pronouns in tandem. In other words, use *he or she* (or *she or he*) when referring to an indefinite person. For example, "Every driver should buckle *his or her*

seat belt before *he or she* starts the engine." A problem arises, however, in sentences like this: "Each participant should ask *himself or herself* whether *he or she* really needs *his or her* umbrella." If you continued in this way, the pronouns could become cumbersome, perhaps even distracting the listeners from your ideas. This problem has caused many people to prefer either of the two remaining alternatives:

2. Use plural pronouns. Say simply, "All drivers should buckle *their* seat belts before *they* start the engine." This alternative has the advantage of being simple, while offending no one.

3. Use the pronoun you. For example, "Whenever *you* get behind the wheel, *you* should buckle *your* seat belt before starting *your* engine." For speeches, this is often the best of the alternatives—it's not only simple and inoffensive, but also direct and personal.

You may use jargon when you are talking to an audience made up entirely of people who share your specialty, but you should avoid jargon as much as possible in speeches to people of varying backgrounds. If you are forced to use a technical word because of the nature of your talk, you should always define it. One student speaker worked part-time in a hospital, and gave a speech on a medical situation that she had agonized over—dealing with "no code" patients. Much to the frustration of the audience, she failed to define *no code*—until she was asked about it during the question-and-answer period. It turns out that *no code* is the term written on a patient's chart to indicate that no artificial life-support measures should be used if his or her condition at some point is determined to be hopeless. In other words, doctors and nurses should not make heroic efforts to keep such patients alive if they become comatose and irreversibly brain-damaged. The speaker had failed to define *no code* because she assumed that everyone knew what it meant.

Be careful about using sports terms that the general public may not know. For example, if you argued for "a full-court press against organized crime," only people familiar with basketball would know that the term means "trying to keep opponents from advancing."

Always explain abbreviations the first time you use them, even if they are fairly well-known acronyms like NATO and UNICEF. Some members of the audience may be unaware of what they stand for, and sometimes an abbreviation has several meanings. For example, *CO* is a popular military term that stands for "commanding officer," but it also means "conscientious

A museum guide must be sure to avoid using jargon or technical terms when introducing art masterpieces to the general public.

objector," someone who refuses to participate in war. Another popular abbreviation is *PC*, which can mean "personal computer," "politically correct," "program console," "personal copier," "privileged character," or "penal code."

A friend who is a real estate agent tells a story which may be fictional, but it illustrates why we need to explain abbreviations: A college student was hired to work as an intern at a real estate agency for the summer. On the first morning of his new job, his boss sent him a message, "Mr. John Smith is in my office. Please get BLT for him." The young intern dutifully left the office, went down the street to a restaurant, and purchased a bacon, lettuce, and tomato sandwich. When he returned, he carried the sandwich into the boss's office, where the boss and Mr. Smith were conferring. "Here's Mr. Smith's BLT," said the young man. "Thanks," said the boss, laughing. "Now would you please to go the files and get Mr. Smith's Block, Lot, and Tract file?"

Using Vivid Language

Vivid words have the magical ability to paint pictures in your listeners' minds—clear, memorable pictures. Let us examine two techniques, imagery and rhythm, which can help you create these pictures.

Create Imagery

You can bring an abstract idea to life by using precise, descriptive words to create images. For example, David Fields, a criminal justice major who had visited several prisons, painted a chilling picture of prison life:

> Prison is a jungle. When you're inside, you're as vulnerable as a lion tamer who steps inside a cage with snarling lions. At any moment the prisoners might erupt in violence. You can find yourself with a dozen knife wounds as a result of an argument over something insignificant. For example, you get a box of chocolate-chip cookies from home, and another prisoner wants those cookies and will stab you with a crude, homemade shank if you don't hand them over. There is always noise in prison—even in the dead middle of night; you never have peace and quiet. Glaring lights are on all the time; you're never allowed the luxury of sleeping in the dark. And the place stinks with the odor of fear.

Field's picture conveys the reality of prison life better than a long recital of dry statistics could ever convey.

Two devices that are especially effective for creating mental pictures are the simile and the metaphor. With a *simile*, you make a direct comparison of things that are dissimilar, using the words *like* or *as*. For example, "The stars are like diamonds in the sky." Like a simile, a *metaphor* compares dissimilar things, but it leaves off the words *like* and *as*. Thus, the simile just described can be changed into the following metaphor: "The stars are diamonds in the sky."

If fresh images are involved, similes and metaphors can be quite vivid. Here are some examples of the effective use of these devices:

> Marriage is a cozy, calm harbor where you are protected from the storms of the outside world. (*Pamela Smith, student speaker*)

> The snow covered up all the brown humps and furrows of the field, like white frosting on a chocolate cake. (*Joshua Burns, student speaker*)

> Manic-depressives are like passengers on an emotional roller-coaster that goes up, up, up to a high of exhilaration and then down, down, down to a low of despair—without ever stopping to let them off. (*Sarah Gentry, student speaker*)

Beware of *mixed metaphors*. These occur when the speaker combines two images that don't logically go together. Such an arrangement either confuses the listeners or leaves them smiling in amusement. President Dwight Eisenhower once said that "the Japanese have a tough row to hoe to keep their economic heads above water." This incongruous mixture of images paints the absurd picture of farmers scratching at the soil while struggling to keep from drowning. To correct the problem, one would have to say something like this: "The Japanese will have to swim vigorously to keep their economic heads above water."

Ernest Bevin, former foreign minister of Great Britain, once used this mixed metaphor: "If you let that sort of thing go on, your bread and butter will be cut out from under your feet." This ridiculous picture of people standing on their own food could be altered in the following way: "Your bread and butter will be snatched from your table."

Avoid *clichés*, which are trite, worn-out words or phrases that have lost their freshness and vividness. Here are some examples:

- ▶ bored to death
- ▶ better late than never
- ▶ last but not least
- ▶ raining cats and dogs
- ▶ at the crack of dawn
- ▶ throw caution to the winds
- ▶ beat the bushes
- ▶ slow but sure

To eliminate clichés, try to find fresh, lively alternatives. Instead of saying, "His tie stuck out like a sore thumb," say something like "His tie was as garish as a clown at a funeral."

Use Rhythm

You can make your language vivid by taking advantage of rhythmic patterns. One such pattern is *parallel structure*, wherein words, phrases, or clauses are arranged in the same form. Here are some examples, placed in poetic form to emphasize the parallels:

> Duty,
> Honor,
> Country.
> These are the watchwords of the American soldier.

> We want a government . . . of the people,
>   by the people,
>   for the people.

> We need parents who will . . . praise honest efforts,
>   punish bad behavior, and
>   ignore inconsequential acts.

Parallel structure can intensify the speaker's emotions, as in this example by student speaker Georgia Adams:

> When I see fish dying in our streams because of acid rain, I am enraged. When I see trees dying on our highest peaks because of acid rain, I am enraged. When I see animal habitats destroyed because of acid rain, I am enraged.

In addition to using parallel structure, Adams also used another effective rhythmic technique—*repetition*. Notice that by repeating "I am enraged," she conveyed the full measure of her anger.

In the next section of this chapter we will discuss repetition of key ideas to help the audience remember; here we are talking about repetition for its emotional, rhythmic effect. It is called "artful repetition" by Ivette Rodriguez, a former presidential speechwriter who is now head of public relations for the giant aerospace company McDonnell Douglas in Huntington Beach, California. Here is a sample from one of her speeches:

> Back in the first century A.D., a Greek philosopher expressed this time-honored truth: "Only the educated are free." Yes, only the educated are free. Free to

leave the welfare lines and find gainful employment. Free to choose meaningful careers. Free to reap the benefits of our economic and political system.[24]

If you go back and read the passage aloud, you will *feel* the rhythm of artful repetition.

Oral versus Written Language

One of the biggest mistakes some speakers make is to treat oral language in a speech as being no different from written language. Although the two forms of communication are similar, oral language has two significant requirements:

1. Oral language requires more elaboration than written language. If you are watching a football game on television and you fail to see a key block that makes a touchdown possible, you have the luxury of watching an instant replay in slow motion. If you are reading a complicated passage in your chemistry text and you find yourself hopelessly confused, you can go back a few paragraphs and study the material again. Unfortunately, these opportunities are not available when you listen to a speech. If you fail to understand what a speaker is saying, you are out of luck. There is no instant replay. There is no way to back up a few paragraphs.

Because of this handicap, oral language requires more elaboration than is necessary in written language. If a statement is too terse, the audience has trouble absorbing it. Consider the following example, which is the opening sentence of an article about immigrants:

> The first generation tries to retain as much as possible; the second to forget, the third to remember.[25]

That terse sentence is excellent in an essay. The reader can study it at leisure if the meaning does not pop up immediately. But can you imagine sitting in an audience and immediately understanding it? It is too compact for easy comprehension. It would have to be spoken in an expanded form such as this:

> When immigrants come to America, how do they treat their cultural heritage from the old country? The first generation of immigrants tries to retain as much as possible of the customs, cuisine, and language of the old country. But the second generation wants to forget all of that; these children of immigrants want to become "100 percent American," with no reminders of their foreign roots. But then along comes the third generation; these grandchildren want to celebrate the past, to find out all they can about their old-country heritage.

With this expanded version, the audience would be able to absorb the information.

One of the best ways to elaborate an idea is to develop it with support materials such as examples, narratives, and statistics. In general, oral communication requires more support materials than written communication. Suppose you wanted to make the following point:

Alaska is our largest state in land area, but it's the lowest in population density.

Everyone knows the first part of this statement, but do people really grasp just how sparsely settled Alaska is? To show them, you can elaborate with statistics and contrasts:

Alaska is so enormous that the 21 smallest states in the U.S. could fit inside its borders. Yet it has a tiny population—only about 400,000. More people live in the city of Pittsburgh, Pennsylvania, than in the entire state of Alaska. To get an idea of just how sparsely populated Alaska is, consider this: If New York City had the same ratio of residents per square mile, only 255 people would be living in all five boroughs of the city.[26]

If you limit yourself to one sentence, your point might fail to stick. If you elaborate by giving some interesting support materials, you increase your chances of driving home the point.

A note of caution: Just because it is a good idea to amplify your spoken message doesn't mean that you should pad your oral language with meaningless or windy phrases. In spoken as well as in written communication, you should omit needless words. Don't say, "In terms of the future, the military expects to meet its recruiting goals." Leave off the unnecessary five words at the beginning and say, "The military expects to meet its recruiting goals." Don't say, "in the area of statistics." Say simply, "statistics."

2. Oral language requires more repetition of key ideas than written language.   "If you have an important point to make," British Prime Minister Winston Churchill advised the young Prince of Wales, "Don't try to be subtle or clever. Use a pile driver. Hit the point once. Then come back and hit it again. Then hit it a third time—a tremendous whack."[27]

One of the reasons Churchill is considered one of the greatest orators of the twentieth century is that he followed his own advice. For example, on the subject of resolution, he said:

Never give in! Never, never, never, never, never, never. In nothing great or small, large or petty—never give in except to convictions of honor and good sense.[28]

Too much repetition? For an essay, yes. For a speech, no.

Have you ever wondered why TV viewers are bombarded with the same commercial over and over and over again? Partly to make sure that everyone sees the commercial, but mainly because marketing research shows that "a message must be heard eight times to be unforgettable," according to marketing specialist Christopher Ryan.[29] How many times must a public speaker state an idea to ensure that listeners retain it? It is hard to say exactly because there are many variables, such as how much knowledge the listeners already possess on the subject and how interesting the speech is. Churchill's recommendation—three times—is a good rule of thumb (though some complex messages may need even more repetition).

When you repeat an idea, you may want to use the exact same wording (as when you reiterate a central idea). But sometimes it's effective to change your wording—so that you can provide variety and increase the chances that the audience will understand and remember. One set of words might work well for some listeners, while another set might be needed for other listeners.

Dr. Rachel Marsella, an obstetrician who gives lectures to expectant parents going through Lamaze childbirth training, says of her talks,

> I try to use some medical language to reassure the better educated men and women that I'm a health professional and to show that I'm not talking down to them. But I have to keep in mind the less-well-educated people, too, so right after I use medical language, I'll say, "In other words . . . ." For example, I might say, "About half of all mothers experience post-partum depression. In other words, they feel sad and blue and 'down in the dumps' after the child is born."

Dr. Marsella's technique permits her to repeat an idea, but with a fresh set of words.

In his plays William Shakespeare used this technique to reach both the educated playgoers in the galleries and the "groundlings," the poor, uneducated folks who stood in the "yard" around the stage: After committing murder, Macbeth asks, "Will all great Neptune's ocean wash this blood clean from my hand?" His own answer: "No, this my hand will rather the multitudinous seas incarnadine, making the green one red." The idea that Shakespeare wanted to convey was: This blood on my hand will change the color of the sea from green to red. The phrase *multitudinous seas incarnadine* was designed for the educated spectators, who understood Latin-derived phrases. To reach the uneducated groundlings, he immediately repeated his idea in plain Anglo-Saxon terms—*making the green one red*.[30] By repeating an idea but doing so with variety and grace, Shakespeare ensured that all listeners understood his meaning.

Summary

The words that you use in a speech should be chosen with care and sensitivity. Always use language that is appropriate for your particular audience and occasion, avoiding words that might be over the heads of the listeners or that might offend any member of the audience. To use words accurately, you must be sensitive to both denotations and connotations, and you must use correct grammar.

You can achieve clarity in your language by choosing words that are simple, concrete, and precise. You can achieve vividness by creating word images and by using rhythm.

Oral language and written language are similar in many ways, but there are two significant differences: (1) Oral language requires more elaboration than written language, and (2) oral language requires more repetition of key ideas than written language.

Review Questions

1. Why did Dr. Martin Luther King use different words with different audiences?
2. What is the difference between the denotation and connotation of a word?
3. Where can one find explanations of the synonyms of words?
4. Why is incorrect grammar a handicap for a speaker?
5. What is doublespeak? Give two examples.
6. What are the two major differences between oral and written language?

13

Delivering the Speech

 Methods of Speaking

Memorized / Manuscript / Impromptu / Extemporaneous /

 Voice

Volume / Clarity / Expressiveness /

 Nonverbal Communication

Personal Appearance / Eye Contact / Facial Expressions / Posture /
Movement / Using Notes / Gestures / Beginning and Ending /

 **Question-and-Answer Period**

▶ **Practice**

Roger Howard is one of the bravest speakers I have ever seen. A young man from New York City who had been addicted to heroin as a teenager, he founded a chapter of Narcotics Anonymous, which was devoted to salvaging the lives of drug addicts. He appeared at a government-sponsored symposium that dealt with the use and abuse of heroin. Though he was a high school dropout with limited public speaking experience, he had the courage to stand before 300 highly educated people (government officials, professors, and journalists) and try to convince them that the government should provide funds to help victims of what he called the "heroin epidemic."

When Howard started speaking, his delivery was terrible. His eyes were cast downward at a spot on the floor in front of the first row; instead of standing up straight, he was hunched over the microphone; he used no gestures because his hands were too busy clutching the lectern as if it were a life raft; his voice was raspy and tremulous. He seemed shaky and unsure of himself—I'm certain that he was scared to death and wished to be a hundred miles from that room. Yet, at the same time, I sensed that he felt a strong compulsion to tell his story. And what a story it was—a harrowing tale of slavery to a narcotic habit that was so expensive that he had to commit crimes to get enough money for his daily fix. As he got into his story, I observed a remarkable transformation. He came out of his hunched-over position and stood up straight. His eyes looked directly at the listeners, imploring their understanding and support. His hands started moving with power and emphasis. His voice gained strength and confidence. The audience responded by listening with rapt attention. There was absolute stillness in the room. At the end of the speech, the listeners gave him a round of hearty, appreciative applause. His speech was a success.

As you read this chapter, I hope you will keep Roger Howard in mind because he exemplifies an important point: *The key to good delivery is a strong desire to communicate with the audience.* Though Howard started out with ragged, unpolished delivery, he had a burning desire to communicate with the audience, and before long he was unconsciously using good delivery techniques. I have observed this phenomenon time and time again: speakers who lack professional polish and training but who care deeply about conveying their ideas to the audience almost always do an adequate job with their delivery. A General Motors executive, R. T. Kingman, expressed it this way: "If a speaker knows what he wants to say, really wants to say it, and wants everybody in the room to understand what it is he wants to say, all the other things like looking people in the eye and using good gestures will just come naturally."[1]

The speaker's desire to communicate is emphasized so that you can put the ideas of this chapter into proper perspective. The dozens of tips about delivery in the pages that follow are important; you should study them carefully. But bear in mind that a strong desire to communicate with your audience is the dynamo of power that makes it possible for you to deliver speech with strength and effectiveness.

Methods of Speaking

There are four basic speaking methods used by public speakers today.

Memorized

A few speakers memorize an entire speech and then deliver it without a script or notes. But if you are like most speakers, memorizing a speech is a bad idea for these reasons:

▶ You are forced to spend an enormous amount of time in committing the speech to memory.

▶ At some point in your speech, you might suddenly forget what comes next. This could cause you to become acutely embarrassed or even panic-stricken. Once derailed from your speech, you might be unable to get back on track.

▶ Even if you remembered your entire speech, you would be speaking from your memory, not from your heart. This could cause you to sound remote, lifeless, unenergetic—more like a robot than a human being.

Memorizing does have one virtue: it lets you figure out your *exact* wording ahead of time. But this gain in precision fails to outweigh the disadvantages. Though I know of several popular speechmakers who memorize their speeches, I don't recommend this method for anyone. Certainly not for the inexperienced speaker.

Manuscript

Some speakers like to put their entire speech on a manuscript. This method, says Elayne Snyder, a speech consultant, is used primarily "if you are to testify at a congressional committee hearing or other official hearing where every word will appear in permanent form in an official record, or if you have been asked to deliver a paper at a scientific or educational conference and every word will appear in a conference journal."

There are two ways to deliver such a speech. The first is to simply read the manuscript, but this approach, says Snyder, "destroys spontaneity and enthusiasm." The speaker fails to look at the audience, fails to speak with adequate expression, and often reads too quickly.[2]

The second technique is to have the written text in front of you, but not actually read it. Here is how this method works: You practice the speech over and over until you are thoroughly familiar with it. When you give the speech, you glance at the text to refresh your memory but most of the time you look at the listeners and speak to them as if the words were coming from the heart—fresh and newly minted. This technique (which differs from the memorized method in that you familiarize yourself with the speech instead of committing it to memory) is very effective, but I must warn you: It is much more difficult than it looks. Some actors, experienced politicians, and professional speechmakers use this method with great success, but most speakers—even ones with a lot of experience—fail to pull it off. They sound dull and lifeless, rather than natural and spontaneous.

Unless you are a veteran orator, don't use a manuscript. You might fail to maintain good eye contact with your audience, and your words—if they are read instead of spoken naturally—might be hard for the audience to absorb.

Impromptu

Speaking *impromptu* means speaking on the spur of the moment—with no opportunity for extensive preparation. For example, without warning you are asked to give a talk to your fellow employees about your recent convention trip to New Orleans. Or during a meeting, you are asked to give your view of a situation. Here are some guidelines for impromptu speaking:

Organize your speech.   Because you usually don't have much time before standing to speak, you should quickly develop three items (on a piece of paper or in your mind)—*point, support,* and *conclusion.* Ask yourself:

▶ What *point* do I want to make? In a short speech, make only one assertion. Don't bring in points that you lack the time or knowledge to handle.

▶ How can I *support* my point? Explain or prove your point by using specific details, examples, anecdotes, and other support materials.

▶ What is my *conclusion*? This can be a restatement of the point and/or an appeal to the audience to take action. Formulate your closing sentence in your mind *before* you start speaking; it prevents you from rambling and being unable to make a graceful ending.

Never apologize.   Asking your listeners to forgive you for lack of preparation is unnecessary—they know you had no chance to prepare, and besides, they are not expecting a polished masterpiece. Apologizing makes you appear insecure and unconfident.

Don't rush.   Try not to gallop through your remarks. Speak at a steady, calm rate. At the beginning, and at various intervals, pause for a few seconds to collect your thoughts. If you can employ pauses without a look of panic on your face, you actually enhance your credibility—you come across as thoughtful and careful.

Whenever possible, link your remarks to those of other speakers.   Listening carefully to what other people say in a meeting can pay dividends. When you are asked to comment or to give a talk, you can often take a statement made by a previous speaker and build upon it or try to refute it. (By the way, failing to listen carefully can hurt you. For example, if you are daydreaming during a meeting, and someone suddenly turns to you and asks, "What do you think about this proposal?" you can look very foolish if you are unable to respond, or if you respond in a way that reveals that you had not been paying attention.)

Don't feign knowledge.   During a meeting or during a question-and-answer period, you may be asked to comment on a matter that you know nothing about. Simply say, "I don't know." Don't feign knowledge by "winging it"—by rambling on and on as a way of pretending that you know the answer. Some speakers think that admitting ignorance will hurt their credibility, but the opposite is often true. If you fail to admit your ignorance and try to hide it behind a smokescreen of verbal ramblings, you can make yourself look insincere and foolish. In some situations you can say, "I don't know the answer to that, but I'll research it and get back to you as soon as I can."

Be brief.   Some impromptu speakers talk too long, repeating the same ideas over and over, because they are afraid that they are doing a poor job and therefore must redeem themselves, or because they lack a graceful way of closing the speech. Whatever the case, you can never help yourself by going on and on. Speak briefly and then sit down.

Try to foresee situations where you are likely to be called upon to speak impromptu.   Plan in advance what you will say. For example, when you return from a convention and you are driving to work, rehearse in your mind what you will say if the boss asks you to make a little speech about your trip.

Extemporaneous

The extemporaneous method is the most popular style of speaking in America today. The idea is to sound as if you are speaking spontaneously, but instead of giving the clumsy, faltering speech that many off-the-cuff speakers give, you present a beautifully organized, well-developed speech that you have spent many hours preparing and practicing.

You speak from notes, but these notes don't contain your speech written out word for word. Instead they contain only your basic ideas, expressed in a few key words. When you speak, therefore, you make up the exact words as you go along. You glance at your cards occasionally to remind yourself of your next point, but most of the time you look at the listeners, speaking to them in a natural, conversational tone of voice.

This conversational tone is valued in a speech because it is the easiest kind for an audience to listen to, understand, and remember. When you speak conversationally, you are speaking directly, warmly, sincerely. You are speaking as closely as possible to the way you talk to your best friends: your voice is full of life and color; your words are fresh and vital rather than stale and warmed-over.

Though the extemporaneous method is popular and effective, it provides no guarantee of success. In fact, if you are not careful, it can lure you to failure. For this method to work, *you must spend a lot of time preparing and rehearsing your speech.* Mark Twain said, "It takes three weeks to prepare a good ad-lib speech." In other words, if you want to *sound* as if you are ad-libbing beautifully, you have to spend a lot of time in preparation and practice. Speakers who use the extemporaneous method correctly are like the Olympic divers you see on television. These athletes make their high dives into the pool look natural and easy, but in reality they have achieved their graceful, "effortless" coordination through hours of hard practice. In public speaking, if you don't put forth time and effort in preparing and practicing, you are really no better off than if you give an impromptu speech. For example, if you fail to prepare a well-organized outline, you might find that your ideas don't hang together and that your words are fuzzy and imprecise. If you fail to practice, you might find that your delivery is ragged, with awkward silences and many "uhs."

Speaking extemporaneously permits more flexibility than reading from a written speech because you can adjust the speech to meet the needs of a particular audience. If, for example, you see that some of your listeners don't understand a point, you can restate your message in different words or you can insert additional explanations. If you are the last speaker of the evening at a banquet and you sense that your audience is about to go to sleep because of the long-winded speakers who preceded you, you can shorten your speech by cutting out some of your minor points.

Voice

Some people think that to be an excellent speaker, you must have a golden voice, so rich and resonant that it enthralls anyone who listens to it. This is not true. Some of the greatest orators in history had imperfect voices. Abraham Lincoln's voice was described by his contemporaries as "thin, high pitched, shrill, not musical, and . . . disagreeable"[3] and Winston Churchill "stammered and even had a slight lisp."[4] In our own day, I have observed a popular evangelist whose voice is thin and weak, a successful TV commentator who talks in an irritatingly abrasive manner, and a leading politician who speaks with an unpleasant nasal whine. Yet all three are in demand as public speakers. It is nice to have a rich, resonant voice, but there are other characteristics of the human voice which are of greater importance for effective speechmaking. Your voice should have proper volume; it should be clear and understandable; and it should be expressive.

Volume

The larger the room, the louder you have to speak. You can tell if your volume is loud enough by observing the people in the back row. Are they leaning forward with quizzical expressions as they strain to hear your words? Then obviously you need to speak louder. In some cases you may want to ask directly, "Can the people in the back row hear me all right?" There are some circumstances in which you may have to raise your voice to overcome unavoidable noises, such as the hum of air conditioners, the chatter of people in a hallway, the clatter of dishes and silverware during a banquet, or even the sound of a band blaring in the next room.

Speaking loud enough for all to hear does not mean shouting. It means *projecting* your voice a bit beyond its normal range. If you have never spoken to a large group or if your instructor tells you that you have problems in projecting your voice, practice with a friend. Find an empty classroom, have your friend sit in the back row, and practice speaking with extra force—not shouting—so that your friend can hear you easily. (Or set up a tape recorder in the back of the room and practice projecting your voice toward it.)

If a speech requires the use of a microphone, go to the meeting site early and spend a few minutes testing it before the listeners arrive. Adjust it to your height; if someone readjusts it during the ceremonies, spend a few moments getting it just right for yourself. Your audience will not mind the slight delay. When you speak into a mike, it is not necessary to have your lips almost touching it; in fact, your voice will sound better if your mouth is 6 to 12 inches away. Position the mike so that you can forget that it is there. This frees you to speak naturally, without having to bend over or lean forward. At large meetings, you don't need to raise your voice while talking into a microphone. In fact, says professional speaker Arnold "Nick" Carter, "the invention of the microphone made it possible for me to speak to 18,000 people with a whisper."[5]

Clarity

Here is the kind of dialogue you might hear on any college campus in America:

"Watcha doin?"

"Stud'n a liddle histry."

"Howbout that lass test? Wajagit?"

"Dunno, probly flunked."

"Jeatyet?"

"Nah."

"Lessgo getta pizza."

Most of us are lazy in our daily conversations; we slur sounds, drop syllables, and mumble words. While poor articulation may not hurt us in conversation as long as our friends understand what we are saying, it can hinder communication in a speech. We need to enunciate our words crisply and precisely to make sure that everything we say is intelligible to our listeners.

If you tend to slur words, you can improve your speech by reading poems or essays aloud fifteen minutes a day for three weeks. Say the words with exaggerated emphasis, and move your mouth and tongue vigorously. Enunciate consonants firmly and make vowel sounds last longer than normal. In real situations you should not exaggerate in this way, but the practice will help you avoid the pitfalls of slurring and mumbling.

While poor articulation stems from sloppy habits, mispronunciation is a matter of not knowing the correct way to say a word. Here are some common pronunciation mistakes[6]:

	Incorrect	*Correct*
across	uh-crost	uh-cross
athlete	ath-uh-lete	ath-lete
burglar	burg-you-lur	burg-lur
chef	chef	shef
chic	chick	sheek
drowned	drown-did	drownd
electoral	e-lec-tor-ee-al	e-lec-tur-ul
environment	en-vire-uh-ment	en-vi-run-ment
et cetera	ek-cetera	et-cetera
evening	eve-uh-ning	eve-ning
grievous	greev-ee-us	greev-us
height	heighth	height
hundred	hun-derd	hun-dred
library	li-berry	li-brar-y
mischievous	miss-chee-vee-us	miss-chuh-vus
nuclear	nu-cu-lar	nu-cle-ar
perspiration	press-pi-ra-tion	per-spi-ra-tion
picture	pitch-er	pic-ture
pretty	pur-tee	prit-ee

	Incorrect	*Correct*
professor	pur-fess-ur	pruh-fess-ur
quiet	quite	kwy-it
realtor	reel-a-tor	re-al-tor
recognize	reck-uh-nize	rec-og-nize
relevant	rev-uh-lant	rel-uh-vant
strength	strenth	strength

If you are like most people, you use words which you have picked up from books but have never heard pronounced. If you rely on your own guess, it can sometimes cause embarrassment, as in the case of one student who had read all about the Sioux Indians, but apparently had never heard the tribal name pronounced. He called them the "sigh-ox" Indians. On other occasions you may confuse words that sound a lot alike. For example, one of my students said that a man and woman contemplating marriage should make sure they are compatible before they say their *vowels*. (One of the listeners couldn't resist the temptation to ask, at the end of the speech, whether consonants were also important for marriage.)

Such mistakes can be avoided by looking up a word's meaning and pronunciation in a dictionary.

Expressiveness

The most boring voices in the world are probably those of elementary school children when they stand on a stage for a holiday skit and mouth sentences they have been required to memorize, often using words whose meanings they are blithely unaware of. Their lines are uttered in a flat monotone, without any flair or meaning.

In sharp contrast, a dynamic speaker has a voice that is warm and expressive, producing a rich variety of sounds. Audiences find such a voice more interesting to listen to than a monotonous one, and therefore they are more likely to respond favorably to what the speaker says. To achieve expressiveness, one must make good use of the following elements.

▶ Pitch

The highness or lowness of your voice is called *pitch*. The ups and downs of pitch—called *intonation patterns*—give our language its distinctive melody. Consider the following sentence: "I was angry." Say it in a variety of ways—with anger, with sarcasm, with humor, with disbelief. Each time you say it, you are using a different intonation pattern.

In conversation, almost everyone uses a variety of intonation patterns and emphasizes particular words, but in public speaking, some speakers fail to use any variety at all. They speak in a monotone—a dull, flat drone that will put many listeners to sleep. Even worse, they run the risk of appearing insincere. They may use dramatic words, for example, like "This is a terrible tragedy for America," but they may say them in such a casual, offhand way that the audience will think they don't really mean them.

One of the problems with a monotone is that some words fail to receive the emphasis they deserve. For example, take a sentence like this: "Mr. Smith made $600,000 last year, while Mr. Jones made $6000." Speakers who talk in a monotone will say the two figures as if there were no difference between $600,000 and $6000. But listeners need help in *hearing* the disparity. A speaker should let his or her voice place heavy emphasis on the $600,000.

▶ **Loudness and Softness**

Besides having the proper volume, so that everyone in the audience can hear you, you can raise or lower your voice for dramatic effect or to emphasize a point. Try saying the following out loud:

> (*Soft:*) "Should we give in to the kidnappers' demands?
>
> (*Switch to loud:*) NEVER!"

Did you notice that raising your voice for the last word conveys that you truly mean what you say? Now try another selection out loud:

> (*Start softly and make your voice grow louder as you near the end of this sentence:*) Edwin Arlington Robinson's character Richard Cory had everything that a man could want—good looks, lots of money, popularity.
>
> (*Now make your voice switch to soft:*) But he went home one night and put a bullet through his head.

Changing from loud to soft helps the listeners *feel* the tragic discrepancy between Richard Cory's outer appearance and his inner reality.

▶ **Rate**

How quickly or slowly should you speak? The ideal speed for giving a speech is like the ideal speed for driving a car—it all depends on conditions. Driving a car at 55 miles per hour is fine for a highway but too fast for a school zone. In similar fashion, a rapid rate of speaking is appropriate in certain conditions—if, for example, you are describing a thrilling high-speed police chase. A slow pace, on the other hand, is preferred if you are introducing a technical, hard-to-understand concept.

One of the biggest mistakes inexperienced speakers make is speaking too rapidly. It is especially important that you speak at a slow, deliberate rate during your introduction (except in special situations, as when you lead off with an adventure story). Have you ever noticed how TV dramas start out very slowly? They don't divulge important details of the story until you are three or four minutes into the show. One obvious reason for this is to have mercy on the viewers who have gone to the kitchen to get a snack and are slow in returning to the TV. But the main reason is to give the viewers a chance to "tune in" to the story, to get adjusted to what is happening on the screen, to get accustomed to the characters. If too much action or dialogue takes place in the first minute, viewers are unable to absorb the story. In like fashion, you need to give your audience a chance to "tune in" to you, to get accustomed to your voice and subject matter. If you race through your introduction, they might become lost and confused, and they might decide to spend the time daydreaming rather than struggling to follow your race-horse delivery.

Speaking slowly—and using pauses, especially at the beginning—will make you come across to the audience as someone who is confident and in control, as someone who cares about whether the listeners understand.

You can avoid speaking too rapidly by practicing your speech at home. Use a tape recorder and listen to yourself. Have friends or relatives listen to your speech; ask them to tell you if you are speaking too fast for easy comprehension.

Some people speak too rapidly because they write out all or most of their speech on note cards or on a sheet of paper and then when they rise to speak, they succumb to the temptation of reading rapidly from their script. The solution is to have brief notes, not a written script, when you stand up to speak.

▶ **Pauses**

When you read printed material, you have punctuation marks to help you make sense out of your reading—commas tell you when to pause, periods when to stop, and so on. In a speech, there are no punctuation marks; listeners must rely on oral cues to guide them. One of these cues is the pause, which lets your listeners know when you have finished one thought and are ready to go to the next. Audiences appreciate a pause. It gives them time to digest what you have said. And it gives you a moment to think of what you are going to say next.

A pause before an important idea or the climax of a story can create suspense. For example, student speaker Stephanie Johnson told of an adventure that happened while she was camping:

> It was late at night when I finally crawled into my sleeping bag. The fire had died down, but the moon cast a faint, spooky light on our campsite. I must have been asleep a couple of hours when I suddenly woke up. Something was brushing up against my sleeping bag. My heart started pounding like crazy. I peeked out of the slit I had left for air. Do you know what I saw? [*pause*]

By pausing at this point, Johnson had the audience on the edge of their chairs. What was it? A bear? A human intruder? After a few moments of dramatic tension, she ended the suspense:

> By the light of the moon, I could see a dark little animal with a distinctive white stripe. [*pause*] It was a skunk.

A pause can also be used to emphasize an important statement. It is a way of saying, "Let this sink in." Notice how student speaker Erik Swenson used pauses in his speech:

> Albert Einstein was once asked whether he thought that World War III would be fought with nuclear weapons. [*pause to give the listeners a chance to think about the momentous nature of the question*] Einstein, the man who made possible the construction of the atomic bomb, gave this answer: "I don't know what weapons will be used for World War III, but I do know what weapons will be used for World War IV: [*pause to create dramatic tension and suspense*] sticks and stones." [*pause to let the audience reflect on the irony*]

Swenson's dramatic pauses captivated his audience. Notice that his final pause gave the listeners time to reflect on Einstein's insight.

In some speeches, you might find yourself pausing not because you want to, but because you have forgotten what you were planning to say next and you need to look at your notes. Or you might pause while searching your mind for the right word. Such a pause may seem like an eternity, so you are tempted to fill in the horrible silence with verbal fillers like "uh" or "er" or "um." Try hard not to make these sounds. There is nothing wrong with silence; there is no need to be embarrassed by it. The audience does not mind. In fact, a few such pauses can enhance your credibility, making you seem more conversational and natural, and less artificial and contrived. You look as if you are concerned about giving the audience the most precise words possible.

▶ Conversational Quality

Many inexperienced speakers give their speeches in a dull, plodding, color-less voice. Yet five minutes afterward, chatting with their friends in the hall, they speak with animation and warmth.

What they need to do, obviously, is bring that same conversational quality into their speeches. How can this be done? How can a person sound as lively and as "real" when talking to thirty people as when chatting with a friend? If this problem applies to you, here are two suggestions:

1. Treat your audience not as an impersonal mass, not as a blur of faces, but as a collection of individuals. Some students sound wooden and artificial when giving a speech, but during the question-and-answer period they respond to questions in a natural, conversational manner. Why does this happen? One reason is that they are engaged in a conversation with the person who asked the question. They are now talking one-on-one. To capture this style of talking during the speech itself, here is a mental ploy you can use from the very beginning: look at one or two or three individuals in different parts of the room and act as if you are talking to them one-on-one. You should avoid staring, of course, but if you look at them briefly, it will help you develop a conversational attitude. As the speech goes on, you can add other faces to your "conversation."

   2. Be yourself—but somewhat intensified.   To speak to an audience with the same natural, conversational tone you use with your friends, you must speak with greater energy and forcefulness. We are not talking now about projecting your voice so that the people in the back of the room can hear you, but rather about *intensifying* the psychological dimensions of your voice—the emotional tones and the vibrancy. How can you do this? Here are two ways:

   First, let your natural enthusiasm come forth. If you have chosen a topic wisely, you are speaking on something you care a great deal about and want very much to communicate to the audience. When you stand in front of your audience, don't keep a lid on your feelings. Don't hold yourself back; let your voice convey all the enthusiasm that you feel inside. Many speakers are afraid they will look or sound ridiculous if they get involved with their subject. "I'll come on too strong," they say. But the truth is that your audience will not react this way; they will be impressed by your energy and zest. Think back to the speakers you have heard: Didn't you respond favorably to those who were alive and enthusiastic?

   Second, practice loosening up. Some novice speakers sound and look stiff because they simply have had no practice in loosening up. Here is something you can try: find a private location (such as a room at home or a clearing in the woods or an empty classroom late in the afternoon when no one else is around). For subject matter, you can practice a speech that you are working on, recite poetry, read from the morning newspaper, or simply ad-lib. Whatever words you use, say them dramatically. "Ham" it up. Be theatrical. Act as if you are running for President and you are trying to persuade 10,000 people to vote for you. Or act as if you are giving a poetry reading to 500 of your most enthusiastic fans. You will not speak so dramatically to a real audience, of course, but the practice of "letting go" will help you break out of your normal reserve. It will help you learn to be yourself, to convey your natural enthusiasm.

Nonverbal Communication

Nonverbal communication consists of the messages that you send without words—what you convey with your eyes, facial expression, posture, body movement, and tone of voice.

   The words of a speech, says Roger Ailes, a communications consultant who has advised various presidential candidates, "are meaningless unless the rest of you is in synchronization."[7]

Corporate executives, he says, "often get up and send all sorts of weird signals to their audience. My favorite is, 'Ladies and gentlemen, I'm very happy to be here.' But they're looking at their shoes as they say it. They have no enthusiasm whatsoever. They look either angry, frightened, or depressed about being there."[8]

When there is a discrepancy between words and nonverbal behavior, the audience "will always go with the visual signals over the verbal ones," says Ailes. "They'll say to themselves unconsciously, 'He's telling me he's happy to be here, but he's really not. Therefore, he's either uncomfortable or a liar, or both.' "[9]

To get your nonverbal signals synchronized with your words, you need to show enthusiasm (with your eyes, facial expression, posture, and tone of voice) as you speak to your audience. Let your body confirm that you believe in what you are saying and that you want your audience to accept your ideas.

If you are truly enthusiastic about your speech and eager to share it with your audience, much of your body language will take care of itself, as we discussed at the beginning of this chapter. But you may be asking, "What if I don't really feel happy and confident? I can't lie with my body, can I?" This is a good question, because there are times in your life when you will resent having to give a speech, as when the boss orders you to give a presentation to the board of directors or when an instructor assigns you to give an oral report to the class. Also there are times when you simply don't feel like standing up in front of a group. Maybe you failed to get much sleep the night before, and you have no zip, no spark. At times like these, what should you do?

Pretend. Yes, pretend to be confident in yourself and in your ideas. Pretend to be glad to appear before your audience. Pretend to be enthusiastic. But isn't this phony? Isn't this forcing the body to tell a lie? Yes, but we often must be "deceitful" in order to carry out life's tasks. We force ourselves to be cheerful and animated for a crucial job interview, for conferences with the boss, for an important date with someone we love, and for myriad other situations in life. By *acting* as if you are confident, poised, and enthusiastic, you will often find that after a few minutes, the pretense gives way to reality. You truly become confident, poised, and enthusiastic. Consider the comedians and talk-show hosts who appear night after night on television. Do you think they are always "up?" No, they are like you and me. They have their bad days, their sluggish days, their down-in-the-dumps days, their head-cold and stomachache days, but they force themselves to perform; they pretend to be enthusiastic. After about 60 seconds (most of them report), the pretense gives way to reality, and they truly *are* enthusiastic. (A word of advice: If this transformation fails to happen to you—if you don't feel enthusiastic after a few minutes—you should still pretend.)

How do you carry out this pretense? How can you make the body "lie" for you? The answer is to be sensitive to the "signals" that the body sends out to show confidence and energy, and then to force yourself to use these signals. To familiarize yourself with these signals, take a look at the major nonverbal aspects of public speaking discussed below.

Personal Appearance

Your audience will size up your personal appearance and start forming opinions about you even before you open your mouth to begin your speech. You should be clean, well-groomed, and attractively dressed.

Janet Stone and Jane Bachner, who conduct workshops for women executives, have some good advice for both men and women:

> As a general rule of thumb, find out what the audience will be wearing and then wear something yourself that is just a trifle dressier than their clothes. The idea is to establish yourself as "The Speaker," to set yourself slightly apart from the crowd, to show them that you are taking their invitation seriously enough to dress up a little for them, and yet to look enough like them to establish yourself as a person they can identify with.[10]

Your attire should always be appropriate. In other words, don't wear anything that would distract or offend the audience. A T-shirt with a ribald or controversial slogan printed on the front, for example, might direct attention away from the speech itself, and it might offend some members of the audience.

Eye Contact

Look at your audience 95 percent of the time, with the other 5 percent devoted to occasional glances at your notes. Having good eye contact with your listeners is important for three reasons: (1) It creates an important bond of communication and rapport between you and them. It is, in the words of Jack Valenti, president of Motion Picture Association of America, a "figurative handshake."[11] (2) It shows your sincerity. There's an old saying, "Don't buy a used car from a dealer who won't look you in the eye." We distrust people who won't look at us openly and candidly. If you want your listeners to have confidence in what you are saying, look at *them*, not at a spot on the back wall. (3) It enables you to get audience feedback. Looking directly at your listeners makes you instantly aware of any lapses in communication. For example, did a number of listeners look puzzled when you made your last statement? Then you obviously confused them; you need to explain your point in a different way.

The biggest spoiler of good eye contact is looking at your notes too much, which is usually caused by one of the following: (1) *Not being prepared*—This can be corrected, of course, by rehearsing your speech so many times that you need only glance at your notes to remind yourself of what comes next. (2) *Nervousness*—Some speakers are well-prepared and don't really need to look at their notes very often, but they are so nervous that they scrutinize their notes to gain security and avoid the audience. One way to correct this is to put reminders, in giant red letters, on your notes—LOOK AT AUDIENCE—to jog you out of this habit.

Another killer of eye contact is handouts. We discussed in Chapter 8 why you should never distribute a handout during a speech unless it is simple and short. This rule is so important—and so frequently violated—that I want to emphasize it once more. Here's what advertising executive Ron Hoff says:

> Think twice before you hand out papers for your audience to study—or give them other inducements to break eye contact. They may get so engrossed in the papers that they never come back to you. And, no matter what they say, people can't read and listen to you at the same time. Eye contact is valuable—be wary about giving it away.[12]

Eye contact is more than darting furtive glances at the audience from time to time. It is more than mechanically moving your head from side to side like an oscillating fan. You must have meaningful contact similar to the eye-to-eye communication you engage in with your friends. For a large audience, the best technique is to have a "conversation" with three or four people in different parts of the room (so that you seem to be giving your attention to the entire audience). Veteran speaker James "Doc" Blakely of Wharton, Texas, explains how to do this:

> Many speakers, especially inexperienced ones, don't see an audience at all. To them, it is just a blur of faces. I have found that the real key in natural, conversational speaking is to pick out the friendliest faces in the audience and speak to them as if you were speaking only to that person. It's like everyone else is eavesdropping on the conversation. By shifting eye contact from one point to another scattered throughout the room, but still speaking to those friendly faces, you give the listeners the feeling that you are speaking to them as individuals.[13]

Picking out faces in different parts of the room is a good technique for large audiences, but you should actually look at *every* listener when the audience is small. Professional speaker Danny Cox uses a technique called "locking" whenever he speaks to a small gathering:

> I learned something once from a piano player. I couldn't believe how she held an audience in a cocktail bar. It was so quiet in there you couldn't believe it.

realized one night what she was doing. She was looking at each person and as soon as she made eye contact with them, she smiled at them. And then moved on to the next one, and smiled. She was "locking" everybody in. This is a good technique in public speaking—very simple, too.[14]

Facial Expressions

Let your face express whatever emotion is appropriate at any given moment in a speech. A student told me he was planning to speak on how to perform under pressure; his primary example was the thrilling moment in high school when he kicked the winning field goal in the final seconds of a championship football game. When he described that triumphant feat, his face was suffused with excitement, but when he got up in front of the class and told the same story in his speech, his face was blank. Gone was the joy, gone was the exhilaration. By having a facial expression that was incongruous with the event he was describing, he weakened the impact of the story.

If you are speaking about sad or sober topics, your face should not be grinning; if you are speaking about happy items, your face should not be grimacing. And whatever you are talking about, your face should not be devoid of any emotion—it should be animated. "Animation," says speech consultant Dorothy Sarnoff, "is the greatest cosmetic you can use, and it doesn't cost a cent. Animation is energy in the face. . . . It's action that comes not only through the eyes, but around the mouth and the whole face. It tells the listener you're glad to be right where you are—at the lectern, around a conference table or across a desk."[15] How can you make your face become animated? By choosing a subject that you care a great deal about, by having a strong desire to communicate your message to your listeners, and by delivering your speech with energy and enthusiasm.

Posture

Stand in front of your audience poised, with your weight equally distributed on your feet. Your body language should convey the message, "I am confident; I am in command of this situation." This does not mean that you should be cocky and arrogant, but simply that you should convey an appearance of relaxed alertness.

If you are speaking at a lectern, here are some things *not* to do: Don't lean on it. Don't slouch to one side of it. Don't prop your feet on its base. Don't rock back and forth with it.

Some speakers like to sit on the edge of a desk to deliver a speech. This posture is fine for one-hour classroom lectures because the speaker gets a chance to relax, and his or her body language bespeaks openness and informality. But for short speeches, especially the kind you are expected to deliver

TIPS FOR YOUR CAREER

TIP 13.1: Decide Whether and How to Use a Lectern

For career and community speeches, should you use a lectern? Experienced speakers disagree. Some say that a lectern gives you dignity and a convenient stand for your notes, especially on formal occasions such as an awards ceremony or a funeral. Others spurn a lectern because it creates a physical barrier. "I don't want anything coming between me and my audience," a politician told me. British speech consultant Cristina Stuart says, "I am 5'2" and some lecterns are 4'0" high, so how can I be a powerful speaker if my listeners can only see my head peeping over the edge?" Her advice: "Even if you are over six feet tall, try to stand to one side of the lectern so that you can refer to your notes and your listeners can see all of your body."

Here is a technique that has become popular: Using the lectern as "home base," walk a few paces to the left or right of it each time you make a point. In other words, glance at the notes on the lectern to remind yourself of the point you want to make, move away from the lectern a few paces, make the point, then walk back to the lectern to pick up your next point.

If a lectern is movable, some speakers remove it and simply hold their note cards in one hand (leaving the other hand free for gesturing). For a large audience, if the lectern is unmovable and has a stationary microphone, says Stuart, "you have no choice but to stand behind it. Stand on a box if you are short so that your upper body can be seen."

With some large audiences, you can arrange for a remote or mobile microphone so that you can move away from the lectern.

in a public speaking class, stand up straight, primarily because it is easier to be alert and enthusiastic if you are standing up than if your body is in a relaxed sitting position.

Movement

You don't have to stand in one place throughout your speech as if you were glued to the spot. Feel free to move about. You can walk to the chalkboard and write a key word, or walk to your visual aid. Occasionally you can move left or right from the lectern to a new position in front of the audience.

Movement gives your body a chance to dissipate nervous energy. It can also be used to recapture your listeners' attention if they are getting bored or tired; an animated speaker is easier to follow than an unanimated speaker who stays frozen in one spot.

You can use movement to emphasize a transition from one point to the next. For example, walking three steps to the left of the lectern while giving the audience a verbal "bridge" to your next point is a good way to emphasize that you are moving from one idea to another.

Movement can also be used to drive home an important point. At a crucial juncture in your speech, when you want strong audience involvement, you can take a few steps toward the listeners as you state a key idea. Moving toward them signals nonverbally that you are keenly interested in having them understand and accept what you are saying.

All your movements should be purposeful and confident—not random and nervous. If you roam back and forth across the front of the room like a tiger in a cage, your audience will be distracted and even annoyed. Don't sway back and forth; don't rock on your heels. In short, make your movements add to your speech, rather than subtract from it.

Using Notes

For classroom speeches, your instructor will tell you whether you may use notes and whether you may use a lectern.

For speeches in your career, the note system that was explained in Chapter 11 is highly recommended. It is a system that most professional speakers use. (Even speakers who talk without looking at notes often have notes with them as insurance—in case they lose their train of thought.)

If you do take cards or sheets of paper to a lectern, arrange them in whatever way works best for you. Some speakers place them in a stack on the lectern and consult one at a time. Other speakers spread them out so that several are visible at a time.

Whatever note system is used, remember our earlier warning: *Use notes sparingly*. Look at your audience 95 percent of the time.

Gestures

What should you do with your hands during a speech? First of all, make sure they do nothing to distract the audience: Don't let them jingle keys or coins, riffle note cards, fiddle with a watch or jewelry, adjust clothing, smooth hair, rub your chin, or scratch any part of your body. The best thing you can do with your hands is to let them be free to make gestures whenever you feel like making them. This, after all, is how you make gestures in conversation—naturally and without thinking. To make sure that your hands are free for gesturing, you can let them hang by your side or allow them to rest on the lectern. Beware of doing things that prevent your hands from being free to gesture: (1) Don't grip the lectern with your hands. (2) Don't clutch your notes with both hands. (3) Don't stuff both hands into your pockets.

Gestures are good if they reinforce your message or help the audience understand what you are saying; gestures are bad if they draw attention to themselves. If, to show anger, you slam your fist down on the lectern,

Gestures help a speaker reach out to the audience.

knocking over a glass of water and scaring the audience, you have called attention to the gesture and distracted the audience from your message.

If you use a lectern, don't let it hide your gestures. Some speakers rest their hands on the lectern and make tiny, flickering gestures that cannot be seen by the audience. This makes the speaker look tentative and unsure. Better no gestures at all than half-hidden ones.

When you make gestures, use your entire arm, advises British speech consultant Cristina Stuart. "Don't tuck in your elbows to your waist or make jerky, half-hearted, meaningless gestures," she says. "I remember a tall woman in one of my courses who, through shyness, stood hunched up making tiny movements with her hands. We advised her to stand tall, make eye contact, and use her arms to express her enthusiasm. The result was startling—she became regal and was very impressive. Without even opening her mouth, she looked like a self-confident, interesting speaker."[16]

Some speeches call for lots of gestures, some call for little or none. If you were describing your battle to catch a huge fish in the ocean, you would find your hands and arms constantly in motion. If you were giving a funeral eulogy, on the other hand, you might not make any gestures at all.

Most gestures should not be mechanically planned in advance because you are not using gestures naturally, your timing might be off. One student gave a speech in which he planned ahead of time to slam his fist on the lectern at the climax of his remarks. He said to the audience, "We must close down all nuclear plants!" But then he waited a few seconds before he slammed his fist down on the lectern, as if he had forgotten to do so until he had seen the cue on his note cards. The effect was comical rather than serious.

Though most of the time you should not plan gestures in advance, there are a few occasions when this is appropriate. If you have three major points to make, you can practice in advance holding up the correct number of fingers to assist the audience in following your points. If you are discussing two contrasting ideas, you can hold up your left hand when you say "On the one hand . . ." and then hold up your right hand when you say "On the other hand . . . ."

The larger the audience, the more sweeping your gestures. The evangelists who use windmill-like arm movements in addressing their multitudes in arenas are doing so for a good reason. They are able to establish a bond with people who are hundreds of yards away; small gestures would be lost in the vastness of the arena.

One last comment about gestures: if you are the kind of person who simply does not gesture much, don't worry about it. You have got enough on your mind without having to add this item to your list of worries. Just be sure to keep your hands free (not clutching notes or the lectern), so that if a gesture wells up inside you and cries out for expression, you will be able to make it naturally and forcefully.

Beginning and Ending

First impressions are important in many human events. The first impression we make on a person at a party, for example, often determines whether that person will want to spend much time chatting with us. In a speech, as one IBM executive told me, "You have only one chance to make a first impression." You make this first impression as you walk to the front and as you say your first few sentences.

When you rise from your seat, avoid sighing, groaning, or mumbling words of regret. Walk to the lectern (or speaking position) with an air of confidence—don't shamble like a condemned prisoner en route to the scaffold.

Avoid the mistake of rushing forward and starting to speak even before you get to the front. Listeners need time to get settled, so that they can clear their minds of other things and tune in to you.

When you face your audience, pause a few seconds before speaking. Don't say a word—just stand in silence. Some inexperienced speakers are terrified by this silence; they view it as a horrible event that makes the audience think they are too frozen with fear to speak. If you have this concern, relax. A brief period of silence is a very effective technique which all good speakers use. It is a punctuation device, separating what went before from what is to come—your speech. It creates drama, giving the audience a sense of expectancy. It is a dignified quietness that establishes your confidence and authority. In some cases, you may need to wait longer than a few seconds. If you are speaking to a civic club, for example, and a large number of people are arriving late, it is best to wait until the noise created by the latecomers has settled down. Or if many members of the audience are still whispering comments related to the previous speaker, simply stand and wait until you have their attention.

During these opening moments of silence, you have a chance to make sure your notes are in order and to review once again what you will say in your introduction. The next step is very important. Before you say a word, give your audience a friendly, confident look (if possible, smile) and then, continuing to look at your listeners instead of at your notes, say your first few sentences. You should have practiced your introduction thoroughly, so that you can say it without looking down at your notes. It is important to establish eye contact at this point. By looking at the listeners directly, your body language is saying, "I'm talking to you—I'm not up here just going through the motions of making a speech. I want to communicate. I want to reach out to you."

While first impressions are vital, final impressions are also important. Like your introduction, your conclusion should be well rehearsed (though not memorized), so that you can say it without looking at your notes. At the end of your speech, pause a few moments, look at your audience, and say, "I wonder what questions you have" or "I'll be happy to answer your questions now." Avoid gathering up your papers and leaning toward your seat—this sends a nonverbal message: "Please don't ask me any questions."

Question-and-Answer Period

In classroom speeches, the question-and-answer period usually represents a small percentage of the total time spent in front of the audience, but in some presentations in business, professional, and technical fields, the question-and-answer period is *the* most important part. Your speech is just a prelude—a little warm-up to get the audience ready for the questions. In some sales presentations, for example, the speaker will talk for, say, 10 minutes and then the question-and-answer period will go on for over an hour, with the listeners getting down to the nitty-gritty ("Okay, you say this machine will never wear out, but what happens if . . .").

Many listeners are so accustomed to listener-speaker interaction that they will interrupt during a speech to ask questions. In some technical presentations or classroom lectures, such interruptions might be appropriate and acceptable, but in other speeches, they are a nuisance. The continuity of the speaker's remarks is broken because listeners are prematurely asking questions that will be answered later in the speech. If you feel that your speech would be marred by interruptions, you should announce (in the orienting material of your introduction), "I know many of you will have questions. I'd like to ask you to hold them until I finish my presentation and then I'll be happy to try to answer them."

Here are some guidelines:

▶ Find out ahead of time if the person planning the program will want or permit a question-and-answer period, and if so, how much time will be allotted.

▶ Decide in advance if you want to invite comments as well as questions. If you do, you can say, "I would like to hear your questions or comments." (In some situations, you may not want comments because they could mushroom into long-winded rebuttals that detract from your message and leave no time for short, clarifying questions.)

▶ Plan for the question-and-answer period as carefully as you plan for the speech itself. Jot down all the possible questions that might come from the audience, and then decide exactly how you will answer them if they are asked. Tom Kirby, a St. Petersburg, Florida, executive, recommends that you ask an associate to prepare a list of questions based on your talk, thus giving you a realistic preview of the questions you might be asked by your listeners.[17]

▶ Try to regard the question-and-answer period as a blessing, not a curse. It gives you valuable feedback—it helps ensure that the message you intended the listeners to receive is indeed the one they end up with. If a misunderstanding has occurred, you have an excellent opportunity to clear it up.

▶ Don't feel defeated if you are not asked any questions. It could mean that you have covered everything so well that the listeners truly have nothing to ask.

▶ Give the audience time to think of questions. Some speakers wind up their conclusion, hastily ask if there are any questions, impatiently wait a few seconds, and then dash back to their seats. They don't really give the audience a fair chance. When you ask for questions, pause for as long as 10 seconds. If you get the feeling that no questions at all will be asked, you can say "Thank you" and sit down. But if you sense that the audience is simply shy (some listeners want to ask questions but are afraid that their question will be considered "dumb"), you may want to give them some encouragement. One way is to say, "While you're thinking of questions, let me answer one that a lot of people ask me. . . ." In some community and career contexts, you may even want to involve the listeners by asking *them* a question; for example, "What do *you* think of my proposal?"

▶ When a person asks a question, look directly at him or her, but when you give your answer, look at the entire audience, so that no one feels left out.

▶ In a large room, when a question is asked, repeat it for the benefit of listeners who may not have heard it. Repeating it also gives you time to think of your answer. If a question is unclear to you, ask the listener to clarify it.

▶ Don't reward some questions with "That's a good question" or "I'm glad you asked that," because the questioners who receive no praise from you will feel as if their questions have been judged inferior.

▶ If you don't know the answer to the question, say so. Your listeners will not think less of you for an honest admission of ignorance on a particular point; they *will* think less of you if you try to fake expertise. In some situations, you may want to ask the audience for help: "I don't know the answer—is there anyone here who can help us out?"

▶ If a listener points out a flaw in the logic of your argument or casts doubt on some of your facts and figures, try to avoid being defensive. If the listener seems to have merit to his or her point, say so. You can say something like, "You've got a good point. I'm going to have to think about this some more." Or, "You may be right—that statistic could be outdated. I'll have to check it. Thanks for mentioning it." Not only is such a conciliatory approach honest, but it is also a good way to gain respect from the listeners. No one expects you to be perfect; if a listener finds an error in your speech, it does not mean that your whole effort has been discredited.

▶ Don't let one listener "hog" the question-and-answer period, especially if a number of other people have questions. If a person persists in asking one question after another or launches into a long monologue, you should interrupt and say, "Let's give others a chance to ask questions; if we have time later, I'll get back to you" or "Why don't you and I talk about this in greater detail after the meeting?"

▶ Decline to answer questions that are not appropriate for a discussion in front of the entire audience—for example, questions that are too personal or that require a long, technical explanation that most of the listeners would find boring and tedious. You can deflect such questions by politely explaining your reasons; for example, "That's a little too personal—I'd rather not go into that" or "I'm afraid it would take us too much time to go into the details right now." In some cases, you might tell the questioner to see you afterward for a one-on-one discussion.

▶ Don't let the question-and-answer period drag on interminably. If you have been allotted an hour, say, for both your speech and the question-and-answer period, end the session promptly at the end of an hour, even if some listeners still have questions. (As we have already di cussed, it is important that you avoid going over your time limit.) If your speech is the last item on the program and you sense that some listeners would like to continue the question-and-answer period, you could say, "I'm going to end the formal part of my presentation now because I promised I would take up only one hour of your time and I know that some of you have other business to take care of. However, if any of you would like to stay, you can move to the seats here at the front and we'll continue with an informal question-and-answer period."

Practice

After you have written your outline and made notes based on it (as discussed in Chapter 11), you should spend a great deal of time rehearsing your speech. Practice, practice, practice—it's a crucial step that some inexperienced speakers leave out. Practice makes you look and sound fluent, smooth, and spontaneous. Practice bolsters your confidence, giving you a sense of mastery and competence. Here are some tips:

▶ Start early. If you wait until the eve of your speech, you will not have enough time to develop and polish your delivery. Allow yourself at least 4 days of practice before your speech date.

▶ Practice going through your entire speech at least four times, more if necessary. Space your practice sessions; in other words, avoid doing most of your practicing on a single day. You will make greater progress if you have time intervals between practice sessions.

▶ "Practice ideas, not words" is a maxim worth heeding; in other words, learn your speech point by point, not word for word.[18] Remember that your goal in extemporaneous speaking is not to memorize or read a speech. Every time you say your speech (whether in practice or in delivery to an audience), the wording should be different. The ideas will be the same, but not the exact words.

▶ Time yourself during practice sessions. If your speech exceeds the time limit set by your instructor or by the group that invited you, go back to your outline and notes and trim them down.

▶ During most of your practice sessions, go all the way through the speech. Don't stop if you hit a problem (you can work it out later). Going all the way through helps you see whether your ideas fit together snugly and whether your transitions from point to point are smooth.

▶ Some speakers find it helpful to practice in front of a mirror or to use a video camcorder or audiotape recorder. Whether or not you use one of these techniques, you should practice at least once in front of a *live*

Some speakers find that practicing in front of a mirror is an effective way to prepare for a speech.

audience—friends or relatives who can give you a candid appraisal. Remember the point we made in an earlier chapter: Don't say "Tell me how I do on this," because your evaluators will probably say "Good job—I liked the speech" to avoid hurting your feelings. Instead give them a specific assignment: "Please note at least three positive things and at least three negative things." Now your listeners have an assignment that they know will not hurt your feelings, and you are likely to get some helpful feedback.

▶ Some speakers find it helpful to make a trial run in the very room in which they will give the speech. This would be an especially good idea if you have visual aids and equipment; you can practice the mechanics, for example, of showing overhead transparencies.

▶ In addition to practicing the entire speech, devote special practice time to your beginning and ending—two parts that should be smooth and effective.

▶ Be sure that you don't put too many words down on your notes. Have just the bare minimum necessary to jog your memory. Practice from the actual notes that you will use in the speech. Don't make a clean set right before the speech; the old marked-up notes are more reliable because you're very familiar with them from your practice sessions.

TIPS FOR YOUR CAREER

TIP 13.2: Deal with Distractions in a Direct, but Good-humored Manner

In classroom speeches you will have an attentive, courteous audience, but at some point in your career, you may encounter an audience that contains a few rude listeners who chat among themselves while you are trying to speak, thus causing a distraction for other listeners.

Professional speakers stress that you should *not* ignore the disturbance that the rude listeners are creating. Confront these listeners, but do so in a calm, friendly, good-humored manner.

One technique is to simply stop your speech and look directly at the rude listeners (try to look friendly and not irritated). This nonverbal nudge is often all it takes to cause the persons to stop talking. Sometimes people sitting near the offenders will pick up on your cue and help you out by turning and saying "shh."

Professional speaker Rosita Perez of Brandon, Florida, says that you may lose the respect of your entire audience if you ignore the talkative few. "Confront them *kindly*," she advises. "Say, 'It seems to me you must have a lot of catching up to do with your friends. I wonder if you would visit outside so I can continue?' " In most such cases, the listeners will stay in the room and give the speaker respectful silence for the rest of the speech.

Speech consultant Sandy Linver says that with a large audience

> I take the trouble to gently zero in on . . . the chatterers and pull them back in. I say something like, "Are you with me? . . ." If it's a small group, side conversations often are

important to the subject at hand, so it is important not to ignore them. If I were speaking at a business meeting of fifteen people or so, I might say to the three people talking among themselves, "That looks as if it might be important. Would you like to share it with the group?" Often they are discussing something I have said that needs clarification or elaboration, and the whole group benefits when they are encouraged to speak up.

Some speeches are marred by the incessant crying of a baby. Even though members of the audience turn and give annoyed, disapproving looks, the parents of the baby sometimes refuse to take the infant out of the room. Actor and orator Steve Allen once handled this situation by saying,

> As the father of four sons I've more than once been in the position of the parents of that child. Personally I could go on even if there were several children crying at the same time, but I know that most people are too distracted by that sort of thing to concentrate on what is being said. So if you wouldn't mind taking the child out—at least until he stops crying— I'm sure the rest of our audience would appreciate it.

This remark, says Allen, prompted applause from the audience and "gracious cooperation from the parents."

Summary

The key to good delivery is a strong desire to communicate with the audience. Speakers who concentrate on getting their ideas across to their listeners usually find themselves using good delivery techniques.

There are four methods of delivering a speech: memorized, manuscript, impromptu, and extemporaneous. Of the four, extemporaneous is the most popular and usually the most effective because the speaker delivers a well-prepared, well-rehearsed speech in a lively, conversational manner.

In delivering a speech, your voice should be loud enough for everyone to hear; your words should be spoken clearly so that they are easily understood, and your voice should be expressive so that you sound interesting and lively.

Nonverbal communication is the message you give with your body by means of personal appearance, eye contact, facial expressions, posture, movement, and gestures. All these elements should convey confidence and a positive regard for the audience. Of special importance is eye contact. You should look at your listeners during 95 percent of your speech to maintain a bond of communication and rapport with them and to monitor their feedback.

Practice is a vital part in the success of your speech. You should practice the entire speech over and over again—until you can deliver it with power and confidence.

Review Questions

1. What are the disadvantages of impromptu, manuscript, and memorized speeches?
2. What ingredient is essential for the success of an extemporaneous speech?
3. Why is it a serious mistake to speak too rapidly at the beginning of a speech?
4. What are the characteristics of good eye contact?
5. What can speakers do with their hands to make sure that they are free for gesturing?
6. Why should a speech be learned and practiced point by point, instead of word for word?

Speaking to Inform

At a shopping mall I happened to encounter Pete Gentry, a former student of mine. "Listen," he said, "Do you remember that speech Julie Parris gave about whatever-it's-called—the way you help a person who's choking on food?"

"Yes," I said, "The Heimlich maneuver."

"Well," continued Gentry, "it was a lucky thing I learned about it because a couple of months ago I used it on my kid brother. He got some food caught in his throat and was turning white as a sheet. I grabbed him and did what Julie taught us—made a fist on his stomach and forced the air up from his lungs. It worked—it cleared his windpipe. He could have died if I hadn't known exactly what to do."

Thus was a life saved because a speaker had presented information so clearly that a listener was able to remember it months later. Gentry had forgotten the name of the technique, but so what? He had remembered the essence of Julie Parris's speech—how to rescue a choking person.

Parris's talk on the Heimlich maneuver is an example of an informative speech, one of the most popular kinds of speeches given in the classroom and in the community. In the informative speech your task is primarily to educate—to give new information to your listeners and help them understand it.

What you hope to achieve is what Parris achieved: having your audience remember the essence of your speech months later. To reach this goal, your speech must be interesting (so that the audience *wants* to listen) and it must be clear (so that the audience can understand you). In this chapter, we will look at four types of informative speeches and then discuss guidelines to help you create speeches that are clear, interesting, and memorable.

Types of Informative Speeches

Informative speeches can be categorized in many different ways, but in this chapter we will concentrate on four of the most popular types: definition description, process, and expository.

Definition Speech

Suppose that one of your friends confides that she has dyslexia, but you don't know the meaning of this word. You would probably ask, "What do you mean by *dyslexia*?"

Your friend could give you a dictionary definition—"the impairment of the ability to read"—but that would not do much to satisfy your curiosity You would want her to give examples such as this: "When I was in eleme tary school, I scrambled letters when I tried to read; the word *was* looked to me like *saw*." You would want her to relate how the affliction has affected her life: "I flunked first grade and I thought I was dumb. I had a terrible inferiority complex." And so on.

What your friend would be giving you is an *extended* definition, one that is richer and more meaningful than a dictionary explanation. That is what a definition speech is all about—giving an extended definition of a concept so that the listeners get a full, richly detailed picture of its meaning. While a dictionary definition would settle lightly on the listeners' brains and probably vanish overnight, an extended definition is likely to stick firmly. Here are some sample specific-purpose statements for definition speeches:

- ▶ To define homeopathic medicine for my listeners
- ▶ To explain to the audience the chief characteristics of wetlands
- ▶ To define radio astronomy for my listeners
- ▶ To explain genetic testing to my audience

Any of the support materials that we discussed in Chapter 7 (such as narratives, examples, description, and statistics) can be applied to defining a topic. If you were speaking on phobias, for example, you could give *examples* of the types of phobias, such as claustrophobia and agoraphobia, and *narratives* from the lives of phobic individuals.

In a speech on employee theft, Karen Kimmey of Arizona State University defined theft in an unexpected way, and she gave an example to help listeners understand her definition:

> Susan was your typical office employee; punched in on her timecard, spent eight hours at her desk, got paid fairly well for her time, and left without snagging so much as a pencil to take home with her. Yet she was deliberately stealing from her employer every day. You see, while being paid for her work in financial services, she was busy running three personal businesses from her desk, selling exercise equipment, videocassettes and designer clothing over the phone, all on company time.[1]

Sometimes the best way to define a topic is to compare or contrast it with a similar item. If you were trying to define what constitutes child abuse, for example, it would be helpful to contrast abuse with firm, but loving, discipline.

Often you can enhance a definition speech by breaking a subject into subcategories. In a speech on vegetarianism, Chad Gordon helped his listeners understand his subject by defining three distinct styles of eating:

Specific Purpose: To define vegetarianism for my listeners
Central Idea: People may choose from three different styles of vegetarian eating.

Main Points: I. The most common style is a semivegetarian diet.
  A. No red meat is eaten.
  B. Poultry, fish, milk, and eggs are allowed.
 II. The second most common style is the lacto-ovo vegetarian diet.
  A. No animal flesh is eaten.
  B. Eggs and milk products are allowed.
 III. The least common style is the vegan diet.
  A. No animal flesh is consumed.
  B. No animal products are eaten.

The above covers merely the high points of the outline. In the full speech, the speaker discussed the three types in detail, giving the listeners a good extended definition of vegetarianism.

Description Speech

Describing a person, place, object, or event is a technique that can be used in any kind of speech. In a definition speech on alcoholism, for example, you might include a description of an alcoholic. In some cases, however, you may want to devote your entire speech to description. Here are some specific-purpose statements for description speeches:

▶ To tell my listeners how a volcanic eruption looks, sounds, and feels
▶ To describe to my listeners the visual and physical pleasures of whitewater rafting
▶ To inform my audience about working conditions in the emergency room of a major hospital
▶ To describe to my audience the highlights of the life of aviation pioneer Amelia Earhart

If you were describing an object or place, you might want to use the *spatial* pattern of organization. Here is an example of the spatial pattern as used in an outline on robots in nuclear power plants. The speaker describes the robot from bottom to top:

Specific Purpose: To describe to my listeners the robots used for inspecting nuclear power plants
Central Idea: Robots are used for inspecting nuclear power plants to protect humans from radiation exposure.
Main Points: I. The robot stands on five spider-like legs capable of walking.

    II. The midsection of the robot contains a computerized
        control system.
   III. The "head" of the robot carries lights, a TV camera,
        and sensing devices.

Describing a person, living or dead, can make a fascinating speech. If you were describing a historical figure, you might want to use the *chronological* pattern; in a speech on Albert Einstein, for example, you could discuss the major events of his life—in the order in which they occurred—from birth to death. Or you might prefer to use the *topical* pattern, emphasizing two major features of Einstein's career:

Specific Purpose: To describe to my audience the accomplishments of Albert Einstein

Central Idea: Albert Einstein was one of the most influential thinkers in human history.

Main Points: I. Einstein revolutionized the field of physics with his theories, especially the Theory of Relativity.
          II. Einstein was a persuasive advocate of world peace and global cooperation.

Process Speech

In a process speech, you are concerned with explaining the steps or stages by which something is done or made. There are two kinds of process speeches. In the first kind, you show the listeners how to *perform* a process so that they can actually use the skills later (this is sometimes called a *demonstration* speech). Here are some examples of specific-purpose statements for this kind of speech:

▶ To teach my listeners how to refinish furniture
▶ To demonstrate to my audience the proper ways to lift, sit, and sleep in order to avoid back strain
▶ To show my audience how to grow dwarfed (bonsai) trees
▶ To demonstrate to my listeners how to bake bread cheaply and quickly

In the second kind of process speech, you provide information on "how something is done" or "how something works." Your goal is to *explain* a process so that the listeners understand the process, not necessarily so that they can perform it themselves. For example, let's say that you outline the steps by which counterfeiters print bogus money. You are showing these steps to satisfy the listeners' intellectual curiosity and also to teach them how to spot a counterfeit bill, not so that they can perform the job them-

A demonstration (or process) speech is enhanced by having listeners actually perform an action, such as giving CPR (cardiopulmonary resuscitation) to a dummy.

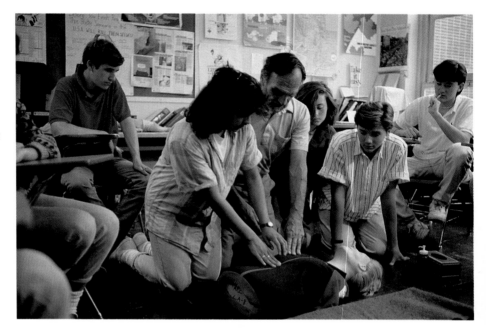

selves. Here are some samples of specific-purpose statements for this kind of speech:

▶ To explain to my audience how filmmakers create the illusion of Superman flying

▶ To explain to my listeners how surgeons perform "face lifts" to smooth out facial wrinkles

▶ To explain to my listeners how the great pyramids of Egypt were built

▶ To explain to my listeners how airport investigators detect drugs and explosives

If your instructor consents, you may want to use humor to make serious points in a process speech. For example, if your speech purported to be on the topic of "how to flunk a test," you could discuss such items as "Be sure to party all night on the eve of the test." Though you don't state it explicitly, your true point, of course, is that a person should get plenty of sleep before taking a big test. One student gave a process speech on how to burglarize a house or apartment; by speaking tongue-in-cheek from the burglar's point of view, he effectively conveyed his real message—how to make sure your home is protected from burglars.

Here are some guidelines on preparing a process speech:

1. Be sure to include all steps, even obvious ones. A lawyer bought a huge aquarium for his new office and then went out and spent hundreds of dollars at a pet shop on an assortment of exotic tropical fish. He returned to his office, filled the aquarium with water, and dumped the fish in. When all the fish died, he called the pet shop and found out why. The directions for the aquarium had neglected to mention that tap water must sit 24 hours before fish are inserted so that all the chlorine can evaporate. Otherwise, the fish will die of chlorine poisoning. Whoever wrote the directions for the aquarium probably assumed that any fish lover would be familiar with this piece of information, but such an assumption was a mistake.

In a process speech, give all the steps involved, including the ones that are simple and self-evident. What seems obvious to you may not be obvious to some of your listeners.

2. Use visual aids whenever possible. Because processes are often complicated, use visual aids, if at all possible, to help the listeners understand and retain your points. One of the most effective visual aids is the demonstration, wherein you actually perform the process while talking. For example, if you wanted to teach cardiopulmonary resuscitation (CPR), you could demonstrate the steps on a dummy while you go through your explanations.

3. Involve the audience in physical activity whenever possible. If you involve the audience in a physical activity, you capitalize on more than just the listeners' sense of hearing and seeing; you also bring in touch and movement. There is an ancient Chinese proverb that says:

I hear—and I forget.
I see—and I remember.
I do—and I understand.

The wisdom of this saying has been confirmed by psychologists, who have found that of the three main channels for learning new information, the auditory is weakest, the visual is stronger, and physical action is strongest of all. The best approach is to bring all three together. For example, if you were explaining how to do stretching exercises, you could explain the techniques (auditory) as you give a demonstration (visual); then you could have each listener stand and perform the exercises (physical action). Some audience involvement can be accomplished while the listeners remain in their chairs; for example, if you are speaking on sign language, you could have the listeners practice the hand signals as you teach them.

Note of caution: Get your instructor's approval before you use any physical activity in a classroom speech. When you give a talk in the community beyond the college campus, use your best judgment. Make sure that you don't ask your audience to do something that would be embarrassing or awkward for some of the listeners. If, for example, there are physically handicapped people in the audience, would they be able to perform the task? One speaker, who was ecstatic about the hug-everybody philosophy of Leo Buscaglia, tried to get the entire audience to exchange hugs. Some of the listeners were embarrassed.

4. Proceed slowly. Always bear in mind that much of what you say might be new to the listeners. If you are giving instruction about how to make leather belts, for example, you might be describing activities that are so easy for you that you could perform them blindfolded, but they might be completely foreign to some members of the audience. That's why you should talk slowly and repeat key ideas if necessary. Give the listeners ample time to absorb the points and form mental images.

5. Give advance warning of difficult steps. When you are ready to discuss especially difficult steps, you can use transitions to give the listeners a warning. For example, you can say, "The next step is a little tricky" or "This next step is the hardest one of all." This alerts the listeners that they need to pay extra-special attention.

Expository Speech

An expository speech (also called an oral report or lecture) involves explaining a concept or situation to the audience. For this speech, your instructor may want you to choose a topic that you are not thoroughly familiar with and then conduct research (in the library and/or by means of interviews) to gain command of the subject.

The expository speech may contain many features of the definition, descriptive, or process speeches. For example, if you chose to speak on the topic "how the bail system works," you would be explaining a process. What makes the expository speech different from the other types is that you must conduct in-depth research, using books and articles and interviews, rather than rely on your own personal experiences.

Here are examples of specific-purpose statements for expository speeches:

▶ To explain to my listeners the "catastrophic" theory as to why dinosaurs became extinct
▶ To inform my audience of the causes of starvation in Africa and Asia
▶ To explain to my listeners how a consumer's credit rating is determined and used

▶ To report to the audience on the causes and impact of illiteracy in the United States

▶ To inform my audience on how conventional physicians are using acupuncture as a medical tool

Expository speeches are often organized in the *topical* pattern. As we saw in Chapter 9, you use the topical pattern to subdivide a central idea into main points, using logic and common sense as your guides. Here is an outline for an expository speech that uses the topic pattern:

Specific Purpose: To inform my audience about the dangers of quicksand
Central Idea: Found in almost every state of the United States, quicksand is a terrifying natural trap from which people can extricate themselves if they follow the correct steps.
Main Points:
I. Quicksand is as treacherous as the movies depict it to be.
   A. It has swallowed people.
   B. It has swallowed cars and trucks.
II. Quicksand is deceptive.
   A. The surface can appear as solid as the surrounding terrain.
   B. Underneath the surface is a sandy brew that is formed by water flowing upward from hidden springs.
III. If you step into quicksand, you can follow four easy steps that will save your life.
   A. Get rid of extra weight such as a backpack or coat.
   B. Throw yourself flat on your back and "float."
   C. Press your arms out onto the surface of the quicksand.
   D. Moving with snail-like slowness, roll your way to firm ground.

Notice that there are elements of description (point I), definition (point II), and process (point III) in this outline.

Another pattern is the *fallacy-fact* pattern (or it could be called *myth-reality*). In this pattern the speaker cites a popular fallacy and then presents facts that refute it. Here is a sample outline from a speech given by Sarah Stepanovich, in which she refutes three popular misconceptions about sharks:

Specific Purpose: To refute, for my audience, common fallacies about sharks
Central Idea: Sharks are not as dangerous to humans as most people think they are.

Main Points:
(Fallacy) I. It is a widely believed fallacy that there are hundreds of shark attacks each year, most of which are fatal.
(Facts)   A. Worldwide, shark attacks average twenty eight each year.
    B. Only three or four are fatal.
(Fallacy) II. It is a widely believed fallacy that when a shark attacks one person, it will attack anyone else who is nearby.
(Facts)   A. Sharks select a single person and ignore others.
    B. Rescuers are usually unharmed.
(Fallacy) III. It is a widely believed fallacy that sharks attack people when they get hungry.
(Facts)   A. Very few attacks are made by sharks that are hungry.
    B. In most attacks, the shark takes one bite and then leaves.

Guidelines for Informative Speaking

In informative speaking, strive to make your message clear, interesting, and memorable. You can achieve this goal by applying the principles that we have covered so far in this book, being especially careful to select good support materials (Chapters 7 and 8). In addition to techniques already covered, here are some guidelines that should be useful for informative speeches.

Relate the Speech to the Listeners' Self-Interest

Many listeners approach a speech with an attitude of: "Why should I care? Why should I pay attention? What's in it for me?" The best motivator in a speech, therefore, is something that has an impact on their lives.

"When I was in the Navy," a friend recalls, "I was assigned to duty as a parachute packer. On our first day, we were given a talk on what people do to prepare themselves for jumping out of planes with a parachute. I didn't pay much attention because I figured my only contact with parachutes would be packing them. Then the next day they announced that in a few weeks *we* would have to parachute out of a plane! They wanted to make us appreciate— the hard way—just how important it is to pack a parachute correctly and carefully. When I heard this, I was scared, and I kicked myself for not paying attention to all that stuff they had said about getting ready for a jump."

Whoever gave that lecture failed to provide the audience with motivation to listen closely. The lecturer should have said something like this: "You may think your only contact with parachutes is packing them, but you're wrong. In a few weeks you will all jump out of an airplane with a parachute. Now here's how you do it. . . ." Hearing such a comment, my friend undoubtedly would have listened to the lecture with wide-eyed attention. Here's another case:

> Hoang Pham, a computer programmer, gave a talk to a business group on "bugs," or tiny glitches, in computer software. He knew that some listeners might be tempted to tune him out, figuring that his speech was about an esoteric subject of no real consequence to them. So, to make sure that everyone in his audience realized that the bugs could someday affect their lives, he said, "According to the *Wall Street Journal*, Verdon Kidd, an East Texas bus driver was using a computerized radiation-therapy machine to fight his skin cancer last spring; the therapy was going along okay until a defect in the machine's software caused Kidd to receive a massive dose of radiation that killed him. This is not just an isolated case: the *Journal* says that during the past five years, 'software defects have killed sailors, maimed patients, wounded corporations, and threatened to cause the government-securities market to collapse.' " Realizing that computer "bugs" could have a life-or-death and dollars-and-cents impact on their lives, the business executives in the audience probably listened intently to the rest of the speech.[2]

If possible, relate every speech to the listeners' self-interest. Show them that what you have to say is important to their own lives.

Make Information Interesting

Many speeches are boring because the speakers deal primarily with *generalities*, which by themselves tend to be dull and vague. To make a speech lively, give the audience lots of *specifics*—verbal support materials such as narratives, examples, quotations, statistics (see Chapter 7), and visual aids (see Chapter 8). While some generalities may be necessary in a speech, they should always be coupled with vivid specifics. Here is an example of a generalized statement:

> Some dogs are trained by their owners to be aggressive and dangerous. The dogs are chosen and bred for their hostile tendencies. These dogs sometimes attack without warning.

By itself, this statement is colorless and not likely to make much of an impression on the listeners' minds. As a contrast, let's look at a portion of a speech by Gina Hawkins, a professional dog breeder:

Some dogs are trained to be vicious. For example, some pit bulls (the popular name for American Staffordshire Terriers) have been bred and trained to be savage attack dogs. Last April, a two-year-old girl in Michigan was killed instantly when the family's pit bull suddenly turned on her and bit her in the throat. That same day, Dr. William Eckman was attacked by two pit bulls; nine people spent 25 minutes trying to pry off the dogs with poles and brooms. Dr. Eckman died soon thereafter, from the wounds. Last year, a 71-year-old woman in Stone Mountain, Georgia, was dragged across her driveway by a pit bull and bitten so severely that she needed 100 stitches. Of the 34 fatal canine attacks in the U.S. in the last five years, pit bulls inflicted 27 of them.[3]

This excerpt shows the use of interesting support materials—examples and statistics. In the same speech, Hawkins also used visual aids—pictures of two breeds that are often confused. The first photograph showed a snarling pit bull; Hawkins pointed out the blunt face and unfriendly "look" of this breed. For contrast, she displayed a poster of Spuds McKenzie, the famous bull terrier of TV commercials, so that the audience could see that bull terriers have elongated oval heads and a gentle, friendly look—characteristics that distinguish them from their cousins, the pit bulls.

A note of caution: give details, but not too many. You don't want to bore your audience with a tedious overload. "The secret of being tiresome," the French philosopher Voltaire said, "is in telling everything." Edit your material: Instead of giving all fourteen quotations that you have compiled for a point, cite just one or two.

Assess the Knowledge of Listeners

Analyze your listeners thoroughly before a speech (as discussed in Chapter 4) to find out what they know and what they don't know. This will keep you from committing two common mistakes.

1. Don't give information that the audience already knows. A famous psychiatrist who had developed innovative programs for training mentally retarded individuals gave the keynote speech at a state convention of the Association for Retarded Citizens. For one hour, he explained the revolution that had taken place in recent years in educating retarded students.

At the conclusion of his speech, he was given polite applause, but throughout the hall, at the individual tables, there were mutterings of discontent. The famous man had spent an hour imparting information that all the delegates already knew. "What a waste of time!" exclaimed one disappointed listener, who had been hungry for new insights. Apparently the psychiatrist had failed to analyze his listeners; he thought they were primarily parents who knew little about the scientific aspects of retardation. If he had analyzed them correctly, he would have known that half the audience consisted of knowledgeable professionals—psychologists, social workers, and teachers—and the other half consisted of parents who had spent months or years learning the basic information.

2. Don't talk over the listeners' heads.   Avoid using words, concepts, references, and allusions that the audience doesn't understand. It is easy to commit this mistake if you assume that your listeners possess a common body of information.[4] Recent polls have shown that many Americans, especially high school students, lack a body of knowledge that earlier generations possessed. Here are some examples:

► A Gallup poll found that 40 percent of American high school students did not know that Israel is a Jewish nation (they thought it was an Arab state), and 10 percent thought that Latin is the language spoken in Latin America.[5]

► A National Geographic Society study estimated that 24 million American adults (one in seven) cannot find their own country on a world map.[6]

► Half the college students surveyed by the National Endowment for the Humanities were unable to name the century in which the American Civil War took place.[7] In a Gallup poll, one in four Americans surveyed

Speakers such as this marine biologist must be careful to neither overestimate nor underestimate the intelligence of the listeners.

could not name the country from which the United States declared independence in 1776.[8]

▶ In a survey by the U.S. Department of Education, one in five high school seniors thought that removing vegetation would increase wildlife populations.[9]

If you find out in advance what your audience doesn't know, you can define words or explain concepts whenever necessary. You can give background information and examples.

What should you do when your audience is mixed—that is, some know your information already and some don't? How can you give explanations in a way that does not insult the intelligence of the listeners who already know the material? In some cases, you can give information in a casual, unobtrusive way. For example, let's say you are planning in your speech to cite a quotation by Adolf Hitler. Most college students know who Hitler was, but some do not. To inform the latter without insulting the intelligence of the former, you can say something like this: "In the 1920s, long before Adolf Hitler rose to power in Germany and long before he launched the German nation into World War II, he made the following prophetic statement. . . ." An indirect approach like this permits you to "sneak" in a lot of background information.

In other cases, you may need to be straightforward in giving definitions or explanations. For example, if you need to define *recession* for a speech on economic cycles, do so directly and clearly. Knowledgeable listeners will not be offended by a quick definition as long as most of your speech supplies them with new material; in fact, they probably will welcome a chance to affirm the accuracy of their own understanding of the term.

Use the Familiar to Explain the Unfamiliar

A few years ago an Israeli leader toured the United States to drum up support for increased military aid to Israel. Dorothy Sarnoff, an American consultant who was hired to help him prepare his speeches, gave him the following advice:

> If you describe Israel at its narrowest point by saying, "Israel is so narrow that we can be [easily] attacked," the Americans won't get it. . . . Instead say "Israel is so narrow that if you were driving on a[n American-style] highway, it would take you only twenty minutes to get from one side of Israel to the other."[1]

Sarnoff's advice was sound. When you want to explain or describe something that is unfamiliar to your audience, relate it to something that is familiar. You can use some of the devices we discussed in Chapter 7, such as comparisons, contrasts, and analogies. If, for example, you point out that divers in Acapulco, Mexico, astound tourists by diving into water from rocks 118 feet high, that statistic does not have much impact unless you point out that a 118-foot plunge is equal to a dive from the roof of an 11-story building.[11]

To give listeners a mental picture of what the inside of a tornado is like, Dale Higgins said: "A tornado's funnel is like the vortex you see when you let water go down a drain." Since everyone has seen the swirling action of water going down a drain, the comparison helped the audience visualize a tornado's vortex.

Sample Informative Speech

Rob Fontaine prepared and delivered a speech on food poisoning, drawing from an interview with a dietician and from magazine articles. The outline is presented first, followed by a transcript of the actual speech.[12]

The Outline

How to Avoid Food Poisoning

General Purpose: To inform
Specific Purpose: To explain to my listeners how to avoid food poisoning in their homes
Central Idea: A person can avoid food poisoning at home by maintaining the proper temperature of foods and by being careful not to contaminate foods.

INTRODUCTION

I. There are 20 people in this room. Six of us this year will eat contaminated food. I base this prediction on studies done by health educators at New York's Mount Sinai School of Medicine. They estimate that this year 75 million Americans—30 percent of the population—will suffer from diarrhea, nausea, stomach cramps, and vomiting as a result of food poisoning, mainly from salmonella and other bacteria. Unfortunately, food poisoning can cause more than stomach distress. It can lead to a variety of long-term health problems such as joint, heart, and kidney disease. And it can sometimes be fatal: every year 9,000 Americans die from food poisoning.

II. Is the situation worse than it was in the past? Yes, for two reasons, according to health authorities. Number one: some strains of poisonous bacteria are becoming more toxic. Number two: the United States is importing more and more foods from other countries, many of which have low sanitary standards. We have no control over the way food is prepared in a restaurant, but we do have control over how we prepare food at home. I'd like to show you two ways you can prevent food poisoning in your home: First, maintain the proper temperature, and second, be careful to avoid contamination. My information comes primarily from an interview with Katherine Buckner, a dietician with Tri-County Hospital, and a magazine article by three health educators at Mount Sinai School of Medicine.

(Transition: Let's take a look at my first recommendation.)

BODY

I. Many cases of food poisoning could be prevented by maintaining proper temperature to kill or neutralize harmful bacteria.
  A. Avoid raw or partially cooked meats.
    1. Use a meat thermometer to insure proper cooking. [hold up meat thermometer as visual aid]
      a. Beef and pork should reach 160°.
      b. Veal and lamb should reach 170°.
      c. Poultry should reach 180°.
    2. Avoid eating raw shellfish.
      a. Even shellfish from clean waters can contain harmful bacteria.
      b. Cook raw shrimp until pink and firm.
  B. Never leave food to thaw on a counter for longer than 2 hours.
    1. "Always thaw food in a refrigerator," says Katherine Buckner, the hospital dietician. "It takes longer, but it prevents bacterial growth."
    2. If you have a microwave oven, you can of course use it for thawing.
  C. Undercooked or raw eggs are a major source of food poisoning.
    1. Ms. Buckner advises you not to use raw eggs to make homemade mayonnaise or other dishes.
    2. When you do use an egg for a recipe, be sure that you cook it through and through.
  D. You should buy a thermometer and use it for both hot and cold. [regular thermometer as visual aid]
    1. In your refrigerator always keep foods at 40° or below, and in your freezer at 0° or below.
    2. Hot foods on a buffet or chafing dish should be kept at more than 140°.
    3. A thermometer may sound like a lot of trouble.
      a. Ms. Buckner says people are in such a hurry nowadays, they don't heat things up enough.
      b. The extra time and trouble can spare you from food poisoning.

(Transition: While temperature is important, you also need to avoid contaminating food.)

II. Many cases of food poisoning could be prevented by being careful not to contaminate food.
  A. A major source of contamination is a wooden cutting board.
    1. Juices from one food can contaminate another.
    2. Use an acrylic board and clean it frequently with hot water and bleach. [hold up an acrylic board as visual aid]

    B. Ms. Buckner says many cases of food poisoning occur in the summertime at backyard cookouts.
       1. People will take chicken in a big bowl out to the barbecue.
       2. When the chicken is cooked, they will put it back into the same bowl.
       3. Thus bacteria from the uncooked chicken juices (at the bottom and sides of the bowl) will contaminate the cooked meat.
    C. Wash away contaminants.
       1. Always wash your hands before handling any food.
       2. Always wash fruit and vegetables.
       3. use a brush to scrub root vegetables like carrots and potatoes to get all dirt particles off. [use a brush and potato as visual aid]
       4. Frequently clean kitchen surfaces, appliances, and accessories like kitchen mitts.
       5. Scrub your entire kitchen every week.
(Transition: Let's review what we've covered today.)

CONCLUSION

I. Avoid raw or partially cooked meats. Avoid raw shellfish. Avoid raw or undercooked eggs. Don't thaw food on an open counter—use the refrigerator or a microwave oven. In the refrigerator, keep foods at 40° or below and in your freezer keep them at 0° or below. Contamination can be avoided if you use an acrylic board and keep it clean. If you keep your kitchen clean, especially preparation surfaces. If you wash fruits and vegetables and scrub root vegetables. And if you keep raw food juices from contacting cooked meat (remember the backyard barbeque fiasco?).
II. At the beginning I said that health experts would predict that six of us will eat contaminated food this year. If we all follow the tips I've given you today, we can beat the odds and have *zero* food poisoning.

BIBLIOGRAPHY

Katherine Buckner, dietician, Tri-County Hospital, personal interview, February 7, 1992.

"Food Safety," *Mayo Clinic Health Letter*, May 1991, p. 4.

"Is Our Fish Fit to Eat?" *Consumer Reports*, February, 1992, pp. 103–120.

Rosalinda Lawson, R.D., Elyse Sosin, R.D., M.A., and Fran G. Grossman, R.D., M.S., Mount Sinai School of Medicine, "Food Poisoning Alert," *Redbook*, November 1990, pp. 46–57.

VISUAL AIDS

Meat thermometer
Scouring brush and potato
Regular thermometer
Acrylic cutting board

The Speech as Delivered

Here is a transcript of the speech as it was delivered.

COMMENTARY

To grab the attention of his audience, the speaker personalizes some statistics.

By showing how widespread and serious food poisoning is, the speaker gives listeners a powerful incentive to listen.

A rhetorical question is a powerful device to pique audience curiosity.

A preview of the body of the speech helps listeners follow the rest of the speech.

Citing reputable sources adds credibility to the speech.

How to Avoid Food Poisoning

There are twenty of us here in this room today. Did you know that six of us will eat contaminated food sometime this year? I can make this prediction on the basis of research done by health educators at Mount Sinai School of Medicine in New York City. They estimate that this year 75 million Americans—that's 30 percent of the population—will suffer from diarrhea, nausea, stomach cramps, and vomiting as a result of food poisoning. This food poisoning is caused mainly by salmonella and other bacteria. Unfortunately, food poisoning can cause more than gastrointestinal agony. It can lead to some serious long-term health problems such as joint, heart, and kidney disease. And sometimes it can be fatal: every year 9000 Americans die from food poisoning.

Are things worse now than they used to be? Yes, and there are two reasons why this is true. Number one: some strains of poisonous bacteria are becoming more toxic. And number two: the United States is importing more and more foods from other countries, and many of these countries have very poor sanitary conditions. You and I don't have any control over the way food is prepared in a restaurant, but we do have control over how we prepare food at home. Today I'd like to show you how you can prevent food poisoning in your home. First, it's important that you keep food at the proper temperature and second, you must avoid food contamination. I got most of my information from an interview with Katherine Buckner, who is a dietician with Tri-County Hospital, and a magazine article by three health educators at Mount Sinai School of Medicine.

Let's take a closer look at my first recommendation, which is that many cases of food poisoning can be prevented if you keep food at the proper temperature. This is important because the correct temperature will kill or neutralize harmful bacteria.

You should stay away from meats that are raw or partially cooked. If you use a meat thermometer like

The speaker gives specific details rather than vague admonitions.

this [*speaker holds up a meat thermometer*], you can make sure you have the correct temperature. Beef and pork should reach 160 degrees before you take them out of the oven. Veal and lamb should reach 170 degrees. Poultry should reach 180.

Don't eat raw shellfish. Some places advertise that their shellfish comes from clean waters, but even so, it can still contain harmful bacteria. If you're like me, you love shrimp. You should always cook raw shrimp until it is pink and firm.

Here's something I'll bet a lot of you didn't know. If you need to thaw a package of frozen food, you should not leave it out on a counter for over two hours. Ms. Buckner, the hospital dietician, says, "Always thaw food in a refrigerator. It takes longer, but it prevents bacterial growth." If you have a microwave oven you can of course thaw food in it.

A major source of food poisoning, especially at summer outings, is undercooked eggs or raw eggs. Ms. Buckner says don't use raw eggs to make homemade mayonnaise or hollandaise sauce or other dishes. If you do need to use an egg for a recipe, be sure that you cook it thoroughly.

Visual aids provide variety and help listeners remember key points.

The health experts at Mount Sinai recommend that you buy an ordinary thermometer and use it to test for both hot and cold. [*Speaker displays a thermometer.*] You should always keep foods in your refrigerator at 40 degrees or below. And keep foods in your freezer at zero degrees or below. If you ever serve hot foods at a party on a buffet or a chafing dish for over thirty minutes, you should maintain a temperature of more than 140 degrees. Now, I know that using a thermometer may sound like a hassle, but the extra time and trouble can save you a lot of grief. Ms. Buckner says people are in such a hurry nowadays, they don't heat things up enough. Play it safe—take the time.

The speaker uses a bridge, a transitional device to transport the listeners from one section of the speech to the next.

Now that we've looked at the importance of temperature, let's take a look at how to avoid contaminating food, the second major cause of food poisoning. Do you use a wooden cutting board in your kitchen? Well, get rid of it. It is a major source of contamination. You cut up some chicken and the juices stay on the board and mix with the apple that you cut next. Instead of a wooden board, where bacteria can hide in the cracks, use an acrylic board. And be sure to clean

Notice how direct and conversational the speaker's words are—very easy for listeners to understand and absorb.

A dash of humor can enliven a speech.

A summary helps the audience remember key points.

Using the statistics from the introduction, the speaker makes an effective, graceful ending.

it frequently with hot water and bleach. [*Speaker displays an acrylic board.*]

Next we come to a biggie. Ms. Buckner says that many, many cases of food poisoning happen in the summertime at cookouts in the backyard. Here's what happens: you put pieces of chicken in a big bowl, and then you walk out to the barbecue grill. You cook the chicken until it's well-cooked. But then look what happens. You put the good, safe chicken back into the original bowl, which has all that uncooked juice at the bottom and on the sides. So you're fouling (pardon the pun) . . . you're fouling your good pieces of chicken with all those bacteria in the juice.

It's also important that you wash away contaminants. Before you handle any kind of food, always wash your hands. Always wash fruit and vegetables. For root vegetables like carrots and potatoes, use a brush to scrub away the dirt that can contain bacteria. [*Speaker uses a brush and a potato to demonstrate scrubbing.*] Clean all kitchen surfaces frequently; also clean appliances and things like kitchen mitts. In fact, scrub your entire kitchen at least once a week.

Now let's review the key points I've made today about how you can avoid food poisoning: Don't eat meats that are raw or partially cooked. Stay away from raw shellfish. Don't eat raw eggs or undercooked eggs. Instead of thawing food on an open counter, use your refrigerator or microwave oven. In your refrigerator, keep foods at 40 degrees or below. Keep foods in your freezer at zero or below. Use an acrylic cutting board instead of a wooden board, and be sure to keep it clean. Always keep your kitchen clean, especially surfaces where you prepare food. Always wash fruits and vegetables, and be sure to scrub all the dirt off of root vegetables. And be sure to keep raw juices from contaminating cooked food (just remember the barbecued chicken disaster).

In my introduction, I said that according to the predictions of health experts, six of us will eat contaminated food at some point this year. If all of us take the precautions I've talked about, we can beat the odds. Wouldn't it be wonderful if all twenty of us have *zero* food poisoning?

TIPS FOR YOUR CAREER

TIP 14.1: For Long Presentations, Plan a Variety of Activities

Your boss asks you to conduct a 3-hour workshop Friday afternoon to explain important procedures to a group of new employees. What do you do? Do you spend 3 hours talking? No, not unless you want to put them to sleep.

For long presentations, provide a variety of activities to keep your audience awake and attentive. Here are some suggested activities:

1. Invite audience participation. At various intervals, or even throughout the entire presentation, you can encourage listeners to ask questions or make comments. By letting them take an active role, instead of sitting passively for 3 hours, you invigorate them and prevent them from daydreaming.

2. Use visual aids whenever possible. Visuals give variety and sparkle.

3. Give coffee or "stretch" breaks at various intervals. A good rule of thumb for marathon sessions is to give a 15-minute break after every 45-minute period, even if the audience does not seem tired. In other words, don't wait until fatigue sets in. If you wait until the audience is nodding, you might lose their interest for the rest of the day. When you give a break, always

announce the time for reassembly; when that time arrives, politely but firmly remind any stragglers that it is time to return to their seats. If you don't remind them, you will find that a 15-minute coffee break can stretch to 30 minutes.

4. Call on people at random. If your presentation is in the form of a lecture, you can use the teachers' technique of calling on people at random to answer questions. This causes every listener to perk up because he or she is thinking, "I'd better pay attention because my name might be called next, and I don't want to be caught daydreaming." An embellishment of this pedagogical ploy is to call the person's name *after* you ask the question. (If you call the name before the question, everyone in the audience except the designated person might breathe a sigh of relief and fail to pay close attention to the question.)

5. Encourage listeners to take notes. Some speakers pass out complimentary pens and pads at the beginning of their presentations in the hope that the listeners will use them to write down key points. There is, of course, a side benefit: Taking notes helps the listeners stay alert and listen intelligently.

Summary

The informative speech is one of the most popular kinds of speeches given in the classroom and in the community. Your goal in this kind of speech is to give new information to your listeners and help them understand and remember it. Four subcategories of the informative speech are definition, description, process, and expository.

In developing an informative speech, you can draw from all of the techniques and methods discussed in the book so far, plus the following guidelines: (1) Relate the speech to the listeners' self-interest, if at all possible. Show them explicitly the connection between your material and their personal lives. (2) Make the information interesting by using verbal and visual supports. (3) Assess the knowledge of your listeners. Don't give them information they already know, and don't talk over their heads. (4) Use the known to explain the unknown. When you want to explain or describe something that is unfamiliar to your audience, relate it to something that is familiar.

Review Questions

1. What is an extended definition? Why is it preferable in a speech to a dictionary definition?
2. What are the two kinds of process speeches?
3. List the five guidelines for preparing a process speech.
4. Why is it important to relate a speech, if possible, to the listeners' self-interest?

15

Speaking to Persuade

 Types of Persuasive Speeches

Speech to Influence Thinking / Speech to Motivate Action /

 Patterns of Organization

Motivated Sequence / Problem-Solution Pattern / Statement-of-Reasons
Pattern / Comparative Advantages Pattern /

 Sample Persuasive Speech

The Outline / The Speech as Delivered /

After suffering a heart attack because of a diet high in saturated fats and cholesterol, Philip Sokolof, an industrialist in Omaha, Nebraska, launched a determined, one-person crusade to reduce fats and cholesterol in processed foods. He used many avenues of persuasion: speeches, TV interviews, phone calls, letters, and advertisements.

"Single-handedly," says *Time* magazine, "Sokolof has persuaded many of the nation's food processors and fast-food chains to change both their ways and the ingredients of their products." Because of Sokolof, McDonald's began offering the McLean Deluxe, a hamburger that contained only 9 percent fat. Because of Sokolof, fast-food giants Burger King, McDonald's, and Wendy's switched from animal fat to vegetable oil for cooking French fries. Because of Sokolof, Nabisco and dozens of other food manufacturers announced they would no longer cook with tropical oils (which are high in saturated fat).[1]

His most impressive victory occurred when he persuaded Congress to pass a strict food-labeling bill, making it possible for consumers to know the exact amounts of saturated fats and cholesterol in a product. The sponsor of the bill, Representative Henry Waxman of California, said, "This bill is a tribute to Sokolof's tenacity."[2]

Sokolof's success demonstrates the power of persuasion—getting people to think or act a certain way. Throughout your life, you face many tasks that require persuasion, ranging from one-to-one situations (such as convincing a bank executive to give you a loan for a new car), to small-group presentations (persuading your fellow employees to join with you in a grievance about working conditions), to large audiences (talking your club into holding its annual picnic at a particular site). In this chapter we will examine types of persuasive speeches and patterns of organization. In the next chapter we will look at techniques for developing persuasive speeches.

Types of Persuasive Speeches

Persuasive speeches can be categorized in a variety of ways. One hand[y] scheme divides them according to two objectives: (1) to influence thinkin[g] and (2) to motivate action. Sometimes these categories overlap (for exampl[e] you often have to influence thinking before you can motivate action).

Speech to Influence Thinking

The speech to influence thinking is an effort to convince people to ado[pt] your position on a particular subject. (If some listeners agree with your ide[as] even before you speak, your job is to reinforce what they already think.) [In] some cases, you may want to implant ideas that are completely new to particular audience; for example, you argue that within a few decades medical science will extend the average human life span to 140 years. In other cases, you may want to cast new light on an old issue; for example, you argue that the United States could have won independence from Great Britain without going to war.

Here are some sample specific-purpose statements for this kind of speech:

▶ To convince my listeners that immigrants continue to enrich American society and business life

▶ To convince my audience that panic attacks are caused by physiological, rather than psychological, factors

▶ To convince my listeners that the greatest team in the history of the National Football League was the 1989–1990 San Francisco 49ers

▶ To convince my audience that a resurgence of racist and xenophobic sentiments in European countries threatens the continuation of democracy in those countries

A subcategory of the speech to influence thinking is the *speech of refutation,* in which your main goal is to knock down arguments or ideas that you feel are false. You may want to attack what another speaker has said, or you might want to refute popularly held ideas or beliefs which you think are false. One student, for example, tried to explode the myth that mentally retarded people can contribute little to the work force.

Here are some sample specific-purpose statements for speeches of refutation:

▶ To convince my listeners to reject the view that alcoholism is a moral weakness instead of a disease

▶ To persuade my audience to reject the false picture of pigs as dirty, stupid animals

▶ To convince my audience that contrary to popular belief, solar power is a viable, inexpensive source of energy

▶ To persuade my audience to disbelieve the claims by so-called psychics that they are able to predict future events

Refuting an argument is easier when you are dealing with facts than when you are dealing with deeply held beliefs. Suppose, for example, that you want to demolish the commonly held idea that during the American Revolution, solid ranks of redcoated British soldiers marched to battle in open fields, while crafty American patriots hid behind nearby trees in guerrilla fashion and shot the unsuspecting British with ease. You could refute this idea by citing the works of scholars and by pointing out that the British army in North America had adapted to guerrilla-style warfare during decades of fighting Native Americans—long before the American Revolution. Since this is a matter of historical record, your persuasive task is easy. But suppose that you wanted to persuade an audience to reject the belief that children should be reared by their parents; instead, you argue, children should be reared by communes like the kibbutzim in Israel. Though you may win some respect for the value of your idea, you are highly unlikely to demolish the deeply held belief that children should grow up under the wings of their parents. Core beliefs are extremely difficult to change.

Speech to Motivate Action

The speech to motivate action is like the above speech in that it tries to win people over to your way of thinking, but it also attempts one of the most challenging tasks of persuasion—getting people to take action. This action can be either positive or negative: You can urge people to *start* doing something (start using dental floss, start investing in the stock market, start recycling aluminum cans), or to *stop* doing certain things (stop smoking, stop tailgating, stop wasting time).

Here are some sample specific-purpose statements for speeches to motivate action:

▶ To persuade my listeners to sign a petition aimed at forcing drivers over 75 to be retested each year for their driver's license

▶ To persuade my audience to try white-water rafting

▶ To persuade my listeners to stop using too much salt in their foods

▶ To persuade my audience to treat AIDS patients with dignity and respect

▶ To persuade my listeners to demand the right to see the computer files that have been compiled on them by credit-rating companies and government agencies

Sometimes you want prompt action from your listeners ("Please vote for my candidate in today's election"); at other times, you simply want them to respond to any appropriate point in the future ("Whenever you see a child riding a bike, please slow down and drive very cautiously").

Here are some suggestions on getting action:

Instead of hinting or implying, ask for precisely what action you want. You can't just "give the facts" and assume that your listeners will deduce what action should be taken; you must tell them *exactly* what you want them to do, as this anecdote demonstrates:

In his first campaign for the state legislature in Pennsylvania, James C. Hum went door to door in an effort to upset a six-term incumbent. At some house he was invited inside for a chat. He remembered one woman who was especially hospitable to him. While chatting with him over a cup of coffee at her kitchen table, she showed interest in his education and qualifications.

One night Humes was attending a political meeting where both he and his opponent had to make an appearance. At a booth being operated by the opposition, he noticed the woman who had been so hospitable to him. He was surprised as well as disappointed that she was working for his opponent. "I went over to greet her and said, 'You know I hoped you would be working for me.' "

" 'But Mr. Humes,' she replied, 'you never asked me to.' "[3]

An old English proverb says, "Many things are lost for want of asking." Countless speakers, says Dr. Jerry Tarver of the University of Richmond, "are reluctant to 'ask for the sale.' They appear to have a naive faith that if audiences are given some pertinent facts and a few exhortations that all will be well. These speakers fail to realize that when conditions are right, conviction can be turned into action."[4]

If you are speaking to an audience consisting of couples, and your subject is the shortage of foster parents for children without parents, don't be content to merely extol the virtues of foster parenting and hope some of the listeners will volunteer someday. Ask your listeners to become foster parents (and tell them how and where to sign up).

Whenever possible, get a response—even if it's a small, token action—before listeners leave the room.   Here is what happens in a typical speech aimed at motivating action:

Imagine that you give a stirring speech on the destruction of elephant herds by greedy poachers and ivory traders. At the end you urge all listeners to go home and write a letter to the Secretary General of the United Nations calling for concerted international effort to save the elephants. And you ask them to telephone their friends to encourage them to do likewise. The listeners leave your speech highly motivated, vowing to themselves to write that letter and make those phone calls. But, unfortunately, very few ever do so. Everyone has good intentions, but life is busy and there are urgent personal matters to be taken care of. After a couple of weeks, the vows are forgotten.

I'm not suggesting that you refrain from asking listeners to make a response in the future. It's always a good idea to encourage people to take action tomorrow and next week and next year. But also try to get them to do something immediately—before they leave the room, before their commitment cools. You could say, "On your way out, please sign the petition on the table at the rear of the room." Even better if time permits, is to circulate the petition before they stand up to leave.

Striking while the iron is hot often brings you an important reward. Researchers have verified that if you persuade a person to take a positive step, even if it's a small one like signing a petition, you increase that person's commitment to your cause.[5] He or she now has made an investment of time and energy. If opponents try to persuade the person to believe just the opposite of what you have espoused, he or she is highly resistant to change (unless, of course, there is some compelling counterargument). Why? Because human beings feel a strong need to be consistent.[6] Going over to the other side would be inconsistent with an action like signing your petition.

Let's examine some on-the-spot responses that can help strengthen your listeners' support of your position.

▶ *Petition.* Some people frown on this idea because they feel that petitions have become a cliché, and besides, public officials just dump them in the trash. I disagree. I think petitions sometimes are effective in bringing about a policy change. If a U.S. senator gets petitions with 500 signatures from the folks back home, he or she sits up and pays attention—these are 500 potential voters. Lawmakers and officeholders often switch their positions after receiving a big stack of petitions. But even if officials don't respond as you wish, getting signatures on a petition is never a futile gesture, because you have increased the listeners' commitment to your idea.

▶ *Show of hands.* "Studies show that something as simple as having people raise their hands is more likely to get long-range results than depending, as too many speakers do, on mere mental assent," says Dr. Jerry Tarver.[7] Ask for a show of hands only when you're sure that most listeners will be eager and unembarrassed to make a public commitment.

▶ *Sign-up sheet.* For some later activity such as volunteer work, you can ask people to write down their name and phone number. This can be effective because even if their ardor cools somewhat, most people will honor their promise to help.

▶ *Written assignment.* Some speakers pass out paper and pens, and ask listeners to write down what action they intend to take as a result of the speech. It is hoped, of course, that the listeners will view the paper as a promise to themselves, and take it to their offices or homes and eventually act upon it. (While this technique may sound weak, the act of crystallizing one's thoughts and writing them on paper strengthens a person's resolve.)

Don't pressure listeners. Despite the desirability of getting audience action, don't browbeat, intimidate, manipulate, or beg. Don't single out and embarrass those listeners who decline to take action. Listeners who feel pressured often are so resentful that they decline to support your cause simply out of spite.

Patterns of Organization

Organizing a speech effectively can enhance your persuasiveness. While any of the organizational patterns we studied in Chapter 9 can be used, the patterns below are especially strong in persuasive speeches.

Motivated Sequence

The *motivated sequence* is a commonsense approach to persuasion that was developed by the late Alan Monroe.[8] It is a good method to use when you want to sell a product or service, or when you want to mobilize listeners to take a specific action (vote for your candidate, pick up litter). It has the virtue of being suitable for any type of audience—unaware, hostile, apathetic, neutral, or favorable. There are five steps in this pattern:

1. *Attention.* Grab the audience's attention at the beginning of your introduction, as discussed in Chapter 10.
2. *Need.* Show your audience that there is a serious problem that needs action.
3. *Satisfaction.* Satisfy the need by presenting a solution, and show how your solution works.
4. *Visualization.* Paint a picture of results. Help the listeners visualize the good things that will happen when your solution has been put into effect. If possible, show how they personally will benefit.
5. *Action.* Request action from the listeners. Be specific; "Sign this petition" or "Write your legislators today—here are their addresses" or "You can volunteer in Room 211 this afternoon."

If you analyze commercials on TV, you will see that the motivated sequence is used frequently, especially in political appeals. The five steps might appear like this:

1. *Attention* (grab the listeners' attention)—The eyes and ears of the viewers are captivated by the image of two cars crashing head-on in a spectacular collision.
2. *Need* (describe the problem, showing the need for action)—As the shrouded bodies of the victims are grimly placed in hearses, a voice intones, "Safety experts say that these people would have survived if their cars had been equipped with air bags. All cars should have air bags as standard equipment."

FOR YOUR CAREER

TIP 15.1: Use Role Play to Change Behavior

If you own a restaurant and you want to persuade your waitpersons to handle cantankerous customers with friendliness, you can give examples of how to treat diners, you can give exhortations to be friendly, you can show training films. But none of these techniques are as effective as having your employees engage in role play. In other words, stage mock situations: One person plays the role of the crabby complainer ("There's too much dressing on this salad!") while a waitperson acts the correct role (saying, while smiling, "I am so sorry—let me bring you another salad"). After each waitperson's performance, give a critique, and if anything is wrong, ask him or her to try again.

While role play might be inappropriate or too time-consuming for a classroom speech, you can use it effectively in career and community settings. Here are some cases:

▶ At Hunterdon Medical Center in Flemington, New Jersey, medical students are

transformed—temporarily—into disabled persons by being obliged to wear smeared goggles to distort vision, wax plugs to dampen hearing, and splints to create a walking handicap. Then they are forced to live as actual patients in the hospital, interacting with physicians and other patients. The role play is designed to shape the behavior of the future doctors, so that someday they will have understanding, sensitivity, and compassion when treating patients.

▶ Throughout America, fire marshals urge families to have fire drills in which everyone leaves the dwelling quickly and assembles in a designated spot. To avoid the potential tragedy of children running back inside to rescue a pet or toy, parents are encouraged to do role play with their children by saying things like "The dog is still in the house!" and then having the child rehearse staying in place.

3. *Satisfaction* (satisfy the need by presenting a solution)—"If you vote for Michael Matthews for the U.S. Senate," the voice continues, "he will fight for passage of a law requiring every new vehicle sold in this country to be equipped with air bags."

4. *Visualization* (help the audience visualize the results)—As the announcer says, "If Michael Matthews is elected, lives will be saved," the screen shows a (simulated) collision, but this time air bags inflate and prevent the occupants of the cars from being injured.

5. *Action* (request audience action)—The commercial closes with a direct appeal, "If you want to protect yourself and your family from a horrible death in a car accident, go to the polls November 4 and vote for Michael Matthews for U.S. Senate."

The following partial outline shows the essence of a speech that used the motivated sequence:

INTRODUCTION

Attention

I. How safe would the world be if the following countries possessed nuclear weapons? Iran, Iraq, Libya, Syria, Algeria, North Korea, India, Pakistan, Brazil, Argentina, and South Africa.

Need

II. These countries have one thing in common: they may soon join the so-called nuclear club. They either have the power to produce nuclear weapons or they are trying to buy nuclear weapons. By the end of the century, according to experts interviewed by *Time* magazine, all of these countries could have The Bomb. As you know, some of these countries are unstable and a danger to their neighbors. Even if they never attack us, think what will happen if they attack each other. Aside from the horrible human death toll, think of the radioactivity that would be released into the atmosphere, poisoning the entire planet.

BODY

Satisfaction

I. The United Nations should take action to stop these countries from producing and possessing nuclear weapons.

Visualization

II. The world has a precedent for stopping unstable countries from developing nuclear weapons.
   A. In the Persian Gulf War, the U.S. destroyed Iraq's nuclear facilities.
   B. After the war United Nations inspectors toured Iraq to make sure the nuclear weapons plants were not reactivated.

CONCLUSION

I. We must keep nuclear weapons out of the hands of unstable countries.

Action

II. Please sign this petition that will be sent to the President and our members of Congress, urging them to support United Nations' action to prevent nuclear proliferation.

For another speech that uses the motivated sequence, see the sample outline and transcript at the end of this chapter.

Problem-Solution Pattern

For many audiences the most persuasive approach is the *problem-solution* pattern. You show that a problem exists, and then you present the solution. This pattern is especially effective when listeners don't know that a particu-

When listeners take an action, even a small to-ken response like raising their hands, they in-crease their commitment to the speaker's cause.

lar problem exists or when they don't know how serious it is. Here is the partial outline of a speech on day care centers, given by student speaker Ed Webster:

Specific Purpose: To persuade my audience to support strict standards for day-care centers

Central Idea: Day-care centers should be carefully monitored to insure that children receive high-quality attention, nutrition, and mental stimulation.

Main Points:

(Problem) I. Many day-care centers are shortchanging the children under their care.

    A. Many offer children little or no interaction with adults.

    B. Many offer an inadequate diet.

    C. Many provide little or no mental stimulation.

(Solution) II. Congress and state legislatures should pass tough laws that require day-care centers to offer high-quality ser-vices or be forced out of business.

In the speech itself, under the first main point, Webster gave examples and statistics that showed the audience that the problem was more serious than most people realized. Under the second main point, he gave specific steps as to how his proposed standards could be enforced.

Statement-of-Reasons Pattern

The statement-of-reasons pattern is a variation of the topical pattern we discussed in Chapter 9. It can be used for any persuasive speech, but it is especially useful when the audience leans toward your position but needs some justification for that leaning. In one community speech Anne Monaco, educator at a zoological park, knew that her listeners favored keeping zoos open, and she wanted to give them ammunition in case a zoo opponent ever tried to persuade them otherwise. Here is the essence of her outline:

>*Specific Purpose:* To persuade my listeners to support the continuation of zoos
>
>*Central Idea:* Despite the protests of some animal liberation groups, zoos are worth preserving for the sake of both animals and humans.
>
>*Main Points:*
>(*1st reason*)   I.   Zoos help people learn to value and conserve wildlife.
>(*2nd reason*)   II.   Zoos keep some endangered species from becoming extinct.
>(*3rd reason*)   III.   Zoos don't cause animals to suffer stress, boredom, and premature death.

In her speech, Monaco developed each reason with examples and statistics.

Comparative Advantages Pattern

When listeners already agree with you that a problem exists but aren't sure which solution is best, you can use the comparative advantages pattern to show that your recommended solution is superior to others. Let's say that your listeners agree with you that criminals must be punished, but they don't know whether prison is the best choice or whether some alternative sentence (such as probation, home confinement, or community service) would be better. If you feel that the latter is the preferred option, you can use the comparative advantages pattern:

>*Specific Purpose:* To persuade my audience that nonviolent offenders should be given alternative sentences instead of being sent to prison
>
>*Central Idea:* An alternative sentence for nonviolent offenders is more beneficial to society and the offenders themselves than a prison sentence would be.
>
>*Main Points:*
>(*1st advantage*)   I.   An alternative sentence costs taxpayers about $19,000 less per offender each year than a prison term.

(2nd advantage)	II. Alternative sentences prevent offenders from learning criminal skills in prison and coming ou embittered against society.
(3rd advantage)	III. Alternative sentences make it easier for offenders to get jobs because they don't carry the stigma of being an ex-con.

Each main point shows the superiority of alternative senter ces over prison sentences.

Sample Persuasive Speech

In a speech to motivate action, Christina Ramirez showed her audience how the incidence of car thefts could be reduced. Her outline is presented first, followed by the speech as delivered.[9] In the commentary alongside the outline, note the discussion of the five steps of the motivated sequence.

The Outline

We Can Defeat Auto Thieves

General Purpose: To persuade
Specific Purpose: To convince my audience that the numbe of car thefts in the U.S. can be sharply reduced
Central Idea: We can drastically reduce the incidence of car thefts in the U.S. by safeguarding our cars, beefing up law enforcement, and insisting on mandatory pr son terms for car thieves.

MOTIVATED SEQUENCE	INTRODUCTION
Attention *The speaker grabs the listeners' attention with some interesting statistics and a rhetorical question.*	I. The FBI says that every year about two million motor vehicles are stolen in the United States—one every 15 seconds. They are stolen in big cities, small towns, suburban areas, and in the country. Will your car be the next one stolen?
	II. Car theft has become a major social and economic problem, but I believe we can drastically reduce the number of cars that are stolen by taking three steps: first, make our cars less vulnerable to a potential thief; second, beef up law enforcement, and third, insist on mandatory prison terms for car thieves. My information comes from a brochure pu

lished by the National Automobile Theft Bureau (NATB), several magazine articles, and an interview with Paul Lyman, a special agent with the Federal Bureau of Investigation.

(Transition: Let's begin by looking at the scope of this problem.)

BODY

Need
The speaker shows that the problem is serious and action needs to be taken.

I. Car theft has become a major social and economic problem.
   A. An increasing number of thefts are committed by well-organized theft rings.
      1. FBI Agent Lyman says stolen cars are easily disposed of.
         a. About 175,000 cars each year are driven to Canada or Latin America, with some being shipped to other parts of the world.
         b. The hottest market is for parts and accessories.
         c. Most cars are taken to "chop shops," says Russell McKinnon, executive vice president of the Automobile Dismantlers and Recyclers Association, which is fighting to expose crooked parts dealers.
         d. Stripping a car is more profitable than selling it whole.
         e. A $12,000 car built from replacement parts would cost $70,000.
         f. Cars are dismembered quickly (less than one hour).
         g. No trace of original ownership remains.
         h. Parts are sold to individuals or used-parts dealers.
      2. If you have an old-model car, it is not immune to theft.
         a. A theft ring gets an "order" for parts from your model of car, so your car becomes a prime target.
         b. Some stolen cars are used to commit other crimes, so your older, inconspicuous car is very desirable.
   B. The NATB estimates that last year car thefts cost the public $8 billion.

1. This includes out-of-pocket expenses because insurance payments rarely cover the
full cost of replacing the car.
2. Everybody's insurance rates go up as the
theft rate goes up.
    a. Because I am under 21, my car insur-
    ance is over $1,000 a year.
    b. Some insurance costs are due to acci-
    dents, but thefts also play a part.
3. All of us must pay taxes to cover police and
court expenses related to car theft.
(Transition: The problem is great—can anything be
done about it?)

Satisfaction
*The speaker presents
her solution to the
problem.*

II. The incidence of car thefts can be reduced.
    A. Make your car less vulnerable.
        1. Always lock your car and take your keys.
            a. 75 percent of cars stolen are unlocked
            (says NATB).
            b. 35 percent have the key in the ignition.
        2. Install a security system.
            a. Cost is $50 to $500.
            b. Best kind has no alarm, but disengages
            the starter and fuel pump when you re-
            move key.
            c. Security systems do not always deter
            (some thieves use tow trucks), but a
            study in Dallas, Texas, showed that secu-
            rity systems can reduce a car's chances
            of being stolen by 90 percent.
        3. Use common sense.
            a. NATB says most cars are stolen after
            dark, so always park near lights.
            b. Leaving valuables and packages where
            thieves can see them makes your car a
            tempting target.
    B. Beef up law enforcement.
        1. Most local and state police lack personnel
        to effectively handle the problem.
        2. Agent Lyman says, "Most cities simply don't
        have enough officers to effectively fight this
        problem."
        3. FBI statistics: only 13 percent of thefts result
        in arrests.
        4. We need to give police more money ear-
        marked for investigation of theft rings, and
        more officers need to be hired.

C. Insist on mandatory prison terms for convicted thieves.
1. According to a study conducted by the National Commission on Law Enforcement and Justice, 78 percent of persons convicted of car theft never serve time because of overcrowded prisons.
2. They are given probation.
3. Certainty of going to prison might deter some thieves.
4. At the very least prison terms would get these thieves out of business for long periods of time.
5. We might have to build more prisons, but the cost would be worthwhile.

(Transition: You might be saying, "These ideas are fine, but how do we know they will work—has anyone tried them?")

III. Determined anti-theft efforts have been successful.
A. In Michigan, according to *The New York Times*, a concerted effort to fight car thieves has paid off.
1. Michigan assigns ninety-two police officers and seven prosecutors to a task force aimed at arresting and prosecuting car thieves.
2. The program began 5 years ago; since then, Michigan has gone from second to ninth among states in its rate of car thefts.
B. We would save money and grief.
1. In short run, we might pay more tax money.
2. In long run, we would pay less insurance money.
3. Once criminals see that car theft was not so easy and so rewarding, the crime would decline.
4. More of us would avoid the pain of having our car stolen.

(Transition: Let's review what we've covered today.)

CONCLUSION

I. I urge you to safeguard your car. Always lock it and take your keys with you. Install a security system. And I urge you to sign a petition that will urge our elected officials to do the important things I

Visualization
The speaker helps the audience visualize how conditions will be if her plan is adopted.

Action
The speaker urges action by the audience.

have talked about—beef up law enforcement and require mandatory sentences for convicted thieves.

II. Remember: two million cars are stolen every year in the United States. Let's work together to reduce this figure. The car we spare may be our own.

BIBLIOGRAPHY

Paul Lyman, special agent, Federal Bureau of Investigation, personal interview, December 16, 1991.

"Making Cars Hard to Steal," *The New York Times*, February 9, 1991, p. 16.

Martin Porter, "The Rape of the Lock: You Can Protect Yourself against Auto Theft," *Gentlemen's Quarterly*, April 1990, p. 165.

"Preventing Automobile Theft," brochure of the National Automobile Theft Bureau, undated.

VISUAL AIDS

Posters showing the main points.

The Speech as Delivered

Here is the transcript of Christina Ramirez's speech. Notice that the speaker uses the ideas of the outline without using the exact wording. In an extemporaneous speech, the speaker does not read or memorize a speech, but speaks from brief notes.

COMMENTARY

The speaker gives interesting statistics that she relates directly to every listener.

Giving the central idea and key points helps the listeners absorb the body of the speech.

Citing her reliable sources adds to her credibility.

We Can Defeat Auto Thieves

Every year in the United States, according to the FBI, two million motor vehicles are stolen. That's one every 15 seconds. They are stolen in all parts of the country—big cities, small towns, suburban areas, and rural areas. Will your car be the next one stolen?

Car theft has become a major social and economic problem, but I don't think it's a necessary evil that we must live with. I believe we can drastically cut down the number of cars that are stolen if we take three steps: first, we should make our cars less vulnerable to being stolen; second, we should beef up our law enforcement, and third, we should insist on mandatory prison terms for car thieves. My information comes from an interview with Paul Lyman, who is a special agent with the Federal Bureau of Investigation; several magazine articles; and a booklet put out by the National Automobile Theft Bureau, or NATB.

Signing a petition helps solidify support for a speaker's proposal. A petition drive can sometimes cause public officials to change policies or laws.

Giving precise details makes the speech interesting and believable.

Let's begin by taking a look at the scope of this problem. In our country today, automobile theft has become a major social and economic problem. One of the reasons why the problem is so big is that more and more thefts are being committed not by amateur thieves but by well-organized, professional theft rings. Mr. Lyman, the FBI agent I interviewed, told me that stolen cars are easily disposed of. Every year about 175,000 cars are driven to Canada or Latin America, with some being shipped to other parts of the world. They are kept in one piece. Of the cars that stay inside our borders, most of them are dismembered because parts and accessories are very much in demand. Most stolen cars are taken to "chop shops," according Russell McKinnon, executive vice president of the Automobile Dismantlers and Recyclers Association, which is fighting to expose shady parts dealers. Mr. McKinnon says that stripping a car is more profitable than selling it in one piece. If you tried to build a $12,000 car from the ground up with replacement parts, it would cost you $70,000. You can easily see how a car is worth more in pieces than as a whole. Chop shops are very efficient: each car is dismembered quickly, usually in less than an hour. They leave no trace of original ownership. The parts are then sold to individuals or used-parts dealers.

The speaker wisely anticipates the reaction of some listeners.

Some of you might be saying, "Well, I don't need to worry because I have an old car that nobody would want to steal." Wrong. Let's say you have an old Subaru. If a theft ring gets an "order" for parts from your model and year of Subaru, your car becomes a prime target. Also, remember that stolen cars are often used to commit other crimes, so your older, inconspicuous car might be very desirable to thieves.

The speaker shows that car theft hurts everyone.

Car thefts hurt more than just the person whose car is gone. The NATB estimates that last year car thefts cost the public 8 billion dollars. First of all, there are out-of-pocket expenses that the owner has to pay because insurance payments usually don't cover the full cost of replacing the car. Second, everybody's insurance rates go up as the theft rate goes up. I'm under 21, so I have to pay over $1,000 a year in insurance premiums. One reason I pay so much is the large number of accidents, but thefts also play a part. Third, everybody must pay taxes to cover police and court expenses that are caused by car theft.

You can see that the problem is big—is there anything we can do about it? Yes, I believe that the incidence of car thefts can be reduced if we do three things. First, we need to make our cars harder to break into and steal. Common sense tells you that you should always lock your car and take your keys, but most people don't do this. The NATB says that 75 percent of stolen cars are unlocked, and that 35 percent have the key in the ignition.

The speaker gives the listeners helpful tips.

To further safeguard your car, you should install a security system, which costs anywhere from $50 to $500. The kind with an alarm is not recommended because if the alarm is always going off falsely, you might be tempted to disconnect the system. The best system has no alarm; instead, it disengages the starter and the fuel pump whenever you remove your key from the ignition. It is true that security systems don't always deter theft because some thieves use tow trucks to take your car away. But a study done in Dallas, Texas, found that security systems can reduce a car's chances of being stolen by 90 percent.

You can also safeguard your car by using common sense. The NATB says that most cars are stolen after dark, so you should always park in a lighted area. Don't leave valuables and packages where thieves can see them because this makes your car a tempting target.

My second proposal is that we beef up law enforcement. Most local and state police lack personnel to handle the problem. Mr. Lyman, the FBI agent, says, "Most cities simply don't have enough officers to effectively fight this problem." Statistics compiled by the FBI show that only 13 percent of thefts result in arrests. If we give police more money earmarked for this problem, they can hire more officers and be able to break up some of these theft rings.

My third proposal is that we absolutely insist on mandatory prison terms for anyone convicted of car theft. In a study conducted by the National Commission on Law Enforcement and Justice, it was found that 78 percent of persons convicted of car theft never served time because of overcrowded prisons. Murderers and armed robbers are given higher priority for prison, so car thieves are simply given probation. If we mandated prison terms, car thieves would face a greater likelihood of serving time, and this might deter them from this crime. If nothing else, prison terms would put these thieves out of business for long periods of time. Yes, we might have to build more prisons, but the cost would be worth it: we would save money in the long run by cutting down on car thefts.

The visualization step in this speech is powerful because it shows the listeners that the speaker's ideas have been tried elsewhere—and they work.

Up to this point, you might be saying to yourself, "Well, these ideas are fine, but how do I know that they will work? Have they been tried anywhere?" Yes, these ideas have been successful. *The New York Times* reports that in Michigan a determined effort to fight car thieves has paid off. Michigan assigns ninety-two police officers and seven prosecutors to a task force aimed at arresting and prosecuting car thieves. The program began five years ago. Since then, Michigan has shown success: it went from being the number two state in the nation in its rate of car thefts to being number nine. If we duplicated the Michigan program in every state, we would save a lot of money and grief. In the short run, we might pay more tax money, but in the long run, we would pay less insurance money.

And if criminals saw that car theft was not so easy and so rewarding, the crime would decline, and more of us would avoid the pain of having our car stolen.

Let's review what we've discussed today. You should always safeguard your car. Every time you leave it, lock it and take your keys with you. Install a security system. And I urge you to sign a petition at the end of the hour. This petition will be sent to our county and state leaders and legislators; it calls for them to do the important things we've discussed today—beef up law enforcement and require mandatory sentences for convicted thieves.

At the beginning I told you that two million cars are stolen every year in the United States. We can all work together to reduce this figure. The car we spare may be our own.

Giving listeners a chance to act before they leave the room is a powerful way to increase their commitment to a speaker's proposal.

The speaker closes gracefully with a reference to the statistic given in the introduction.

▶ **For other sample persuasion speeches, see the outline and transcript at the end of Chapter 11 and the prize-winning persuasive speech in Appendix B.**

 FOR YOUR CAREER

TIP 15.2: Provide Supplementary Material at the End of a Speech

At the end of a speech, especially a persuasive talk to a community or business audience, it is sometimes effective to offer the listeners supplementary materials that support or elaborate your message. Here are some possibilities:

1. Pass out a brief written summary of your key ideas. This reinforces your message and gives the listeners, many of whom probably did not take notes, an accurate record of what you said. A summary is especially helpful for technical presentations that include complex ideas and detailed statistics.

2. Pass out supplementary readings. If you get your listeners interested or excited about a particular subject, they will appreciate receiving copies of articles that they can read to delve further into the subject.

3. Offer a bibliography of your sources. You might say, for example, "I don't have time to name all the books and articles from which I got my information, but I have a bibliography which I'll place on the table at the front, and you're welcome to pick this up after I finish." Such a list is not only helpful to listeners who want to pursue your subject further, but it also suggests to the audience that you are a careful researcher who is concerned about getting the information correct.

Summary

Persuasion—getting people to think or act in a certain way—is one of the most frequent tasks of the public speaker. Two major types of persuasive speeches are the speech to influence thinking and the speech to motivate action.

In the speech to influence thinking, your primary goal is to convince people to adopt your position. A subcategory of this kind of speech is the speech of refutation, in which your aim is to knock down arguments or ideas that you feel are false. In the speech to motivate action, you should tell the listeners exactly what action you want them to take. Whenever possible, encourage them to take some action—even if it's a small, token action—immediately.

Of the many patterns that can be used for the persuasive speech, four are especially effective: the motivated sequence, problem-solution pattern, statement-of-reasons pattern, and comparative advantages pattern.

Review Questions

1. What is the goal of the speech of refutation?
2. In a speech to motivate action, why should you try to get listeners to take action immediately?
3. Give three examples of immediate, on-the-spot audience action.
4. What are the five steps of the motivated sequence?
5. When is the comparative advantages pattern most effective?

16

Developing the Persuasive Speech

▶ **Knowing Your Audience**

▶ **Building Credibility**

▶ **Providing Evidence**

▶ **Using Sound Reasoning**

▶ **Appealing to Motivations**

▶ **Arousing Emotions**

Dr. Frank C. Laubach was an educator who launched a nationwide crusade in the 1950s to teach illiterate adults how to read. In the early days of his crusade, when he went to factories to try to recruit illiterates for his reading classes, he would make the following appeal: "Would any of you people like to learn how to read?" Much to Dr. Laubach's disappointment, only a few of the illiterates in each factory would sign up—even though the classes were free.

What was wrong? Didn't the illiterates know that their inability to read was a big handicap in an advanced industrial society such as ours? Yes, Dr. Laubach reasoned, these people were keenly aware that their illiteracy condemned them to spend their lives on the margins of society. Why, then, did they pass up a chance to take free classes to better themselves?

As Dr. Laubach analyzed his audiences, he realized that most illiterates were ashamed to admit in public that they could not read. So he altered his pitch. At a factory in Charlotte, North Carolina, he asked, "Would any of you people like to learn to improve your reading?" This time, scores of illiterates stepped forward. The new pitch was effective because it enabled the men and women to maintain their self-respect. Instead of embarrassing themselves with an open admission that they could not read, they could identify themselves simply as people wanting to improve a skill. Thenceforth, Dr. Laubach used the revised version for all his spiels, with the same good results. (At first glance Dr. Laubach's change of words seems a bit deceitful, but it really was not; all the illiterates certainly could have read their own names and a few other simple words, so it was not stretching the truth to talk of "improving" their reading.)

This story demonstrates that persuasion involves more than simply "giving the facts." To get people to think or to act a certain way, you must know who they are and how to reach them.

In this chapter we will examine some practical techniques for reaching the audience in a persuasive speech. Here are six key questions that can guide you in your preparation:

1. Who are my listeners?
2. How can I make myself and my ideas believable?
3. What evidence would be most likely to convince these listeners?
4. What form of reasoning would be most compelling?
5. How can I appeal to the listeners' motivations?
6. How can I arouse their emotions?

To help you answer these questions, let us examine each point in greater detail.

Knowing Your Audience

As Dr. Laubach discovered, the first step in persuasion is understanding your listeners. To truly understand them, you must find out where they are standing, then go over to that spot, stand inside their shoes, and see the world as they see it. Only after you have seen the world from their perspective will you have a ghost of a chance of leading them to where you want them to stand.

Here are some strategies for understanding your audience:

▶ Analyze Listeners

How can you find out where listeners stand? Using the techniques discussed in Chapter 4, gather information about your audience. You can, for example, interview some of the listeners to determine how much they know on your subject and what their beliefs and attitudes are. Or you can use a questionnaire to poll all members of the audience.

▶ Use a Persuasion Scale

A persuasion scale for analyzing an audience can be helpful. Below is one that I have modified from a scale created by Sandy Linver, president of Speakeasy, Inc., a consulting firm with offices in Atlanta and San Francisco.[1]

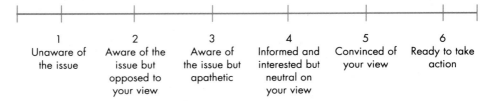

1	2	3	4	5	6
Unaware of the issue	Aware of the issue but opposed to your view	Aware of the issue but apathetic	Informed and interested but neutral on your view	Convinced of your view	Ready to take action

On the scale, mark where the listeners are in relation to your specific purpose *before* you speak. Then mark where you hope they will be *after* you speak. Knowing a starting point and an ideal finishing point will prevent you from having the kind of frustration that one speaker experienced:

> Because of water-purification problems in one region of a state, a public-health official sought speaking engagements at various public meetings. At a PTO (parent-teacher organization) meeting of an elementary school in a rural community, he displayed various kinds of water purifiers and discussed how much they cost. "I thought the people would be very interested, but most of them looked bored and listless; I could tell that I was convincing very few people to buy a purifier," he said. "Later I found out that the people didn't really know the facts about their drinking water. They didn't know that it was not as pure as it should be—it sometimes contained microbes that can cause gastrointestinal illness. I should have told them about the problem before offering a solution."

This official made the mistake of thinking that his audience was at stage 6 (ready to take action by buying a water purifier) when really they were at stage 1 (unaware of the dangers in their drinking water). Obviously he should have started at stage 1 and moved toward stage 6.

Set a realistic goal. Don't feel that you are a failure if your listeners fall short of stage 6. With some listeners, helping them go from stage 1 to stage 5 is a fine accomplishment. With other listeners, persuading them to move from stage 2 to stage 4 is a great triumph.

▶ Plan Strategy

While some entire audiences may fit neatly into one category or another, many audiences are segmented—that is, you may find sixteen listeners opposed to your view, fifteen apathetic, eight already convinced, and so on. (For the scale above, you can use color pens for each segment—for example, mark red for the starting point and finishing point for listeners who oppose your position, blue for neutral listeners, and black for favorable listeners.)

When you have several different segments, to which group should you devote your energies? An easy answer: try to meet the needs of everyone. While this is an admirable (and sometimes attainable) goal, it cannot always be achieved. Often there are priorities and variables beyond your control. Let's say that for a speech on a highly technical subject, you ascertain that three listeners are totally uninformed on your topic while the remaining nineteen are well-informed. If you have been allotted only 10 minutes, you would be foolish to spend most of your time giving basic information to the three uninformed listeners. If the situation is reversed, with nineteen uninformed and three well-informed, you should, of course, focus on the majority.

The best approach is this: Try to meet the needs of all listeners, but when this is impossible, choose the group that is most important. If, for example, you are trying to persuade a group of homeowners to buy mortgage insurance from your company, aim your remarks at those listeners who are predisposed to buying insurance but haven't yet chosen a company to buy from. Don't devote all your time and energy trying to win over those stubborn members of the audience who swear they will never buy insurance under any circumstances.

Despite the difficulty of meeting the needs of several different segments, there are some strategies you can employ. Using our persuasion scale, let's examine how to reach listeners with *starting* points at each of the six stages. As a continuing example, let's imagine that you want to convince listeners that utility companies should use wind power to supplement or replace oil, coal, natural gas, and nuclear power.

1. Unaware of the issue. For people in the dark on your topic, start by explaining the situation and showing why your ideas are important. Later in the speech, try to persuade them to adopt your view.

For your speech on wind power, you can pitch the following remarks to those listeners who know nothing about the issue:

> The old windmill is making a comeback in the form of advanced wind turbines that can create energy to light our homes and fuel our factories. Wind turbines are clean and reliable; they can be located in most parts of the country, and they lessen our dependence on dirty fuels like coal and dangerous energy sources like nuclear power. Best of all, wind is free.

2. *Aware of the issue but opposed to your view*.   Find out the listeners' reasons for opposing your view and then aim at refuting them. When listeners are strongly skeptical of or hostile to an idea, a smart plan often is to delay divulging your central idea until the end of your speech (this idea will be discussed later in this chapter under inductive reasoning.)

Always show respect for opponents and their views. *Never* insult or belittle those who disagree; sarcastic or belligerent remarks make people defensive and all the more committed to their side. Try to persuade these people, but if that fails, be content if you can move them a few inches toward your camp. Sometimes the best you can hope for is to plant some seeds of doubt about their position which might someday sprout into full-blown conversion to your side.

In your wind power speech, let's assume you discover that some listeners oppose your view because they think wind power is impractical and too expensive. To overcome the first objection, you can say:

> According to *Time*, new technology has made wind turbines more efficient and practical than they used to be. The chief of renewable-energy programs at the U.S. Department of Energy, J. Michael Davis, says that within 30 years, these new wind turbines could provide a quarter of the nation's power needs.

To counter the notion that wind power is too expensive, you can say:

> Wind power used to be much more expensive than other energy sources, but this is no longer true. According to *Time*, wind machines operating in California today can produce energy at a cost of 7 cents per kilowatt, and within two years, that will fall to 5 cents—the same cost as oil.

3. *Aware of the issue but apathetic*.   "Who cares?" is the attitude of listeners in this category. To break through their crust of apathy, show that the issue has an impact on their personal lives.

In your wind power speech, you can say, for the benefit of listeners who are apathetic about wind power,

> Our reliance on oil can hurt all of us physically and financially. Oil and its byproducts pollute our air and endanger our health. And imagine what will

happen if there is a new war or some other upheaval in the Middle East. Oil will become scarce, and all of us will end up paying more money for gasoline. We need to find alternatives to oil, and one of the best alternatives is wind power.

4. *Informed and interested but neutral on your view.* People at this stage need little background information; you can plunge directly into convincing them that your position is correct or superior to other views.

Concerning your wind power speech, let's imagine that you have listeners who are well-informed on alternative energy sources, but they see all the alternatives—wind, solar, geothermal, hydrogen, and so on—as equally promising. Your job is to show them that wind power is superior to the others—or at least deserves a special push behind it.

> A government survey estimates that 10 Midwestern states can more than meet all their electric power needs from wind. Also, studies show that wind turbines are cheaper to construct and operate than solar collecting stations and other energy plants.

5. *Convinced of your view.* For listeners who agree with you, try to reinforce their belief and, if possible, give them new reasons for supporting your position. Although they agree with your view, some listeners may not have considered or endorsed a plan of action; with them, your task is to demonstrate that your plan offers the best course of action.

For your wind power speech, let's imagine that you have identified some listeners as sharing your enthusiasm for wind power. With them, you should try to sell your specific plan:

> I believe that our state should give tax deductions to utility companies that derive at least 10 percent of their power from wind turbines. This would give companies an incentive to invest in wind power.

6. *Ready to take action.* For speeches aimed at motivating action, this is the stage you want all listeners to reach (although, as we noted above, you may not be able to bring every listener this far). Show listeners how, when and where to take action. For listeners who are poised to act on your wind power proposal, give a specific plan of action:

> I have a petition that will be sent to our governor and state legislators urging them to enact a law giving utility companies the tax break I have discussed today. If you would like our state to rely more and more on safe, clean, cheap wind power, please sign this petition before you leave the room.

As we noted above, it is often difficult (and sometimes impossible) to meet the needs of all listeners when their starting points are at different stages on our scale. But sometimes you can do so. All of the wind power examples above could be integrated into one speech, permitting you to meet the needs of listeners at all six stages.

Building Credibility

Before 1971, acupuncture, a medical treatment in which hair-thin needles are inserted into the skin at various points, was virtually unknown in the United States, even though it had been practiced in China for pain relief and anesthesia for over 2000 years. The few medical authorities in the United States who knew about the technique dismissed it as exotic hokum—absolutely worthless.

In 1971, *New York Times* columnist James Reston was on assignment in China when he needed an emergency appendectomy. Writing about the operation a few days later, Reston reported that an acupuncturist's needles had effectively blocked pain.

His article quickly changed the way most western health experts looked at acupuncture. Instead of dismissing the procedure as nonsense, they now saw it as rich with possibilities. A few years later, acupuncture was being used widely in hospitals and clinics throughout the United States.

Before Reston's article, a few travelers to China had written about the virtues of acupuncture, but they were ignored. Why was Reston's column so persuasive? Was it because he was known as a medical authority? No, he had no medical training. Was it because he had reported extensively about medicine? No, his field was national and international politics. It was because Reston had high *credibility*. For many years his column—appearing in one of the nation's foremost newspapers—had been read and respected by thousands of Americans who considered him reliable, trustworthy, and wise. Their reaction was probably something like this: "If James Reston says acupuncture isn't absurd, then it's not absurd."

The remarkable impact of one person's article illustrates the power of credibility—a major source of persuasiveness in all human communication, especially a speech. Before listeners can accept your ideas, they want to know whether you are reliable, competent, and trustworthy.

In your career, when you want to persuade people who know you well, your credibility boils down to how they perceive you—how they assess your character (or ethos). If you are a person who is known for honesty, fairness, and competence, you enter the speech with a powerful asset. If you are known for dishonesty, unfairness, or incompetence, you enter with a heavy liability.

In the speech itself, credibility is enhanced if your delivery is enthusiastic and if your speech is clear, well-organized, and well-reasoned. In addition, you can build credibility by following these guidelines:

FOR YOUR CAREER

TIP 16.1: Don't Expect Universal Success

You can't count on winning the approval of every listener. Even Abraham Lincoln's Gettysburg Address was a failure to some. An editorial in the Chicago *Times* on the day after his speech said, "The cheek of every American must tingle with shame as he reads the silly, flat and dishwatery utterances of the man who has to be pointed out to intelligent foreigners as the President of the United States."

▶ Explain Your Competence

If you have special expertise, be sure to let your audience know about it—modestly, of course. Don't boast or brag, just give the facts. Telling about your special competence enhances your credibility because it shows that you are speaking from personal experience. It says, "I've been there—I know what I'm talking about." Here is how student speaker Lauren Shriver bolstered her credibility during a speech:

> Deep-sea diving is not dangerous—if you follow all the safety rules. I've made over 50 dives myself, and I feel very safe because I'm very careful each time. I never allow myself to get slack and overconfident.

Shriver's information about her dives was necessary to give credibility to her remarks. Notice how she inserted her personal background in a modest way.

If you lack personal knowledge of a subject and therefore must rely on the authority of others, you can enhance your own credibility by showing that your sources are competent. For example, in arguing that computers in the future will be capable of humanlike thinking, Don Stafford knew that his ideas might sound farfetched coming from a student, so he said:

> My information comes from the work of Dr. Patrick Winston, who for the past ten years has been director of the Artificial Intelligence Laboratory at Massachusetts Institute of Technology. Let me explain an experiment that Dr. Winston carried out. . . .

By quoting from an eminent authority, Stafford was able to give his speech instant credibility.

▶ Be Careful with Speech Material

Sloppiness with facts and figures can make your whole speech less believable In a speech on child abuse, one student said that 55 percent of Americar parents abused their children—a statistic that listeners scoffed at during the question-and-answer period. (A few days later, the student sheepishly admitted to the instructor that the original source estimated 5.5 percent rather than 55; the overlooked decimal point made a huge difference.) When listeners believe you are wrong on a point, even when it's a small matter, they tend to distrust everything else you say.

Another destroyer of credibility is oversimplification. One student, who gave a talk on the desirability of eating whole-wheat bread, said at one point, "In the 1700s, rich people ate white refined bread, which caused them to grow sickly and weak. Meanwhile the poor people ate whole-wheat bread, which caused them to grow strong. Eventually the poor people overthrew the rich people in the revolutions at the end of the century." Although diet may have played a part in health and disease during the 1700s, it is an oversimplification to say that white bread was the main factor in the revolutions that rocked the world in that century. There were, of course, many complex social and economic factors involved. When you oversimplify in this way, listeners view you as unreliable.

▶ Show Your Open-Mindedness

"If you would convince others," Lord Chesterfield once said, "seem open to conviction yourself."[2] In other words, show that you are a reasonable person who is open-minded and receptive, and quite capable of being wrong. This approach is not only an ethical one, but it is also highly effective in building credibility. Audiences distrust fanatical know-it-alls who never admit that they might be mistaken.

In a community speech, Patricia Caldwell argued for the right of parents to teach their children at home instead of sending them to school. After citing cases where home-taught children excelled in college, she showed her open-mindedness by conceding that some parents are bad teachers:

> In one well-publicized case in Chicago a few months ago, the authorities brought legal action against a husband and wife for not sending their children to school. Their idea of a home school was to make the children—ages 7, 9, and 10—work all day instead of teaching them to read and write.[3]

Was it stupid for the speaker to relate an incident that seemed to negate her central idea (that some parents can do a better job of teaching than the public schools)? No, because she went on to say that bad parent-teachers are rare, and that periodic state inspections can weed out such cases. Rather than having damaged her case, her concession strengthened it, for she showed herself to the audience as a fair-minded individual who could be trusted. If you were a listener, wouldn't you trust her more than someone who said *all* parents are good teachers?

It is especially important to be reasonable and open-minded during the question-and-answer period. I have seen some speakers do a good job in their speech, but when they are asked questions by listeners, they become rigid and defensive, refusing to admit error, refusing to concede that a listener has a good point. These speakers severely damage their own credibility and undo much of the persuasiveness of the speech itself.

▶ Show Common Ground with Your Audience

When you are introduced to someone at a party, you try to find things that you have in common. You ask each other questions ("What is your major?") until you hit upon some interest that you share. Often a person introducing you will try to help you find common ground ("Bill, I'd like you to meet Susan. She's like you: *loves* to ski"). We try to find common ground because it not only helps us to make conversation but it also helps us to feel comfortable with another person.

In a speech, listeners respect and trust a speaker who is similar to themselves. Your job is to show that to some degree you are like your listeners. This does not mean compromising your beliefs; it means highlighting those characteristics you share with the audience. This is especially important if some of the listeners are hostile to your ideas. Say, for example, that you are speaking on gun control, and you know that half the listeners are already against your position. Here's what you can say: "I'm talking on gun control today. I know that a lot of you are opposed to the position I'm going to take. I ask only that you hear me out and see if my arguments have any merit whatsoever. Though we may disagree on this subject, you and I have at least one thing in common: We want to see a reduction in the number of violent, gun-related crimes in our society." With this kind of statement, you not only pinpoint common ground (opposition to crime), but you also appeal to the audience's sense of fair play.

One of the best ways to build credibility is to show the listeners that you identify with them—that you share (or have shared) their ideas or feelings. For example, Actress Carol Burnett made the following revelation in a talk on how relatives of an alcoholic should deal with the problem drinker in their lives:

> You may wonder why I'm here to talk about alcoholism. It's easy to explain Both of my parents died when they were 46 years old because they were both drunks.[4]

Thus, Carol Burnett demonstrated that she was not an aloof, imperiou star being paid to talk to the "lowly" masses about a problem that *they* had She showed, by means of a revelation that must have been painful to make that she shared the heartbreak of so many people in her audience—the heartbreak of being related to an alcoholic. Her revelation undoubtedl caused her audience to draw closer to her emotionally and to become espe cially receptive to the rest of her talk.

Providing Evidence

When you make an assertion in a speech, it is not enough to say, "Trust me on this" or "I know I'm right." The audience wants *evidence*, or proof. Evidence can be presented in the forms we discussed in Chapter 7: narratives, statistics, examples, testimony, and so on. For each main point in your speech, choose the evidence that is most likely to prove your point with a particular audience. Ask yourself these questions:

1. Is the evidence *accurate*? Erroneous information would obviously undermine the credibility of your entire speech.
2. Is the evidence *up to date*? A research study conducted in the field of medicine in 1936 is almost certain to be outdated.
3. Is the evidence *typical*? An athlete may attribute his success to consuming five banana milkshakes a day, but is his diet common among athletes or is he probably the only one in the world with such a diet?

Here are some tips on using evidence:

Choose evidence from reliable, reputable sources. While listening to TV news one night, I was astounded to hear this story:

> A New York doctor reports that a patient experienced epileptic seizures whenever she heard the voice of Mary Hart, co-host of the TV show *Entertainment Tonight*. The seizures ceased when she stopped watching the show.

My immediate reaction was total disbelief. What nonsense! Hearing a person's voice cannot cause a seizure. But then the news anchor added:

> The woman was the subject of an article in the *New England Journal of Medicine* by Dr. Venkat Ramani, professor of neurology at Albany Medical College in New York.

Just as suddenly as I had disbelieved the story, I now believed it. Why? Because the *New England Journal of Medicine* is one of the mostly highly respected medical journals in the world and would not publish an article unless its editors considered it to be sound and reliable.

Evidence—especially the hard-to-believe variety—becomes much more convincing to the audience if you cite a reliable source. Even better would be *several* sources.

Be sure to give full details; instead of saying, "a judge," give her name and title: "Sharon Brown, Chief Justice of our state's Supreme Court."

Provide a variety of evidence. In some cases a single example or statistic might be sufficient to bolster an argument, but in most persuasive situations, multiple support is needed.

Use a vivid personal narrative whenever possible. Imagine that you are planning a speech on drunk driving. If you want to convince your listeners that they stand a chance of being victimized by a drunk driver, which of the following would be the more persuasive piece of evidence?

1. You relate the sad, shocking details of an automobile accident in which a drunk driver hit your car and killed one of your passengers.
2. You cite the fact that 25,000 people are killed in America each year in alcohol-related car accidents.

Though you would need to use both items in your speech, the more persuasive item for most listeners would be item 1. But, you might ask, how can one, solitary case be more persuasive than a statistic encompassing 25,000 people? Psychologists have conducted scores of experiments which indicate that one vivid narrative, told from the speaker's personal experience, is much more persuasive than its statistical status would imply.[5] "All other things being equal," writes social psychologist Elliot Aronson, "most people are more deeply influenced by one clear, vivid personal example than by an abundance of statistical data."[6]

While using a variety of evidence in your persuasive speeches, remember that your most powerful evidence might be found in your own pool of personal experiences.

Using Sound Reasoning

Reasoning, the act of reaching conclusions on the basis of logical thinking, is a part of everyday life. If you take an umbrella with you on a walk because you notice heavy clouds massing in the sky, you are using reasoning to prevent yourself from getting soaked by the rain that will soon fall. While it is true that people are not always logical and rational, it is also true that they frequently can be persuaded by a message that appeals to their powers of reasoning.[7]

Let's look at two popular types of reasoning and then examine some common fallacies of reasoning.

▶ Deduction

Imagine that you are driving a car on a highway at a speed about 15 miles per hour over the speed limit. Suddenly you see a police car parked behind a billboard; as you whiz past, you notice that a radar device is protruding from the police car. You slow down, but you know it is too late: You are certain to be stopped. Sure enough, you glance in your rear-view mirror and see a second police car with lights flashing; the officer motions you to pull over.

How did you know that you were going to be stopped? By using *deduction*—a chain of reasoning that carries you from (1) a generalization to (2) a specific instance (of the generalization) to (3) a conclusion. In a formal logic, this chain of reasoning is expressed in the form of a syllogism:

> *Major premise (generalization):* Motorists who are speeding when they pass a radar point are stopped by police.
> *Minor premise (specific instance):* I was speeding when I passed a radar point.
> *Conclusion:* Therefore, I will be stopped.

Deduction is one of the most powerful tools of persuasion that a speaker can use. If you can convince your listeners to accept the major and minor premises, the conclusion is inescapable. The listeners are compelled by logic to accept it.

Until her death in 1906, Susan B. Anthony was one of the foremost fighters for the right of women to vote—a right that was not fully secured until 1920 when the Nineteenth Amendment to the Constitution granted nationwide suffrage to women. In speeches delivered throughout the United States, she used deductive logic as her persuasive strategy.[8] If we put the essence of her speeches in the form of a syllogism, it would look like this:

> *Major premise (generalization):* The Constitution guarantees all U.S. citizens the right to vote.
> *Minor premise (specific instance):* Women are U.S. citizens.
> *Conclusion:* Therefore, women have the right to vote.

To us today, this syllogism looks simple and obvious: How could Susan B. Anthony fail to persuade every listener? But bear in mind that in the nineteenth century many people viewed women as less than full-fledged citizens. In her speeches, she had to devote her energies to convincing her audience of the major premise and the minor premise. Those listeners whom she won over were then obliged by force of logic to accept her conclusion.

In a speech, deductive reasoning is convincing *only if both premises are accepted by the audience as true.*[9] Would an audience be likely to accept the following chain of reasoning?

> *Major premise:* Cardiovascular exercise improves eyesight.
> *Minor premise:* Jogging is a form of cardiovascular exercise.
> *Conclusion:* Therefore, jogging improves eyesight.

The minor premise is true, but the major premise is false, so the entire syllogism is flawed. An audience would reject the conclusion.

Of what value is a syllogism to you? In preparing a persuasive speech, you can use the power of deductive logic in two ways:

1. Putting your audience's reasoning into a syllogism helps you plan your persuasive strategy. Let's suppose that you are preparing a speech aimed at persuading your business associates to support a no-smoking rule inside your office building. As part of your audience analysis, you interview some of the smokers who will be in the audience; later, on paper, you translate their reasoning into the form of a syllogism:

> *Major premise:* Any legal activity should be permitted.
> *Minor premise:* Smoking is a legal activity.
> *Conclusion:* Therefore, smoking should be permitted.

When you analyze this syllogism, you see that your best point of attack is against the listeners' major premise. Your main counterargument will be: Legal activities should be permitted, yes, but not if they hurt someone else (you, of course, will show how secondhand smoke harms nonsmokers).

By seeing the architecture of your listeners' thoughts, you have enhanced your chances of tearing down what you consider a wall of unreason.

2. Putting your own thoughts into a syllogism helps you create a persuasive structure. Not every speech can be fashioned into a syllogism, but sometimes a syllogism gives you a handy framework for the task of persuasion. To continue with our smoking example, you could create the following syllogism:

> *Major premise:* An activity should be prohibited if it hurts others.
> *Minor premise:* Smoking in the office building hurts others.
> *Conclusion:* Therefore, smoking in the office building should be prohibited.

You now have a potent argument. If you can convince the listeners of the major premise and the minor premise, they are led by force of logic to accept the conclusion.

▶ Induction

While deductive reasoning moves from the general to the specific, *inductive reasoning* proceeds from the specific to the general. Imagine that you are a pediatrician seeing patients one January morning in your office:

> ▶ The first patient, age 9, complains of a runny nose, sore throat, headache, and muscular pains. You discover she has a fever of 103°.

▶ The second patient, age 7, has similar complaints and a fever of 102°.

▶ Third patient—same symptoms, plus a fever of 101.5°.

▶ Fourth patient—similar complaints and a fever of 102.5°.

▶ Fifth patient—similar symptoms and a fever of 103°.

You know from your medical training that these complaints are classic symptoms of influenza (or flu). You know that influenza is an epidemic disease, striking many people in a community, usually in winter. Based on what you have seen, you reason inductively that your community is experiencing an influenza epidemic. You use *specific* evidence (or isolated observations) to reach a *general* conclusion. In reaching this conclusion, however, you must take an *inductive leap*. You cannot prove that there is an epidemic simply because of what you have seen. You are probably right, but your conclusion has to remain tentative (until further evidence is gathered, and the county health department declares an epidemic) because there is always the chance that some other explanation can account for your five patients' illness. Perhaps they have nasty colds or suffer from some new virus; perhaps no other patients with those symptoms will show up at your office during the remainder of the week. The chances are overwhelming that an influenza epidemic *is* the explanation, of course, but the point is that

Inductive reasoning is used frequently by scientists in their investigations and can be a powerful tool for speakers who wish to build a persuasive argument.

induction, unlike deduction, never leads to a certain conclusion, only a *very likely* one.

The inductive method is used frequently by scientists. They make isolated observations and then form a hypothesis. They may note, for instance, that the average temperature is rising each year in Sydney, Tokyo, Cairo, Rome, Copenhagen, Montreal, Lima, Mexico City, and Los Angeles. Therefore—now they take an inductive leap—the entire globe is warming up.

The inductive method has often led to discoveries: In World War II, British airplanes had cockpit covers made of plastic. During combat a cover would sometimes shatter, causing pieces of plastic to become lodged in the pilots' eyes. In pilot after pilot, a British physician observed that the eyes were not damaged or infected by the plastic fragments. This observation led to the use of plastic to make artificial lenses, including contact lenses, for people's eyes.

Some public speakers construct their inductive arguments by following three steps: (1) ask a question, (2) answer the question by collecting as much specific evidence as possible, and (3) reach a conclusion based on the evidence. Here is an example:

Question: Do air bags in cars save lives?
Evidence:
Item 1: Joan Baxter of San Diego survived a head-on crash because of the air bag in her car.
Item 2: Dr. Arnold Arms, a Kansas City physician, survived a 35 mile-per-hour crash into a city bus; the bus suffered $15,000 damage, while Dr. Arms was spared any injury because of the air bag in his car.
Item 3: Mrs. Mattie Lansing of Chicago was involved in a head-on collision at 50 miles per hour, but suffered no injuries because of the air bag in her car.
Conclusion: Air bags save lives.

Is this all you need for evidence? No, although the inductive reasoning up to this point is powerful, you would need to show that your examples are not isolated flukes. You could, for example, cite statistics from national authorities, such as "The Department of Transportation estimates that 11,000 lives would be saved each year if air bags were used in all cars."

When you use inductive reasoning, you will convince an audience only if your evidence is strong. If you have weak evidence, your conclusion will be weak. In the preceding example, if you had used vague statements like "The manufacturers of air bags assure us that the bags will save lives," your evidence would have been too flimsy to support the conclusion.

While inductive reasoning can be used for all or part of any kind of persuasion speech, there are two situations in which it is especially effective.

1. Consider using inductive reasoning when your audience is skeptical or hostile to your central idea. Earlier in this book, we stressed the value of stating your central idea in the introduction of your speech; there is, however, an important exception to this "rule." When you have an audience that is likely to be skeptical or hostile to your central idea, a wise strategy is to lead them through an inductive chain, saving your central idea for the latter part of the speech.

Let's say that you own a business, and you have decided that henceforth all of your sales representatives must send orders to the home office on laptop computers that can be linked to telephone lines. Though you will dictate your decision, you still want to "sell" your staff on the idea—to convince them that your decision is a good one—so that they will cheerfully implement it.

You plan to announce your decision at the next sales meeting, but you know that many of the sales representatives are hostile to the idea of using computers. If you make your announcement in the introduction of your speech, many sales representatives will react with internal disagreement and anger, and some will tune you out. Instead of listening to your explanation, they will mutter to themselves, "What nonsense! The boss wants to burden us with the latest electronic gimmicks." So, instead of making your announcement right away, you use an inductive line of reasoning:

"I've been doing some research," you tell the sales force, "to see which companies process their orders quickly and how they do it." Then you cite some specifics:

► Last year, Acme Company switched to a new system for placing orders, and now orders are processed 2 days faster than before.

► Brown Corporation reports that customers are extremely happy over the speed with which orders are filled. The president of the corporation, Jim Brown, says, "Our revenues have risen dramatically this quarter, and we owe it all to our new ordering system."

You continue to pile case upon case, and then you divulge one final, powerful piece of evidence: "What do all these companies have in common? They all installed a new ordering system that works like this: each sales rep has a lap-top computer that can be linked by telephone to the home office." Now you are ready to take the inductive leap and draw a conclusion from the evidence: "Using lap-top computers means faster processing of orders, faster delivery of goods, happier customers, and—ultimately—greater profits." With such persuasive logic in front of them, the sales force should be receptive to your announcement: "We will require all of you to use lap-top computers that can be linked by telephone to the home office."

An inductive line of reasoning helps listeners keep an open mind. By seeing you build your case block by block, they are more respectful and appreciative of the central idea when it is finally presented to them. This doesn't mean they will always agree with you, of course, but it does mean that those who are hostile or skeptical to your ideas will probably see more merit to your case than they would if you announced your central idea in the introduction.

2. *Use inductive reasoning when you wish to show the drama of discovery.* As we mentioned above, the inductive method is the one scientists use to make discoveries; they make one observation after another until they take the inductive leap and create a conclusion (or hypothesis). Sometimes public speakers follow such a path to discovery, and a description of the steps can be interesting to the audience. Here are the inductive steps taken by one speaker:

▶ Last winter I woke up every morning with a severe headache.

▶ When I visited some relatives in another state for a few days, I noticed that I would wake up *without* a headache.

▶ I asked myself: How is my house different from my relatives' house?

▶ My house is tightly sealed, with no chance for inside air to escape, while my relatives' house is loosely sealed.

▶ As an experiment, I cracked my windows a few inches during day and night, and my headaches disappeared.

▶ An article in the *Journal of the American Medical Association* cites eight different studies that describe headaches and malaise experienced by people who had been living in tightly sealed homes. The culprit: cooking gases and other irritating chemicals that stay bottled up indoors.

▶ Conclusion: A tightly sealed home in the winter can cause some people to suffer headaches.

The speaker then urged the audience to keep their homes ventilated in the winter to prevent headaches.

Quick tip: If you have trouble remembering the difference between deduction and induction, keep in mind that they travel in opposite directions. Deduction (think of the word *deduct* in the sense of taking *away*) leads *away* from a generalization; it goes from general to specific, applying a general principle to a specific case. Induction (think of the first two letters *in*) leads *into* or toward a generalization; it goes from specific to general, accumulating specific instances that point toward a general idea.

▶ Fallacies in Reasoning

A fallacy is an error in reasoning that renders an argument false or unreliable. You should become adept at recognizing fallacies (1) so that you can avoid using them in your own speeches and (2) so that you can prevent yourself from being influenced by them when you listen to the speeches of others. Here are some of the more common fallacies:

1. *Hasty generalization.* A hasty generalization is a conclusion that is reached on the basis of insufficient evidence. For example, "The mayor was convicted of accepting bribes, and a city council member was indicted for vote fraud. So we can conclude that all the politicians in this city are corrupt." The fact that two politicians are corrupt does not prove that all are. Make sure that you have ample evidence before you reach a conclusion.

2. *Sweeping generalization.* A sweeping generalization is a statement that is so broad and so categorical that it ends up being unfair and inaccurate. It often includes words like *always, never, all,* and *none.* In a speech on America's neglect of old people, one student said, "America is the only country in the world that has no regard for its elderly family members. All other countries have great respect for the age and wisdom of the elderly."

The speaker had a good point to make—that we need to take better care of our elderly—but he damaged his credibility by indulging in such an outrageously unfair generalization. Is it true that *all* Americans have *no* regard for the elderly? Don't some Americans have high regard for old people? Even if his accusation were true, how can he say that America is the *only* country exhibiting such neglect? Has he researched the situation in such nations as Zaire, Luxembourg, and Sri Lanka?

To make his argument reasonable and accurate, the speaker would need to modify the generalization to say: "Some Americans don't give their elderly family members the honor and attention that they deserve." Now the generalization would be acceptable to most listeners.

3. *Attack on a person.* Some speakers try to win an argument by attacking a person rather than the person's ideas. For example: "Rodney has lived in upper-class luxury all his life, so how can we believe anything he says about changing the welfare system for the poor? He obviously knows nothing about poverty." This tactic, sometimes known as *argumentum ad hominem* (argument against the man), is unfair and unethical. Rodney's arguments should be judged on how sound his ideas are, not on any aspect of his personal life.

Attacks on a person are often used in the courtroom to discredit a witness ("Ladies and gentlemen of the jury, this witness admits that he's an atheist, so how can we trust him to tell us the truth?") and in politics to discredit a foe ("My opponent has gambled in Las Vegas at least five times. Do you want such a person to manage your tax dollars?"). Though this tactic may be effective in the hands of such speakers, it should never be used by the ethical speaker, not only because it is dishonest and unfair, but also because it can backfire and cause careful listeners to lose respect for the speaker.

4. False cause. Beware of the fallacy of assuming that because events occur close together in time, they are necessarily related as cause and effect. A U.S. President takes office, and four months later the unemployment rate goes up 1 percent. Can we say that the President's policies caused the rise in unemployment? It is possible that they did, but many other factors may have caused the problem—for example, the economic policies of the previous administration.

The fallacy of false cause can also occur when a speaker oversimplifies the causes of complex problems. Take, for example, a speaker who says that *the* cause of cancer is negative thinking. That explanation is simple and understandable—and wrong. Although negative thinking—and the stress and tension that go with it—may be implicated someday as contributing factors in cancer, medical researchers say that no one thing has been isolated as *the* cause of cancer. The disease is probably caused by an interaction of several factors, including genetic predisposition, susceptibility of the immune system, the presence of a carcinogenic virus, and environmental irritants. Cancer is too complex to be explained by a single causative factor.

5. Building on an unproven assumption (also called begging the question). Some speakers act as if an assertion has been proved when in fact it has not. Suppose that a speaker made the following statement: "Since the Japanese never make a product that will last a long time, we should stop buying Japanese products and start buying American-made products." The speaker is acting as if the impermanence of Japanese products is an established fact, when in reality many listeners would probably disagree. An ethical speaker would first try to prove that Japanese products are less enduring than American products and then urge the audience not to buy Japanese-made goods.

When a speaker commits this fallacy, careful listeners are resentful because they feel as if they are being tricked into giving assent to a proposition that they don't believe.

6. False analogy. When speakers use a false analogy, they make the mistake of assuming that just because two things are alike in minor ways, they are also alike in major ways. For example, some people say, "Feed a dog every day and it will be your friend forever. Likewise, if we give generous aid, especially food, to foreign countries, they will always be our friends." This analogy is erroneous. Although it is true that dogs and humans are similar in some respects, they are different psychologically in many important ways. While dogs may never bite the hand that feeds them, the same cannot be said of humans. In fact, receiving food from the United States has sometimes caused peoples in other lands, embarrassed by their poverty, to resent and even hate their American benefactors.

Here is another false analogy: "We can communicate effectively via satellite with people on the other side of the planet, so it should be easy for parent and children to communicate effectively within the intimate environment of their own homes." Upon close examination, this analogy falls apart. Satellite communication between nations is a purely technical matter of transmitting radio and television signals, whereas communication among family members is far more complex, involving psychological subtleties that are beyond the reach of technology.

7. *Either-or reasoning.* The either-or fallacy occurs when the speaker states that there are only two alternatives, when in fact there may be many. For example: "Either we wipe out our national deficit or we watch our economy die." Is there truly no other way? Is it not possible that we can trim the deficit, without totally eliminating it, and still preserve our economic health? Stating an argument in stark, either-or terms makes a speaker appear unreasonable and dogmatic.

Here is another example: "Intelligence is determined by either heredity or environment, and I say that heredity is the key. How smart you are is determined by your genes." Most psychologists would disagree with this statement because intelligence seems to be determined by a complex interplay of both genetic and environmental factors. People like Albert Einstein or Margaret Mead probably would never have thrived intellectually if their entire lives had been stunted by extreme poverty and malnutrition.

8. *Straw man.* Some people try to win arguments by creating a *straw man*, a ridiculous caricature of what their opponents believe, and then beating it down with great ease. For example, one speaker, while arguing in favor of the death penalty for convicted murderers, said, "These people [who oppose the death penalty] say that a murderer is not really to blame for his crime. They say that society is to blame for not providing better educational and economic opportunities. So the murderer shouldn't be executed; he shouldn't even be sent to prison. We should simply say to him, 'Naughty boy, you did a no-no. Don't do it again.' "

Was this a fair summary of the beliefs of his opponents? Of course not. Most opponents of the death penalty favor long prison sentences for murderers. A speaker like this creates a straw man in order to look like a victor. Careful listeners, however, will spot the deception and lose confidence in the speaker.

Appealing to Motivations

Motivations are the needs, desires, or drives that impel a person toward a goal or away from some negative situation. People have hundreds of motivations, including love, happiness, health, social acceptance, financial security, adventure, and creativity.[10] If you show your listeners how your ideas can help them satisfy such needs and desires, you increase your chances of persuading them to adopt your point of view. Here are some examples of how student speakers appealed to the motivations of their audiences:

▶ To raise money to buy food for starving people in Africa, LeeAnne Washington appealed to the motivation that most Americans have to help those less fortunate than themselves.

▶ To try to persuade listeners to use seat belts at all times in a car, Jason Bradley appealed to the strong drive that people have to protect themselves from harm.

▶ To try to convince listeners to invest in real estate, Glenda Jorgensen tapped the public's desire for financial security and wealth.

Let's examine some of the more common motivations that audiences have. (This is a partial list; there are dozens of other motivations.)

▶ *Love and esteem.* People want to love and to be loved, to have good friends, to be esteemed at work and at home.

▶ *Health.* Your listeners want to avoid sickness, maintain their fitness and their health, and live a long time.

▶ *Safety.* People want to be protected from crime, and they want to use products that will not injure or kill them.

▶ *Success.* Most men and women wish for success of some sort, depending upon their individual definition of the term; for one person, success means making a million dollars, while for another, it is becoming the best violinist in an orchestra.

▶ *Financial security.* Most men and women desire a degree of financial security, though they would disagree on just how much money they need to achieve it.

▶ *Self-improvement.* Most people want to improve themselves, whether by learning a new skill or learning more effective ways of coping with life.

▶ *Recreational pleasure.* People of all ages love to get away from the stress and toil of work by taking vacations, going to movies, eating at fine restaurants, and so on.

▶ *Altruism.* Many people have a sincere desire to help others, whether through donating blood in their communities or through sending food to starving children in a faraway land.

Here are some tips for motivating an audience:

Focus on* listeners' *needs, rather than on your own. Imagine the following scenario:

At a large metropolitan newspaper, Smithers is sports editor and Parks is business editor, and they have the same problem in their departments: being shorthanded. This means that they and their staffs are overworked and stressed-out. Each editor decides to appear before the senior management council to request the hiring of a new reporter.

In her plea, Smithers tells the managers that she and her staff are constantly frazzled because of long hours and a crushing workload.

Taking a different approach, Parks says that if a new reporter is hired for her department, news coverage can be expanded and this, in turn, can help entice more people to subscribe to the newspaper.

Which editor is more likely to win her case? Parks—because she appeals to the needs of the managers (the need to provide good coverage and the need to sell more newspapers). Smithers' case is weakened by focusing on her own needs.

Appeal to more than one motivation.   Whenever possible, appeal to several motivations at the same time. Listeners who are not reached by one appeal can still be influenced by another. Suppose, for example, that you were trying to persuade your listeners to take up bicycling. Here are some of the motivations that you could identify, coupled with appropriate appeals:

Motivation	*Appeal*
Feeling good	Bicycling works out tension and makes you feel energetic and happy.
Looking good	Bicycling burns lots of calories, so it's ideal for weight control. It also tones up leg muscles.
Long-term health	Bicycling is excellent exercise for heart and lungs, thus helping prevent cardiovascular disease.
Friendship	Being on a bicycle is an instant passport to the world of cyclists. It's easy to strike up conversations with other riders, and you can often make new friends. Cycling also provides an enjoyable activity to share with old friends.
Adventure	With a bicycle you can explore out-of-the-way places, travel long distances in a single day, and experience the thrill of flying down a steep mountain road.
Competition	If you enjoy competing, there are bike races in almost every city or town.

By appealing to more than one motivation, you increase your chances of persuading the audience. For example, the listener who is already in superb health may not be reached by the first three items, but might be swayed by one of the last three.

Determine the strongest motivational appeals. As part of your audience analysis in the early stages of preparing a speech, ask yourself, "What are the *strongest* motivational appeals that I can make to this particular audience?" Then decide how you can work those appeals into your speech. As an example, let's take a look at how one speaker handled this matter: Vanessa Rivers is a real estate agent who frequently gives a talk in her community on the advantages of living in a condominium (a unit in an apartment building that a person owns instead of rents). Here are her main points, followed by an explanation of the motivational appeal in each.[11]

I. Owning a condo is more advantageous financially than renting an apartment. [She explains that a condo owner's monthly mortgage payment is an investment, and that a condo owner can write off these mortgage payments on federal income taxes. Thus she appeals to the audience's desire for *financial security*.]

II. A condo owner does not have to worry about house and yard maintenance. [This point appeals to a person's desire for *independence* (in this case not being tied down to such tasks as mowing a lawn and repairing gutters) and for *leisure time*.]

III. A condo owner, along with all the other residents, owns and has unlimited access to the recreational facilities, which may include a swimming pool, tennis courts, and health club. [This item appeals to the audience's desire for *good health*, *recreational pleasure*, and *companionship*.]

The points Rivers makes encompass what she considered to be the strongest possible motivational appeals to an audience of potential condo buyers.

Anticipate conflicting needs. In analyzing the motivations of your listeners, ask yourself, "Will any need that I plan to emphasize conflict with some of their strongest desires and needs?" If so, confront the problem explicitly in your speech (in other words, don't pretend that the problem doesn't exist). Let's say that you urge your audience to invest in the stock market. From your audience analysis, you know that some listeners have a strong motivation to make money quickly and easily, but at the same time they have an equally strong desire not to "gamble" with their savings. To win over such listeners, you must acknowledge their ambivalence and work to overcome it (perhaps by saying, "I know many of you are worried that investing in the stock market is a gamble—a high-risk roll of the dice—but are you aware that you can choose a low-risk investment such as a mutual fund?").

In some cases you can concede that a conflict exists, but then you can offer a countervailing reward. In the condominiums speech mentioned above some listeners might feel that condos don't satisfy their desire for complete privacy (of the kind they would experience in a private home). The speaker could acknowledge that condos are, as far as privacy is concerned, the same as apartments, but that the advantages of a condo—health facilities, lack of maintenance requirements, tax advantages, and so on—far outweigh the disadvantage of lack of privacy.

Arousing Emotions

Emotions are "stirred up" feelings that can be either positive (amusement, love, joy) or negative (fear, anger, sadness). You can use emotional appeals to stimulate listeners and rouse them to action.

How can emotions be evoked? By using support materials (such as provocative narratives) or powerful language (such as vivid metaphors).

As an example of how emotion can be used effectively, here is an excerpt from a speech by Stacey Brooks, who was arguing for a crackdown on divorced parents who kidnap their children and thereby deprive the other parent of seeing them:

> One morning Martha Greer, a divorced woman, woke up her kids, Samantha, age 8, and Bruce, age 6. She rubbed their backs to help them get awake, then she helped them find their school clothes. She made them a breakfast of orange juice, toast and jelly, bacon, hash browns, and milk. The she walked with them to the place where they caught the bus to school.
>
> That was the last time Martha saw them. They were kidnapped by their father that afternoon as they left school. That was six months ago, and Martha has no idea where they are. The police have not been able to find them. Think how frantic Martha is, think how angry she is, as she wonders where her kids are and how they're getting along without their mother. Imagine how you would feel if your kids were suddenly snatched from your life.

This story was effective in eliciting anger and pity. Here are some tips on arousing emotions:

Always combine emotional appeals with rational appeals.   If you appeal only to emotions, you play a risky game because you give the audience only one underpinning for a belief. Here's an example:

> Two speakers were debating the morality of the death penalty for convicted murderers. The first speaker, who was opposed to the penalty, concentrated on the ghastly horrors of electrocution, showing grisly photographs and giving lurid descriptions of charred flesh and prolonged suffering. The second speaker

Eliciting emotions such as joy is an effective way to supplement appeals to reason.

quickly conceded that electrocution was barbaric and argued instead for the death penalty by means of lethal injection, which he described as more humane. He gave philosophical and moral justifications for the death penalty, and then he aroused emotions in the listeners by describing the terrible ordeal of victims of crime and their families. From comments made by listeners at the end, it was clear that the second speaker had convinced previously neutral listeners to adopt his position.

Regardless of how you feel about this controversial issue, I hope you can see that because the first speaker dealt only with emotions, he let himself be outmaneuvered. There are many sound arguments that can be made against the death penalty; if he had used some of them—in addition to his emotional appeal—he might have won some listeners to his view.

While people can be swayed by emotional appeals, they also need to think of themselves as rational. They need to have reasons for the feelings and passions they embrace in their heart. If you use logic and emotion together, you have a more powerful speech than if you use either alone.[12]

Know how to use fear.   Over the years communicators have wondered how much fear one should evoke in trying to persuade people. For example, if you want to convince an audience to wear seat belts, would you be more successful with some low-fear visual aids, such as a chart on traffic fatalities, or with some high-fear graphics, such as a gory, full-color videotape of victims of a terrible car wreck? Research favors the latter. "The overwhelming weight of experimental data," says psychologist Elliot Aronson, "suggests that . . . the more frightened a person is by a communication, the more likely he or she is to take positive preventive action."[13] Research also indicates that high-fear messages are most effective when they are coupled with specific instructions on how to take action. For example, a high-fear message on rabies would be more persuasive if it included instructions on how to avoid the disease than if it left out such instructions.[14]

Use emotional appeals ethically.   Any emotion can be exploited in the wrong way. Fear and loathing, desirable when targeted at an infectious disease, are undesirable when aimed at a minority group. Unfortunately some politicians have demonstrated that creating or exploiting fears and hatreds can win elections. If you are an ethical speaker, however, you will never let short-term gain entice you into such tactics. If, for example, you are trying to mobilize public opinion to save an endangered species of bird, you will not demonize homebuilders who want to build on the bird's natural habitat; you will not foment hatred by falsely portraying them as merciless killers. Instead you will channel emotional appeals in appropriate ways—by generating sadness over the possible disappearance of the bird or by appealing to the happiness one might feel over saving endangered creatures.

To determine whether you are acting ethically, identify each emotion you want to arouse and then answer the following questions.

- ▶ Is the emotion worthy of compassionate, trustworthy people in the context of your topic? (If some politicians candidly answered this question and acted ethically, they would cease creating scapegoats to vilify in election campaigns.)
- ▶ Does the emotion reinforce, rather than replace, solid evidence and sound logic? (If not, is it because your case is unsupportable and illogical?)
- ▶ In arousing this emotion, are you treating the issue and the opposing side with fairness? (Put yourself in the shoes of an opponent and see if your treatment looks fair from that perspective.)

If you cannot answer yes to all three, your ethical footing is shaky. You should omit the emotional appeal or alter the speech.

Develop the emotional appeals inherent in some pieces of evidence.
Often you don't need to hunt for emotional appeals to add to your accumulation of evidence. All you need to do is develop the evidence already collected so that it moves the listeners. Let's say that while preparing a speech on the appalling murder rate in America, you have found this statistic: About 25,000

homicides occurred in the United States last year. You can state that figure in your speech and then develop it for emotional impact: "That means that every 22 minutes, another American is shot . . . stabbed . . . beaten . . . or strangled to death." By expressing a fact in this dramatic way, you help your listeners feel the magnitude of the problem. Note that vivid language ("stabbed," "beaten," and so on) enhances the emotional impact.

Summary

To be effective in persuasion, you must have a thorough *knowledge of the audience*. Find out exactly where your listeners stand concerning your view. Are they opposed, apathetic, neutral, or already convinced? Then plan a strategy to move them toward your position.

During a persuasive speech, enhance *credibility* with the audience by explaining your competence, by being honest and careful with speech material, by remaining open-minded, and by showing common ground with listeners.

Build your case by using strong *evidence* (such as statistics, examples, and testimony) that is accurate, up to date, and typical. Try to use a variety of sources, all of them reliable and reputable.

Use sound *reasoning* as a powerful tool of persuasion. Two popular forms are deductive reasoning, in which you take a generalization or principle and apply it to a specific case, and inductive reasoning, in which you observe specific instances and then form a generalization. In using logic, avoid these fallacies: hasty generalization, sweeping generalization, attack on a person, false cause, building on an unproven assumption, false analogy, either-or reasoning, or straw man attacks.

Whenever possible, appeal to listeners' *motivations*—their needs, desires, and drives that impel them toward a goal or away from some negative situation. Focus on the listeners' needs, not on your own; if possible, appeal to more than one motivation, and anticipate conflicting needs.

Finally, try to arouse the listeners' *emotions*, making sure that you always combine emotional appeals with rational appeals and that you always use emotions ethically.

Review Questions

1. Why are sarcastic remarks inappropriate when directed toward listeners who are hostile to your view?
2. Why is it a good idea in many cases to tell the audience why you are competent to speak on your particular subject?

3. How is an audience likely to react if you are careless with your facts and ideas?

4. Which is more persuasive with the typical audience—one vivid personal narrative or a series of statistical data?

5. What is the difference between deduction and induction?

6. Why should a speaker never use the logical fallacy called "attack on a person?"

7. List at least five motivations that all listeners have.

8. Why should emotional appeals always be accompanied by rational appeals?

FOR YOUR CAREER

TIP 16.2: In a Debate, Be Reasonable and Fair

Your boss knows that you strongly oppose a proposed policy, and she asks you to debate the issue with a colleague at the next staff meeting. What is your best approach? Should you demolish your foe with a slashing, take-no-prisoners assault, ripping him apart with sarcasm and scorn, while upholding your own view with an air of righteous indignation? No, this approach may sound effective, but it is actually counterproductive.

"Victory is not won by bluster," says Douglas Hunt. "Inexperienced arguers tend to enter the arena like gladiators ready for combat. . . . They often allow their commitment to one side of an argument to blind them to the virtues of the other. They argue so aggressively that the audience dismisses them as cranks." Effective arguers, on the other hand, "are usually cautious, courteous, and reasonable. . . . They understand, anticipate, and even sympathize with the arguments of their opponents. . . . They give the impression of being reasonable people whose judgment can be trusted."

Avoid cheap shots. (A cheap shot is unfair and unwarranted abuse or ridicule aimed at a person; for example, a speaker at a public forum on air pollution ridiculed environmentalists as "mushroom pickers who weep at the thought of a butterfly dying"). If you throw poisoned barbs, listeners who agree with you might laugh and applaud your cleverness, but listeners who are neutral or opposed to your position (the very people you want to win over) might discount everything you say. In fact, your unfairness sometimes elicits sympathy for the other side.

17

Special Types
of Speeches

▶ **Entertaining (or After-Dinner) Speech**

▶ **Speech of Introduction**

▶ **Speech of Presentation**

▶ **Speech of Acceptance**

▶ **Speech of Tribute**

▶ **Speech of Inspiration**

T hough most of the speeches that you will give in your lifetime will probably be informative or persuasive, there are occasions when you may be called upon to give other kinds—an entertaining speech at a banquet, a brief speech introducing the main speaker at a convention, a few words announcing the presentation of an award, a eulogy at a funeral to honor a close friend, an acceptance speech to thank an organization for giving you an award, or an inspirational speech to lift the morale of your subordinates or fellow employees. In this chapter we will take a look at these special types of speeches.

Entertaining (or After-Dinner) Speech

An entertaining speech provides amusement or diversion for the audience. It should be light and enjoyable, and easy to listen to. There should be no lecturing, no preaching, no doomsaying.

An entertaining speech can be given in a variety of circumstances, but it is most often delivered at meetings such as conventions and annual club dinners. It is frequently referred to as an "after-dinner speech" because it is usually given after a luncheon or dinner. People who have just eaten a big meal want to sit back, relax, and enjoy a talk. They don't want to work hard mentally; they don't want to be given anything negative and gloomy. So if you are an after-dinner speaker, don't challenge their beliefs or pump them with statistics. Strive to entertain them.

An entertaining speech can consist of a series of jokes, but joke telling is a difficult and risky business (see Tip 17.2 at the end of this chapter); besides, an entertaining speech does not have to be humorous to be effective. In other words, to entertain you don't have to elicit belly laughs, shrieks of glee, or deep chuckles. You can entertain an audience with stories and word pictures: for example, a well-told story about the calamities that occurred on your first date, a dramatic account of Sir Edmund Hillary's conquest of Mt. Everest, a description of the weird behavior of the South American sloth, or an imaginative forecast of life in America 100 years from now. All these speeches could be given without thigh-slapping jokes, but they nevertheless would be highly entertaining.

Students have given entertaining speeches on such topics as

- ▶ My First Piano Recital—A Total Disaster
- ▶ Hitchhiking from East Coast to West Coast
- ▶ My Grandfather's Favorite Ghost Stories
- ▶ The Wit and Wisdom of Mark Twain
- ▶ The Best Rock Concert I Ever Attended

While entertaining the audience is the general purpose of this kind of speech, this does not mean that you cannot include a few elements of persuasion, information, or inspiration; it just means that you should weave them unobtrusively and gracefully into the cloth of entertainment. To see how one speaker dispensed information in a light, entertaining manner, read the speech "Spoonerisms, Goldwynisms, and Malapropisms" in Appendix B.

Speech of Introduction

The speech of introduction is designed to introduce a speaker to an audience. For example,

▶ At a meeting of her civic club, Paula Moreno spoke briefly on why she was supporting a particular candidate for Congress and then turned the lectern over to the candidate.

▶ Theodore Lansing, a university librarian, stood up in front of 1500 delegates at a national librarians' convention and introduced the keynote speaker, a renowned writer of science fiction.

When you introduce one friend to another, you want them to get interested in each other and to like each other. When you introduce a speaker to an audience, you want to achieve the same goal. You want speaker and audience to be interested in each other and to feel warmth and friendliness.

An introduction should mention the speaker's name several times (so that everyone can catch it), and it should give background information to enhance the speaker's credibility with the audience. Your tone of voice and facial expression should convey enthusiasm for the speech to come.

Here are some guidelines for speeches of introduction:

Ask the speaker ahead of time what kind of introduction he or she would like. Some speakers will write out their introduction and send it to you in advance. While you should not actually read the document (because this would be boring to the audience), you should use it as the basis for your remarks. If the speaker provides you with a lengthy résumé or list of accomplishments, select those items that would be most appropriate for the audience and the occasion. Also, the speaker may want you to establish ground rules about questions; for example, "John will take questions at the end of the speech."

Be sure to pronounce the speaker's name correctly. If you have any doubt about how to pronounce the speaker's name, verify the pronunciation beforehand. If the name is difficult to pronounce, practice saying it in advance so that you don't stumble during the introduction.

Use the name the speaker prefers. If you are scheduled to introduce Dr. Elizabeth Wilson, find out beforehand what she wants to be called. Don't assume that she prefers to be called "Dr. Wilson." It could be that for this particular audience she prefers the informality of "Elizabeth" or even her nickname "Liz."

Set the proper tone. When you introduce someone, you help set the tone for the speech to follow. Be careful to set the right tone—a humorous tone for a humorous speech, a serious tone for a serious speech. Consulting with the speaker in advance will ensure that you understand the tone he or she wants you to set.

Avoid long introductions. A good rule of thumb is to keep an introduction under 3 minutes. After all, an audience wants to hear the speaker, not the introducer.

Avoid exaggeration. If you exaggerate the speaker's abilities or credentials, you build up unrealistic expectations in the audience. Consider this kind of introduction: "Our speaker tonight is a funny person who will have you laughing so hard you'll have to clutch your sides" or "The speaker will give us insights that are wise and brilliant." Such statements raise expectations that are very difficult for the speaker to meet. If the listeners are expecting one of the world's funniest speakers or one of the wisest, they may be disappointed. Overpraising a speaker also puts enormous pressure on him or her. The introduction "Our speaker is a dynamic personality who is known far and wide for her flawless platform technique" not only will cause the audience to focus on the speaker's delivery rather than on the message, but will also place great pressure on the speaker to perform perfectly.

Find out whether the speaker wants you to discuss the topic. Some speakers will want you to discuss the significance of their topic (to help prepare the audience for the speech); other speakers prefer to save all discussion of the topic until *they* step to the lectern.

Never steal the speaker's material. Imagine this scenario: You are about to deliver a speech to an audience of 1000 people, and suddenly you realize that the person introducing you is telling the very anecdote that you had carefully planned as the opener of your speech. How in the world are you going to begin your talk? Such nightmares actually happen, say professional speakers. The introducer uses a joke, anecdote, key statistic, or quotation that the speaker had planned to include. Or the introducer summarizes the subject matter in a way that duplicates or contradicts the subsequent speech. When you are an introducer, stay away from the speaker's material unless you and the speaker have worked out an agreement on exactly what you may cover. Your job is to set the stage, not steal it.

The following introduction of Joseph Conte was delivered at a meeting of a genealogical society:

> Our speaker tonight, Joseph Conte, will talk to us about how to set up a computerized ancestry record. Mr. Conte brings a lot of personal experience to this subject. The great-grandson of immigrants from Italy, he has traced his own family roots back to Florence. He has put all of his genealogical records onto a computer, using a program that was created by a Mormon group in Salt Lake City. Mr. Conte has a background of expertise in scholarly detective work: for the past decade he has been a researcher for the National Archives in Washington, D.C., specializing in 19th and 20th century immigration. Mr. Conte, welcome to our society and thank you for taking the time to share your knowledge with us.

Speech of Presentation

Awards or honors are often bestowed on individuals for their service to a business, institution, community, church, or club. It is customary for a brief speech to be made before the award is presented.

The speech of presentation should give (1) any background information that would help the audience understand the purpose or circumstances of the award, (2) the criteria used for selecting the recipient, and (3) the achievements of the recipient. In many cases, it is customary to withhold the name of the recipient until the very end of the speech, as a way of building suspense.

If humor is used, it should be handled very carefully. If you try to make a joke about the recipient, it may seem as if you are belittling him or her. At one company banquet, a department head gave an award for 10 years of service to a subordinate and used the occasion to tease him with a mock insult—"the only reason we keep him on the payroll is because his father worked here for 40 years." The "humor" was similar to the kind of bantering that the boss and the subordinate engaged in during a typical workday, but at the awards banquet, with his family present, the subordinate felt humiliated.

Here is a speech of presentation delivered by Meredith Brody at the annual meeting of a community theater:

> The John Cleese Award is given each year to the top actor or actress in our theater. As most of you know, the award is given in honor of the British actor

John Cleese of *Monty Python* and *Fawlty Towers* fame. The winner is selected by ballots circulated to all our members. Our winner this year is a seasoned veteran of our stage, a person who always performs with intelligence, audacity, and élan. I am pleased to announce that the winner of the third annual John Cleese Award is . . . James Colton!

Speech of Acceptance

If you are ever given an award, a promotion, or some other sort of public recognition, you may be called upon to "say a few words." Giving a speech of acceptance is difficult because you want to sound appreciative without being syrupy; you want to sound deserving without being egotistical. Here are some guidelines to follow:

Thank those who played a part in your achieving the honor. If a few individuals made your recognition possible, mention them by name; if a lot of people did, mention the most important contributors to your success and say something like this: "There are many others, but they are too numerous to name. Nevertheless, I am grateful to all of them."

Thank the organization giving you the award, and recognize the work it is doing. If, for example, you are cited by the United Way as a top fund-raiser of the year, spend a few moments extolling the great work that United Way does in helping the unfortunate and needy.

Don't exaggerate. If you receive an award for perfect attendance at your club's meetings, don't say, "This is the greatest honor I've ever received or ever hope to receive," unless, of course, you mean it. Exaggeration makes you seem insincere.

Be brief. I have seen some ceremonies marred because an award recipient viewed the acceptance speech as a chance to expound on his or her pet ideas. If you deliver a lengthy oration, the people who gave you the honor might regret that they did. Make a few sincere remarks—and then sit down.

A sample acceptance speech is the one given by Rita Goldberg, who was honored by a chapter of the Lions Club for her work with the handicapped:

I want to thank you for choosing me to receive your Distinguished Service Award. In the past year I couldn't have accomplished half of what I did without the help of Henry and Judith Fletcher. I am grateful to them for their valuable assistance. And I am grateful to you Lions for setting up programs for the visually handicapped. Because of your compassion and your work, you have made it easy for volunteers like me to help the handicapped. Again, thank you for this honor.

Speech of Tribute

A speech of tribute praises or celebrates a person, a group, an institution, or an event. For example, the leader of a veterans' organization might pay tribute on Memorial Day to comrades who had died on the field of battle. At a retirement banquet, you might give a brief talk lauding the work of a colleague who is stepping down after 25 years with your organization.

A speech of tribute should be completely positive. It is not appropriate to point out faults or dredge up old disputes. Concentrate all remarks on the praiseworthy and noble.

In the U.S. House of Representatives, Rep. Barbara Boxer of California delivered the following speech of tribute. (In keeping with the tradition of the House, she addressed her remarks to the Speaker of the House, though she was actually speaking to the entire House.)

In Praise of Mimi Silbert

Mr. Speaker, I rise today to pay tribute to Mimi Silbert. It is a great pleasure to recognize the achievements of this extraordinarily dynamic woman. I congratulate her on being honored by America's Awards at the John F. Kennedy Center for Performing Arts in Washington, D.C., at the end of September. She is one of America's unsung heroines. She truly personifies the American character and spirit.

Ms. Silbert is cofounder and chief executive officer of one of the most successful drug treatment programs in the nation. Delancey Street Foundation was so successful that the U.S. Department of Justice considers it a model for federal rehabilitation programs.

Ms. Silbert's unswerving devotion to Delancey Street is exemplified in many ways. She is a mother, mentor, boss, and counselor to 850 former felons, substance abusers, and the homeless who want to build a new life. At no cost to the taxpayer or client, she presides over programs that teach residents to teach each other how to live drug-free and become a valued member of society.

Because of Ms. Silbert, Delancey Street has maintained its high level of self-sufficiency and profitability. It has such thriving enterprises as a moving company, stained glass, woodworking, and catering businesses. These concerns are all run by the residents.

The most recent example of Ms. Silbert's determination is the completion of Delancey Street's new home in San Francisco, California. This magnificent

A speech of tribute praises or celebrates a person, group, institution, or event. This speaker is honoring his community's airborne paramedics.

structure was described by Pulitzer Prize winning columnist Alan Temko as a "masterpiece of social design." Over 250 residents learned to build this magnificent symbol of self-reliance, commitment, and plain hard work.

Mimi Silbert embodies the spirit of Delancey Street. She is the ultimate role model. She is one of mine.

Mr. Speaker, it is my privilege to honor Mimi Silbert for all her unselfish contributions to our society.[1]

One kind of tribute speech that you are likely to make is a eulogy—a speech of praise for a friend or colleague who has died. A eulogy should be dignified, without exaggerated sentimentality. (Though humor is often out of place in a eulogy, it is sometimes appropriate: One student described the funeral of a uncle who had been a "colorful character," well known for his storytelling abilities; during one of the eulogies for this uncle, the speaker recited some of the humorous tales, and everyone smiled in warm remembrance of the yarn-spinning uncle.)

A eulogy should focus on the *significance* of the person's life and deeds, rather than on a mere recital of biographical facts. In other words, how did this man or woman enrich our lives? What inspiration or lessons can we draw from this person's life?

Speech of Inspiration

The goal of the inspirational speech is to stir positive emotions—to cause people to feel excited, uplifted, encouraged. You may need to give inspirational speeches at various times in your life. Let's say, for example, that you are manager of an office or department and you give your staff an upbeat, "you-can-do-it" speech to motivate them to do good work. Or you coach a children's softball team and you give the boys and girls a "pep talk" before a game to make them feel confident that they can play well.

The inspirational speech is similar to the persuasive speech, with the two purposes often overlapping. The main difference is that in the inspirational speech, you devote yourself almost solely to stirring emotions, while in the persuasive speech, you use emotional appeals as just one of many techniques.

Delivery is an important dimension of inspirational speaking. To inspire other people, *you* must be inspired. Your facial expression, your posture, your tone of voice—everything about you must convey zest and enthusiasm.

An inspirational speech should tap the emotional power of vivid language. An example of effective language can be found in a speech delivered by Dan Crenshaw to a support group of parents of mentally ill children. Here is a section from the speech:

 TIPS **FOR YOUR CAREER**

TIP 17.1: Offer Toasts That Are Sincere and Warm

Someday you may be called on to offer a toast, especially at a wedding reception. The hallmarks of a good toast are sincerity and warmth. A lengthy "speech" is not required; in fact, some of the best toasts are short and simple, such as, "Here's a toast to Maggie and Zack. May your future be filled with much happiness." (By the way, traditional etiquette requires that the word "congratulations" be offered only to the groom—never to the bride.)

Some persons offering toasts tell of their admiration for the honorees and relate some personal anecdotes. This is fine as long as the remarks are sincere and appropriate for the occasion. Avoid clever barbs, risqué comments, and all forms of teasing.

Try to express the best sentiments of the entire audience. "Recently, at a wedding," says New York City editor Mary Farrell, "the best man focused his remarks *only* on the personal relationship he had with the groom—he didn't even mention the bride! In contrast, when the maid of honor toasted the *couple*, she tried to phrase her remarks to reflect the sentiments of everyone present. I felt as though I was giving the toast—along with the entire gathering."

We must learn to live fully and joyfully in the here and now, setting aside all our pain from the past and all our worries about the future. Fulton Oursler said, "We crucify ourselves between two thieves: regret for yesterday and fear of tomorrow."

If we live in the past or in the future, we miss what today has to offer.

We miss the glistening beauty of a puddle of water.
We miss the soothing melody of a love song.
We miss the glint of wonder in a child's eyes.
We miss the lingering aroma of fresh-baked cinnamon rolls.
We miss the beautiful arrangement of clouds in the sky.
We miss the satisfaction of rubbing a dog's fur.

The past is over. Think of it as a bullet. Once it's fired, it's finished. The future is not yet here, and may never come for us. Today is all we have. Treasure *today*, celebrate *today*, live *today*.[2]

Crenshaw made effective use of the techniques of *repetition* and *parallel structure* (which we discussed in Chapter 12).

Summary

While informative and persuasive speeches are the most frequent types, there are speeches when other purposes must be served. When you need to entertain an audience, as in an after-dinner talk, your remarks should be light and diverting; any elements of information or persuasion should be gracefully interwoven into the fabric of entertainment. When you are asked to introduce a speaker, convey enthusiasm for the speaker and the topic, and give whatever background information is necessary to enhance the speaker's credibility. When you make a speech of presentation, focus your remarks on the award and the recipient. When you are called upon to "say a few words" in acceptance of an award or promotion, thank the people who gave you the honor, and acknowledge the help of those who made your success possible. When you give a speech of tribute, praise the person, group, institution, or event being honored, avoiding any negativity. When you speak to inspire an audience, devote yourself to stirring emotions, using a dynamic delivery to convey your zest and enthusiasm.

TIPS FOR YOUR CAREER

TIP 17.2: Inject Humor—If It Is Appropriate

If you can use humor effectively, it is a good way to keep an audience interested in your speech. It creates a bond of friendship between you and the listeners, and it puts them into a receptive, trusting mood. Here are some guidelines:

1. Use humor only when it is appropriate. A speech about a solemn subject such as euthanasia would not lend itself to an injection of humor.

2. Tell jokes at your own risk. A popular kind of humor is the joke—a funny story that depends upon a punch line for its success. If you are an accomplished humorist, you might be able to use jokes effectively, but I don't recommend that any novice speaker use them, for these reasons: (1) jokes usually don't tie in smoothly with the rest of the speech; (2) most speakers (both inexperienced and experienced) cannot tell jokes well, (3) a joke that is successful with your friends might bomb with a large audience, and (4) the audience may have already heard the joke.

I have seen speakers tell a joke that no one laughed at—not one single soul. Maybe the audience had heard the joke before, or maybe it was too early in the morning or too late in the evening. Whatever the reason, a joke that fizzles can be devastating to the speaker's morale. "But it looks so easy on TV," some students say. It looks easy and *is* easy because TV joke tellers have advantages that most speakers lack: They have studio audiences that are predisposed to laugh at virtually any joke the comedians tell (your audiences will probably not be poised for laughter in this way). They have a supporting cast of gag writers who test the jokes out before

they are used. Most important of all, they have years of joke-telling experience before they appear on national television.

3. Use low-key humor. You can use other kinds of humor beside jokes. A mildly amusing story, quotation, or observation can be as effective as a side-splitting joke. The best thing about low-key humor is that it's safe. While the success of a joke depends upon the audience laughing immediately after the punch line, the success of a light story or witty observation does not depend on laughter—or even smiles. Sometimes the only audience response is an inner delight. In a speech urging his listeners to exercise regularly, student speaker Jerry Cohen began with a humorous quotation:

> The late Robert Maynard Hutchins, president of the University of Chicago, once said, "Whenever I feel like exercising, I lie down until the feeling passes." Is this your attitude toward exercise? Do you think of exercise as an odious chore to be avoided if possible?

Notice that Cohen's quotation was the kind of wry humor that does not depend on belly laughs; also notice that he tied the humor in with the purpose of his speech. This is an example of how you can sneak humor in, so that the audience sees it as part of your speech, not as a "joke." If they laugh or smile, fine; if they don't, no harm has been done. It's still enjoyable and relevant.

4. Humor must always relate to the subject matter. In other words, never tell an amusing
(continued)

(Tip 17.2 cont.)

5. Never use humor that might be offensive to any person in the audience. Avoid humor that is obscene or that ridicules members of any group in society (racial, ethnic, religious, political, gender, and so on). Even if the audience contains no members of a particular group, you are unwise to ridicule that group because you risk alienating listeners who disapprove of such humor.

6. Never let your face show that you expect laughter or smiles. Let's say that you cleverly insert a delicious piece of ironic humor into your introduction. After you make your humorous remark, don't stand there with an expectant grin on your face. If no one smiles back or laughs, you will feel very foolish. By the way, if you do fail to get any smiles or laughs, this doesn't mean that the listeners did not appreciate your humor. As I mentioned above, some kinds of humor elicit only an inner delight.

7. If you use jokes, use self-deprecating ones. Though jokes are risky (as discussed above), you can minimize the risks if you make *yourself* the target of your humor. Professional speaker Hope Mihalap says, "I always try to start with a line that will get a laugh, usually something about myself (slightly derogatory, of course)." And former Olympic Gold Medalist John Naber says: "I always begin with a cute joke at *my* expense." Poking fun at yourself is fairly safe because you escape the possibility of telling a joke the audience has already heard, and you avoid offending anyone (as long as you don't resort to vulgarity or obscenity).

Review Questions

1. Why would an informative speech on a difficult, highly technical subject usually be inappropriate for an after-dinner audience?
2. If you are asked to introduce a speaker, why should you coordinate your remarks with those of the speaker?
3. Name four guidelines for the speech of acceptance.
4. What is the difference between an inspirational speech and a persuasive speech?

Speaking in Groups

▶ **Responsibilities of Leaders**

▶ **Responsibilities of Participants**

▶ **The Reflective-Thinking Method**

Define the Problem / Analyze the Problem / Establish Criteria for Evaluating Solutions / Suggest Possible Solutions / Choose the Best Solution / Decide How to Implement the Solution / Decide How to Test the Solution /

▶ **Team Presentations**

Symposium / Panel Discussion /

S mall groups do much of the work of our society, at all levels of government, education, business, and industry. For example, NASA (National Aeronautics and Space Administration) uses small task forces to develop space programs. Colleges and universities use committees to set policy and develop new curricula. Businesses use small sales teams to sell their products.

The value of small groups is even recognized by giant corporations. After studying forty-three successful American companies for their best-seller *In Search of Excellence*, management consultants Thomas J. Peters and Robert H. Waterman wrote, "Small groups are, quite simply, the basic organizational building blocks of excellent companies." The most effective groups, they say, range from four to ten members.[1]

Here are some of the examples that Peters and Waterman cite:

> ▶ 3M Corporation has several hundred four- to ten-person "venture teams" that design and develop new products.[2]
> ▶ Texas Instruments has 9000 teams "zipping about looking for small productivity improvements."[3]
> ▶ To solve problems quickly and effectively, many corporations such as General Motors and IBM bypass the chain of command—the formal organizational structure—and instead form task forces made up of "champions"—a few key employees who are known for their creativity and dedication.[4]

For creativity and problem solving, small groups have obvious advantages over individuals: They provide a pooling of resources, ideas, and labor. Errors can be caught and corrected. Small groups also have advantages over large conglomerations of people: they act with greater quickness and flexibility. In this chapter, we will focus on meetings, the means by which small groups do their collective work. If carried out properly, meetings give group members a chance to discuss ideas, solve problems, reach decisions, resolve differences, and reduce tensions. Meetings provide close eye-to-eye contact with lively interaction between participants.

To perform well in meetings, groups should have (1) a purpose, (2) the cooperation of all members, and (3) effective leadership. Everyone in the meeting should possess a spirit of goodwill, or—to use the term of etiquette expert Letitia Baldrige—good manners. "I have observed," says Baldrige "that every well-run meeting invariably has a combination of a chairman with good manners and participants with good manners—it is like an excellent symphony conductor who needs an excellent corps of musicians in order to make truly beautiful music."[5]

Let us take a closer look at the roles of the leader and the participants.

Responsibilities of Leaders

Meg Slubiski, head of the sales force at a car dealership, called a meeting of salespersons to try to work out a problem that was causing hard feelings among the staff. Whenever a potential customer walked into the automobile showroom, the salespersons would elbow each other aside in an effort to be the one to greet the person (and possibly make a sale). Patiently, Slubiski listened to the complaints and accusations, and then shepherded the group toward a compromise that pleased everyone. The staff would use a rotating system for greeting potential customers so that each salesperson got the same number of contacts as everyone else.

Slubiski demonstrated the importance of firm but friendly leadership in small groups. When you are the leader of a small group, here are some guidelines for planning and conducting a meeting:

Establish an agenda. An agenda is a list of items that need to be covered in a meeting. When there is no agenda, groups often fail to work efficiently and productively. They waste time pursuing irrelevant matters, or they spend all their time and energy on minor items and never get around to the major issues. When you are leader of a group, decide in advance what issues should be discussed (be sure to consult the participants regarding the topics they want to include). Then write out an agenda, ranking items from most important to least important. Be sure the group members receive the agenda well before the meetings so that they can prepare themselves. At the beginning of the meeting, ask the participants if they want to add items to the agenda or make alterations in the order of priorities. If circumstances prevent you from preparing an agenda in advance, take a few moments at the beginning of the meeting to establish the agenda, asking group members for their suggestions and then rank-ordering the items on a chalkboard for everyone to see. Though setting the agenda may take a few minutes, it is time well spent, for it will help the group stick to the relevant and important issues. If your group is working against a deadline, you may need to establish a timetable for the agenda—for example, allotting 10 minutes for discussion of item A, 15 minutes for item B, and so on. (A special kind of agenda, using the reflective-thinking method, will be discussed in detail later in this chapter.)

Start the meeting on time. If some group members fail to arrive at the designated time, you may be tempted to delay the start of the meeting in the hope that they will soon appear. This is a mistake for two reasons: (1) You are being discourteous to the group members who were punctual; their time is valuable and should not be wasted. (2) You are setting a bad precedent for future meetings. If the people who arrived on time see you wait for latecomers, they will perceive you as a leader who starts meetings late, so they also will probably arrive late for the next meeting. If the same thing happens again, some group members will arrive later and later for meetings.

Set a friendly tone.   Start off with a friendly, upbeat welcome. If some of the participants don't know one another, introduce all the members of the group, one at a time, or let them introduce themselves.

Make sure that minutes are kept.   If the group is not a formal committee with a previously designated secretary, the leader should appoint someone to take notes and later prepare minutes of the meeting. Minutes are a record of what was discussed and accomplished during a meeting. They should be circulated to group members as soon after the meeting as possible. While minutes are obviously valuable for absentees who need to get caught up on events, they are also important for people who were present—to remind them of their responsibilities for the next meeting. Minutes should consist of five elements: (1) agenda item, (2) decision reached, (3) action required, (4) person(s) responsible for taking action, and (5) target date for completion of action.[6] At each meeting, the minutes of the previous session should be briefly reviewed to make sure that tasks have been completed.

Make sure all participants know the purpose of the meeting and the scope of the group's power.   Even if you have circulated an agenda in advance, you should still review the purpose of the meeting. Some of the participants may have failed to read the agenda carefully or correctly, while others may have forgotten what it contained. Refresh their memories; make sure everyone knows the task that the group faces. Also review the scope of the group's power, so that participants don't labor under false ideas of what the group can or cannot do. Group members need to know the following: Does the group have the power to make a decision, or is it being asked simply to recommend a decision? Will the group reach a decision and then carry it out, or will someone else actually carry out the decision? Is the group's decision subject to revision by a higher authority?

Encourage participation.   In some groups, especially ones led by a boss, group members say nothing while the leader does all the talking. Such groups are little more than rubber stamps for whatever the leader wants—the meetings are really a waste of time. When you are a leader, don't be dictatorial or directive. Guide the discussion, but don't dominate it. Encourage the free flow of ideas from all members of the group. This is more than a matter of politeness: group-created decisions are usually better than leader-dictated decisions because people tend to support what they have helped create. If, for example, you are the manager of five employees and you call them together and dictate a policy, there may be grumbling behind your back and passive resistance in implementing the policy, but if you call your people together and spend a few hours letting *them* hammer out the same policy, they will feel a strong commitment to it—now it is *their* idea, *their* policy.

Guide the discussion. As leader, you should move the discussion along from point to point on the agenda. If participants go off on tangents, diplomatically pull them back to the task at hand. (You can say something like, "That's an interesting point, but let's stick to our agenda; if we have any time left over, we can come back to your idea.") If a participant talks too much, not giving others a chance to speak, gently but firmly intervene. (You can say, for example, "Good point; if I may interrupt, I would like to hear how the others are reacting to what you just said.") If a participant is shy or unusually quiet, you can try to elicit comments. Don't ask a yes or no question, such as "Do you have anything you would like to say?" Instead, ask open-ended questions such as, "How do you think we can solve this problem?" If the person says, "I don't know," press no further. Thus you avoid badgering or embarrassing the person. It may be that he or she truly has no particular contribution to make on the issue. If participants become hostile toward one another, try to mediate by finding common ground and by helping them concentrate on issues instead of resorting to personal attacks.

Discourage side conversations. Meetings can be marred if two or more people break off from the group's activities and hold a private discussion. This, of course, is rude to the other group members, and it prevents the group from staying together as a unified team. As leader, you should gently shepherd the wayward group back into the fold; for example, if two members are carrying on a private conversation, you can say, "It looks as if you've come up with something interesting. Could you share it with the group?" This technique usually has one of two results: the offenders share their comments with the group, or (if they have been chatting about unrelated matters) they grin sheepishly, decline to reveal the content of their discussion, and return to participation with the group.

Summarize periodically. Since you are playing the role of guide, you should occasionally let the participants know where they are located on their journey toward the group's goal. Summarize what has been accomplished, and indicate work that still needs to be done. For example: "Let's see where we stand. We have decided that item A and item B should be recommended to the board of directors. But we still need to tackle problem C. . . ." Keep your summaries brief—just say enough to help the participants gain their bearings.

Keep meetings short. Probably because of high school and college, where classes are often 50 minutes long, many people act as if 50 minutes were the *required* length of a meeting, and they are reluctant to end a meeting sooner.

This is nonsense: some groups can complete all required work in much less time.

Never exceed one hour without a break. Most small-group meetings should last no longer than one hour. Anything longer will cause fatigue and a dropoff in the group's effectiveness. If one hour is not enough time to handle the group's work, a series of one-hour meetings should be set up. If, for some reason, the group is obliged to conduct all its business in one day or during an afternoon, one-hour sessions should be interspersed with coffee or "stretch" breaks.

End the meeting. At the end of a meeting, summarize what the group has accomplished, make sure that all participants know their assignments for the next meeting, and express appreciation for the work the group has done.

Follow up. After the meeting, make sure that minutes are written and distributed to each participant and that all participants carry out their assignments.

Responsibilities of Participants

In one community, a committee was formed to plan and finance the construction of a new swimming pool for a YMCA. The committee included a cross section of community talent—for example, a financier who was experienced at fund-raising, an engineer who was knowledgeable about pool construction, and a swimming instructor who knew what kind of pool the public wanted. When the committee met, it was effective in overseeing the design and construction of an excellent pool because the participants were able to share their ideas and expertise.

This story illustrates that while leadership of a small group is important, the participants themselves play a vital role. When you are a participant in a small group, here are some guidelines to keep in mind.

Prepare for every meeting. Find out in advance what is going to be discussed at the meeting and then decide what contributions you can make. Jot down items that you think need to be discussed. Do whatever research, background reading, and interviewing that might be necessary to make you well-informed or to bolster your position on an issue. If documentation is likely to be requested for some of your data, bring notes to the meeting so that you can cite your sources.

A small group works best when all participants give full attention and enthusiasm to the business at hand.

Arrive on time. Meetings cannot work effectively if some participants straggle in late. Make sure that you arrive at the appointed time. Even better, arrive a bit early; this will give you a chance to chat informally with your fellow participants and create a mood of friendliness.

Participate in group discussion. Don't sit back and let others carry on the work of the group. Throw yourself wholeheartedly into the discussion, contributing your ideas and opinions. This does not necessarily mean giving a brief speech or saying something brilliant. You can enter the discussion by asking questions, especially when points need to be clarified, by expressing support for ideas that you like, and by paraphrasing other members' ideas to determine if you understand them correctly.

If possible, speak up early in the meeting. If you have the opportunity to make a contribution to the group, do so at the earliest possible time. This serves as an "icebreaker," causing you to draw closer (psychologically) to the other members of the group and making you more attentive to the discussion. The longer you wait to speak, the harder it becomes to enter the discussion.

This does not mean that you should blurt out the first thing that pops into your head; never speak impulsively or aimlessly. But when a chance to make a genuine contribution arises, take advantage of it.

Exhibit positive nonverbal behavior.   Nonverbal cues, such as clothes, facial expression, posture, and eye contact, speak as powerfully as words. In a meeting, avoid slumping in your chair because that conveys boredom, negativity, or lack of confidence. Instead, sit in an alert but relaxed posture that shows you are both comfortable and confident. Whether you are playing the role of speaker or listener, look people in the eye. Your facial expression should convey openness and friendliness.

Don't treat your own ideas as beyond criticism.   Some group members act as if criticism of their ideas is an attack upon themselves, so they fight ferociously to defend their position. What they really are defending is not their ideas, but their ego. Unfortunately when people are busy defending their ego, they refuse to listen to what their critics are saying, they refuse to budge an inch from their position, and they sometimes prevent a group from making progress. When you present your ideas to a group, recognize that no human is perfect and that a wise and mature person readily admits the possibility of being in error.

Don't monopolize the meeting.   Give others a fair chance to state their views.

Stick to the point.   A common problem in meetings is for participants to stray off the subject and get bogged down in irrelevant matters. Before speaking, ask yourself if what you plan to say is truly related to the purpose of the meeting.

Treat all group members fairly.   All too often, some group members form coalitions with people who already agree with them, and then they freeze out the rest of the group (by not listening carefully to what they say, by not giving them sufficient eye contact, and by not soliciting and respecting their ideas). Aside from being rude, this cold shoulder treatment cripples the effectiveness of the group; members who feel frozen-out tend to contribute little. Treat each person in the group with dignity and respect, offering a friendly ear and an open mind to his or her ideas.

Express dissenting views.   Some groups members never raise objections or express views contrary to the majority. There are a number of reasons for this timidity: fear of being ridiculed, fear of antagonizing others, or fear of displeasing the leader (especially if he or she is the person's boss). When you disagree with an idea being discussed by the group, it is a mistake to remain silent. Group decisions that are made in a mood of pseudo-unanimity are often poor decisions.

Avoid personal attacks. Conflict—a clash of ideas or opinions—is healthy in group discussion. It exposes weaknesses in plans; it separates the workable from the unworkable. While conflict is desirable, it should always be centered on *issues*, not on personalities. In other words, disagree without being disagreeable.

Whenever possible, express objections in the form of a question. While you should certainly speak up when you think an idea is poor, there is a diplomatic way to offer criticism. If you blurt out, "Oh no, that will never work," you might deflate the person who suggested the idea and even provoke hostility. A better approach is to ask a question such as "How could we make this work?" As the group members try to answer the question, there is a spirit of cooperation, and often they come to the conclusion you hoped they would reach—that the idea *is* unworkable—without hostility or bad feelings.

Don't work from a hidden agenda. A group's work can be sabotaged if some members pretend to be committed to the goals of the group, but in reality have hidden agendas—that is, unannounced private goals that conflict with the group's goals. Examples of hidden agendas are a desire to gain personal power over other participants, a striving to impress a superior, and a secret wish to see the group fail.

Don't carry on private conversations. Group unity can be undermined if two or three participants engage in a whispered conversation, which is rude and insulting to the speaker. It is also damaging to the work of the group since it cuts off teamwork and a spirit of cooperation.

The Reflective-Thinking Method

When a group must solve a problem, one of the most effective techniques is the *reflective-thinking* method. Derived from the writings of the American philosopher John Dewey, this method is a step-by-step procedure for groups to use in solving problems.[7] To illustrate the steps, imagine that you and I and several other people are joint owners of a restaurant, and suppose that we have a problem that must be solved: many customers have been complaining about slow service.

▶ Define the Problem

A group will sputter and falter unless everyone has a clear idea of exactly what is wrong; so your first step is to define the problem. Sometimes a problem is obvious; for example, "What prices should be set for each item on the menu at our restaurant." But sometimes a problem is vague; for example, "We need to improve our restaurant." This statement is so vague that it would probably mean different things to each of the owners. To one, it might mean that we need to improve the food; to another, it might mean that we need to improve the skills of our servers (those employees sometimes called waiters and waitresses). One of the best ways to define a problem is to phrase it in the form of a question. In the case of our restaurant's problem, we could ask, "What steps can be taken to improve the service in our restaurant?"

▶ Analyze the Problem

A problem-solving group should scrutinize the problem in order to learn as much as it can. Some of the questions that should be asked are: What is the nature of the problem? How severe is the problem? What are the causes?

In our restaurant, we need to focus on causes so that we can correct the situation. Is slow service caused by the servers? If so, is it because they are lazy or inefficient, or is it because they are forced to serve too many tables? Or can the slow service be blamed solely on the kitchen staff? Are *they* the lazy or inefficient ones? Are *they* understaffed? At this point, if we cannot get a clear picture of the cause of the problem, we need to stop the problem-solving process and get answers to these questions before continuing. Let us assume that we ascertain the cause of the problem: the kitchen staff is slow in getting items into the hands of our servers.

▶ Establish Criteria for Evaluating Solutions

Suppose that you are asked by a friend to pick up "a good movie" for her while you are visiting a videotape store. What should you do? Grab the first videocassette you see? No, before going to the shop, you would need to find out your friend's tastes—her criteria for what constitutes a good movie. For example, does she enjoy comedy? If so, does she lean toward subtle British humor or slapstick Hollywood farces? Armed with the answers to such questions, you can choose a movie likely to appeal to her.

The same strategy works well for problem-solving groups. Instead of rushing to find a solution, a group should first decide the criteria—the standards or conditions—by which to judge a solution. To establish criteria, a group should ask: What must a proposed solution do? What must it avoid? What restrictions of time, money, and space must be considered? If there is more than one criterion, all should be rank-ordered in terms of importance.

In our restaurant example, the most obvious solution might be to hire more cooks, but what if we simply cannot afford to hire any new people? I at this stage we establish criteria, we can avoid pursuing solutions that are ultimately impossible. For our restaurant's problem, let us set the following standards, rank-ordered from most important to least important: (1) Orders must be taken to tables 10 minutes quicker than at present. (2) We must take action immediately. (3) We must not lower the quality of food. (4) Whatever solution we come up with must cost no more than $1000.

▶ Suggest Possible Solutions

The next step is for group members to suggest possible solutions. It is important for groups to show patience and avoid leaping at the first solution that comes along. Spreading out on the table a wide variety of possible solutions can enhance the chances of the group arriving at a sound decision. One of the best techniques for generating these potential solutions is *brainstorming*, wherein participants rapidly throw out ideas and the group leader writes them on a chalkboard. For brainstorming to work effectively, there should be an atmosphere of total acceptance—no one analyzes, judges, ridicules, or rejects any of the ideas. Let us say that for our restaurant we generate a dozen potential solutions, ranging from "use frozen (instead of fresh) foods" to "hire an efficiency consultant to teach the kitchen staff to work faster."

▶ Choose the Best Solution

After the brainstorming session, a group should analyze, weigh, and discuss the various ideas in order to come up with the best solution (or solutions). Each possibility should be measured against the criteria previously established. In our restaurant example, let us say that the idea of using frozen foods is examined. Since the chef tells us that frozen food is not as tasty as fresh, we would now reject the idea because it would violate our criterion about not compromising the quality of our food. The idea about hiring an efficiency expert would be rejected because one of our criteria stipulates immediate action. Let's say that another idea is to buy two more microwave ovens to speed up the kitchen's work. The two ovens would cost a total of $750; this would permit us to meet the under-$1000 requirement, and the chef assures us that two ovens would help her get the food out to the customers quickly, without lowering the quality. So we choose this option.

▶ Decide How to Implement the Solution

A solution may sound fine at the talking stage, but can it be realistically implemented? Our next step is to decide how to put the solution into action. In our restaurant's case, we authorize our bookkeeper to write the necessary check and we verify that a certain restaurant supply store can send us the ovens within 24 hours.

▶ Decide How to Test the Solution

Many groups hammer out a solution to a problem, but never follow it up to determine whether their solution really solved the problem. The last task of the problem-solving group is to decide how to find out if the solution, when put into effect, really works. In our restaurant's case, we can create customer response cards to be placed at each table. The customers are asked to rate, among other things, whether the service was fast enough to suit them. We decide that if 99 percent of our customers express satisfaction with the service, then our solution has indeed worked. (We aim for 99 percent rather than 100 percent because we know from our studies of restaurant management that there is always an irritable 1 percent of customers who are never happy with the service—no matter how fast it may be.)

Team Presentations

While most group work is done in private, there are some occasions when you may act as part of a team in making a presentation to an audience. Two of the most popular forms of team presentations are the symposium and the panel discussion.

Symposium

A symposium is a series of brief speeches on a common topic, each usually discussing a different aspect of the topic. In some cases, the speakers might be members of a problem-solving group who present their ideas and conclusions to a larger group. A symposium usually features a question-and-answer period after the speeches, and sometimes includes a panel discussion.

When you prepare and deliver a speech as part of a symposium, use the same skills and techniques as those of solo speechmaking, but work in advance with other members of your team to avoid duplication of material.

Panel Discussion

A panel is usually made up of three to eight members and is led by a moderator. Though there are many different methods of conducting panel discussions, a common pattern is to have the panelists give a brief opening statement and then permit them to discuss the subject among themselves, with the moderator serving as referee. At the end of the discussion, the audience is usually invited to ask questions.

Because of the variety of viewpoints and the liveliness of informed conversation, audiences enjoy a good panel discussion.

▶ Guidelines for the Moderator

Much of the success (or failure) of a panel discussion is determined by the moderator. He or she must keep the discussion moving along smoothly, restrain the long-winded or domineering panelist from hogging the show, draw out the reticent panelist, and field questions from the audience. Here are some guidelines to follow when you are a moderator:

Arrange the setting.   You and the panelists can be seated at a table facing the audience. Or, even better, you can be seated in a semicircle so that all members of the panel can see one another, while still remaining visible to the audience. A large name card should be placed in front of each panelist so that the audience can see the participants' names.

Brief panel members in advance.   Well before the meeting, give panel members clear instructions on exactly what they are expected to cover in their opening remarks. Are they supposed to argue the "pro" or "con" position? Are they supposed to speak on only one aspect of the topic? (For information-giving discussions, you may want to assign each panel member a subtopic, according to his or her area of expertise, so that there is not much overlap among speakers.) Instruct the panelists not to bring and read written statements because this would kill the spontaneity that is desired in a panel discussion, but tell them that they are free to bring notes.

Before the meeting, prepare a list of items that you think should be discussed.   By so doing, you can make sure that no important issues are inadvertently omitted. If the discussion begins to lag or to go off into irrelevancies, you will have, at your fingertips, material from which to derive questions.

Prepare and deliver an introduction.   At the beginning of the program, introduce the topic and the speakers, and explain the ground rules for the discussion; be sure to let listeners know if and when they will be permitted to ask questions.

Moderate the discussion.   Give each panelist a chance to make an opening statement (within the time constraints previously announced), and then encourage the panelists to question one another or to comment on one another's remarks. Be neutral in the discussion, but be prepared to ask questions if there is an awkward lull or if a panelist says something confusing or leaves out important information. Listen carefully to what each panelist says so that you don't embarrass yourself by asking questions on subjects that have already been discussed.

Maintain friendly, but firm, control.   Don't let a panelist lead everyone off on a tangent that is far afield of the speech topic. During the question-

and-answer session, don't let a member of the audience make a long-winded speech; interrupt kindly, but firmly, and say, "We need to give other people a chance to ask questions." If a panelist exceeds the time limit for opening remarks or monopolizes the discussion time, gently break in and say, "I'm sorry to interrupt, but let's hear from other members of the panel on their ideas concerning. . . ." If a panelist is reticent and says very little, draw him or her out with specific, pertinent questions.

Be respectful of all panelists, including those with whom you disagree. Think of yourself not as a district attorney who must interrogate and skewer criminal defendants, but as a gracious host or hostess who stimulates guests to engage in lively conversation.

Ask open-ended questions (ones that require elaboration) rather than questions that elicit a simple yes or no. For example, ask "How can we make sure our homes are safe from burglars?" rather than "Is burglary on the increase in our community?"

End the program at the agreed-on time. Wrap up the proceedings on time and in a prearranged way, perhaps by letting each panelist summarize briefly his or her position. Another option is for you to summarize the key points made during the discussion (to do this, you would need to take notes throughout the program). Thank the panelists and the audience for their participation. If some members of the audience are still interested in continuing the discussion, you may want to invite them to talk to the panelists individually after the program is over.

▶ Guidelines for Panelists

If you are a member of a panel, here are some guidelines to keep in mind.

Prepare for the discussion in the same way you prepare for a speech. Find out all that you can about the audience and the occasion: What particular aspect of the topic are you expected to speak on? Who are the other panelists and what will they cover? Will there be questions from the audience? What are the time constraints?

Prepare notes for the panel, but not a written statement. If you write out your remarks, you may be tempted to read them and thereby spoil the spontaneity that is desired in a panel discussion. In addition to notes, you may want to bring supporting data (such as bibliographical sources or statistics) to draw from in case you are asked for substantiation of a point.

Respect the time limits set by the moderator. If, for example, you are asked to keep your opening remarks under 2 minutes, be careful to do so.

In the give-and-take of the discussion, be brief.   If the other panelists or listeners want to hear more from you, they will ask.

Stay on the subject.   Resist the temptation to ramble off into extraneous matters.

Be respectful and considerate of your fellow panelists.   Don't squelch them with sarcasm, ridicule, or an overbearing attitude. Don't upstage them by trying to be the one to answer all the questions from the audience.

Listen carefully to the comments of other panelists and members of the audience.   If some people disagree with you, try to understand and appreciate their position instead of hastily launching a counterattack. Then be prepared to follow the next guideline.

Be willing to alter your position.   If you listen with an open mind, you may see merit in others' views and you may decide that you need to modify your original position. Though such a shift may seem like an embarrassing loss of face, it actually causes the audience to have greater respect for you. It shows you are a person who possesses intellectual courage, flexibility, and integrity.

Summary

Small groups are important elements in business and professional life, and much of the work of small groups is done in meetings. To lead a meeting, establish an agenda and make sure that it is followed; encourage all members to participate in group discussions, and guide the discussion to make sure that it stays on the subject. When you are a participant in a small group meeting, enter the discussion with a positive attitude and an open mind.

One of the most effective agendas for problem solving is known as the reflective-thinking method. It involves seven steps: defining the problem, analyzing it, establishing criteria for evaluating solutions, suggesting possible solutions, choosing the best solution, deciding how to implement the solution, and deciding how to test the solution.

Sometimes groups appear in public to discuss or to debate an issue. Two popular formats for team presentations are the symposium (a series of brief speeches on a common topic) and the panel discussion (an informal presentation involving a moderator and panelists).

Review Questions

1. Why is an agenda necessary for a meeting?
2. Why should a participant speak up, if possible, early in a meeting?
3. If you disagree with what everyone else in the group is saying, what should you do?
4. What is the best way to express objections to an idea?
5. What are the seven steps of the reflective-thinking method?
6. What are the duties of the moderator in a panel discussion?

 FOR YOUR CAREER

TIP 18.1: Strive to Improve Your Communication Skills Throughout Your Career

As you give speeches during your career, I hope that you will try to become better and better as a communicator. Here are three suggestions:

1. Seek opportunities for speaking. The best way to improve your skills is to actually give speeches: so look for opportunities in your career and in your community. An excellent place to practice is in a Toastmasters club, where your speaking skills will be critiqued in a friendly, supportive atmosphere. For the name and phone number of the club nearest you, write Toastmasters International, P.O. Box 9052, Mission Viejo, California 92690.

2. Seek feedback. See the guidelines in TIP 1.1 in Chapter 1.

3. Be a lifetime student of public speaking. You can improve your own speaking skills by studying the speechmaking of others. Whenever you listen to a speech, make notes on what works and what doesn't work. Which delivery techniques were effective? Which were ineffective? What speech material seemed to please the listeners? What seemed to bore them? Keep your notes in a file for future reference, so that you can profit from both the successes and failures of others.

APPENDIX A

Speaking in Front of a Camera

The next time you go for a job interview, you might find yourself sitting in front of a video camera because more and more businesses are using video-tapes to select their employees. "The video interview has some advantages over the face-to-face chat," says *Time* magazine. "The tape can be passed around to several executives for review, crucial parts of the interview can be watched more than once, and if a candidate looks hopeless in the first five minutes, the employer can hit fast forward and move to the next applicant."[1]

Once you have a job, you may appear again on television. Many companies communicate by means of teleconferences—video hookups that enable em-ployees in different parts of the country to talk to one another on screen. Each year almost one million business meetings are conducted in the United States by means of teleconferences.[2]

A growing number of firms also use videocassettes for in-house communi-cation and training. For example, Sonoco Corporation sends news to its plants throughout the world by means of a monthly videocassette that fea-tures interviews with executives, human-interest stories about workers, safety tips from engineers, and footage of new equipment in operation. "The beauty of a videocassette 'newsletter,'" said one Sonoco official, "is that you can show it to every shift and it builds a team spirit. Our people are thrilled to see themselves and their fellow workers on television."

There is also a chance, of course, that you will appear someday on regular television. You might be asked by a local TV station, for example, to give comments related to your job, your club, your church or synagogue, or your neighborhood. Or you might be asked to participate in a debate over some local controversy.

Here are some guidelines:

Find out in advance the production "rules." The director or interviewer can tell you how the program will be produced. He or she should explain any hand signals that you need to know—such as the signal for "Fifteen seconds left" or "Stop speaking—time is up." In all programs, the camera that has a red light on is the one operating at the moment.

Find out in advance whether the program involves direct or indirect TV. There are two distinct types of television programs.[3] *Direct TV* means that you look straight into the camera and speak directly to the TV viewers. This kind of program is used for news reports and teleconferences. *Indirect TV* means that you converse with an interviewer or with fellow panel members while the television camera looks on. Indirect TV is the more popular type; it is used for talk shows, interviews, and many documentaries. It is important for you to know which type of TV program you are on so that you can observe the next two guidelines.

For direct TV, look at the camera. If you fail to look steadily at the camera in a direct-TV program, you come across to viewers as evasive, untrustworthy, or unprepared. The only exception to this rule would be glancing down at notes occasionally and briefly. In some cases you may want to look at cue cards or a TelePrompTer placed next to the camera's lens—so that you give the impression that you are looking directly into the camera (the newscasters you see on television appear to be talking straight into the camera but they are actually reading the news from a TelePrompTer).

For indirect TV, never look at the camera. One of the reasons for the popularity of indirect TV is that it creates the illusion that the viewer is eavesdropping on a conversation. Thus, to avoid destroying this illusion, you must never look into the camera. Give your full attention to the interviewer or other participants.

If possible, practice in the studio. Being ushered into a TV studio, with its bright lights, massive equipment, and bustling technicians, can be unnerving for the person who has never had TV experience. If possible, practice sitting and speaking in the studio a few days before the production. If your program will be a *direct* show, practice looking at the camera lens. If you can rent or borrow a video camcorder, practice on videotape and watch yourself in playback to correct any problems in your delivery.

Dress conservatively. The colors that show up best on television are the medium hues—pink, green, tan, and gray. Avoid extremely bright colors such as red and extremely dark colors such as black. Because it reflects other colors, white is a poor choice. Stay away from fine prints such as checks or plaids—they can cause visual distractions. Avoid sparkling or noisy jewelry. Both men and women sometimes need makeup such as powder to cut down on shininess and glare.[4]

Arrange to have a cup of water handy. When I appeared on a live TV talk show recently, I found that the heat of the bright lights, plus my nervousness, made my mouth go dry. With envy, I observed that the host o the show had a cup of water underneath her chair; during commercial breaks, she would reach for her cup and take a sip. Learning from her example, I arranged to have a cup of water nearby during my next TV appearance.

Always keep your "real" audience in mind.   Let us say that you take part in a videotaped program about your company's new product. If you are interviewed by a colleague about the product, your real audience is not the colleague but the people who will be watching the program. So while you are ostensibly chatting with your colleague, you need to fashion your remarks to reach your true viewers. What are their needs and interests? How can you entice them into buying the product?

Speak conversationally.   Jack Valenti, president of the Motion Picture Association of America, makes frequent appearances on television in programs such as the Academy Awards presentations. "The indispensable element of television speaking," he says, "is [to be] conversational, as if you were in a living room talking to a half-dozen people." But how can you be conversational if you are on a *direct* TV program, needing to speak straight into the unblinking gaze of a camera? "I think it useful," says Valenti, "to have someone (preferably two or three people), either friends of yours or studio technicians, stand slightly behind and around the camera. When your cue comes, and the red light [goes on], talk to them. If they are grouped closely around the camera, you will not be diverting your own gaze too far to the left or right of the lens but will be able to talk to living people rather than that robotlike, sterile companion." If no one is available to stand near the camera, says Valenti, "imagine the camera eye to be a window through which you are speaking to the cameraman on the other side of the lens" or "pretend that someone you trust is sitting in front of you. Speak to that imaginary friend."[5]

Be yourself.   Try to be relaxed and natural. Don't paste a smile on your face and wear it throughout the program; smile only when it is appropriate. Don't feel that you must be an expert on everything discussed. If the interviewer asks a question and you don't know the answer, simply say so.

Never assume that the eye of the camera is no longer on you.   During interviews, many people assume that because another person on the show is talking, the camera is no longer focused on them, so they scratch their head or look around the studio or grin at someone off camera. Meanwhile, of course, the TV camera is mercilessly televising this rudeness and inattentiveness, the camera operator having broadened the focus to include all participants. Always assume that you are being televised—not only to avoid making a fool of yourself but also to keep from distracting viewers from the content of the program.

Scale down movement and gestures.   The kind of vigorous movement and powerful gestures that are excellent in a speech to an auditorium of 500 people will make you look like a buffoon if repeated in front of the TV camera. In the language of television, these actions are "too hot" for the medium. Any gestures you make should be small and low-key. Jack Valenti says, "It is fine to express passion in your cause, but without flailing of arms and head. On television, passionate belief is better expressed by a gaze or an emotional inflection of a phrase than by an outthrust fist or jaw."[6] Avoid sudden, swift movements such as crossing your legs rapidly; this can have a jarring effect on the viewers. If you must make such movements, make them very slowly.

Sit in a relaxed, confident posture.   Neither sit in a rigid position that suggests nervousness and anxiety, nor go to the opposite extreme and slouch in a casual position that suggests boredom and lack of interest. Try to make yourself comfortable, yet alert—the way you would sit if you were carrying on an animated conversation with your best friend.

Use the microphone correctly.   There are two facts about microphones that you need to know: (1) A microphone picks up all sounds, not just your words. Avoid coughing, rustling papers, whispering side comments to someone off camera, and brushing against the microphone. (2) A microphone works best if you don't put your mouth right next to it. Some people think that they must almost eat the mike in order to get their words picked up. In reality, today's microphones are engineered so that they work best when you speak at some distance from them. The best advice is to simply speak in your normal voice and forget all about the microphone. (If, however, you are required to hold a microphone, hold it about one foot below your mouth and speak over it, instead of into it.)

Ignore distractions.   When the red light goes on, concentrate all your attention on reaching your audience. Ignore the crew members and the machinery.

Speak briefly.   If you are long-winded, rambling, or tedious, your viewers will tune you out—out of their minds and out of their TV screens. Be brief. Be concise.

APPENDIX B

Sample Speeches

This persuasive speech, delivered by Jeffrey E. Jamison, a student at Emerson College, won first place in the 118th annual contest of the Interstate Oratorical Association in 1991. It is reprinted with permission from Winning Orations 1991.

ALKALI BATTERIES
POWERING ELECTRONICS AND POLLUTING
THE ENVIRONMENT

Jeffrey E. Jamison

1 One day the Energizer bunny will die.

2   Since its inception in 1989 the lovable little pink bunny has not only interrupted television commercials and movie previews, but has also significantly helped to increase sales of Energizer batteries. Unfortunately, the creative people at [the Energizer's advertising agency] may have hit closer to home than they realized when they developed the "it's still going" campaign.

3   We all know that one day the batteries inside the bunny will run out, (and we will just throw them out), but unfortunately these batteries are still "going" . . . going into landfills and incinerators, where the dangerous chemicals they contain are still going . . . going into the air we breathe, the water we drink, and the food we eat. Michael Fisher, executive director of the Sierra Club, warns in a personal interview that unsafe disposal of alkali batteries will become one of America's most serious environmental threats during the next three to five years.

4   In order to understand how truly devastating the threat from batteries is to our environment and to ourselves, we need to first identify what it is about the batteries themselves which makes them so dangerous to the environment, then focus on the problems with our current disposal methods. Finally, we need to consider the steps we must take to insure that our health and our environment are still "going" far into the future.

5   The threat to our health and to the environment that batteries present begins with the batteries themselves. In short, batteries are composed of very dangerous elements. David Macaulay explains in his book *The Way Things Work* that common alkali batteries are composed of three different

elements: cadmium, mercury, and lead. Cadmium, which forms the core of the battery, acts as the energy source. Mercury, which circulates around the cadmium, stabilizes the reaction, producing a steady energy flow. Lead forms the protective casing of the battery. Unfortunately, as the *Wall Street Journal* pointed out on June 4, 1990, these same three elements are among the most dangerous substances in our environment. According to the *Journal of the American Medical Association,* lead in the environment causes damage to both our immune and neurological systems; cadmium is responsible for cancer as well as liver and kidney disease, and mercury can cause kidney and lung disease as well as neurological and genetic disorders. The *Boston Globe* warns on March 19, 1990, that mercury, lead, and cadmium can enter our respiratory system through the air we breathe, or by ingestion of contaminated food or water. Unlike other elements which our bodies can naturally flush out, these heavy metals accumulate in our systems. When the toxicity levels of these elements reach a certain point, the effects are fatal.

6   While the batteries are inherently dangerous, when they are in your Walk-man, flashlight, fire detectors or toys, they really pose no serious health or environmental threat. For batteries were designed with a lead casing to contain the hazardous materials during their use. However, it is when you dispose of these batteries that dangerous substances they contain are being released into our environment.

7   In his 1990 book *The Green Consumer*, John Elkington, from the United Nations Environment Program, explains that we currently dispose of batteries in two ways: they are either buried in landfills or they are incinerated. And here is where the problem begins. Those batteries that are buried in landfills corrode, allowing mercury, lead, and cadmium to seep into nearby groundwater which contaminates our drinking water as well as the food chain. Even supposedly safe landfills, which are lined to prevent substances buried there from entering the ecosphere, are not safe. The *Boston Globe* warned in its March 19, 1990, edition that mercury simply eats through the protective lining into the environment. In addition, the hole the mercury creates can allow other dangerous substances to enter the environment.

8   While disposal in landfills is dangerous, *The Green Consumer* adds that the second disposal method, incineration, is even more dangerous. Ironically, the battery industry recognizes the potential harm of incinerated batteries, and prints a warning label on batteries that reads "Do not dispose in fire." When batteries are incinerated, the heavy metals they contain gasify and escape into the atmosphere, providing a more direct path into our bodies.

9   Now how much damage can one alkali battery do? Not much. However, *Seventh Generation Magazine* (June of 1990) says considering that we throw away three billion house batteries each year, the consequences are disastrous. The *New York Times* warns that each year we are adding 150 tons of mercury, 130 tons of lead, and 170 tons of cadmium to the environment. Sean Hecht from the Environmental Action Coalition explained in a personal interview that we have not had one battery death because it is impossible to trace the

path of the mercury, lead, and cadmium back to the batteries. However, he adds, considering that 50 percent of the mercury and 25 percent of the cadmium dumped into the environment each year come from alkali batteries, this is a problem that clearly affects all of us.

10   We have to realize that everything we throw away is recycled into the environment, through our air and water. We can no longer believe that once something is out of sight it is out of mind. It is this philosophy that has placed us in the environmental bind that we are in today. We need to realize that these batteries are like time bombs, and they are activated once they are thrown into the garbage. The February 25, 1989, issue of the *New York Times* claims that one of the primary reasons we are oblivious to the situation is that we are "dependent on them to power scores of modern devices, from talking dolls and Walkmans to camcorders and laptop computers." *Business Japan* (March of 1990) claims that recent technology has invigorated the battery industry to the tune of 5 billion dollars a year. And with more technology on its way, that figure is expected to triple within the next three to five years. On top of the fact that we are becoming increasingly dependent on these batteries, we think nothing of throwing them away, for they are referred to and even called disposable batteries. This is a contradiction: while we can throw the batteries away, we can never dispose of the mercury, lead, and cadmium. For they are still active in the environment years after we throw the batteries away.

11   What is almost as shocking as the battery problem itself is that a few simple steps can make a significant difference. Rhode Island, Florida, and New York have banned the incineration of household batteries. In addition, New York state is currently considering a battery bill, similar to the bottle bill of the 1980s. The battery bill would require that we pay a deposit, which is returned to us once we turn in our used batteries. While these are steps in the right direction, we cannot wait for our legislatures to act. We can all take steps individually to solve the problem. The *Recycler's Handbook* advocates recycling. We recycle paper and plastic—why not batteries? Recycling is simple. Collect your used batteries in a plastic container. Once the container is full, contact your local household hazardous waste facility (every municipality has one, and you can find this number in your local phone directory). Then place the container on the curb and the batteries will be picked up, with the mercury, lead, and cadmium extracted and recycled. This is important considering that 50 percent of all the mercury and 25 percent of all the cadmium used in the United States goes into the production of alkali batteries. The elements will be reused and not just dumped into the environment.

12   While recycling is a step in the right direction, we must also take steps to cut down on our dependency on alkali batteries. The 1991 book *Ecologue* explains that the most economically and environmentally sound solution is to use rechargeable batteries. One rechargeable battery will last as long as a hundred alkali batteries. So you're getting more bang for your buck, and at the same time you are not shocking the environment. Rechargers and rechargeable batteries can be purchased in most hardware, appliance, and

department stories. The batteries cost around two dollars apiece and the rechargers will run around 20 dollars. The initial cost may seem high, but the return is invaluable both economically and environmentally.

13 Every day millions of batteries are dumped into landfills and incinerators; in turn every year hundreds of thousands of tons of mercury, cadmium, and lead needlessly enter our air, water, and food supplies. We can no longer continue to consume these heavy metals. And the longer we wait to act, the worse the situation will become because the elements will continue to build up in the environment and our bodies.

14 These batteries can be very useful and valuable as long as we are responsible with them. As we've seen today, the batteries themselves are inherently dangerous; however, the real problem lies in the unsafe disposal of these batteries. After you walk out of the room today and the batteries in your Walkman, flashlight or Nintendo Gameboy run out, don't throw them out, save them for a recycling day. When you go to replace these batteries, make sure you use rechargeable batteries. By recycling and recharging, we can make sure that not only [the] Energizer bunny but our health and the environment are still "going."

An entertaining speech does not have to be a series of jokes. It can be a light, diverting tale or a playful look at human foibles. In this speech, Jessica McFadden takes her listeners on a tour of a few amusements in the English language. The speech was delivered in a class at Asheville-Buncombe Technical Community College in Asheville, North Carolina.

SPOONERISMS, GOLDWYNISMS, AND MALAPROPISMS

Jessica McFadden

1 Wouldn't it be nice to have your name enter the English language as a noun? People like Candido *Jacuzzi*, Samuel *Maverick*, Charles *Boycott*, Patrick *Hooligan*, and Jules *Leotard* ended up with their names in the dictionary as common nouns. I'd like to tell you about three people whose last names have entered our language, but I don't think you will envy them.

2 *Do you know what a spoonerism is?* It is the accidental transposition of sounds in a spoken sentence. Instead of saying, "There is a pouring rain," you say, "There is a roaring pain." The term spoonerism is named after the Reverend William Archibald Spooner, a British clergyman who lived around the turn of the century. Spooner was famous for linguistic disasters like this: After performing a wedding ceremony, he was supposed to say, "It is customary to kiss the bride," but he advised the groom: "It is kisstomary to cuss the bride." Once he wanted to say "The Lord is a loving shepherd," but it came out as, "The Lord is a shoving leopard."

3   Poor old Spooner made these mistakes so often that his church was packed by people eager to hear the latest slip. He rarely disappointed them. When he wanted to say, "crushing blow," it came out as "blushing crow." And one time he was trying to speak respectfully of his monarch Queen Victoria, except instead of saying "our dear queen," he said "our queer dean."

4   The most famous spoonerism in American history occurred during the Presidency of Herbert Hoover. Radio announcer Harry Von Zell said, "From the White House in Washington, we bring you the President of the United States, Mr. Hoobert Heever."

5   Do you know what a *goldwynism* is? This is a garbled statement that makes no sense. It was named after Samuel Goldwyn, the famous Hollywood movie producer. Here are some of his mangled statements:

> ▶ "If Roosevelt were alive today, he'd turn over in his grave."
> ▶ "They are always biting the hand that lays the golden egg."
> ▶ "In two words: impossible."
> ▶ "Include me out."

6   You have probably heard people utter goldwynisms. One of my favorites was blurted out by Yogi Berra, the baseball player. Speaking of a certain restaurant, he said, "Nobody goes there anymore—it's too crowded."

7   Finally, we come to the *malapropism*, which is the comical misuse of a word that sounds similar to another word but has a different meaning. If you say, "under the *affluence* of alcohol" instead of "under the *influence*," you are guilty of a malapropism. It is named for Mrs. Malaprop, a character in a British play who said things like this: "as headstrong as an *allegory* on the banks of the Nile." Here are some wonderful malapropisms I found in *The Guinness Book of Words* and *Anguished English*:

> ▶ "They severed his juggler vein."
> ▶ "The agnostics in the church are very poor."
> ▶ "The first thing they do when a baby is born is to cut its biblical cord."
> ▶ "His mother got it all on videotape for prosperity."
> ▶ "The murder defendant pleaded exterminating circumstances."

8   Spooner, Mr. Goldwyn, and Mrs. Malaprop have given us their names to enrich our language. It's fun to have these names available when someone utters a spoonerism like "Please sew me to another sheet" (instead of "Please show me to another seat"), when someone says a goldwynism like "We must take the bull by the teeth," and when someone utters a malapropism such as "I don't like swimming in that pond because it has too much of that green allergy."

NOTES

Preface

1. Survey by Motivational Systems of West Orange, N.J., reported by Warren Struhl, "Clear Impressions," *Desktop Communications*, March–April 1991, p. 69

Chapter 1

1. Sharon Nelton, "Address for Success," *Nation's Business*, February 1991, pp. 43–44.
2. Barbara A. Magill, Roger P. Murphy, and Lilian O. Feinberg, "Industrial Administration Survey Shows Need for Communication Study," *American Business Communication Association Bulletin*, 1975, pp. 31–33.
3. Teresa L. Thompson, "The Invisible Helping Hand: The Role of Communication in the Health and Social Service Professions," *Communication Quarterly* 32 (Spring 1984), 148–163; Thomas E. Harris and T. Dean Thomlison, "Career-Bound Communication Education: A Needs Analysis," *Central States Speech Journal* 34 (Winter 1983), 260–267.
4. Dan B. Curtis, Jerry L. Winsor, and Ronald D. Stephens, "National Preferences in Business and Communication Education," *Communication Education*, January 1989, pp. 6–14; Garda W. Bowman, "What Helps or Harms Promotability?" *Harvard Business Review*, January–February 1964, p. 14; Edward Foster et al., *A Market Study for the College of Business Administration, University of Minnesota, Twin Cities* (Minneapolis: College of Business Administration, University of Minnesota, 1978); *Instruction in Communication at Colorado State University* (Fort Collins, Colo.: College of Engineering, Colorado State University, 1979).
5. William R. Kimel and Melford E. Monsees, "Engineering Graduates: How Good Are They?" *Engineering Education*, November 1979, pp. 210–212.
6. Jack Valenti, *Speak up with Confidence* (New York: William Morrow 1982), p. 99.
7. Gerald Ford, Quote of the Month, *Communication Briefings*, January 1989, p. 8.
8. John F. Kikoski, "Communication: Understanding It, Improving It," *Personnel Journal* 59 (February 1980), 126–131.
9. Slogan used in an advertisement by Hitachi, Ltd., Tokyo, Japan included in a stereo system package (undated).

10. David W. Richardson, professional speaker, Westport, Conn., in reply to author's survey, November 1984.
11. Adapted from Tamar Jacoby, "Waking up the Jury Box," *Newsweek*, August 7, 1989, p. 51.
12. Nido R. Qubein, *Communicate Like a Pro* (Englewood Cliffs, N.J.: Prentice-Hall, 1983), p. 67.
13. James ("Doc") Blakely, professional speaker, in audiotape, "Anatomy of a Bomb, Analysis of Success," copyrighted 1983 by Blakely.
14. Michael McGuire, "The Ethics of Rhetoric: The Morality of Knowledge," *Southern Speech Communication Journal* 45 (Winter 1980), 133–149.

Chapter 2

1. Morris K. Holland, *Using Psychology* (Boston: Little, Brown, 1985), p. 33.
2. Keith Davis, quoted by Thomas Montalbo, "Listening: Not a Spectator Sport!" *The Toastmaster*, July 1987, p. 9.
3. D. A. Roach, "State of the Art in Listening Comprehension: A Compendium of Measures," paper presented at the International Listening Association Convention, Denver, 1981.
4. Lyman K. Steil, "Your Personal Listening Profile," booklet published by Sperry Corporation, Lake Success, N.Y., undated, p. 5.
5. Lyman K. Steil, interview in *U.S. News & World Report*, May 26, 1980, p. 65.
6. M. Scott Peck, M.D., *The Road Less Traveled* (New York: Simon & Schuster, 1978), p. 128.
7. Roger Ailes, *You Are the Message* (Homewood, Ill.: Dow Jones–Irvin, 1988), pp. 47–48.
8. Robert Bostrom and Carol Bryant, "Factors in the Retention of Information Presented Orally: The Role of Short-Term Listening," *Western Journal of Speech Communication* 44 (Spring 1980), 137–145.
9. Margaret Lane, "Are You Really Listening?" *Reader's Digest*, November 1980, p. 183.
10. Ralph G. Nichols, "Listening Is a 10-Part Skill," in James I. Brown, ed., *Efficient Reading* (Boston: Heath, 1962), p. 101.
11. Ibid., pp. 101–102.
12. Enid S. Waldhart and Robert N. Bostrom, "Notetaking, Listening, and Modes of Retention," paper presented to the International Listening Association, Washington, D.C., 1981; Francis J. Divesta and G.

Susan Gray, "Listening and Note Taking II: Immediate and Delayed Recall as Functions of Variations in Thematic Continuity, Note Taking, and Length of Listening Review Intervals," *Journal of Educational Psychology* 64 (1973), 278–287.

13. Wayne Austin Shrope, *Speaking & Listening* (New York: Harcourt Brace Jovanovich, 1970), p. 232.

14. This story was related to me by a psychology professor who says it is true. Jan Harold Brunvag, a University of Utah professor who collects "urban legends," reports in *Curses! Broiled Again!* (New York: Norton, 1989, pp. 311–313) that similar stories have been told throughout the United States for at least twenty years, and he thinks they may be apocryphal. From my discussions with several psychology professors, I am convinced that such experiments have been tried at various colleges, though some of the accounts undoubtedly get exaggerated as they are repeated. Brunvag himself reports that such an experiment was tried, with partial success, on Professor Lester J. Hunt at Northern Arizona University.

15. Lyman K. Steil, "Ten Keys to Effective Listening," undated pamphlet published by Sperry Corporation, Lake Success, N.Y., p. 10.

16. Anonymous speaker quoted by Ronald B. Adler, *Communicating at Work*, 2d ed. (New York: Random House, 1986), p. 88.

Chapter 3

1. Roger Ailes, *You Are the Message* (Homewood, Ill.: Dow Jones–Irvin, 1988), p. 132.

2. Ibid., pp. 132–133.

3. Roper Organization survey, cited in untitled research note, *Psychology Today*, March 1989, p. 14; "What Are Americans Afraid of?" *The Bruskin Report* 53 (July 1973); Susan R. Glaser, "Oral Communication Apprehension and Avoidance: The Current Status of Treatment Research," *Communication Education*, October 1981, pp. 321–341.

4. Reggie Jackson, interview during an ABC sports telecast, October 2, 1984.

5. Don Beveridge, professional speaker, Barrington, Ill., in response to author's survey, November 1984.

6. Elayne Snyder, *Speak for Yourself—with Confidence* (New York: New American Library, 1983), p. 113.

7. I. A. R. Wylie, quoted in Bert E. Bradley, *Fundamentals of Speech Communication: The Credibility of Ideas*, 4th ed. (Dubuque, Iowa: Brown, 1984), p. 385.

8. The term *stage fright* originated in the world of theater, but it is used today to designate the nervousness or fear experienced by a person before or during an appearance in front of any kind of audience. Other terms that are sometimes used to describe this condition are *speech fright, speech anxiety,* and *communication apprehension.*

9. Joel Weldon, professional speaker, Scottsdale, Ariz., in response to author's survey, November 1984.

10. Joel Weldon, in audiotape, "Elephants Don't Bite: Joel Weldon Live," copyright 1984 by Joel H. Weldon & Associates, Scottsdale, Ariz.

11. Michael T. Motley, "Taking the Terror out of Talk," *Psychology Today*, January 1988, p. 49.

12. Ali MacGraw, quoted in James Link, "Dealing with Stage Fright," *Cosmopolitan*, October 1982, p. 112.

13. Steve Allen, *How to Make A Speech* (New York: McGraw-Hill, 1986), p. 9.

14. Philip Zimbardo, *Psychology and Life*, 11th ed. (Glenview, Ill.: Scott, Foresman, 1985), p. 448; and miscellaneous other sources.

15. Joe W. Boyd, professional speaker, Bellingham, Wash., in response to author's survey, November 1984.

16. Hugh Downs, quoted in Max D. Isaacson, *How to Conquer the Fear of Public Speaking* (Rockville Centre, N.Y.: Farnsworth, 1984), pp. 70–71.

17. Ralph R. Behnke, Chris R. Sawyer, and Paul E. King, "The Communication of Public Speaking Anxiety," *Communication Education* 36 (April 1987), 138–141; Theodore Clevenger, Jr. "A Synthesis of Experimental Research in Stage Fright," *Quarterly Journal of Speech* 45 (April 1959), 135–136.

18. Dick Cavett, as quoted in Steve Allen, op. cit., pp. 9–10.

19. Earl Nightingale, *Communicate What You Think* (Chicago: Nightingale-Conant Corp., 1976), Audiocassette 11.

20. Dr. Henry Heimlich, professional speaker, Cincinnati, Ohio, in reply to author's survey, November 1984.

21. Danielle Kennedy, professional speaker, San Clemente, Calif., in reply to author's survey, November 1984.

22. Bert Decker in *Decker Communication Reports*, November 1986, p. 5.

23. Maggie Paley, "Modern Image Signal: Voice," *Vogue*, August 1984, p. 412.

24. Motley, op. cit., p. 49.

Chapter 4

1. Helayne Spivak, "The Art of Standing Out in a Crowd," *Working Woman*, June 1991, p. 68.

2. Thomas Leech, *How to Prepare, Stage, and Deliver Winning Presentations* (New York: American Management Association, 1982), p. 253.

3. Carl Sagan, *Cosmos* (New York: Random House 1980), p. 196.

4. Janet Elliott, "That's No Lady, That's My Wife," *Toastmaster*, August 1986, p. 15.

5. Karen Carlson and Alan Meyers, *Speaking with Confidence* (Glenview, Ill.: Scott, Foresman, 1977), p. 73.
6. Fred Ebel, "Know Your Audience," *Toastmaster*, June 1985, p. 20.
7. Paul Gillin, "Sparse Attendance May Turn out to Be the Kiss of Dearth [*sic*] for Softcon Shows," *PC Week*, April 9, 1985, p. 18.
8. John Naber, professional speaker, Pasadena, Calif., in reply to author's survey, November 1984.
9. Earl Nightingale, *Communicate What You Think* (Chicago: Nightingale-Conant Corp., 1976), Audiocassette 11.

Chapter 5

1. Charles Osgood, *Osgood on Speaking* (New York: William Morrow, 1988), p. 35.

Chapter 6

1. Herb Brody, "Getting the Facts," *PC/Computing*, August 1989, p. 86.
2. Thomas Hunter, quoted in "Conducting Interviews," *Speechwriter's Newsletter*, May 2, 1986, p. 3.

Chapter 7

1. Jon M. Shepard, *Sociology*, 2d ed. (St. Paul, Minn.: West Publishing, 1984), p. 164.
2. News article distributed by The Associated Press, July 8, 1984.
3. Report cited by Shepard, op. cit., p. 164.

Chapter 8

1. Anita Taylor, *Speaking in Public* (Englewood Cliffs, N.J.: Prentice-Hall, 1984), p. 174.
2. William J. Seiler, "The Effects of Visual Materials on Attitudes, Credibility, and Retention," *Speech Monographs* 38 November 1971), 331–334.
3. "The Effects of the Use of Overhead Transparencies on Business Meetings," Wharton Applied Research Center, University of Pennsylvania, September 1981. See also, George L. Gropper, "Learning from Visuals: Some Behavioral Considerations," *AV Communication Review* XI, Summer 1963, pp. 75–95.
4. Hower J. Hsia, "On Channel Effectiveness," *AV Communication Review*, Fall 1968, pp. 248–250.
5. Ron Hoff, *"I Can See You Naked": A Fearless Guide to Making Great Presentations* (Kansas City, Mo.: Andrews and McMeel, 1988) pp. 183–184.
6. Ibid., pp. 184–185.
7. Ibid., p. 185.
8. Bill Crider, "Professional Presentations," *PC World*, August 1984, pp. 248–254.
9. "Achieving the Proper Image," *PC Magazine*, September 27, 1988, p. 124.

10. Sandy Linver, *Speak and Get Results* (New York: Summit Books, 1983), p. 107.
11. Laurel T. Griffith, "Audiovisual Checklist," *The Toastmaster*, April 1988, pp. 25–26.
12. Kirsten Schabacker, "A Short, Snappy Guide to Meaningful Meetings," *Working Woman*, June 1991, p. 73.

Chapter 9

1. Shelly Chaiken and Alice Eagly, "Communication Modality as a Determinant of Message Persuasiveness and Message Comprehensibility," *Journal of Personality and Social Psychology* 34 (1976), 605–614.
2. John P. Houston et al., *Essentials of Psychology*, 2d ed. (Orlando, Fla.: Academic Press, 1985), p. 185.
3. Harry Sharp, Jr., and Thomas McClung, "Effect of Organization on the Speaker's Ethos," *Speech Monographs* 33 (1966), 182–184.

Chapter 10

1. Don Aslett, *Is There a Speech inside You?* (Cincinnati: Writer's Digest Books, 1989), p. 30.
2. Joel Weldon, in audiotape "Elephants Don't Bite: Joel Weldon Live," copyright 1984 by Joel H. Weldon & Associates, Scottsdale, Ariz.
3. The puzzle analogy is derived from Len Gougeon and Kevin Nordberg, "Microcomputers and the Teaching of Speech," *Communication Education*, January 1987, p. 74.
4. Hon. Ben Nighthorse Campbell of Colorado, in U.S. House of Representatives, *Congressional Record*, June 27, 1991, p. E2421.
5. The musical analogy is derived from Michael Adams, *The Writer's Mind* (Glenview, Ill.: Scott, Foresman, 1984), p. 126.
6. John E. Baird, "The Effects of Speech Summaries upon Audience Comprehension of Expository Speeches of Varying Quality and Complexity," *Central States Speech Journal* 25 (1974), 124–125.
7. Adapted from Edward L. Friedman, *The Speechmaker's Complete Handbook* (New York: Harper & Row, 1955), p. 16.
8. Adapted from Tari Lynn Porter, "By Hook or By Look," *The Toastmaster*, July 1987, p. 5.
9. Introduction and conclusion printed with the permission of Thomas Vandenberg.

Chapter 11

1. Stan Lee, *The Best of the Worst* (New York: Harper & Row, 1979), p. 51.
2. Outline, notes, and classroom speech by Patricia Clark Zarnowski used with her permission.
3. Mike Edelhart and Carol Ellison, "Build Images with Words at the Core," *PC/Publishing*, April 1990, p. 75.

Chapter 12

1. Julian L. Simon, *How to Start and Operate a Mail-Order Business* (New York: McGraw-Hill, 1981), p. 196.
2. Ibid., p. 216.
3. Janet Elliott, "That's No Lady, That's My Wife," *Toastmaster*, August 1986, p. 15.
4. Kenneth McFarland, *Eloquence in Public Speaking* (Englewood Cliffs, N.J.: Prentice-Hall, 1961), p. 186.
5. Don Bagin, "Here's a Frightful Implication," *Communication Briefings*, December 1989, p. 3.
6. Reid Buckley, *Speaking in Public* (New York: Harper, 1988), p. 133.
7. Roy Fenstermaker, professional speaker, Lakewood, Calif., in response to author's survey.
8. Edward T. Thompson, "How to Write Clearly," reprint of advertisement by International Paper Company, undated.
9. William Zinsser, *On Writing Well*, 3d ed. (New York: Harper & Row, 1985), p. 110.
10. *Doublespeak* is a hybrid word based on "doublethink" and "newspeak" from George Orwell's novel *1984*.
11. *Quarterly Review of Doublespeak* is available at $8 a year from National Council of Teachers of English, 1111 Kenyon Road, Urbana, IL 61801.
12. William Lutz, *Doublespeak* (New York: Harper, 1989), pp. 1–7.
13. "The Two Sides of Warspeak," *Time*, February 25, 1991, p. 12.
14. Lutz, op. cit., pp. 2–3.
15. Adapted from Hugh Rawson, *A Dictionary of Euphemisms and Other Doubletalk* (New York: Crown, 1981), p. 146.
16. "Military Doublespeak, *Quarterly Review of Doublespeak*, October 1988, p. 5."
17. Gary Jennings, *World of Words* (New York: Atheneum, 1984), p. 119.
18. Lutz, op. cit., p. 6.
19. "The Two Sides of Warspeak," op. cit., p. 12.
20. Lutz, op. cit., p. 6.
21. Reported in *Editor's Workshop*, May 1990, p. 16.
22. "Doublespeak Here and There," *Quarterly Review of Doublespeak*, April 1991, p. 1.
23. Adapted from Gary Jennings, op. cit., pp. 123–124.
24. Quoted by Carol Richardson, "Words to the Wise," *The Toastmaster*, December 1990, p. 22.
25. Theodore Solotaroff, quoted in Frederick Crews, *The Random House Handbook*, 6th ed. (New York: McGraw-Hill, 1992), p. 276.
26. Statistics courtesy of student speaker Frank Harrison.
27. Winston Churchill, as quoted in William Safire and Leonard Safir, *Good Advice* (New York: Times Books, 1982), p. 253.
28. Ibid., p. 294.
29. Christopher Ryan, president of Direct Marketing Solutions, as quoted in "Let's Repeat the Message," *Communication Briefings*, March 1990, p. 4.
30. This example is adapted from a discussion of Shakespeare in the "Muse of Fire" episode of the PBS television series *The Story of English*, narrated by Robert MacNeil.

Chapter 13

1. R. T. Kingman, quoted in Thomas Leech, *How to Prepare, Stage, and Deliver Winning Presentations* (New York: American Management Association, 1982), p. 223.
2. Elayne Snyder, *Speak for Yourself—With Confidence* (New York: New American Library, 1983), p. 69.
3. Waldo W. Braden, "Abraham Lincoln," in *American Orators Before 1900*, edited by Bernard K. Duffy and Halford R. Ryan (New York: Greenwood Press, 1987), p. 267.
4. Steve Allen, *How to Make a Speech* (New York: McGraw-Hill, 1986), p. 12.
5. Arnold "Nick" Carter, vice president, Nightingale-Conant, Chicago, in response to author's survey, November 1984.
6. Most items are adapted from Jeffrey C. Hahner et al. *Speaking Clearly: Improving Voice and Diction*, 2d ed. (New York: Random House, 1986), pp. 331–337.
7. Roger Ailes, *You Are the Message* (Homewood, Ill.: Dow Jones–Irwin, 1988), p. 20.
8. Ibid., p. 30.
9. Ibid.; Robert Rosenthal and Bella M. DePaulo, "Expectations, Discrepancies, and Courtesies in Nonverbal Communication," *Western Journal of Speech Communication*, 43 (Spring 1979), 76–95.
10. Janet Stone and Jane Bachner, *Speaking Up* (New York: McGraw-Hill, 1977), p. 55.
11. Jack Valenti, *Speak up with Confidence* (New York: William Morrow, 1982), pp. 74–75.
12. Ron Hoff, "*I Can See You Naked*": A Fearless Guide to Making Great Presentations (Kansas City, Mo.: Andrews and McMeel, 1988), p. 101.
13. James ("Doc") Blakely, professional speaker, Wharton, Texas, in response to author's survey, November 1984.
14. Danny Cox, professional speaker, in audiotape of speech entitled "Perils of the Platform," delivered to a National Speakers Association convention and provided in response to author's survey, November 1984.
15. Dorothy Sarnoff, *Never Be Nervous Again* (New York: Crown, 1987), p. 43.
16. Cristina Stuart, *How to Be an Effective Speaker* (Lincolnwood, Ill.: NTC Business Books, 1989), p. 67.

17. Tom Kirby, "117 Ideas for Better Business Presentations' pamphlet distributed by Tom Kirby Associates, St. Petersburg, Fla.
18. Adapted from "Be Prepared to Speak," videotape produced by Kantola-Skeie Productions, San Francisco, and David DeJean, "Selling Your Ideas," *PC/Computing*, August 1989, p. 76.

Chapter 14

1. From "Time Theft: The Silent Thief," a speech by Karen Kimmey, Arizona State University, first-place winner in the 117th Annual Contest of the Interstate Oratorical Association, reprinted from *Winning Orations 1990*, Interstate Oratorical Association, p. 4.
2. Reprinted with permission from Hoang Pham.
3. Reprinted with permission from Gina Hawkins.
4. Adapted from Reid Buckley, *Speaking in Public* (New York: Harper, 1988), pp. 37–38; and Rudolf Flesch, *The Art of Readable Writing* (New York: Harper & Row, 1949), p. 12.
5. "What We Don't Know," Associated Press article in the *Charlotte Observer*, July 28, 1988, p. 1.
6. Untitled research note, *Psychology Today*, March 1989, p. 14.
7. John Camper, "The Discovery of America? Don't Ask Collegians," *Chicago Tribune*, October 9, 1989, p. 1.
8. News item from the *San Francisco Chronicle*, reprinted in *The Progressive*, September 1991, p. 10.
9. National test results released by the U.S. Department of Education, February 8, 1990.
10. Dorothy Sarnoff, *Make the Most of Your Best* (New York: Doubleday, 1981), p. 51.
11. The Diagram Group, *Comparisons* (New York: St. Martin's Press, 1980), p. 22.
12. Outline and speech used by permission of Rob Fontaine.

Chapter 15

1. Leon Jaroff, "A Crusader from the Heartland," *Time*, March 15, 1991, pp. 56–58.
2. Ibid., p. 58.
3. James C. Humes, *Roles Speakers Play* (New York: Harper & Row, 1976), p. 6.
4. Dr. Jerry Tarver in "Writing for Results," *Speechwriter's Newsletter*, December 25, 1987, p. 3.
5. Erwin P. Bettinghaus, *Persuasive Communication*, 3d ed. (New York: Holt, Rinehart and Winston, 1980), pp. 32–33.
6. Elliot Aronson, *The Social Animal*, 6th ed. (New York: Freeman, 1992), pp. 115–169.
7. Dr. Jerry Tarver, op. cit., p. 3.
8. Douglas Ehninger, Bruce Gronbeck, and Alan Monroe, *Principles of Speech Communication*, 9th brief ed. (Glenview, Ill.: Scott, Foresman, 1984), pp. 249–259.
9. Outline and speech reprinted by permission of Christina Ramirez.

Chapter 16

1. Scale adapted from Sandy Linver, *Speak and Get Results* (New York: Summit Books, 1983), pp. 46–47.
2. Lord Chesterfield, quoted by William Safire and Leonard Safir, in *Good Advice* (New York: Times Books, 1982), p. 60.
3. Reprinted with permission from Patricia Caldwell.
4. Carol Burnett, as filmed in the video program "Drink, Drank, Drunk," KQED-TV, Pittsburgh, 1974.
5. Elliot Aronson, *The Social Animal*, 6th ed. (New York: Freeman, 1992), p. 90.
6. Ibid., p. 91.
7. Jeanne Fahnestock and Marie Secor, "Teaching Argument: A Theory of Types," *College Composition and Communication* 34 (February 1983), 20–30.
8. For this example I am indebted to Thomas Montalbo, *The Power of Eloquence* (Englewood Cliffs, N.J.: Prentice-Hall, 1984), p. 64.
9. Aristotle, *Analytica Posteriora*, Book I, in *Introduction to Aristotle* (New York: The Modern Library, 1947), pp. 9–34.
10. Abraham H. Maslow, *Motivation and Personality* (New York: Harper & Row, 1970).
11. Reprinted with permission from Vanessa Rivers.
12. Courtland L. Bovée and John V. Thill, *Business Communication Today* (New York: Random House, 1986), p. 249.
13. Aronson, op. cit., p. 85.
14. Ibid., p. 85.

Chapter 17

1. Hon. Barbara Boxer, speech delivered in the U.S. House of Representatives, September 17, 1991, as printed in the *Congressional Record*, September 17, 1991, p. E3059. Reprinted with permission.
2. Remarks courtesy of Dan Crenshaw, mental health counselor.

Chapter 18

1. Thomas J. Peters and Robert H. Waterman, Jr., *In Search of Excellence* (New York: Warner Books, 1982), p. 126.
2. Ibid., p. 127.
3. Ibid.
4. Ibid.
5. Letitia Baldrige, *Complete Guide to Executive Manners* (New York: Rawson Associates, 1985), pp. 191–192.

6. Adapted from Harold Tyler, as quoted in *Decker Communications Report*, March 1984, p. 1.
7. John Dewey, *How We Think* (Boston: Heath, 1933), pp. 106–115.

Appendix A

1. "Video Headhunting," *Time*, January 13, 1986, p. 52.
2. John F. Budd, "Video: A Corporate Communications Tool," *Vital Speeches of the Day*, July 15, 1983, p. 593.
3. "The Media and the Message: The Executive on Television," supplement to *Decker Communications Report*, November 1985, p. 2.
4. Ibid., p. 3.
5. Jack Valenti, *Speak up with Confidence* (New York: William Morrow, 1982), p. 101.
6. Ibid., p. 122.

Tips for Your Career

Tip 1.1: Jerry Tarver, Ph.D., "Face-to-Face Communication," in Carol Reuss and Donn Silvis, *Inside Organization Communication* (New York: Longman, 1985), p. 221.
Tip 1.2: Arnold "Nick" Carter, vice president, Nightingale-Conant Corp., Chicago, in response to author's survey, November 1984; Hope Mihalap, professional speaker, Norfolk, Va., in response to author's survey, November 1984.
Tip 2.1: William McWhirter, "Major Overhaul," *Time*, December 30, 1991, p. 57.
Tip 3.1: Larry McMahan was a student in one of my public speaking classes when he related his technique to me.
Tip 3.2: Carl Van Doren, *Benjamin Franklin* (New York: Viking, 1938), p. 650; and Edmund Fuller, editor, *Thesaurus of Anecdotes* (New York: Avenel, 1990), p. 21; speech excerpt reported with permission of Diana Perkins Hirsch.
Tip 4.3: James ("Doc") Blakely, professional speaker, Wharton, Tex., and Rosita Perez, professional speaker, Brandon, Fla., in response to author's survey, November 1984.
Tip 5.1: Jane Tompkins, "Teach by the Values You Preach," *Harper's*, September 1991, p. 30; Sandy Linver, *Speak and Get Results* (New York: Summit Books, 1983), pp. 39–43.
Tip 7.1: Robert R. Updegraff, "The Conscious Use of the Subconscious Mind," in Barry M. Smith and Betty Hamilton Pryce, *Reading for Power* (Providence, R.I.: P. A. R., Inc., 1982), p. 241; Joe W. Boyd, professional speaker, Bellingham, Wash., in response to author's survey, November 1984.

Tip 8.1: Preston Bradley, vice president, Graystone Corporation, in personal correspondence with the author.
Tip 9.1: Adapted from Donald M. Murray, *Writing to Learn*, 2d ed. (New York: Holt, Rinehart & Winston, 1987), p. 182.
Tip 10.2: Ron Hoff, *"I Can See You Naked": A Fearless Guide to Making Great Presentations* (Kansas City, Mo.: Andrews and McMeel, 1988), pp. 105–106; Tom Kirby, "117 Ideas for Better Business Presentations," pamphlet distributed by Tom Kirby Associates, St. Petersburg, Fla.
Tip 11.1: "American Preaching: A Dying Art?" *Time*, December 31, 1979, p. 64.
Tip 12.1: Ron Hoff, *"I Can See You Naked": A Fearless Guide to Making Great Presentations* (Kansas City, Mo.: Andrews and McMeel, 1988), p. 189.
Tip 12.2: Frederick Crews, *The Random House Handbook*, 6th ed. (New York: McGraw-Hill, 1992), p. 347.
Tip 13.1: Cristina Stuart, *How to Be an Effective Speaker* (Lincolnwood, Ill.: NTC Business Books, 1989), p. 69.
Tip 13.2: Rosita Perez, professional speaker, Brandon, Fla., in response to author's survey, November 1984; Sandy Linver, *Speak Easy* (New York: Summit Books, 1978), p. 121; Steve Allen, op. cit., p. 120.
Tip 15.1: Anastasia Toufexis, "A Lesson in Compassion," *Time*, December 23, 1991, p. 53.
Tip 16.1: Quoted by Clifton Fadiman, editor, *The American Treasury, 1455–1955* (New York: Harper & Brothers, 1955), p. 152.
Tip 16.2: Douglas Hunt, *The Riverside Guide to Writing* (Boston: Houghton Mifflin, 1991), p. 158.
Tip 17.2: Hope Mihalap and John Naber, professional speakers, in response to author's survey, November 1984.

Photo Credits

Page   0: Chuck Fishman/Woodfin Camp & Associates
Page   3: Tommy Thompson/Black Star
Page 00: Lester Sloan/Woodfin Camp & Associates
Page 27: Sepp Seitz/Woodfin Camp & Associates
Page 00: Bob Daemmrich/The Image Works
Page 47: Mickey Pfleger/Photo 20/20
Page 51: Dave Schaefer/Monkmeyer
Page 00: Bob Daemmrich/The Image Works
Page 69: David C. Binder/Stock, Boston
Page 71: Bob Daemmrich/The Image Works
Page 78: Mathew McVay/Stock, Boston
Page 81: Renee Lynn/Photo Researchers
Page 100: Will & Deni McIntyre/Photo Researchers
Page 112: Elizabeth Crews/The Image Works

Page 128: Peter Bryon/Monkmeyer
Page 137: Elena Rooraid/PhotoEdit
Page 148: Robert Holmes/Photo 20/20
Page 160: John Elk/Stock, Boston
Page 174: Sullivan/TexaStock
Page 187: Bob Krist/Black Star
Page 198: Bob Daemmrich/Stock, Boston
Page 204: John Ficara/Woodfin Camp & Associates
Page 224: Sepp Seitz/Woodfin Camp & Associates
Page 239: Tony Freeman/PhotoEdit
Page 250: D. & I. MacDonald/The Picture Cube
Page 264: Carol Lee/The Picture Cube
Page 272: Bob Daemmrich/The Image Works
Page 292: Bob Daemmrich/Stock, Boston

Page 298: D. Ogust/The Image Works
Page 302: Bob Krist/Black Star
Page 308: Richar Hutchings/Info Edit
Page 315: Robert Houser/Comstock
Page 326: Michael Newman/PhotoEdit
Page 336: Spratt/The Image Works
Page 343: Farrell Grehan/Photo Researchers
Page 348: Bob Daemmrich/The Image Works
Page 363: Bob Daemmrich/Stock, Boston
Page 374: David Wells/The Image Works
Page 378: R. Michael Stuckey/Comstock
Page 386: Bob Daemmrich/Stock, Boston
Page 392: Richard Howard/Black Star
Page 399: Hewlett Packard/PhotoEdit

INDEX